The Causes of the Civil War

The Causes of the Civil War

The Political, Cultural, Economic and Territorial Disputes between North and South

PAUL CALORE

McFarland & Company, Inc., Publishers
Jefferson, North Carolina, and London

LIBRARY OF CONGRESS CATALOGUING-IN-PUBLICATION DATA

Calore, Paul, 1938–
    The causes of the Civil War : the political, cultural, economic
and territorial disputes between North and South / Paul Calore.
        p.   cm.
    Includes bibliographical references and index.

    ISBN 978-0-7864-3304-9
    softcover : 50# alkaline paper ∞

    1. United States—History—1815–1861. 2. United States—
History—Civil War, 1861–1865—Causes. I. Title.
    E415.7.C35   2008
    973.7'11—dc22   2008005192

British Library cataloguing data are available

On the cover: Battle of Opequan or Winchester, Va., Kurz & Allison,
color lithograph, 1893 (Library of Congress); (inset) Abraham Lincoln, June 3, 1860 (Granger Collection). Front cover by TG Design

Manufactured in the United States of America

McFarland & Company, Inc., Publishers
    Box 611, Jefferson, North Carolina 28640
    www.mcfarlandpub.com

Contents

Preface

What do you think were the underlying factors that caused the American Civil War? If a southerner in 1861 was asked that question, the most obvious answer may have been Lincoln's decision to invade the South with Union troops and to blockade southern ports with Union warships. As a consequence, he would answer, the southern states were forced to form an army to protect southern rights and to defend the honor of southern families and their homeland.

It's quite likely the North blamed the South for the attack on Fort Sumter or, more significantly, for their seceding from the Union—an unlawful act that if left unchallenged would have had damaging consequences on the rest of the country. The crisis was impossible to resolve diplomatically, the northerners argued, and it left the president little choice under the Constitution but to take necessary military actions to preserve the Union.

Of course, some truth can be found in both' views, at least in the immediate sense of the times. But even in a more enlightened age, a simple explanation for the cause of the war remains elusive because one simply does not exist. On the surface it is easy and quite understandable for many people today to refer to those aggressive events as the causes of the bloodiest conflict in our nation's history. This book, however, will demonstrate they simply *started* the war. The causes went much deeper.

It is extremely difficult to ignore that by 1860, particularly after Lincoln was elected to the presidency and when the cries for secession were the most alarming, the political environment was a very combustible one. The nation had reached a point where in all likelihood any significant sectional crisis would ignite a major calamity. And, since the outbreak of the war could be linked directly to this emotional and hostile environment, this book examines the underlying source of this antagonistic climate, specifically the long series of contentious sectional conflicts which were cultivated over years of antebellum politics and the degree of hatred and resentment those conflicts created.

1

Although many of the disputes over conflicting ideology were fiercely debated by our nation's political leaders and in some half-hearted sense ultimately resolved or simply put off for another day, the hateful tenor of their confrontations left a bitterness neither section was able to put aside. Over time, this ever-suppressed sense of hostility created a volatile mindset on both sides needing only one final straw, one spark to unleash its fury.

Indeed, there were many instances when, despite their differences, the North and South shared common cultural values and lived and worked together harmoniously. Nevertheless, over the years the ongoing political tensions between the two sides bred an overriding environment of mutual animosity, of continuous bickering, and of distrust. The accretion of this resentment over the decades only exacerbated their mutual enmity and in turn created an ever-widening breech between the people of the North and the South. Although there was one flag, the country ultimately became divided into two separate and quite different "nations," each striving to obtain the political and economic power necessary to satisfy its own unique sectional interests.

In the end, following years of agitation, it was a war waiting to happen.

Sectionalism and the resulting conflicts derived from a combination of cultural, economic, political, and territorial disputes. Southern slavery and northern views on its morality were, of course, at the root of these sectional conflicts. It was the fundamental cultural element of sectionalism, the ongoing battle between a slave-labor society and a free-labor philosophy. One side believed in the necessity of a coerced working class to permit a higher class to promote progress, civilization, and refinement. The other insisted that the desire to better oneself was paramount and was limited only to the degree of effort applied in a competitive and free society. The "peculiar institution," however, was the engine that drove the southern economy and the southern way of life, a concept completely alien to northern Christian values and beliefs but one the South would defend to the death.

Nothing, however, aggravated the South more than northern resistance to the Fugitive Slave Act, which had long been an overwhelming cause of resentment on both sides of the Mason-Dixon Line. The opposing views on this issue not only aggravated the already hostile sentiments over slavery but also the slaveholders' frustrations over their inability to secure the rights to regain control over their runaway slaves.

Likewise, the intrusiveness of northern abolitionism and its deleterious effect on the southern way of life also contributed greatly to the growing abhorrence between the two sides. Abolitionism instilled a deep sense of fear and foreboding among the southern slave holders, a fear created and worsened by the incessant anti-slavery rhetoric designed to incite their slaves to revolt. From the early Quaker evangelists to the Underground Railroad, from William Lloyd Garrison and the flood of antislavery literature to John Brown and his murderous rampage, the cause of abolitionism only stoked the flames of sectional hatred.

On the economic front, shortly after their inception in 1816, protective tariffs were one of the principal sources of sectional conflict. Southerners viewed them as unfair taxes on their consumption, and they believed the northern-inspired tariffs stole hard-earned money from the pockets of poor southerners to enrich the wealthy northern industrialists. Since the southern people imported most of their goods in exchange for cotton, the cost of the tariffs was ultimately passed along for them to pay. These high tariffs, southern aristocrats complained, were hurting the South and were nothing more than examples of what northern corporate greed and a corrupt central government could accomplish when working together to satisfy their own self interests, and all at southern expense.

The chartering of the Second Bank of the United States, the distribution of surplus government funds to the states, the control over federal deposits, and the establishment of new banking laws that often impacted their clashing economic goals also kept both sides in a continuous state of agitation.

Passions also ran high over such sectional issues as expansionism, federal subsidies for internal improvements, political parity, and states' rights, particularly the right to nullify laws seen as unconstitutional and the right to secede from the Union.

When Mexican lands became involved, sectional conflicts were ratcheted up to an entirely new level. Now taking center stage were issues that included apportioning western lands, the Wilmot Proviso, popular sovereignty, guaranteed federal protection for slavery, the prohibition of slavery expansion, state sovereignty, and the interpretations of constitutional and congressional powers.

In writing this book my goal was two-fold. I wanted first to reduce the complex subject of sectionalism to its most fundamental form, and secondly, to illustrate how the most troubling political, cultural, economic, and territorial issues of the times influenced the relations between the North and South. Specifically, I wanted to explain how each section interacted with the other over these issues, how bitter sectional disputes fomented a mutual sense of distrust, anger, and resentment, and how after decades of repressing these emotions, the pent-up anger suddenly exploded in a series of widely diverse and aggressive events between December of 1860 and April of 1861. Hopefully, I have accomplished my goal without compromising historical accuracy.

This work does not pretend to be a deep analytical study of the causes of the war, which I leave to the more learned historians. Rather, it is a concise narrative on the antebellum politics that nurtured the growth of sectional conflicts. It was the cumulative effect of these conflicts that formed the psychological mindset for the inevitability of war.

Since much of this material is readily available in many secondary sources, the use of footnotes was considered unnecessary. Also, instead of choosing to go into exhausting detail, I chose to portray these sectional conflicts as a sequence of historical snapshots, a mini-history, so to speak, each in context with the political events of the times. There are always instances where several noteworthy events are taking place during the same time period and at different locations. Presentation of this material in a chronological format, therefore, simply by its very nature, will always require unavoidable overlap. Nevertheless, compressing many years of antebellum history into eighteen concise chapters was indeed a most challenging effort. I hope the readers find the result of this effort satisfactory.

As in my previous works, I sought to give the readers a brief glance back into a truly incredible period in U.S. history in a book that is both easy to read and easy to understand.

1

Slavery and Its Impact on Sectionalism (1619 to 1830)

Mere shadows of the men they used to be, the twenty chained and shackled survivors, weak from near starvation, frightened and confused, disembarked from a Dutch vessel onto the shores of Jamestown, Virginia. These pitiful creatures were the remnants of a group of one hundred Africans stolen from a Spanish slave ship on the high seas. Short on provisions to sustain himself and his crew, the captain dropped anchor at Jamestown to exchange them for food. It was August of 1619 and these men, the first of hundreds of thousands of Africans that would follow, were beginning a tragic chapter that would forever influence the course of American history.

Following the Portuguese and Spanish occupation of the Caribbean, a thriving trans–Atlantic slave trade developed during the sixteenth and seventeenth centuries primarily designed to import human laborers to work as slaves on the numerous sugar plantations on the islands. These twenty young men, part of a larger group that on most ships ranged between 450 and 600, had been destined for a life of slavery on any one of these islands in the Caribbean chain.

The earliest reference to Africans in the North was in 1637, following the Pequot War, in Mystic, Connecticut. Angry over the steady encroachment of European settlements, the Indians mercilessly attacked the small village of Wetherfield. Several months later, local militia from the surrounding area joined forces and launched a bloody counterattack that nearly wiped out all the Pequot warriors. While the women and children were enslaved, most of the surviving men and boys were shipped to the West Indies aboard the *Desire* in trade for Africans and other goods. Arriving back in Massachusetts in 1638, the *Desire*'s manifest listed a cargo of "salt, cotton, tobacco, and Negroes."

Yet, during those pre–Revolutionary colonial years, when survival was an ever-increasing struggle, procuring Africans proved to be a costly proposition and for that reason the practice wasn't entirely embraced. By 1650, therefore, only an estimated 300 Africans were in the colonies, mostly in Virginia.

Instead of buying African laborers the early colonists found it more cost-effective to hire and pay a modest wage to small numbers of local workers to clear the land and to plant and harvest crops, while the relatively small number of blacks in the South continued to work as household servants. Kidnapped Indians and those captured in battle were also forced to work on the farms with one significant caveat; under Virginia law in 1676 prisoners of war were judged to be slaves for life. In that ruling, the members of the General Assembly declared, "And bee it further enacted by the authority aforesaid, that all Indians taken in warr be held and accounted slaves dureing life." The Indians, however, were seldom cooperative, an attribute based on the fact that farm labor in their culture was considered to be women's work. Another drawback was their familiarity with the surrounding territory, a condition that made escape easy and commonplace. Over time the local hired hands either drifted away to other places or to other jobs, and the number of available Indians steadily decreased from escapes, white-man diseases, and battle deaths. Consequently, to maintain an adequate quantity of workers, a third source of labor also had to be utilized.

Called indentured servants, during most of the seventeenth century they would make up the majority of the southern labor force. Indentured servitude in the colonies attracted Europeans, mostly English males desperate to leave behind a life of economic or political hardship. They provided the landowner with cheap labor for a number of years, generally not more than seven or eight, in return for their passage to the colonies. In fact, it was a win-win business arrangement for everyone. It was certainly a very lucrative deal for the landowners. Besides receiving a relatively inexpensive, albeit temporary, labor force, they could also increase their land holdings. Under the usual agreement, landowners typically received a freehold of 50 acres or more for each servant under contract. And it was certainly beneficial for the English redemptioners or free-willers as they were called, who not only had their transatlantic voyage paid for but also had a chance to begin a new life in a new world. Furthermore, during their time as domestics or field hands, they were fed, clothed, and provided shelter at the expense of the landowner. Since there was always a great demand for skilled labor, if the indentured servant had such skills as carpentering or as a blacksmith, he was highly prized. When their term of service expired they were freed and given "freedom dues," which usually included new clothes, a small piece of land, an assortment of supplies, and tools to clear the land and build a cabin. A gun was also included for hunting as well as protection against marauding Indians. Because there was a scarcity of women, however, the majority were unable to find wives and settle down with a family. Instead, they were inclined to drift from job to job working on farms in exchange for room and board. In addition to the redemptioners, many European criminals were also sentenced to work in the colonies as an alternative to imprisonment in English dungeons, as were prisoners of war and vagrants under a system called enforced servitude.

During the years of colonial rule, a number of laws were enacted in Virginia which settled the numerous questions over the management of a growing slave population. In 1662, for example, one law resolved the issue of inherited slavery by simply stating, "All children borne in this country shalbe held bond or free only according to the condition of the mother." Although teaching Christianity to slaves was encouraged and widely practiced, another law refused to permit freedom to a slave because of his conversion, which was altogether contrary to the practice in England. Even the "casuall killing of slaves" was permitted under a ruling in 1669 that declared, "If any slave resist his master (or other by his masters order correcting him) and by the extremity of the correction should chance to die, that his death shall not be accompted ffelony, but the master (or that other person appointed by the master to punish him) be acquit from molestation, since it cannot be presumed that prepensed malice (which alone makes murther ffelony) should induce any man to destroy his owne estate." Under the same philosophy, further statutes by the members of the General Assembly also permitted the wounding or killing of runaway slaves who resisted their capture as if such an occurrence never happened. A year later a Virginia law appeared on the books that for the first time referenced the existence of black servants as slaves for life. The law declared that "all servants not being Christians imported into this colony by shipping shall be slaves for their lives." And if a slave was caught stealing a hog, he would receive 39 lashes. Punishment for the second offense was to stand in the pillory for two hours, "and have both his eares nailed thereto and after the expiration of the said two hours have his ears cutt off close by the nails." Other forms of punishment would include torture, branding, mutilation, imprisonment, being sold away from his or her family, or being murdered, all at the discretion of the master.

As their numbers grew, and they were forced to live and work without even the basics of freedom and dignity, the Africans were becoming less and less tolerant of their conditions. Consequently, it soon became evident that something had to be done to curb the growing problem of runaways. Especially infuriating to the landowners was that frequently the white indentured servants, those unable to adjust to the hard life under a harsh master, were also escaping from the colony with the black slaves. Once apprehended, however, in addition to the penalty of the lash, a new law determined that the indentured servant had to make up the time not only for his own absence but also for the slaves' absence as well since the slaveholder could not add more time onto the slaves' lifetime term. The runaway slave, on the other hand, being the property of the landowner, would undoubtedly suffer a punishment at the pleasure of his or her owner.

The Virginia General Assembly also went on to declare in October of 1705 that slaves were considered property to be bought and sold at the pleasure of their owners. According to this edict, "All Negro, mulatto and Indian slaves within this dominion ... shall be held to be real estate." And to re-enforce their status as property, corporal punishment or even worse was often used as the surest and quickest means to complete their "education." In addition, slaves could not testify in court, make contracts, leave the premises without permission, buy or sell goods, assemble together without a white present or physically assault a white person. These are but a few of the many restrictions under a set of laws called the Slave Codes.

Toward the end of the seventeenth century, the southern colonies had grown to such an extent that the small number of indentured servants on hand could no longer provide the labor needs of their benefactors. Furthermore, to compound the crisis, the pool of people willing to work in the fields of the South was rapidly dwindling. Conditions in Britain had improved to the point where many Englishmen now believed indentured labor in the colonies no longer held the same appeal as it once did. Consequently, to the landowners desperate for field hands, the African slave trade now held the allure of an inexhaustible supply of laborers who would not only be permanent, but also self-perpetuating.

Waiting in the wings were the British slave merchants who by that time had taken over the trans–Atlantic slave-trading business from the Portuguese and the Dutch and as such were experiencing lucrative profits. The trade was chartered by the king of England as the Royal African Company. It was estimated that from the mid–seventeenth century to 1807, when Britain abolished the slave trade, some two million slaves were transported to British sugar plantations in the Caribbean.

Most of the unfortunate Africans transported into slavery were those surreptitiously snatched from their huts in the middle of the night. To carry out these heartless kidnappings, so-called slave-hunters were employed to raid the many and widely scattered jungle villages for their hapless and unsuspecting victims. These forays were usually conducted in such areas as Senegal, the Niger delta, the Gold Coast, Gambia, and even as far south as the Congo River and Angola. The captives would be manacled together in groups of two or four, marched to collection centers along the west coast of Africa and held in enclosed pens called barracoons. Following incarceration for weeks or even months under extremely inhumane conditions, a price or trade was finally agreed upon between the slave merchants and any one of the African chiefs participating as slave-dealers in the business.

Sailing out of Liverpool with such items as weapons, liquor, cloth, and manufactured goods, the British slave merchants negotiated trade deals with the African slave-dealers for the black men and women confined in the barracoons. At that point, terrified over the unknown circumstances that awaited them, the Africans were brought aboard a slave ship where they were forced to lie on their backs below deck, each head positioned between the legs of another to the rear. During their journey across the Atlantic, sailings that could take anywhere from one to three months, many Africans died from malnutrition or disease from lying in human excrement while many others, unable to cope with their condition or not wanting to confront a life in captivity, committed suicide by jumping overboard. At the end of this so-called Middle Passage, the surviving Africans were sold as slaves in the numerous colonies throughout the Caribbean, such as Jamaica, Cuba or Haiti.

Typically, when a ship reached an American slave market, like those established in Philadelphia, Charleston, Richmond, and New Orleans, the captive Africans were unloaded, washed, shaved and rubbed down with an oil to cover bruises caused by the long voyage across the Atlantic. Once the men were secured with handcuffs and with heavy iron shackles around their necks, they were led to the auction house. The women, on the other hand, wore long ropes around their necks with their petrified children clinging desperately to the dangling end trailing behind. In the meantime, the upcoming auction was well advertised on numerous posters strategically placed all over town and in many local newspapers. Business boomed during this period as local hotels, rooming houses, and the numerous saloons were overwhelmed with scores of visitors from the surrounding cities and farms. Excited with anticipation as the slaves were being assembled in a large building or fenced-in yard, the planters strained and shoved to get a better look at the latest supply of "farm equipment." Suddenly, a drum roll would clatter over the chaos signaling the start of this grotesque and cruel spectacle and the potential buyers surged forward eager to begin their shopping. Following an inspection of the slave's teeth, muscles, and overall fitness, the highest bidder went home with his newly acquired property.

In the 1680s, home was usually on the tobacco plantations in the Chesapeake colonies of Virginia, Maryland, and northeast North Carolina, where large numbers of slaves first appeared. This was soon followed by a growing slave-driven economy along the coast of South Carolina, Georgia, and southern North Carolina, where indigo and rice were cultivated, and still later around the area of Louisiana where sugar was the principal crop. Slavery emerged on a much smaller scale in the North where climate and soil conditions precluded large-scale profitability. The relatively few slaves in the North grew corn and wheat while others served as house servants or day-laborers on various dairy or horse farms or as longshoremen in the bustling ports of Boston and Philadelphia. More often than their southern counterparts, by the antebellum years many of the northern slaves had acquired enough skills to work as weavers, tailors, and bakers.

Despite the progressive thinking of the sophisticated elites, such as Thomas Jefferson, many of the signers of the Declaration of Independence owned a number of slaves even though they believed slavery was morally wrong. In this regard, some people today, specifically those using a twenty-first century level of morality, consider Jefferson somewhat hypocritical for writing in the Declaration of Independence that "all men are created equal."

In the psyche of the Founding Fathers, however, Jefferson's words simply reflected the social point of view prevalent in both the North and the South during the mid–eighteenth century when birthright and pedigree meant a great deal to men of high social status. The elitists saw themselves in terms of their social class. While not of nobility, they were members of the gentry, the ruling class, while other men were classified as artisans, shopkeepers, or yeomen, followed by indentured servants, and finally slaves. In this context, therefore, the word equal was rather limited in its meaning. Jefferson was actually referring only to white Protestant men of European ancestry. They were the ones created equal. Indeed, slave-men were not considered as equals in Jefferson's sense of the word, men who were considered inferior beings and who, a decade later would be constitutionally defined as only three-fifths of a man nor for that matter were Native American men equal; they were considered by most people as sub-human savages. Therefore, although this was the so-called age of enlightenment, in one sense our young nation was an unwitting victim of an unjust and less enlightened age of morality when the phrase "all men are created equal" was very narrowly defined.

It would take another eighty-eight years and a bloody civil war before President Abraham Lincoln, speaking at a cemetery in Gettysburg, Pennsylvania, redefined the true meaning of these words for all future generations.

Although most of these learned and honorable statesmen considered slavery to be wrong, eight of our first twelve presidents owned slaves themselves, a practice dutifully protected by the U.S. Constitution. Years later, Jefferson conceded that he had "long since given up the expectation of any early provision for the extinguishment of slavery among us." Further, "The laws do not permit us to turn them loose, [even] if that were for their good." To illustrate how sensitive the issue of slavery was, and how it had influenced colonial statesmen, the word "slave" was completely avoided in the Constitution and instead, in an instance of colonial political correctness, was politely referred to as a "person held to service or labour...."

Although the African slave trade was accepted as a legitimate business practice in the Deep South, where there was always a desperate need for more laborers and servants, this deplorable and dehumanizing enterprise was beginning to receive widespread opposition and harsh criticism. The outcry against the slave trade came not only from the North, which was always notoriously opposed to it, but also from the Upper South as well, in states such as Maryland, Delaware, and Kentucky.

Therefore, in 1776, the second Continental Congress agreed to address this very controversial issue. Instead of outlawing the slave trade outright, however, the delegates conveniently side-stepped the issue and voted merely to denounce the importation of slaves onto American shores. It wasn't until 1787 when the Constitutional Convention convened that the question of the African slave trade was taken up anew. Even though a number of the fifty-five delegates attending the four-month meeting were inclined to end the practice right then and there, in deference to the powerful slave traders among them who feared it would doom slavery at the expense of the southern planters, the convention chose to acquiesce to the traders once again by agreeing to a compromise. As a consequence, the new Constitution allowed the Congress to consider legislation outlawing the African slave trade, but only after twenty years had passed. Predictably, between 1787 and 1807, the South managed to ratchet up its demand for more slaves than ever before, importing tens upon tens of thousands. In fact, during the intervening twenty years more Africans disembarked on southern shores than in any other similar timeframe in American history. And as expected, in 1807 Congress finally passed a bill outlawing the African slave trade effective January 1, 1808.

Also of concern to the South was the impact the U.S. Census would have on its ability to gain seats in the House of Representatives. Since the number of representatives from each state would be determined by its population, the more populated North wanted only free men counted. The South, on the other hand, was adamantly opposed to this idea and demanded slaves be counted as well. Again, a compromise was arranged when it was decided to count each slave as three-fifths of a person.

While the Constitutional Convention met in Philadelphia, Congress was also in session debating an ordinance historians today refer to as the single most significant piece of legislation enacted during the post–Revolutionary period. This ordinance was important for at least three reasons. One, it provided the means by which five future states would be created out of the yet unorganized Northwest Territory and would also serve as the blueprint for annexation of additional states into the Union. Ultimately, these new states were Ohio, Indiana, Illinois, Michigan and Wisconsin, and marked the beginning of the western expansion in the United States. Secondly, and perhaps more significantly, the ordinance prohibited the spread of slavery into this vast open and unregulated expanse north of the Ohio River. Called the Northwest Ordinance of 1787, it easily gained the approval of Congress on July 13, but in deference to the South the new law also contained a third important provision, a stipulation that all slave owners had the right to reclaim their fugitive slaves. Under this law, "any person escaping ... from whom labor or service is lawfully claimed in any one of the original States, such fugitive may be lawfully reclaimed and conveyed to the person claiming his or her labor or service as aforesaid." This provision of the ordinance wasn't exactly a new one but simply reflected Article IV, Section 2 of the Constitution which declared, "No Person held to Service or Labour in one State, under the Laws thereof, escaping into another, shall ... be discharged from such Service, but shall be delivered up on Claim of the Party to whom such Service or Labour may be due."

Nevertheless, despite this provision in the ordinance and the constitutional right to repossess a fugitive slave, no mechanism for enforcing the law was ever established. And without the power to enforce the law the provision was quite meaningless. In the South this oversight was of major concern and demonstrated to Southerners how weak the federal government was on this issue. It was also quite ironic that of all the issues the South stood for, the keystone of its political philosophy was states' rights and a weak federal government, except of course in this instance. On this point, Southerners were willing to ignore their own principles and to insist on a stronger central government to enforce the capture and return of their runaway slaves.

Finally, after five more years of southern pressure to correct this ambiguity, the Fugitive Slave Act of 1793 was passed by the Second Congress. This stronger edict now gave the owner the unrestricted right to cross into another state to reclaim his "property" and to deliver it before "any magistrate of a county, city or town" in order to prove his ownership.

Now empowered to apprehend their runaway slaves, the owners employed professional slave-catchers to search for the fugitives and to bring them before the court. Corrupt slave-catchers, however, frequently failed to accurately identify their captives, as did a few inept judges, and at other times neglected to go to court altogether, simply conducting their prisoners south and into slavery. Free blacks in the North were fully aware of these numerous and seemingly random kidnappings and for years had to live and move about in constant fear of being picked up off the street or taken from their homes. Furthermore, since anyone caught aiding a fugitive would be fined $500, the fugitive slaves had to be extremely cautious about the people they enlisted for help.

Northerners were enraged over this new law. It failed to protect the civil liberties of innocent free blacks, they complained, who were helpless victims falsely accused of being fugitives. With no rights to a jury trial, no rights to testify on their own behalf, and no protection under habeas corpus, the accused free blacks were soon subjected to widespread abuse. Over the following years several northern states fought back against this appalling attack on the integrity of freedom by enacting their own personal liberty laws which gave the free blacks their rights in court, required a certificate of removal from the court before removing any suspect, and even imposed criminal penalties on slave-catchers for kidnapping. As reviled as this law was to northerners and as difficult as it was to enforce for southerners, the Fugitive Slave Act would continue to be a major source of sectional conflict for another fifty-seven years at which time a new, stronger, and even more controversial fugitive slave law was enacted.

By the late eighteenth century, two momentous technological events occurred that redefined the South, the southern economy, and the institution of slavery itself. The first was the introduction of steam power in Great Britain, one of the most significant factors contributing to the beginning of the Industrial Revolution. Steam-powered textile factories, now able to process cotton into fabric much more efficiently and at a lower cost, resulted in an explosive demand for more cotton. Then, by using an improved version of the cotton gin, beginning in 1794, southern planters were delighted to discover that it was now possible to process enormous quantities of raw cotton on a scale unimaginable in the past.

Initially cultivated in small quantities in the fields of Georgia and North Carolina, cotton production now escalated to new heights. Planters throughout the Deep South soon discovered that with Eli Whitney's gin, cotton would now be the king of all southern crops. In great demand, less costly to process, and a more profitable bottom-line, planters rushed to concentrate on this new cash crop. In time, wide expanses of cotton were being cultivated in Florida, Texas, and Arkansas as well, and then in Louisiana, Alabama, and Mississippi, all of which pointed to a greater demand for slaves to work the fields and the resultant lock on the southern rationale for defending their peculiar institution.

Despite the long-held perception of large plantations with hundreds of slaves, only one-fourth of the southerners actually owned slaves, and of these, nearly 90 percent owned fewer than twenty. The larger cotton plantations usually owned around fifty to several hundred. Although the poor non-slaveholder, the white yeoman farmer, longed to have his own slaves and to join the ranks of the wealthy and powerful privileged, he was content with knowing he was still superior to the black, was not a slave, and any power he did possess came simply from being white.

In the South, owning slaves, whether it was one or one hundred, was an acceptable practice taken for granted as a way of doing business. To most people it was a sign of the times. Southern planters were merely utilizing an available labor force in a land with an abundance of fertile soil, but constrained by an inadequate supply of laborers. Besides, as devout Christians, the owners felt they were following the religious truths contained within the Bible, which did not condemn slavery. The slave owners believed they also had every right to enslave non–Christians, or captives taken in an honorable war. It was, after all, a belief formed from a long-standing British tradition and one they would continue to maintain.

Under the watchful eye of an overseer, the slaves were in the fields from sunrise to sunset and at harvest time they were expected to work an eighteen-hour day. They also cut and hauled wood, constructed roads and buildings, shod the horses, dug canals and ditches, slaughtered livestock, and repaired nearly everything on the estate. While the youngest, most able-bodied men and women were used primarily for work in the fields, the older slaves were more likely utilized as cooks, dressmakers, maids, or household servants in the master's family mansion, generally called the great house, while others worked in the family vegetable and herb gardens. Many women spent their time carding the wool and making it into yarn, or doing chores that prepared the master's family for the winter, such as salting the beef and putting up the preserves. Their diets, crude, make-shift quarters, and tattered clothing were wholly inadequate as was the treatment for their health. Consistently exposed to unsanitary conditions, inadequate nutrition, and hours of hard labor in the extreme heat and humidity of the South, slaves were extremely susceptible to many diseases and illnesses. Slave women, besides living under these dreadful conditions, also had to endure the constant threat of being sexually exploited by masters and overseers. This abusive practice was widespread and taken advantage of by many of those in power. Tragically, the slave men were powerless to intercede on behalf of the women they loved. One ex-slave recounted, "No colored man wishes to live at the house where his wife lives, for he has to endure the continual misery of seeing her flogged and abused, without daring to say a word in her defence."

Despite the risks involved, however, there was always a certain degree of rebellious behavior the slaves would demonstrate against their owners in retaliation. Slaves would constantly steal food or household items, pretend they were ill, take longer to perform their tasks, or even damage the crop.

The very young of the slaves were always free to play, even with the white children living in the great house, unaware of their slave status. But as they grew older and witnessed the abuse of their parents at the hands of the owner or the overseer, the cruel reality of their existence became apparent. For most slave children, work in the fields began around the tender age of ten. At this stage they quickly learned that in addition to their parents their lives were also influenced by a second level of authority, the master and his overseers.

Although many slaves lived a very harsh existence, most slaves lived in two different worlds. One life was spent as a strictly regimented and coerced laborer in a white man's world, the other commencing after working hours when they enjoyed the few meager pleasures afforded to them in a black man's world. Their family and their religion were, of course, always the source of their strength and perseverance in a life of unbelievable hardships. Their families were typically large, usually consisting of around seven or eight children all living in a simple dirt-floor cabin. Slave quarters were small and poorly constructed, usually measuring around eighteen by twenty feet. As primitive as they were, the cabins were far better than having to sleep in the barns, lofts, sheds, or outdoors as the slaves were forced to do in earlier times. Normally consisting of only one room, the cabins were usually grouped in clusters always some distance from the great house. This segregated arrangement not only provided the master's family with a partition separating them from the slaves, but at the same time afforded the slaves relative privacy and a quasi-sense of freedom they very much enjoyed among themselves. Away from the constant threat of beatings and the dominating eye of the overseer they laughed and argued, told stories, played games and music, sang songs, complained, worried, and loved. Soon an underground black culture formed as a testament to their survival in an otherwise cruel world.

Around 1830, three decades after the beginning of the so-called antebellum period, the slave owner's compassion for his slaves was much more evident than at any other time, a by-product of a renewed Protestant evangelical movement called The Second Great Awakening. Perhaps the most dominant form of Christian expression in the United States, the revival movement was led by such distinguished preachers as Charles G. Finney and Nathaniel Taylor. It was a doctrine devoted to reshaping American society through a greater commitment to abolitionism, and to pursue other reform programs such as temperance, charitable work, and educational improvements. Through the persuasive power of their sermons the revisionists were steadfast in urging others to abandon their sinful ways and to fight the moral degradation and the evil sin of owning slaves. Consequently, although the pillory and whippings were the punishments of choice on the slaves, and would remain so for some time, incidents of other, more severe abuses, such as branding and castration, were significantly diminished as a result of the Christian movement. And instead of the arrogant display of bravado over the harsh discipline inflicted on their slaves, there were some owners who now found it more fashionable to boast over the kindnesses afforded to them.

During these years the owners became more and more aware of the importance of protecting and caring for their slaves on a more humane level and of their obligation to introduce the Bible into their lives. Although sermons in southern churches never criticized slavery, they did stress the Christian duty of masters to instruct their slaves in the word of the Gospel, and such virtues as personal honesty, freedom of conscience, and devotion to their faith, their family and their southern heritage. But, the slaveholders were not exactly deaf to the inflammatory preaching from the northern pulpits against slavery. They were certainly mindful of the words expressed against the institution as being immoral; that not only owning slaves but also any connection with slavery was an abominable sin and guaranteed eternal damnation in hell. Therefore, to absolve their conscience of personal sin and to cleanse their souls, slaveholders, as devout Christians, became more and more defensive of their peculiar institution, and resented northern abolitionists for simply refusing to mind their own business.

As a result of the evangelical sermons, combined with the close association with their slaves, many slaveholders considered them part of their extended family and as such mandated their schooling in Christian beliefs. Since most owners believed literacy encouraged independence, however, the slaves were rarely taught to read and write. Instead the nearest they got to a formal education was when the owner assembled his slaves in a group to read and discuss the Bible with them. Even special church services were arranged for them to attend, but frequently many slaves resisted this gesture, preferring instead to hold secret prayer meetings where their own form of Christianity was preached with a gospel steeped in strong African overtones.

Medical care for the slaves had not improved appreciably over the years, not because of the master's negligence, but due to the general lack of medical knowledge. In any case, a master now took greater interest in the health of his slaves and provided them with whatever medical care he could obtain. This may have been more difficult in the Louisiana area, however, where working conditions were at their worse. Not only was it very hot and humid, but the wet rice fields created a breeding ground for malaria and a very high rate of child mortality.

One important factor that contributed enormously to an improvement in the diet and health of the slaves during the antebellum period was the large quantity of food available. The slaves were normally given weekly food rations of corn meal and pork or bacon, and to supplement their rations many slaves were permitted to tend their own vegetable gardens, raise chickens, and fish in the nearby waters. In addition, from time to time the slave owner would distribute luxuries such as coffee or confectionaries. All of these practices, in turn, contributed to healthier, happier and more productive slaves. One occasion the slaves particularly looked forward to each year was Christmas when they were given a week off to enjoy the holiday in their own fashion.

Also, instead of the tattered rags of the colonial era, antebellum slaves were issued an allotment of suits and dresses per year as well as ill-fitting shoes and long-shirts for the children. Although most of the clothes were bought pre-made, many articles were hand-sewn by the slave women from coarse woolen material manufactured in the North specifically for slave owners.

As for marriage among the slaves, it was quite rare in the early colonies because of the numerical disparity between the sexes. But in the antebellum years, as more and more women were sold into slavery, owners became more cognizant of the importance of slave marriage and family in terms of its impact on the slaves' work ethic, cooperation, and productivity. In this regard, marriage was encouraged and formed the beginnings of the African American family culture. At the same time, the master's capital investment would increase substantially in value as the number of his slaves multiplied. One freedman explained years later, "Slaves always wanted to marry a gal on 'nother plantation cause dey could git a pass to go visit 'em on Saddy nights."

Although an owner held some slaves apart from the rest, like those he may have grown up with from childhood, he took great interest in the welfare of all his slaves. But there were also times when his actions were somewhat contradictory and tempered by a power balance both understood. This was particularly true when the master had to reduce his inventory of surplus slaves or when he suffered a financial loss. During these troubling times it became necessary for one owner to sell his human property to another slave owner at the local auction house where the slaves were examined, prodded, poked, and treated no differently than the horses or hogs would be at their auction.

The slave auction was perhaps the most heart-wrenching experience for any slave, but it was particularly dreadful for a slave family. Young, able-bodied men who were well valued on the auction block would never see their wives and children again, and on occasion mothers were torn away from their babies, or youngsters sent off, never to return. If in the rare instance a family was kept together, they were almost always transported far from their extended families. For this reason merely the threat of being sold was cause for enormous anxiety. In some cases slaves were known to mutilate themselves in a desperate attempt to reduce their value and the likelihood of being sold at auction.

The introduction of coerced labor into American society in 1619 started the long, incremental process that would eventually lead to two distinct Americas. Although sharing a common flag, a common language, a common European ancestry and a common Protestant Christianity, slavery would force the North and the South to grow apart, more alienated, more intolerant, more hostile, and more different.

Most of their differences evolved from the clash of two vastly conflicting ideologies. Southern aristocracy was infested with an enormous cancer that had grown from over 200 years of perpetuating the exploitation of human bondage. In the perception of the Northerners, this cancer and its debilitating side effects influenced and skewed the cultural, political, and social values of southern society, a condition that was an extreme contradiction to northern religious and moral principles.

In their defense, the Southerners were forced to continually defend slavery and their way of life and to engage in a seemingly neverending battle with outside agitators that threatened their very existence. Southern aristocracy believed that "labor in every society, by whomsoever performed, is necessarily unintellectual, groveling, and base." And while northern wage-laborers must work in factories or starve, in conditions that were as bad as or even worse than those for a majority of slaves, one Virginian wrote, "Slaves are supported whether they work or not." Their slaves were far better off working for a caring master, they argued, one who gave them shelter, medical care, and clothing. One southern newspaper bitterly wrote, "Free Society! We sicken at the name. What is it but a conglomeration of greasy mechanics, filthy operatives, small-fisted farmers, and moon-struck theorists...? The prevailing class one meets with [in the North] is that of mechanics struggling to be genteel, and small farmers who do their own drudgery, and yet are hardly fit for association with a Southern gentleman's body servant." South Carolina senator James Hammond eloquently defended slavery in a speech he gave before the

Senate. "In all social systems there must be a class to do the menial duties, to perform the drudgery of life.... It constitutes the very mudsill of society.... Such a class you must have, or you would not have that other class which leads progress, civilization, and refinement.... Your whole hireling class of manual laborers and operatives, as you call them, are essentially slaves. The difference between us is, that our slaves are hired for life and well compensated ... yours are hired by the day, not cared for, and scantily compensated."

Slaveholders blamed the North for creating a volatile climate in the South that not only impacted the behavior of their slaves but also induced fear and trepidation into the hard working southern people. After all, in the southern psyche, to defend slavery from these outside agitators was to defend the South, and since slavery was the very foundation of their social order, any effort at reform was soundly rebuffed as an effort to endanger their homeland and their way of life. And so, the relentless exchanges of taunts and accusations continued which only created more bitterness and more recriminations. Aware of these profound differences, one Savannah lawyer remarked, "Yankees and Southrons could no more mix than oil and water. They have been so entirely separated by climate, by morals, by religion, and by estimates so totally opposite of all that constitutes honor, truth, and manliness, that they cannot longer exist under the same government."

In the end, despite all the inflammatory rhetoric against slavery from the abolitionists and in spite of the elimination of the slave trade, slavery was a necessary element in southern society and remained firmly entrenched. It was the engine that drove the southern cash crop economy over which King Cotton reigned. A slave-based society was the means by which the wealthy southern aristocrats could continue to survive in the style they were accustomed to and it would be defended to the death.

Of course there were others factors that also distinguished the character and personality differences between the North and South. While the climate conditions in the South accounted for much of its farming proclivities and therefore its unswerving dependence on slave labor, at the same time, nearly 90 percent of the European immigrants seeking greater opportunities for a better life avoided the South. Instead, they preferred to settle in the bustling northern cities of New York, Boston and Philadelphia, from where thousands eventually migrated to the western states and territories. Equipped with countless skills, they provided much of the wage-labor force that helped drive the North towards industrial and economic superiority which in turn only accentuated the disparity between the two sections.

The differences between the two sides, each intricately linked, each affecting the other, when taken in aggregate, placed them at odds politically, socially, culturally, and economically. While many people of the two regions did, in fact, enjoy numerous common interests and enjoyed their mutual contributions and friendships, the net impact of their interwoven differences resulted in political hostility, bitter disputes, petty jealousies, accusations, controversies, and resentment. This intolerable scenario forced each side into an incessant struggle with the other, each straining to uphold its separate and sacred ideals, and in the end only gave birth to years and years of sectional conflict.

By 1830 there were nearly two million slaves in the country, all but eight thousand residing in the states of the South. And of those two million, a quarter of them were in Virginia alone. Deeply troubled over the issues emanating from the divergent views of morality, the North began to perceive the South in a much different light. They looked upon the South as an alien people economically and socially degraded by their own cruel adherence to its degenerative values. It was our system against their system, they said, a free-wage labor philosophy as opposed to one mandating a forced-labor system under the coercive influences of the lash.

The collision, therefore, between forces espousing southern slavery with its inherent cultural and social mutations and the enlightened northern antislavery establishment, was the first major contributing factor that not only differentiated the "two Americas" but also caused the initial sectional fracture that began the process destined to drive the two sides apart. This sectional conflict, joined by a number of others in the coming years, created the hostile conditions that bred frequent, prolonged, and bitter sectional disputes which would ultimately lead the South along the road to secession, a road destined to culminate in a bloody and historic civil war.

2

The Rise and Fall of Abolitionism (1750 to 1848)

As more people became fed up with the barbaric cruelty and immorality of slavery, the humiliating horror of slave auctions, and the social degradation of the South, beginning in the 1750s and continuing through the years leading to the Civil War, challenges to the institution of slavery were a constant cause of sectional conflict.

These challenges were, to a great extent, instigated by Quaker activists such as John Woolman and Anthony Benezet, who preached that slavery was unethical and counterproductive. It was a system of labor, they opined, that eliminated the incentive for self-improvement, which in reality was the catalyst for even greater productivity and economic health. Furthermore, they asserted, slavery was the epitome of depravity, a social and cultural injustice to everyone, and only forced one to work a lifetime for the betterment of someone else with nothing gained in return.

As Woolman declared in 1757, "free Men, whose Minds were properly on their Business, found a Satisfaction in improving, cultivating, and providing for their Families; but Negroes, labouring to support others who claim them as their Property, and expecting nothing but slavery during Life, had not the like Inducement to be industrious."

The birth of the abolitionist movement occurred in parallel with a number of evangelical revivals principally dominated by the Society of Friends in Pennsylvania, called the Quakers. Since slavery was never condemned by the Bible, most Quakers at the time were not particularly averse to the practice. Consequently, during the so-called Great Awakening of the mid–18th century, a period marked by widespread secularization, the Quakers were primarily concerned with teaching their parishioners such virtues as tolerance for others and human kindness, and to encourage the conversion of slaves into the

Christian faith. In time, however, this message of compassion and brotherhood began to resonate within the church in a more profound way and ultimately inspired a small group of Quakers in Pennsylvania to organize against slavery itself.

Founded in 1775 by Benezet, the Society for the Relief of Free Negroes Unlawfully held in Bondage became the first anti-slavery organization in America. Consisting of only ten members, the society interceded in cases where free blacks and Indians claimed to be wrongfully enslaved. With eighteen members nine years later, the society reorganized as the Pennsylvania Society for the Abolition of Slavery. In fact, Benjamin Franklin became one of its presidents and was instrumental in promoting programs to establish black schools and to gain employment for the free blacks in Philadelphia.

Throughout the colonial years, the persistent and anguished drumbeat from the abolitionists over the evils of slavery motivated other religious faiths to lend their support as well. Baptists and Methodists were equally united in the denunciation of slavery, calling the practice inhumane and demeaning to mankind, and preached that everyone was equal before God. In some instances, the evangelical sermons even persuaded devout Christian planters to have second thoughts over the enslavement of other humans. One such master wrote that he "wished that our economy & government differ'd from the present system but alas—since our constitution is as it is, what can individuals do?" At the same time, however, most southerners defended owning slaves; the Rev. Peter Fontaine of Virginia wrote, "It is, to be sure, at our choice whether we buy them or not, so this then is our crime, folly, or whatever you will please to call it.... This is our part of the grievance, but to live in Virginia without slaves is morally impossible."

In response to the example set by the Quaker community, other abolitionist organizations were also formed, all expressing a common goal not only to assist the free blacks and Indians, but also to rescue the African slaves from their bondage. As the number of these diverse groups increased, the principal feature that distinguished one from another was the specific methodology they would employ to implement their abolitionist goals, either through colonization of the slaves, gradual emancipation, or immediate emancipation.

One such abolitionist organization was formed by Benjamin Lundy, a Quaker and owner of a saddling business in St. Clairsville, Ohio. As a successful entrepreneur and family man, Lundy was saddened by the deplorable treatment of the slaves he had encountered over the years and felt compelled to devote the remainder of his life to assisting those held in bondage. Consequently, as a staunch advocate of colonization, in 1815 he established an anti-slave association called the Union Humane Society. Soon Lundy began writing articles in a local newspaper, the *Philanthropist,* urging others to form their own anti-slave organizations and "to meet in convention to discuss policies and formulate a common program." A few years later, in 1821, Lundy began publishing his own highly influential anti-slave journal, the *Genius of Universal Emancipation*, a series of informative writings for "molding public opinion in the desired form."

Coinciding with Lundy's appeal, a group of Presbyterian ministers founded the American Colonization Society (ACS) in 1817. They originally embraced the doctrine of gradualism, or gradual compensated emancipation, but at the same time they feared the dire consequences of unleashing hundreds of thousands of newly emancipated slaves into a white society. Gaining support from such prominent advocates as Thomas Jefferson, James Madison, James Monroe, and Henry Clay, the ACS revised its position after being convinced that the two races could not and should not live together in a white man's country. As a result, their immediate goal, more racist than not, was colonization, to transport free blacks to Africa where, they insisted, the blacks would thrive living in their native lands and among their own people. Indeed, over the years ahead, despite lacking support from other abolitionists or from a great majority of free blacks who resented the practice, the society managed to send an estimated 6,000 blacks to a colony they purchased called Liberia, on the west coast of Africa. Even Abraham Lincoln advocated colonization when as president in 1863 he arranged transportation for a shipload of free blacks to an island off the coast of Haiti. Many white southerners wholeheartedly agreed with the concept of colonization. In the southern perception of the movement, ridding the country of the troublesome free blacks was a significant step in eliminating a source of rebellious influence, the ever present bad examples, and was embraced as a way to strengthen control over their slaves. Considering the size of the free black population, the staggering financial costs and the generally hostile response from the blacks themselves, in the years after 1830 colonization was found to be wholly impractical.

Free blacks in the North were also organizing public forums as well, meeting regularly to voice their concerns over human rights issues. In 1830, for instance, forty blacks from nine states concentrated their own efforts towards fighting for equal rights by organizing a ten-day National Negro Convention in Philadelphia, the first of many to follow. Taking their places at the convention were several former slaves and future civil rights activists such as Frederick Douglass, Sojourner Truth, and Harriet Tubman. From that first meeting other black organizations emerged, such as the American Society of Free People of Colour, whose goal it was to improve their condition in the United States and to purchase land for a settlement in the province of Canada. Later, a much larger organization would be formed with chapters in several states called the American Society of Free Persons of Labor. In fact, the black societies became so popular that one newspaper lightheartedly noted that "colored conventions are almost as frequent as churchmeetings."

As more signs of expanding abolitionist activity spread throughout the country, tensions between the two sections increased dramatically. The South was particularly infuriated by the so-called Underground Railroad, a network of anti-slave activists, mostly Quakers, New England Yankees, and free blacks, who assisted fugitive slaves to move from the South to the northern states and at times into Canada. Launched towards the end of the eighteenth century by the Society of Friends, the system would be dubbed the Underground Railroad following the introduction of the first steam locomotive.

Gradually growing in popularity and scope over the years, especially following the adoption of the Fugitive Slave Act, the Underground Railroad utilized literally thousands of participants and hundreds of escape routes through Virginia, Maryland, and Delaware and most of the northeastern states. Such names as Thomas Garrett, Levi Coffin, Harriet Tubman, and John Rankin are just a few of the many people that risked their own lives to help slaves experience a life of freedom. Led by people called conductors under the cover of darkness, the fugitives, or cargoes, would generally travel around 15 miles. At that point they would be concealed, fed, supplied with new clothing, and rested at a prearranged hideout, or station, usually a home or barn. This process would be repeated over successive nights until the fugitives were safely at their destinations. Often it became necessary for the men to dress as women and vice versa to masquerade their movements. Once settled, they were provided with medical care and helped in finding employment. Although figures vary widely, according to one estimate the South lost over 100,000 slaves between 1810 and 1850, a period when it was most effective.

Occasionally the railroad workers and their cargoes were apprehended by slave-catchers either through a chance encounter or by being betrayed for the reward money. Once in custody they were brought before a court to stand trial. The abolitionists were usually ordered to pay a heavy fine or imprisoned, while the slaves would be returned to the South where their masters were certain to inflict their own special form of punishment. Most fugitives, however, particularly those from the upper South, made the trip north alone. On foot and in the dead of night, the runaways surreptitiously made their way northward, hiding out in the woods or caves during the day. Along the east coast the slaves were often stowed below deck of certain vessels and ferried to Philadelphia, Washington, or Boston.

Although anti-slavery sentiments were quite strong from the early days of colonialism through the decade of the 1820s, the main thrust of the abolition movement did not coalesce into a radical crusade until 1831. The strongest voice in this renewed abolitionist movement and one that attained the greatest national prominence began in January when Boston pacifist William Lloyd Garrison, along with his partner, Isaac Knapp, began publishing their anti-slavery journal, the *Liberator*. Greatly influenced by the evangelist revivals, the twenty-six-year-old Garrison published his anti-slave philosophy, often invoking the teachings of the Bible. Garrison was a close confidant of Benjamin

Lundy and also stressed a non-political and nonresistance agenda, consistently reminding his readers that all men were created equal in God's eyes and that slavery was a scandal and an abomination. Instead of colonization or gradualism, however, Garrison urged all Americans to take up his more radical cause of "immediate, unconditional, uncompensated emancipation."

Considered by most of his contemporaries as an extremist and not one to mince words, Garrison used his weekly journal as a forum for his immediatism philosophy and to explain his opposition to slavery. In 1831 he wrote, "I shall strenuously contend for the immediate enfranchisement of our slave population.... On this subject, I do not wish to think, or speak, or write, with moderation. No! No! Tell a man whose house is on fire, to give a moderate alarm; tell him to moderately rescue his wife from the hands of the ravisher; tell the mother to gradually extricate her babe from the fire into which it has fallen; but urge me not to use moderation in a cause like the present. I am in earnest— I will not equivocate—I will not excuse—I will not retreat a single inch—and I WILL BE HEARD." And on another occasion he told his readers, "Woe to this guilty land...! IMMEDIATE EMANCIPATION can alone save her from the vengeance of Heaven, and cancel the debt of ages!" With these uncompromising words a new phase of abolitionism emerged with a wholly new ambitious and extremist goal.

The majority of northern anti-slave advocates, however, strived for a more gradual freedom for the southern slaves, the gradualist point of view. Although the number of slaves in the North was miniscule in comparison to the South, which made emancipation much easier, with millions of slaves in the South, immediate emancipation would be much more difficult to manage. They felt immediate emancipation was an unrealistic goal which would bring only catastrophic results. The southern cotton-driven economy would be in utter chaos, they opined, and financial ruin a certainty. Suffering as well, and perhaps the most, would be the newly emancipated slaves unable to fend for themselves in an alien southern society mired in hatred and resentment. Without an education, employment, housing, finances, or most other means to support themselves or their families, the emancipated slaves would strike back not only from the intolerance shown to their freedom but also from the accumulated pain and racial injustice suffered over the years. The ex-slaves would revolt against the white society, their former masters for certain, in a murderous and bloody vengeance. In the South, scenarios such as this were a constant reminder of the inherent dangers attributed to the abolitionists and their goals against their slave society and worked only to heighten southern tensions and fears. At the same time southern slaveholders felt even more compelled to strengthen their resolve and to oppose all the abolitionists and their intrusive activities.

Instead, in states such as Pennsylvania and New York, the legislatures were persuaded to implement the gradualist approach. In Pennsylvania, for instance, all future-born slaves after 1780 were freed at the age of twenty-eight, making Pennsylvania the first state to abolish slavery. A similar stipulation was also used in other northern states such as New York, with one exception; male slaves were freed at the age of twenty-five and the females at twenty-one, while the New Jersey legislature determined in 1799 that the boys had to be twenty-eight and the girls twenty-five before they received their freedom. During the years ahead the gradual emancipation of northern slaves continued under these state-enacted laws, a procedure that resulted in freedom for three-quarters of the northern slaves by 1810, and virtually all the remaining slaves by 1835. On the other hand, because Vermont and Massachusetts had relatively fewer slaves, they opted for immediate emancipation by simply outlawing slavery in 1777 and 1781, respectively. At the same time, and in a striking contrast, the slave population in the southern states would climb to just over a million or roughly one-third of the southern population.

In the ensuing years since Garrison began publishing the *Liberator*, a considerable number of other abolitionist periodicals began to flood the country as well. These works included the *Emancipator*, the *Anti-Slave Reporter*, and the *National Anti-Slavery Standard*, to mention only a few. To the angst of the southern aristocracy the abolitionists were not merely preaching libelous diatribe against slavery but were also distributing this unseemly and emotional nonsense throughout the South in order to educate southerners, particularly the slaves, about the evils of their peculiar institution.

In truth, much of the abolitionist information that circulated in the South via pamphlets, periodicals and letters sought not only to enlighten but also to sow the seeds of discord among the citizens of the South and to incite the slaves to revolt against the cruelty of their masters. The net result was that in the 1830s the cumulative impact from scores of distressing assertions in this nineteenth-century media blitz had progressively cultivated a deep paranoia in the southern psyche over the possibility and the horrors of a slave revolt. This anxiety was heightened to near hysteria by such incidents as the publication of *Appeal to the Colored Citizens of the World,* a highly provocative work by former slave David Walker which attempted to incite the slaves to rise up against their masters and to seize their freedom by brute force, and the infamous Nat Turner slave revolt.

Nat Turner was a slave and religious fanatic who claimed to have had a vision of Christ. And in this vision Christ asked him to take up the "fight against the Serpent." In August of 1831, therefore, with a band of some fifty to sixty slaves, the group massacred over fifty white men, women and children, mercilessly killing a mother and her ten children at one Virginia farm alone. The bloody rampage continued for about ten days before they were apprehended, with the exception of Turner who escaped. Caught in a swamp two months after the killing spree began, Turner was tried and convicted. Prior to his execution Turner wrote in his confession that Christ had told him "the time was fast approaching when the first should be last and the last should be first." To the thousands of God-fearing, Bible-toting southerners, Turner's revelation was a matter of much trepidation and compelled planters to institute even tighter controls on their slaves. Fueling the fire of southern apprehension even more was Garrison's opinion of Turner's bloody murdering spree, calling it the "first step of the earthquake, which is ultimately to shake down the fabric of oppression.... The first drops of blood, which are but a prelude to a deluge from the gathering clouds ... " and that a "war of extermination" was underway in a "nation of oppressors."

Continuing to flaunt his anti-slavery prowess and to spread his philosophy of moral suasion, in 1832 along with ten others, Garrison founded the New England Anti-Slavery Society. The following year he broadened the abolition movement into New York and Ohio by joining forces with evangelical preacher Charles G. Finney and two wealthy New York businessmen, Arthur and Lewis Tappan, and by establishing a national organization called the American Anti-Slave Society (AASS).

The Tappan brothers were steadfast in their devotion to the abolitionist movement and because of their fanaticism were deeply despised by the South. Rich and influential from their success in the New York silk trade, they epitomized everything the South hated about the abolitionist and as a result were in constant danger of being kidnapped or murdered. In one violent episode during the notorious New York City riots, the home of Lewis Tappan was broken into, windows smashed, and the furniture hauled out to the street and set on fire.

As the abolitionists continued to ratchet up their antislavery agenda, a suppressed backlash of resentment against the movement began to appear in the North. Beginning around 1834 and extending well into the '40s, support for abolitionism in such places as New England, New York and Pennsylvania, once considered abolitionist bastions, had grown extremely fragile and more and more violence was now directed toward abolitionists. Over the years, many northerners looked upon these anti-slavery activists with ever-growing degrees of disdain and frustration, considering them nothing but trouble makers hell-bent on stirring up matters best left alone. Eventually, this pent-up emotion began to erupt into hostile clashes across the North as advocates of the Underground Railroad were continually harassed by disapproving mobs, a school was attacked for attempting to enroll "colored little misses" into its classrooms, abolitionist publishers found their presses destroyed, a church was blown up because it had been used to hold abolition meetings, and elsewhere anti-slavery speakers were either attacked or forced to cancel their appearances, fearful of being beaten or tarred and feathered. In Illinois a newspaper editor was killed by a rampaging mob and even in Boston, the center of this born-again abolitionism movement, anti-slave meetings were frequently stormed by angry townspeople who disrupted the gatherings with their taunts and curses. Even Garrison himself was attacked there by a lynch party until rescued by the mayor and police. In New York City, organized mobs destroyed many black homes and churches, or theaters where blacks and whites appeared on the same stage. Regarding the abolitionists as dangerous fanatics, the mobs insisted that discussions about slavery must stop. The constant dialogue over slavery had grown exceedingly caustic, they asserted, and would only agitate the sectional conflict and endanger the Union. Many were also concerned that if the abolitionist movement accomplished its goal, thousands of freed slaves would flee the South for the better life in the North. Penniless, homeless, uneducated, and unemployed, they would create an enormous burden on the major cities of the North, a prospect incompatible with the mores of the times. Views against the abolitionist movement were also being expressed from the pulpits of various churches. The Methodists and the Congregational faiths, those that once supported the abolitionist cause, now deplored any intervention into the relationship between master and slave. And the Presbyterians had yet a different position, that slavery was a political rather than a moral issue. The abolitionists, however, whether they supported gradual or immediate emancipation, vowed never to relent in their quest to make the United States a land of the free for everyone regardless of the color of their skin. In reality, however, as righteous as the white abolitionists professed to be in their cause, they could not entirely separate themselves from the mindset of their time.

Below the Mason-Dixon Line, southern reaction to the abolitionist movement, as least in the earlier years, around 1817 when the American Colonization Society was formed, was somewhat supportive. Over time, however, southern citizens became highly agitated by the continuous onslaught of outside meddlers, the incendiary rhetoric, and the resultant threat of insurrection, a climate they claimed interfered with their peaceful and legitimate social order.

Obviously an enemy of the slave owners for his uncompromisingly harsh statements about their peculiar institution, Garrison's popularity in the North and even among some anti-slave circles continued to suffer. Indeed, his demand for immediate emancipation was looked upon by many political intellectuals as too extreme, as rocking the boat on a very sensitive issue and one most likely to lead to disunion. In fact, abolitionism and slavery had become such sensitive issues in some circles that even the northern politicians in Washington displayed a curious sense of uneasiness when discussing them, preferring instead to pursue southern votes and to leave the issues of slavery and emancipation to the southern states to resolve.

Despite the troubling signs of a growing resistance to abolitionism in the North, Garrison's vision for an immediate end to slavery never wavered. "What have I done?" said an incredulous Garrison. "Within four years I have seen my principles embraced by thousands of the best men in the nation. I have seen prejudices which were deemed incurable utterly eradicated from the breasts of a great multitude.... I have seen discussions of slavery going on in public and in private, among all classes and in all parts of the land; and more spoken and written and printed and circulated in one month than there formerly was in many years."

By 1835, the influx of northern abolitionist propaganda into Mississippi had become so offensive that the legislature offered rewards of $5,000 for the apprehension and conviction of anyone distributing anti-slave literature within its borders. The American Anti-Slavery Society was, in all probability, the worst offender with over a million mailings into the South in just 1835 alone.

To combat the flood of anti-slave literature coming into the state, the South Carolina legislature sent appeals to the non-slaveholding states asking them to help contain the flow of this inflammatory material into the South. Although several northern states politely replied to the letter, to the disappointment of South Carolina's recently elected governor, George McDuffie, not one of them acted on the appeal. Meanwhile, Democratic president Andrew Jackson, in a self-serving gesture, stepped into the fray by asking Congress in his annual address for legislation that would restrict the flow of anti-slavery material into the South. The result was a five-member select committee, chaired by John C. Calhoun of South Carolina. Recognizing the constitutional impediments placed on the federal government to legislate on any issues involving slavery, Calhoun decided that instead of proposing a new federal law, which in all likelihood would fail, he would submit a bill that called on the federal government to enforce existing state laws enacted to protect the safety, peace and tranquility of its citizens. Opponents of Calhoun's recommendation were quick to point out that his bill would not only violate the First Amendment right of free speech but would also place the central government on the side of slavery, a direct contradiction of his states' rights principles. Calhoun, however, in his own characteristic logic, responded that by not acting on his bill, the government was doing the same thing by taking the side of the abolitionists. In the end, Calhoun's bill was rejected by the Senate but with 1836 being a presidential election year, administrative orders from Postmaster General Amos Kendall made every attempt to put a stop to all unwanted deliveries of abolitionist materials in a clear pandering maneuver to attract southern voters to the Democratic candidate.

Compounding the problems for the abolitionist movement was dissention within the movement itself. Since its formation in 1833, the American Anti-Slavery Society became increasingly divided ideologically over the methodology for combating a seemingly growing apathetic northern attitude toward slavery. This split created two camps, a radical Garrisonian faction that remained committed to immediate emancipation, and a more moderate but politically-oriented faction controlled by the Tappans. Although the abolitionist movement had succeeded in creating an enormous public dialogue over the morality of slavery, it failed to arouse what the movement really strived for— a national uproar against the practice of slavery itself. The Garrisonians believed this attitude was actually a symptom of another problem: the degenerative and immoral corruptive influences of American values in general. Therefore, they opined, in addition to slavery, the nation's social values must also be reformed by promoting such programs as temperance, equal rights for women and free blacks, better education, and prison reform. One of their first initiatives to implement this new philosophy was to welcome women into the society and to take up their fight for women's rights and equality. On the other hand, the more moderate faction thought the time was right to politicize the movement by forming an anti-slavery party to promote their particular agenda.

The remaining bonds within the AASS finally broke in 1839 when members of the moderate crowd were defeated for seats on the executive committee. Resentful of their rejection, most of the so-called political abolitionists walked out and joined another group called the American and Foreign Anti-Slave Society, also a product of the New York Tappan brothers. In fact that same year they formed the first anti-slavery political party in the United States, the Liberty Party, and nominated James G. Birney in an unsuccessful bid for the presidency in 1840. Running solely on a platform of abolitionism, the party would repeat its losing effort four years later as well. Ultimately, the Liberty Party would merge with anti-slavery Democrats and Whigs in 1848 to form the Free Soil Party.

The economic downturn and the resultant financial panic beginning in 1837 also undermined the efforts of the AASS and, in effect, the abolitionist movement itself. With the country experiencing hard times, abolitionists saw their financial resources severely diminished. Attention to their causes had also become diluted amid the more pressing problems of the economy and the war with Mexico. The focus on abolitionism was further weakened by the popularity of expansionism in the mid–1840s and compounded by a new and predominant issue—the possible extension of slavery into the wide expanse of western territory.

From the seeds of the abolitionism movement, therefore, new civil rights factions began to appear when free blacks and female activists took up their own causes for justice in their fight for equality.

With the AASS severely weakened and losing its focus on black ideals and goals, the free black members determined they had little choice but to leave the organization for a more compatible forum to express their views. Instead they continued to address the issues that concerned them the most through the meetings of the National Negro Convention movement. And following several years of promoting their own agenda under the auspices of Garrison and the AASS, the women in the movement also sensed the society was losing its command of the issues. They were convinced that to better achieve their goals for civil rights and equality, they needed to form their own organization as well. Consequently, in July 1848, Elizabeth Cady Stanton, Lucretia Mott, and others, led a group of female abolitionists at a meeting in Seneca

Falls, New York, and organized the first women's rights movement in the nation.

Finally, by pursuing the more extreme cause of immediate abolitionism as a moral issue instead of a political one, Garrison undermined his leadership of the abolitionist movement. His unswerving resentment of the government, as well, had tainted his ability to accept the concept of a Union as others defined it, particularly one including slavery. Explaining his position on preserving the Union, Garrison remarked several years later, "The issue is this: God Almighty has made it impossible from the beginning, for liberty and slavery to mingle together, or a union to be founded between abolitionists and slaveholders—between those who oppress and those who are oppressed. This Union is a lie; the American Union is a sham, an imposture, a covenant with death, an agreement with hell, and it is our business to call for a dissolution.... I say, let us cease striking hands with thieves and adulterers, and give up to the winds the rallying cry, 'No union with slaveholders, socially or religiously, and up with the flag of Disunion.'"

The loser, of course, was the momentum of the abolitionist movement, a social reformation that would eventually be fragmented and pursued by hundreds of smaller state organizations, many with contradictory tactics, incompatible personalities, and ideologically at odds with one another.

In the end, the greatest success of the abolitionist movement was that it unwittingly became a social awakening of its own. By creating an intense dialogue and meaningful debate over the morality of slavery, forced servitude was now a public issue. Slavery and abolitionism were now discussed freely in the parlors, at the dinner tables, from the pulpits, and pretty much everywhere people congregated, except of course in Congress where they secreted themselves behind the Constitution. On the basis of this dialogue and from the exposure to the flood of anti-slave periodicals, many and varied observations and opinions on these issues were surely formed. Resolutions, however, remained elusive.

As a result, Garrison's power of moral suasion had convinced thousands in the North that slavery was indeed wrong. And in the process the South and the southern way of life was looked upon with utter disdain, repressed anger, and disgust. The South and its people were held responsible for perpetrating this evil and as such the South must be held accountable. But northern emotions were mixed and confused. Along with these hostile passions, the North feared the consequences of what abolitionism would unleash if its goals were attained. It was easy to criticize the evils of slavery and its aristocratic perpetrators, but at the same time they were thankful as well that the very people they criticized were so adamantly defending their peculiar institution.

3

Economic Protectionism (1815 to 1828)

While social and cultural differences over slavery and abolitionism embroiled the two sections in a seemingly never-ending struggle, other forces were also at work that continued to divide the North and South even further. These forces, economic in nature, were founded in policies promoting favored domestic industries over all others through the use of high tariffs and other regulations to discourage competing imports. It was called protectionism. And when coupled with the perceived corruption inherent in the newly established banking laws, sectional discord grew even more intense.

Ongoing disputes with Great Britain, when measured in their totality, eventually forced the United States government into an untenable position. These disputes included disagreements over the U.S–Canadian border in the Northwest Territory, specifically the line dividing the Great Lakes and the present-day states of Ohio, Indiana, Illinois, Michigan, and Wisconsin, and the shelling and capture of the *Chesapeake* by the British man-of-war the H.M.S. *Leopard* off Norfolk, Virginia, in 1807. It was a battle that killed three American crewmen and wounded eighteen others. The final straw, however, was the impressment of American sailors into service aboard English naval vessels.

In response to an ever increasing number of crewmen deserting His Majesty's navy for a much better life aboard U.S. merchant vessels, beginning around 1803 the British government assumed the right to stop and board any American merchant ship on the high seas. Once aboard, proof of citizenship was demanded from every seaman on the vessel. If the lad failed to provide this proof he was automatically assumed to be a British deserter, immediately placed under arrest and taken away. So widespread was this flagrant kidnapping of American crewmen that by the time war was declared the U.S. estimated a loss in the thousands of merchant seamen. In fact, it was the refusal of the *Chesapeake*'s commander to allow a search of his ship that led to the shelling of his vessel and the subsequent injuries and loss of life. At length, angered over this persistent insult to U.S. sovereignty and the failed attempts to reach a diplomatic solution, with the urging of President James Madison, the Twelfth Congress declared a state of hostilities with Britain on June 18, 1812.

From the outset, as the War of 1812 took its toll on the U.S. economy, the Madison administration had to confront at least four major problems.

First, the British blockade of major ports from New York to New Orleans and its ensuing interference with commercial shipping strained the coffers of the U.S. Treasury. With the ports closed and imports limited, the Treasury suffered a substantial loss of tariff revenue needed to pay wartime expenses. This situation was particularly alarming because the solvency of the Treasury depended heavily on customs duties, a primary revenue source for the government. Therefore, to help finance the war the federal government was forced to double the duties on all remaining imports into the country for the duration of the conflict and for one year thereafter.

Secondly, compounding the Treasury's difficulties was the lack of a large central bank that could assist the government in dealing with the war's enormous financial burdens, an institution similar to the defunct First Bank of the United States. The Bank, as it was often referred to, was a private corporation established by Congress in 1791. Located in Philadelphia, the Bank was chartered for twenty years not only to lend funds to the government to help pay the Revolutionary War debt, but also, since each of the state banks issued a different currency, the Bank could stabilize the financial system as well by creating a standard currency. Nevertheless, over the intervening years many influential politicians questioned the constitutionality of the Bank's perceived monopoly on issuing money. Opposition to the Bank also came from the South, a section of the country still clinging to the ideals of limited government. Large banks were corrupt institutions, southerners maintained, inherently empowered to grant special favors to a few wealthy and powerful elites for their own self-interests. The most persuasive outcry against the Bank, however, was over the fact that 70 percent of the Bank's shares were owned by foreign investors. In view of these and other criticisms, the effort to renew the bank's charter was denied in 1811 when Vice President George Clinton cast the deciding vote against renewal of the charter after the Senate vote tied at seventeen. This decision by Congress forced the government to borrow additional funds from state banks (also called private banks) at exorbitant interest rates while the same banks were also dispersing loans to finance scores of high-risk real-estate ventures and to numerous other private investors. Since the federal government did not print paper money and the Constitution prohibited the states that right as well, state legislatures chartered only the banks that issued their own paper bank notes. Although the notes were not legal tender, the demand for credit became so intense that most of these banks became over-extended, printing and issuing bank notes without regard to their own holdings. One of these banks, for example, despite having only $86 in specie to back up its transactions, issued loans totaling $580,000 in bank notes. With so much money in circulation inflation rose dramatically and sent prices 40 percent higher in just two years. To make matters even worse, the state banks refused to exchange their notes in specie and as a result the government was unable to redeem millions of dollars of their deposits, temporarily bankrupting the Treasury.

Also confronting Madison was the significant shortage of goods and products Americans had grown accustomed to in their daily lives, a consequence of the wartime restrictions on foreign imports. Nevertheless, the scarcity of these items, although an inconvenience to a large segment of the general public, proved to be a blessing in disguise. The shortage of imported goods created an enormous upsurge in nationalistic spirit and a massive impetus for American businesses, mostly in the North, to produce goods previously imported from foreign manufacturers. Although prices for these goods were somewhat higher than the imports, a condition attributed to manufacturers passing along their start-up costs, America was now endeavoring to be economically self-sufficient and free from its dependency on foreign manufacturers for many of its consumer needs.

And finally, the war exposed the glaring need for building an infrastructure of roads and canals to transport goods and materials throughout the country.

To make matters even worse, following the Treaty of Ghent, which officially ended the war in 1814, unrestricted foreign trade resumed once again and on an unprecedented scale. Less expensive goods imported primarily from Great Britain now flooded the marketplace. Unable to compete against this onslaught of cheap foreign merchandise, many promising American manufacturers and small entrepreneurs were either forced out of business or found their attempts to participate in the new capitalistic experience threatened. A British minister defended the practice declaring, "It is well worth while to incur a loss upon the first exportation, in order, by a glut, to stifle in the cradle those rising manufactures in the United States which the war had forced into existence."

Recognizing the dawn of a new economic era, one that freed Americans in their pursuit of personal prosperity, in December of 1815, President Madison, known as the father of the U.S. Constitution, asked the Fourteenth Congress to approve his proposal for a sweeping national economic development program. Called the Madisonian Platform, the program was designed to address the wartime problems that impacted the U.S. economy and to put the country on a better road to economic independence.

One element of Madison's proposal called for establishing protections or safeguards to assist the new and developing home-grown industries from the onslaught of foreign competition. Specifically, he asked Congress to continue to levy the tariff imposed during the war on imported goods but at a reduced rate. Although the high wartime rates would be somewhat lower than before, he declared, the proposed levy would still be able to protect the new American manufacturing initiatives, encourage more domestic manufacturing which would further stimulate U.S. industrial growth, substantially reduce reliance on British manufacturers and British goods, and would supply the Treasury with badly needed revenue.

Since the War of 1812 had demonstrated how inadequate the country's internal transportation system was for both interstate commerce and national defense, Madison also called for a number of internal improvements that he thought would help stimulate growth in the South and West. These improvements included such projects as building a more comprehensive system of roads and canals, projects he believed would lower the cost of transportation, facilitate trade, and unite the country both physically and economically. Also recommended was funding to increase the strength of the army and for additional vessels for the navy, a lesson learned from the recent war with Britain that clearly demonstrated the need for military preparedness.

Finally, Madison asked Congress to charter a Second Bank of the United States. The new so-called banker's bank and its branches, besides serving as a safe repository for the nation's funds, would also strengthen the country's banking system by implementing more stringent regulations against the wayward state banks and would promote monetary stability by preventing these smaller banks from over-speculating in the marketplace.

Acknowledging the need to provide some degree of protection to the new industries, Congress dutifully voted to approve Madison's tariff recommendation. Called the Tariff of 1816, the measure was the work of secretary of the Treasury, Alexander J. Dallas, and called for the imposition of import levies ranging between 15 percent and 30 percent on such products as textiles, paper, pig iron, and leather over a span of four years. At the end of the four years the tariffs would be reduced to an average of 20 percent. The fact that the duration of the protection provisions was limited contributed somewhat to the guarded acquiescence of the South, as was a clause which protected the interests of the cotton growers from the importation of cheap Indian cotton by imposing a twenty-five cent base tax on all imported cottons regardless of the invoice values. Nevertheless, there was still resentment over the tariff, chiefly from the agricultural and commercial shipping interests who feared it would make foreign goods much more expensive since the high cost of the tax would be passed on to the American consumer. But, the administration reasoned, European prices would then be comparable for the same U.S. products, and hopefully, the government stressed, Americans would choose the domestic products over the foreign competition. At the same time, proponents would argue, the country benefited from the income the tariff would bring into the Treasury.

The Tariff of 1816, the first truly protective tariff, was deemed more of a compromise between conflicting interests and as a needed stimulus package for the country as a whole. It was designed strictly to raise much needed revenue and to reduce U.S. reliance on British manufacturers, with protectionism only a mild and incidental byproduct. Despite the compromise, however, nobody was completely satisfied and in the years ahead southern resentment over any protective tariff would place the South at odds with both the North and the federal government, a bitter sectional dispute that would last for years.

Despite the scattered opposition over the perceived corruptive nature of the Bank, again chiefly from the South, Congress was in no mood for any further conflict. With little debate, in April a charter for the Second Bank of the United States was approved. The charter would be in force for twenty years beginning January 7, 1817, and gave the Bank the privilege of holding and transferring government funds without paying interest for their use. In return, with $35 million in assets, the charter required the Bank to pay a bonus of $1.5 million per year to the federal government and because one-fifth of the stock was owned by the government, the charter allowed the U.S. president to select five of the Bank's twenty-five directors. In addition, the Bank would assist in collecting taxes, providing credit, and issuing bank notes.

Predictably, the private banking industry rallied strenuously against reestablishing a national bank chiefly because of the unwanted and unfair competition from a federally sponsored institution. Opposition also resurfaced over the constitutionality of using a private commercial bank, dominated mostly by foreign investors who owned nearly 80 percent of the stock, as an instrument for U.S. fiscal operations.

On Madison's request for the military, appropriations were also approved to reorganize the army, strengthen the militia, and construct new forts, as well as build twenty-one new ships for the navy.

Although debate on the internal improvements provision was postponed to the second session of this Congress, most of Madison's economic program was subsequently passed and signed into law by the end of April 1816. The bipartisan endorsement of Madison's economic programs was in large part attributed to the support of three young forward-looking congressional leaders. They each recognized the long-term wisdom of Madison's proposal not only for the economic health of the nation but also for his insight on the need for military readiness. These were preeminent men of a new generation of political leaders, men capable of putting aside their sectional differences for the good of the country.

Acclaimed as the foremost spokesmen for their respective regions they were John C. Calhoun, a co-sponsor of the 1816 tariff, and adopted Kentuckian Henry Clay, the 39-year-old speaker of the House. A congressman from South Carolina since 1811, Calhoun recognized the benefits of a national banking system and the obstacles the measure faced from a southern constituency who saw the Bank as a venture inspired solely by northern manufacturers and politicians for their own financial gain. In this regard, he saw the need to join forces with Secretary Dallas on devising a bank charter acceptable to the South. Entering the House two years after Calhoun, Clay received a bit of notoriety when he served as a peace negotiator at Ghent. Representing the West, he had opposed the Bank in his earlier days but now worked tirelessly to gain the necessary votes for passage of the bill. Also included in this so-called Great Triumvirate was the lone Federalist and northerner, Rep. Daniel Webster. The young lawyer from New Hampshire did not support Madison's protective tariff because, as spokesman for New England interests since 1813, he was against having the nation's industrial base broadened over fears that New England's commercial strength would be diluted. He also voted against the Bank bill and for two reasons. First, the charter did not specifically mandate the payment to the government of taxes in gold or silver, or in bank notes redeemable in specie. Secondly, he was concerned over the integration of government and private powers in such a critical

Left: John C. Calhoun of South Carolina. As congressman, cabinet secretary, vice president, and senator between 1810 and 1850, Calhoun spoke out for states' rights, slavery, and other southern causes. Photograph from 1850 lithograph. Courtesy of the Library of Congress. *Right:* Henry Clay, the "Great Compromiser," was the driving force in Congress as House speaker between 1811 and 1825 and U.S. senator from Kentucky for 16 years. Clay was the first person to lie in state in the Rotunda of the U.S. Capitol. Reproduction of a Brady daguerreotype, circa 1850–52. Courtesy of the Library of Congress.

venture. However, when a supplemen-
tal bill amended the charter, Webster
became more amiable to the bank bill
and would remain a staunch supporter
of banking interests.

During the second session of the
Fourteenth Congress, which convened
in December of 1816, debate on the
remaining element of Madison's economic program was renewed. Introduced by Congressman Calhoun, the
so-called Bonus Bill recommended
that the $1.5 million yearly bonus
money from the Bank be used as a permanent fund to finance internal
improvements in the states instead of
the money going into the Treasury's
coffers. "We are great, and rapidly, I
was about to say fearfully, growing."
Calhoun thundered before his august
audience. "This is our pride and danger—our weakness and our strength....
We are under the most imperious obligation to counteract every tendency
to disunion.... The more enlarged
the sphere of commercial circulation,
the more extended the social intercourse; the more strongly we are bound

Daniel Webster. Massachusetts senator renowned for his oratory skills
and his support of the Union over
the rights of individual states. Along
with Calhoun and Clay, he was the
third member of the Great Triumvirate. Photograph circa 1849–51.
Courtesy of the Library of Congress.

together, the more inseparable are our destinies.... Let us then bind the
Republic together with a perfect system of roads and canals. Let us conquer
space."

Calhoun's nemesis, however, House Speaker Henry Clay, amended the
bill so that in addition to appropriating funds for internal improvements, the
federal government would also become directly involved in their construction
as well. With this new caveat added to the bill, many of Clay's colleagues wondered whether the Constitution granted the government the right to impose
its will upon the sovereign states for internal improvements. Many of his southern listeners, those strictly holding to their states' rights principles, didn't think
so and were prepared to fight for their principles at all costs.

Although Madison agreed with the goals of Calhoun's bill, Clay's amendment added a new wrinkle. Therefore, siding with the southern states' rights
advocates, Madison opposed it on constitutional grounds and promptly vetoed
it on March 3, 1817. With his veto imposed, Madison's own recommendations

for internal improvement legislation would have to wait for the next Congress and a new presidential administration.

Inaugurated the following day, National Republican James Monroe had overwhelmingly defeated New York senator Rufus King, the candidate of the much weakened Federalist Party. A dignified and formal man, Monroe was the last president belonging to the revolutionary generation and the fourth out of the last five presidents from the state of Virginia. He had impeccable credentials having previously served as a member the U.S. Senate, minister to France and Great Britain, and as Madison's secretary of state and secretary of war.

The earlier years of Monroe's first term were described by one newspaper as the Era of Good Feelings, a reflection of the tranquil mood of the country during those good times. Historians generally attribute this mood to two basic factors—the steady decline of the Federalists, a political party centered chiefly in New England, and the enormous increase in popularity of the National Republican Party, which was now virtually the only party of choice. For this reason the Era of Good Feelings was a period distinguished by a relative absence of political discord and hostility, replaced instead by a spirit of political unity. Monroe was delighted with the idea that the country was no longer divided over party politics, which he considered "the curse of the country." But the good feelings, as brief as it was destined to be, may have been merely an artificial perception of political unity, masking potential difficulties fated to befall an administration governing without the competition of a two-party system.

One of the items cited in Monroe's first annual message to the Fifteenth Congress was the Bonus Bill, the internal improvement measure submitted in the previous Congress by Calhoun, who was now Monroe's secretary of war. In his message, to the surprise of many statesmen supporting the bill, Monroe agreed with his predecessor's veto on the same constitutional grounds and even called for a constitutional amendment to remedy the situation. In the process of considering the amendment, in 1818 the House debated a number of resolutions concerning the powers and constitutional authority granted to Congress by the Founders. In its wisdom, the House agreed that its powers extended only to appropriating funds for internal improvements, not for constructing them, yet at the same time rejected the idea of establishing a permanent fund for internal improvements with the bonus money. Eventually, Monroe agreed to a compromise whereby he would approve bills for internal improvements that in his judgment were clearly national in principle, construction projects that benefited the country as a whole. As a consequence, the final provision of Madison's plan was finally acted upon by Congress, and over the next several years nearly a hundred national-oriented projects were undertaken under the heading of general survey bills.

Monroe's popularity in his first two years continued to soar, the reward of an administration that deftly negotiated two important pacts on behalf of the country. One, the Rush-Bagot Agreement, was an accord between Great Britain and the U.S. that halted a growing naval arms race since the War of 1812. Ratified by the Senate in April of 1818, the agreement fixed the strength of their respective naval forces in the Great Lakes, and provided detailed provisions on dismantling surplus vessels. A treaty with Spain was signed in February of 1819. Called the Adams-Onís or Intercontinental Treaty, the Spanish government, represented by Louis de Onís, consented to relinquish its claim to the Oregon Territory north of the 42nd parallel (the northern border of California) and to cede the eastern half of Florida to the United States. In return, the United States, represented by Secretary of State John Quincy Adams, agreed to pay the five million dollars in damage claims submitted by Americans against Spain. Another concession was to renounce all United States claims to the territory of present-day Texas west of the Sabine River, a concession that was most unpopular with many westerners. Spain, on the other hand, retained possession not only of the Texas territory, but also an enormous expanse of desolate real estate in the Far West destined to be at the center of controversy in twenty-seven years.

Based upon the provisions of the Northwest Ordinance, the notion that slavery would ever penetrate the territories north of the Ohio River (the recognized border between free states and slave states popularly known as the Mason-Dixon Line) was considered extremely remote and for that reason the issue was never taken all that seriously. But in March of 1818 the Missouri Territory, a small part of the 800,000 square mile Louisiana Purchase, would change all that when its petition for statehood as a slave state was presented to the U.S. House.

Because more than half of Missouri fell north of the Ohio River, its request for statehood provoked the Congress into a new round of sectional infighting. Almost immediately tempers flared not only over the northward encroachment of slavery but also over the effect Missouri would have on the balance of political power. Although Louisiana was permitted to gain her statehood as a slave state back in 1812, northern politicians were extremely hesitant to allow the further spread of slavery. If Missouri fostered slavery as well, they argued, what would prevent future states in the vast territory of the Louisiana Purchase from going that way as well? It was also quite clear to the North that under such a scenario a potential congressional imbalance in Washington could develop where slave states would hold dominion over the political power in the country.

The prospect of such a development sent both sections into a maddening frenzy and for the first time not only was the spread of slavery debated in the congressional chambers but most significantly, the dire consequences of sectionalism began to rear their ugly heads. "It is a most unhappy question awakening sectional feelings," complained Clay, "and exasperating them to the highest degree. The words, civil war, and disunion, are uttered almost without emotion."

To soothe the growing crisis, in February of 1819, an amendment by Rep. James Tallmadge, Jr., of New York was introduced in the House of Representatives that admitted Missouri into the Union under two rigid conditions. The state would be prohibited from importing new slaves, and henceforth, the state had to grant full emancipation to all slaves born there upon reaching the age of twenty-five. Since Illinois was annexed as a free state only two months earlier, the northern coalition reluctantly agreed to support the Tallmadge amendment as a means to return the Senate's balance of power to parity. Consequently, the amendment easily cleared the House, but following a rancorous debate in the Senate it was soundly defeated. The Constitution gave the individual and sovereign states the right to decide between slavery and no slavery, the amendment's detractors angrily remarked, not the Congress.

In the meantime, that critical balance of power in the Senate was prudently maintained at eleven states each when Alabama, a southern slave state, was admitted into the Union in December.

The issue over Missouri statehood remained on the back burner for nearly a year until Maine also applied to join the Union as a free state. At this point House Speaker Henry Clay, in his own inimitable manner, entered the fray. Being a staunch advocate for granting statehood to Missouri, he insisted Missouri's admittance should not be conditioned on the slavery restrictions now being proposed. And to further emphasize his objection, he pointed out that unless northern dissenters changed their position on Missouri, the South would not hesitate to reject Maine's bid for statehood. Consequently, following stiff negotiations, the bill was amended to exclude the provisions on slavery, a gesture to gather southern support, and to please the North, Sen. Jesse B. Thomas of Illinois added his historic amendment to the annexation bill in February of 1820.

Called the Missouri Compromise, Thomas's amendment proposed admitting Maine as a free state and Missouri as a slave state without any restrictions, thereby maintaining the Senate power balance. In addition, he ordered the territory comprising the Louisiana Purchase divided at the 36° 30' line (the southern border of Missouri). Except for Missouri itself, above that line slavery would be prohibited.

Championed by Clay as speaker of the House, the compromise was unambiguous. It gave each section something of what it wanted and was subsequently adopted. The Missouri Compromise was signed into law on March 6 and Maine was admitted into the Union as a free state nine days later. Maintaining her position on slavery, Missouri entered the fraternity of states in August of 1821. With both sections somewhat appeased, the sectional conflict over political parity was quieted—at least for now.

While the contentious debates over political parity pitted the North against the South, Monroe's elation over the early successes of his administration became severely strained when a new financial crisis began to sweep the nation.

Referred to as the Panic of 1819, this latest downturn not only ended the post-war economic expansion program but also abruptly halted Monroe's Era of Good Feelings as well. Although quite controversial at the time, it was generally accepted that the Second Bank of the United States, together with the smaller western and southern state banks, shared some of the responsibility for the crisis that led to the first great depression in the country's history. This assessment was based chiefly on the banks' demonstration of poor management practices and questionable credit and monetary policies. As in the past, state banking policies were particularly suspicious and for the same infractions. Not only were these banks allowed to print as many bank notes as they wished, they still refused to redeem their notes in gold specie. Furthermore, their loans were so excessive compared to the amount of gold on hand in their vaults that the practice bordered on criminal. Unable to maintain the necessary controls over the state banks and weary of their risky lending policies, especially at the new wildcat western banks, the directors of the Bank called in all of their outstanding loans. This demand from the Bank forced the state banks to do likewise on loans made mostly to land speculators and others in high-risk ventures. Unable to repay their loans, these speculators and other investors defaulted and lost everything. Now trapped in a domino effect, one bank failure led to another which instigated only further grief as thousands of depositors lost their entire savings. In the Midwest bankruptcies occurred almost daily, and in Pennsylvania, property values of $150 an acre in 1815 fell to merely $25 an acre in 1819.

Taking most of the blame, however, was the post-war foreign imports that were still growing at an incredible pace and continuing to stifle many of the new U.S. business ventures. Such enterprises as the New England textile mills, already staggered by the onslaught of foreign competition, were devastated as commodity prices began to fall. Also severely hurt was the cotton market in the South as agriculture prices plummeted as well. Consequently, as labor costs skyrocketed and profit margins disappeared, numerous factories were forced to shut down, Pennsylvania being particularly hard hit. Urban unemployment increased, savings were lost, mortgages were foreclosed, and across the country there were thousands of people lining up at soup kitchens for a meager dinner; others even less fortunate, were confined to debtors prisons. In attempting to describe the crisis John C. Calhoun remarked, "There has been within these two years an immense revolution of fortunes in every part of the Union; enormous numbers of persons utterly ruined; multitudes in deep distress."

To aggravate the government's financial difficulties even further, the Treasury Department reported that although foreign trade was booming, the income from import levies was getting dangerously low. What made this condition particularly critical was that since a previous Congress had repealed the last of the internal taxes, the government was now totally dependent on just the revenue receipts from the customs houses for its support.

To address the obvious lack of adequate protection, the following year an exclusively protectionist tariff on foreign imports was proposed to the Sixteenth Congress. The bill was introduced by Rep. Henry Baldwin of Pennsylvania, chairman of the Committee of Manufactures, and almost immediately the measure instigated a new round of sectional controversy as northern supporters of the bill clashed head-on with the unrelenting southern opposition against any protective tariff.

Baldwin's bill favored domestic manufacturers by mandating cash duties for foreign producers, replacing the two-year credit system currently in place. Once signed into law it was presumed the higher duties would help resolve two of the suspected causes of the Panic. It would replenish the Treasury's coffers and also provide a degree of protection to U.S. business interests. In the House Baldwin's tariff enjoyed the full blessings of Speaker Clay, who upon taking the podium reminded his fellow statesmen that no country on earth "contains within its own limits more abundant facilities for supplying our national wants, than ours does. The war of our Revolution effected our political emancipation. The last war contributed greatly toward our achieving commercial freedom. But our entire independence will only be consummated after the policy of this bill shall be recognized and adopted." Baldwin's bill easily gained the necessary votes to pass; the western states of Illinois, Indiana, Ohio, Tennessee and Kentucky were the most supportive, while the votes from the North, especially New England, were evenly split. Southern backing, as expected, was non-existent.

In the Senate, like their House colleagues, the southern contingent was also solidly against the tariff measure. Becoming extremely wary of the growing application of protectionism and irate over the continuous debates on protectionist tariffs, southern lawmakers maintained that many anti–South lawmakers in Congress were blatantly pursuing a political agenda to protect northern manufacturers, to legislate navigational laws to assist northern ship owners, and to grant subsidies to protect New England fishermen, all at the South's expense. Under this perception, the South overwhelmingly blocked the passage of Baldwin's tariff bill and also threatened to oppose any further attempts to legislate protective tariffs. A line in the sand had now been drawn between the two sections over protective tariffs and over the next three years any efforts to cross it would fail.

Meanwhile, legislative actions to correct the banking procedures, the second suspect in the Panic crisis, were put aside and would not be addressed for another twelve years.

By the end of Monroe's first term numerous political differences and contentious rivalries had split the National Republicans into several warring factions that would ultimately fracture the party. Nevertheless, with one-party rule and so little opposition, Monroe easily won a second term in 1820, amassing an unprecedented electoral vote of 231 to 1.

By 1821, as the financial panic was playing itself out, the demand for additional economic reforms was gaining more and more political momentum. In Washington, protection of American industry against foreign competition was still the principal rallying cry. Since foreign import tariffs were the only source of revenue for the government, and manufacturing interests were steadily growing more significant, the development of a protective tariff had become a real political and practical necessity. The protectionists, largely from the northern states and to an increasing degree from the West, mobilized their troops to fight in yet another sectional conflict over this controversial issue. Steadily growing in power and believing that protectionism and economic independence went hand in hand, they positioned themselves for a confrontation against the mostly southern contingent of free traders who were still boldly standing their ground. With no domestic sales to protect, the South perceived protective tariffs as a tax on their consumption and not only vowed to fight against them but also continued to abandon support for any national economic program. Their hostility and inflammatory rhetoric over these issues was an unmistakable omen that signaled a growing sectional rift and a clear indication that economic sectionalism would continue to dominate the political scene.

Speaking before his assembled colleagues in the elegant chamber of the House, recently renovated into a splendid landscape of marble columns and white Corinthian capitals, Clay was convinced more than ever that the government had to take a more aggressive role in formulating economic development policies. "The truth is," Clay said, "and it is vain to disguise it, that we are ... independent colonies of England—politically free, commercially slaves." Clay envisioned and would work for a more comprehensive national economic program that eliminated U.S. dependency on transatlantic manufacturers, a condition that only nurtured monopolistic aims of foreign interests. His plan would also pursue the advancement of the nation's homeland marketplace, as well as a new program of internal improvements. He believed in a strong central government, one that had to take a more active role in channeling the country's productivity in a way that would benefit the entire nation. Similar to the Madisonian Platform, Clay would call his proposal The American System, the success of which depended on three vital factors—instituting additional protective tariffs to assist the Northeast, legislating internal improvements to assist the South and West, and maintaining a national banking system.

The basic strategy behind Clay's American System was to merge America's agricultural system with America's manufacturing system. Although imbedded with unfair burdens and inequities in the short term, over the long haul he believed the rewards would be substantial. Protective tariffs would give U.S. manufacturing industries the time to grow and mature to the point where they could withstand the stresses of the free marketplace. Without question, Clay declared, it would benefit the country through increased employment and more skillful workers, which would then translate into even more growth. Under this strategy, Clay and his proponents of protectionism compartmentalized the country; the Northeast was best suited for manufacturing and commerce, the West for livestock and grains, such as wheat and corn, and the South for its exports of cotton, tobacco, rice and other staples. According to Clay's proposal, integrating the productivity of the three sections in a balanced and cohesive manner would ensure progressive and viable economic growth. Subsidies for internal improvement projects, like clearing rivers, and constructing roads and canals to make it easier and cheaper for the more distant farmers to ship their produce to market, would also be administered from the income from the sale of public lands.

James K. Polk, a young congressman from Tennessee, disapproved of Clay's idea, calling it "a tripod that stands upon three legs. One is high prices for the public lands to prevent emigration to the West, that a population of paupers may be kept in the East and forced to work for low wages in the factories. Another is high duties, and high taxes to protect the manufacturer and produce surplus revenue. The third is the system of internal improvements which is a sponge to suck up the excess revenue taken from the people."

Southerners also dismissed the American System as yet another scheme favoring Northeastern industrial interests at the expense of their section. Infuriated over all these blatant acts of discrimination, they still refused to support any economic program, particularly for protective tariffs and internal improvements, that had no direct benefit to them.

In the meantime, President Monroe's attention was also focused on the delicate nuances of foreign affairs. To counter suggestions of European interest in the Americas, specifically Russia's claim to the entire Pacific coast from Alaska to Oregon, and rumors of Spain's desire to reclaim her Latin American colonies, Monroe was compelled to respond to this threat of foreign invasion in a declaration of principles known as the Monroe Doctrine, authored by Secretary of State John Quincy Adams. In his annual message to Congress in 1823, Monroe announced that the Western Hemisphere was forever closed to any further European colonization and that the United States would interpret any attempt "to extend their system to any portion of this hemisphere as dangerous to our peace and safety." And for those nations with colonies already in place, they were forbidden to attempt any further expansion. Furthermore, Monroe's doctrine continued, the United States would remain neutral in all wars between European powers and their colonies. It was a stern warning that made many Americans proud and illustrated to the world that American resolve and military might could be assertive and capable of stopping any threat to U.S. security.

Finally answering the call for economic reform, in December of 1823, the

Eighteenth Congress was gaveled into session and a new tariff bill, the most far-reaching protectionist bill of its kind to date, was introduced in the House of Representatives. Since the Treasury was beginning to show a surplus three years after the defeat of the Baldwin bill, the proposed rate increases had little to do with revenue needs. Instead it was a purely protectionist bill designed exclusively to safeguard U.S. industries and jobs. Not only did the measure increase protection to more than sixty new products, it also extended it for the first time to agricultural commodities such as beef, pork, wool, and wheat. Under this bill, the general tariff would range between a whopping 23 percent and 37 percent. Also, the bill attempted to revive the western cordage and cotton bagging industries with a 35 percent levy on such items as hemp, cotton, and wool.

Not surprisingly, the loudest concerns came from the southern congressmen. In extremely forceful tirades they rebuked the tariff supporters on behalf of the cotton-growers, their principle constituents. The southern economy was driven by their cotton exports, they explained in utter frustration. Southern cotton producers sold two-thirds of their product to Britain and in exchange the South bought most of its manufactured goods from the Brits. Since the costs of the high tariffs were being passed on to the consumer, they were the ones actually paying the bulk of the tariffs. Again, it was class legislation that benefited the few, they said, at a cost to the many. Another reason for their concern was that higher tariffs could inhibit further purchases of cotton by Britain as a form of tariff retaliation. Northern manufacturers and western farmers, on the other hand, produced for the domestic markets and were therefore more immune from foreign reprisals than southern planters.

Indeed, many southerners believed any new tariffs to finance northern interests were not only unfair to the South but were also the result of northern manufacturers influencing government political and economical policies for the sole benefit of their own industrial capitalistic elites. It appeared the South was preparing for yet another battle over protectionism and the resulting discrimination to their section.

Clay and his protectionist allies, however, simply shrugged off the southerners by explaining that tariff legislation was the only effective way to obtain "adequate protection against the overwhelming influence of foreign industry," and assured them that in the long run the tariff would greatly benefit the South by establishing a competing American market for their cotton. In the meantime they could easily avoid paying the tariff by simply purchasing the same products from U.S. manufacturers. That scenario, of course, was considered by the South as outright humiliating, one that would force them into the unwanted position of dependency on northern goods produced by northern manufacturers, and they would have none of that.

After two months of debate the new Tariff of 1824 easily passed through the House of Representatives thanks in large part to the support from Clay's western section, specifically the states north of Tennessee. In fact, in some circles it was known as the Sectional Tariff, because the North and the West joined together to pass it over southern objections. Also significant was that as House speaker, Clay controlled the selection of committee chairmen. By cleverly installing fellow protectionists in key positions he was able to steer the bill through the House bureaucracy to its final and successful passage. Nevertheless, the southern votes of seventy-six congressmen clearly illustrated the growing division between the two sections over protective tariffs. Of those seventy-six, all but six voted against the bill.

The third leg of the Great Triumvirate, Daniel Webster, continued to oppose protective tariffs, convinced that the country's economic problems would not be solved by imposing even greater levies on imports which, he said, would only stifle international trade and weaken American prosperity.

Narrowly winning the approval of the Senate, the Tariff of 1824 was signed into law that May. The matter of protective tariffs was far from over, however. The purely sectional vote only forewarned of more troubling times ahead.

The end of another presidential cycle was quickly approaching. As Monroe reflected on his two terms in office, the depression of 1819 was most likely the low point in his tenure, as was the fragmentation of the National Republican Party into strongly opposing factions. Nevertheless, he could undoubtedly offset these disappointments and take some consolation from the very significant accomplishments of his administration. The Monroe Doctrine was most likely the high point of his presidency and would define his legacy. But Monroe could also reflect on the Missouri Compromise of 1820, the Adams-Onís Treaty, the Rush-Bagot Agreement, the acquiescence of the British government to grant American fishermen the right to fish in eastern Canadian waters, the joint occupation of the Oregon wilderness, territorial status for Arkansas, and the protectionist tariff of 1824. Also and perhaps equally significant was that congressional representation in Washington, that all-important Senate parity, was again maintained during Monroe's administration when five new states were added to the Union in quick succession. Mississippi was granted statehood in 1817, Illinois in 1818, Alabama in 1819, Maine in 1820, and Missouri in 1821. The United States now consisted of twenty-four states, twelve free and twelve slave.

Five candidates ran for Monroe's seat in the President's House, now popularly called the White House, three of them from his own administration. (The presidential residence was called the White House after being painted white to cover the scorch marks from a fire set by the British during the War of 1812.)

In previous years the traditional procedure for selecting a presidential candidate was by congressional caucus of the respective party. This time, however, with the National Republican Party fractured into different factions, the candidates, with the exception of William H. Crawford, were put up by legislators from their respective sections. They included Secretary of State John Quincy Adams, the only northerner on the ticket, and from the West, House Speaker Henry Clay, like Adams a strong nationalist. From the South were Secretary of War John C. Calhoun, a staunch advocate of states' rights; Secretary Crawford, of the Treasury Department, along with Adams, thought to be the leading contender; and finally, the hero of the battle at New Orleans in 1815, renowned Indian fighter and senator from Tennessee, Andrew Jackson.

Responding in disgust to Jackson's nomination, Clay couldn't help voice his disdain for Jackson's electors, whom he cried were "people so intoxicated and deluded by a little military glory, that a man totally unknown to the civil history of the country—who knew nothing of the constitution, or laws of the land—and who, in short, had no other recommendation than that which grew out of his fortunate campaign at New Orleans, should be thought of for president of the United States, and even preferred to ... men who had grown gray in the civil departments of government."

By early 1824, it became fairly obvious that voter support for Adams and Jackson had grown enormously while just the opposite was true for the rest of the pack. With his prospects for winning the election drastically weakened, Calhoun dropped out of the race and comforted himself by joining the Adams camp as its vice-presidential candidate, or as he referred to it, the post of "dignified inaction."

When the balloting was over and the final count determined, Jackson won the lion's share of the presidential votes. Although Jackson received the greatest number of votes, 99, he still fell far short of the required majority of 131. Consequently, as directed by the 12th Amendment, the names of the three candidates receiving the most votes, Jackson, Adams, and Crawford, would be placed before the House of Representatives for their consideration. This would be only the second time in U.S. history that a president was selected through this process. (The first time was in 1800 when Jefferson was selected over Aaron Burr.)

There would be one vote from each of the twenty-four states and a majority of states, thirteen in this case, being necessary for election. Of the three candidates submitted, Crawford was immediately eliminated for health reasons. Having just suffered a severe stroke, he was too incapacitated to remain in contention. The race had now boiled down to the two front-runners, Jackson and Adams. Clay, however, who was out of the running, was still adamantly opposed to Jackson winning the presidency because of his supposed ignorance of politics and foreign affairs. To thwart Jackson's bid, therefore, Clay used the power of his position as speaker of the House to persuade his own supporters there to vote for Adams because "killing two thousand five hundred Englishmen at New Orleans was not a proper qualification for the presidency."

Following a string of persuasive arguments for both candidates, on February 9, 1825, the votes were cast and John Quincy Adams, with the necessary thirteen votes, was elected president on the first ballot. Apparently, Clay's eloquence and persuasiveness was enough to convince House electors from six states, three previously supporting Jackson and three of Clay's own followers, to switch their votes for Adams.

Adams enjoyed a remarkable six year career as a Massachusetts senator followed by his appointment as the U.S. minister to Russia from 1809 to 1814, and to England until 1817. Recalled to serve as Monroe's secretary of state, as chief of the American delegation, he was instrumental in negotiating the treaty that ended the War of 1812. Considered by some historians as the nation's greatest secretary of state, Adams was a short, bald and highly intelligent alumnus of Harvard College. Deeply religious, during his days in the White House he would read passages from the Bible, at times in three different languages, being fluent in seven. Despite his religious inclinations, however, in lieu of using the Bible to take his oath of office, at his inauguration he chose a book of laws instead. He was also a man that lacked personal charisma, a trait apparently inherited from his father and one that motivated his opponents to describe him as "a chip off the old iceberg."

In Washington, the Adams presidency met with frustrations right from the start. Three days after being declared president, Adams nominated Clay to be his secretary of state, the most coveted cabinet post of them all. The State Department seat was always highly prized, it being the traditional stepping-stone to the presidency itself. What made Clay's selection so suspicious and so outrageous was that previously Clay had remarked that he "would not cross Pennsylvania Avenue to be in any office under any Administration which lies before us," while at the same time, Clay's backers were climbing onto the Adams bandwagon. Outraged, Jackson smelled political collusion and cried foul amid charges of a "corrupt bargain" between Adams and Clay and pledged to vigorously discredit Clay, the "Judas of the West." The malicious charge by Jackson was wholly untrue, and haunted Clay for years. But as much as he tried, Clay found it virtually impossible to prove otherwise. Nevertheless, in March, Clay's nomination was confirmed by the Senate. Meanwhile, Jackson supporters were beside themselves, infuriated that Adams, the only president to lose both the popular vote and the electoral vote, had stolen the election. Incensed over this travesty, Jackson's supporters immediately placed his name in nomination and began campaigning for 1828, vowing to spend the next four years making every effort to undermine and discredit Adams and his administration as well as the presidential ambitions of Secretary Clay.

In addition, the president's advocacy of protectionist tariffs upset the pro-slavery and states' right southerners. And if that wasn't enough, many of his constituents were also extremely distressed over his support of Clay's American System, as well as using the federal government to drive the long-delayed national economic development program. Making his situation even worse was that the National Republican Party was now clearly divided into two distinct and opposing factions. On one side were Adams and his supporters, on the other their antagonist, the Jacksonian coalition, now being referred to as the Democratic Republicans. The president's problems even came from within his own administration.

Moving into the vice-president's office, Calhoun had a proven record as an able statesman and lawyer and had performed his role as Monroe's secretary of war with great efficiency. Also, as a member of the House, he gained a well respected reputation not only for representing his home state of South Carolina but also the interests of the southern planter aristocracy. But as vice president, Calhoun would oppose Adams throughout his four-year term, reflecting a disgust he felt for the manner in which Adams came into power. What alienated Calhoun from the administration even more was his unswerving dislike for Henry Clay and his policies as secretary of state, which Calhoun suspected were self-serving for his own presidential bid in 1828.

Calhoun's dilemma became much more intolerable when a conference championed by Clay, called the Assembly of American Nations, was organized for June of 1826. The representatives from the U.S. and several Latin American countries were scheduled to meet in Panama City to discuss the diplomatic status between the U.S. and the growing number of new hemispheric states. Calhoun, together with the Jackson coalition in Congress, orchestrated an opposition to this conference in order to injure Clay's image and reputation. But their attempts to prevent the meeting were more or less ignored and the mission was carried out. Incensed over this episode, Calhoun was convinced more than ever that "Mr. Clay governs the President. The latter is in his power. He has thought proper to consider me as his rival; and while Mr. Adams is left to struggle with General Jackson as he can, the weight of the Executive is made to bear, as Mr. Clay desires, and for his own ends." The Panama episode was the final straw for Calhoun. Extremely discontented with the Adams administration, Calhoun now began to consider joining the Jacksonian coalition.

Early in 1827, while visiting his estate in South Carolina, called Fort Hill, Calhoun gained additional insight into the economic plight of his fellow planters as well as their views on the subject of protective tariffs. Cotton production from the upcountry region of the state had fallen precipitously, they lamented, and prices suffered a corresponding decline from around twenty-five cents a pound two years earlier to only nine to twelve cents a pound. Struggling just to make ends meet, many planters chose to move out of South Carolina to cultivate their crops in the more fertile virgin lands of the southwestern states of Alabama and Mississippi. Although their decline in production reflected the worn out condition from years of intensive farming, many of the planters ignored that reality and simply blamed their difficulties on the protective tariffs. Calhoun soon saw his chance not only to strike back at the Adams administration, but also to gain additional approval from his constituents in the South as a fighter against protective tariffs, a strategic move to enhance his standing with the home folks in a future bid for the presidency.

Coincidentally, during this same period the Brits were attempting to destroy the U.S. woolens business by adjusting the duties on raw wool in favor of their own industries. In turn, the American manufacturers of woolen goods forwarded an urgent petition to Congress pleading for help. Members of the House were so eager to rescue the American woolens industry from failure that a new protectionist tariff was approved on February 27 supporting the cause. The new tariff was a measure submitted by Rollins Mallary of Vermont, the new chairman of the Committee on Manufactures, called the Woolens Bill of 1827. In the Senate, however, the tariff bill ran into the usual stiff southern opposition and the floor vote ended in a tie, leaving the deciding tie-breaking vote up to Calhoun. Taking advantage of his constitutional right as president of the Senate, Calhoun struck back and rejected the protective tariff, not only to demonstrate his displeasure at the Adams administration but also for the sake of his fellow southerners, that they should witness his loyalty to the home state. "I hold it certain," he said, "that at present, we are the only contributors to the national Treasury. We alone pay without indemnity, while other sections are more than indemnified for all their contribution, in their character of monopolists and receivers."

The repercussions over the failure of this legislation were not long in coming. Stung by Calhoun's vote, an enormous storm of political outrage resonated throughout the North, and most noticeably from within the Adams administration. The South, on the other hand, gained a resurgence of newfound confidence in Calhoun and rejoiced that their doctrine of states' rights would at last be defended.

Meanwhile, northern displeasure over the rejection of the woolens tariff resulted in a meeting in Pennsylvania where a hundred delegates from thirteen states spent five summer days discussing this latest crisis. Called the Harrisburg Convention, the resolutions agreed upon pledged to initiate steps at the first opportunity to provide the woolens industry with a much larger degree of protection.

In March of 1828, during the first session of the new Twentieth Congress, the Jacksonian majority in the House of Representatives introduced a cleverly engineered tariff bill. It is widely believed by historians that the intent was to create the appearance to the Northwestern section, specifically the states of the Ohio Valley, New York, and Pennsylvania, that the Jackson coalition was actively lobbying for their protectionist interests in hopes of getting their votes. Since Jackson would likely carry the South and its electoral votes and Adams would win New England, this was the section of the country where they were politically weak and from where the coalition needed additional support. Their proposal substantially increased the already high tariffs from 1824 levels of roughly 33 percent on such goods as hemp, raw wool, molasses, and iron. At the same time, and quite significantly, duties on woolens would be maintained relatively low, a factor that would severely hurt the New England woolens industry. The South, in contrast, would not benefit in the slightest from this tariff, but instead would suffer from the higher prices of imported goods they were likely to purchase. But, for the bill to pass the House, which the Jacksonians really wanted, they needed Southern support. The question was how to get it.

In lobbying for the bill, the northern Jacksonians convinced their southern allies that the tariff proposal was sure to fail in the Senate because with the low duties on woolens, the bill would almost certainly generate extreme opposition from the New England states. And even though the bill would fail, the northerners explained, they would still gain the recognition as supporters of protectionist tariffs for the western states.

Quickly recognizing the rebuff to the New England woolens industries, committee chairman Mallary attempted to get the woolens protection resolutions agreed to at the Harrisburg Convention placed into the bill but was soundly defeated by the southern votes. When the roll was finally called the tariff bill was approved by the House, with the southerners fully expecting it to fail in the Senate.

In the Senate, however, Sen. Martin Van Buren, a loyal Jackson supporter from New York, offered an amendment in a last hour maneuver that also imposed higher duties on imported woolens, cotton cloth, and manufactured goods to about 50 percent of their value, a move that completely diluted New England objections and stunned the disbelieving southerners. Now urged to support the measure by Massachusetts manufacturing interests, the Tariff Bill of 1828, called the Tariff of Abominations by the South, was approved in the Senate by a vote of 26 to 21 and Adams signed it into law on May 19.

The new tariff bill was also known by southerners as the Black Tariff and as the Yankee Tariff. Needless to say, whatever it was called, the South was livid over this blatant sleght of hand by the northern Jacksonians and their scheme to protect the northern woolen interests from the British. They were particularly struck by the persuasive power of the New England manufacturing lobby to accomplish these aims. The higher levy not only compelled the South to pay higher prices for manufactured goods but to also expect lower income on the sale of raw materials.

Wild talk abounded at Washington dinner parties from southerners, most half-inebriated, who threatened to walk out of Congress in protest, while in some areas of the South flags were flown at half-staff. Others began to indulge in treasonable talk of secession and claiming that individual states had the right to refuse to submit to laws which worked adversely to their interests. It was a philosophy called nullification, one destined to gain more and more prominence in the years ahead. Even students at South Carolina College vowed to boycott, pledging not to "buy, consume, or wear any article of clothing manufactured north of the Potomac till the rights of our State shall be fully acknowledged." Nevertheless, despite this transgression, the South refused to blame the Jacksonians. Since they favored the Jacksonian position on protective tariffs and states' rights, Southerners were fearful of hurting Jackson's presidential run. Instead, they blamed the Adams administration, Secretary Clay in particular, and Webster, now a senator from Massachusetts, for his supposed financial interests in the New England woolens industry.

The on-going and divisive sectional disputes between southerners demanding reduced tariffs and northerners insisting on protection, the monopolistic perception of the Bank of the United States, the continuing harangue over slavery and the intrusiveness of abolitionism had, without question, widened the sectional schism between the North and South.

For the moment, however, southern opposition to protective tariffs was seen by many as the cause for much of the current anti–South bitterness.

Despised by the South, protectionist tariffs either reduced foreign trade, they claimed, or increased the price of their imported goods. And since imported goods paid for southern cotton, the tariffs worked to the detriment of the southern economy. They were demeaning, unfair, and costly, which only forced the South into a state of enslavement to the North with its resultant financial hardships and humiliation. In the eyes of the southern people, the northern establishment reveled in the enormous success and progress of its free-labor, capitalistic society. And, in their perspective, to satisfy its enormous self-serving appetite, the North never hesitated to take full advantage of its political power in a nationalistic Congress, many times at the expense of southern interests. Northern power brokers, despite pleas for what the southerners defined as fair and equitable treatment, were perceived as money-hungry bureaucrats committed to enhancing their own economic welfare through protective tariffs and other self-serving government laws.

To a northern observer, however, it was the South that chose to shun industrialization and its many rewards in favor of more agricultural pursuits, while enslaving blacks as subjects of his majesty King Cotton. The sum result was backwardness, and a gross lack of social and economic development where most of the people lived in extreme poverty, without education, motivation, and skills.

In the midst of all this unsettling turmoil, with the National Republican Party split and severely demoralized, and Adams weakened from the violent aftermath of the Tariff of Abominations, the administration prepared for the upcoming presidential election.

4

"Old Hickory" Comes to Washington (1829 to 1832)

By the end of the Adams presidency the years of political squabbles and factional rivalries, aggravated by bitter sectional conflicts, split apart the National Republicans and shifted party loyalties among several competing blocs. One such faction, the Jacksonian coalition, or Democratic Republicans, included a dynamic political luminary and party organizer from New York, Martin Van Buren. Recently elected governor after serving in the Senate since 1821, the "Little Magician" was a vital element in Jackson's campaign for the presidency. He represented the northern contingent of Old Republican ideology and spearheaded the drive for voters in this important northern state. Also included in the Jackson camp were the backers of William H. Crawford, the 1824 presidential candidate, as well as Adams's vice president, John C. Calhoun, and his constituents.

During his tenure in the Adams administration, Calhoun's political ambitions became increasingly focused on ascending to the presidency. With his standing in the administration somewhat diminished, however, the heir apparent was more than likely his archrival, Henry Clay. Aside from his aversion to Adams's policies and Clay's self-serving demeanor, Calhoun considered Adams and his secretary of state politically weakened over the dubious circumstances that gained them power in 1824. Given that scenario, he thought Clay was extremely vulnerable in his future bid to succeed Adams, a circumstance he could capitalize on at the end of a one-term Jackson administration. Consequently, shortly after the Panama episode, Calhoun made his move. Taking full advantage of Jackson's pledge to serve for only one term, Calhoun began to maneuver himself into the Jackson coalition for a future bid at the presidency. Assuming that Van Buren already had a lock on the State Department, Calhoun offered to run as Old Hickory's vice-presidential running mate, an offer readily accepted by the Jacksonians.

Also included on the team were several political strategists such as Sen. Thomas H. Benton, a "blustering, bullying, and hectoring" Missourian who had been in a gunfight with Jackson sixteen years earlier, and Sen. John H. Eaton of Tennessee, along with Van Buren, a committed organizer in Jackson's run for the presidency. A trusted and loyal friend of Jackson's, it was Eaton that most thought the instigator in the corrupt bargain charge against Clay in 1825 and again during the upcoming 1828 campaign. A number of prominent political spokesmen, wealthy bankers, and influential newspaper editors rounded out the Jackson camp, all strongly opposed to renewing the Bank charter, laws establishing protective tariffs, as well as internal improvement laws.

In stark contrast were the Adams supporters, loyal nationalists who were adamantly opposed to Jackson's presidential bid. They were such men as Henry Clay, Daniel Webster, and from New York, Sen. Rufus King and publisher Thurlow Weed. In backing Clay's American System they promoted the concept of direct government intervention in advancing the nation's economic development. To this end, they all supported such initiatives as the Bank of the United States, protective tariffs to encourage entrepreneurial initiatives, and distributing federal subsidies from the sale of public lands to the states for constructing roads and canals, a measure Clay vigorously sponsored to enhance commercial relations between the North, South, and developing territories of the West.

The Jackson-Adams campaign, more or less a rematch of 1824, was a dirty one filled with preposterous charges and countercharges. Both sides engaged in exaggerated attempts to demean their opponent and both shamelessly indulged in hypocrisy, exaggeration, and deceit to win over potential voters. Adams was consistently described as corrupt and as a wild spender of taxpayer money to support his taste for gambling, or as a bigot against Catholics, a smear campaign designed to win over the Irish voters. Not only was Adams fair game but also Jackson's political foe, Henry Clay, who was also slandered and castigated in the Jacksonian press in an effort to destroy his reputation and political future. The corrupt bargain accusation was, of course, employed consistently to remind voters of the sleazy collusion between the two. To counter their charges, the Adams supporters persistently portrayed Jackson as a primitive backwoodsman completely devoid of political acumen, without knowledge, experience, and sophistication; they claimed Jackson was not fit to govern the country. Some of his opponents even began calling him a jackass, a symbol Jackson took a liking to and one he decided to use on his campaign posters to represent, like the mule, his own strong will. But in the harsh world of politics the Adams machine was much less sophisticated than Jackson's and less effective in getting out its message and rousing the support necessary to win. (The symbol of the mule is still in use today by the Democratic Party.)

Jackson's popularity as a tough and strong willed frontiersman was cleverly exploited also by establishing hickory clubs, and wherever he appeared hickory poles would dot the landscape. It was a campaign maneuver to reinforce his image as "Old Hickory" and that he was indeed a simple farmer, just like the people he was reaching out to for support. The strategy behind these attempts to lure voters was also designed to portray Jackson as a devoted husband and successful military commander, while at the same time minimizing his specific positions on the relevant issues of the day.

Their strategy obviously succeeded. The appeal of his toughness on one hand and his folksy charisma on the other attracted followers by the thousands. When the final vote was tallied Jackson managed to gather enough support to win 56 percent of the popular vote and a decided margin in the electoral vote (178 to 83). Jackson's

Andrew Jackson, the first Democratic resident of the White House, as he appeared between 1844 and 1845. Jackson's presidency was beset with banking and tariff issues that further divided the nation and instigated southern threats to secede. Courtesy of the Library of Congress.

landslide win, the first election of a military leader to the presidency since Washington, came principally from the southern and western states, while Adams maintained his support mostly in the old Federalist and loyal strongholds of New England.

The most significant factor in this election was that many voter restrictions of the past, such as religious affiliations and property qualifications, were finally removed. And instead of party bosses and legislative cliques selecting the electors, as was the past tradition, the choice was now delegated to the people in 22 of the 24 states (Delaware and South Carolina being the exceptions). With a new sense of political power invested in them, interest in the candidates at the grassroots level surged as more people took advantage of their civic duty.

Recognizing the enormous opportunity for support from this potential pool of first-time voters was also a key to Jackson's win. Van Buren's take charge persona and his consummate organizing skills were instrumental in establishing campaign committees in each of the states. The committees, in turn, developed a new and untried campaign strategy of organizing parades, marching bands, speeches and fireworks, as well as fundraisers, rallies, barbeques, country fairs, and other political events to bolster support for their candidate. "Considerable pains were taken to bring out the people" one of Jackson's campaign workers was overheard to remark.

Since his victory was the result of thousands of first-time voters, the laborers from the farms and shops, Jackson claimed his election clearly demonstrated a win for the working people rather than the more privileged elitists. In that light Jackson felt obligated to his supporters and committed his administration to improve the economic development of this constituency and to combat what he saw as "the rich getting richer and the powerful more potent."

Many of the Washington locals, above all the politically sophisticated, were stunned over Jackson's victory. His having spent barely two years in the Senate, from 1823 to 1825, made them apprehensive over his lack of political experience. The general's reputation as an unsavory frontier ruffian also filled the political elite with alarm. Stories of his duels and violent brawls were now dinner table entertainment. His poor health was another worrisome issue, the legacy of a hard and wild life that left Jackson still suffering from the bullet wounds of his past encounters. Even Washington's high-society snobbery expressed concerns over a Jackson presidency. Notwithstanding the unsavory prospect of entertaining ill-mannered hooligans, the capital city's upper crust complained that their long-established ties with Washington bureaucrats would be severely disrupted if the new president carried out his campaign promise to sweep the incumbents off the government payroll. Meanwhile, Clay and others within the losing team considered Jackson's win a fluke, the result of a horrendous campaign by Adams and nothing more. When Jackson's stand on the issues become known, they argued, his supporters would quickly abandon the Democratic Republicans. It was a prediction completely at odds from the eventual reality.

As for Jackson, his time had finally arrived. Lost in a conflicting maze of sorrow and joy, he gazed blindly from the deck of his steamer. It was January 20, 1829, and "Old Hickory," having left Nashville the previous day, was traveling down the Cumberland River on his way to Washington for his inauguration as the seventh president of the United States. His thoughts that morning, however, were not on the joys of the upcoming ceremony and the gala reception that would follow, but instead were on his beloved wife, Rachel, who for over 35 years kept the home fires burning at their plantation, the Hermitage. Succumbing to a sudden heart attack only a few weeks earlier, she was now in eternal slumber. As he stood alone, shrouded in the morning fog, the sixty-two-year-old Tennessean understood full well that the United States was entering a new era and that he would be its guardian over the next four years.

The country was indeed changing. The population was nearly 13 million, an increase of over 60 percent in 30 years. New York City, followed by Baltimore, Philadelphia, and Boston, was a thriving metropolis of over 200,000 people. It was a prosperous center of commerce, banking, and free enterprise. In New England, textile mills such as those in Waltham and Lowell, Massachusetts, and Pawtucket, Rhode Island, as well as the world's largest cotton mill in Saco, Maine, were continuing to demonstrate their growing industrial capabilities. Immigrant pioneers were beginning to flood the Northeast, and thousands were migrating westward seeking a new and better life. Steamboat travel, now a relatively common mode of passenger transport, had made the country a bit smaller and if the upcoming trials of the new steam-driven locomotive, the "Best Friend of Charleston," were successful, a revolution in modern technology could shrink the country even more. In the northern states slavery was continuing to diminish as more and more of its victims were granted their freedom. Their release from bondage appeased many of the pontificating abolitionists, but to the unemployed white men who were destitute and seeking jobs, the competition was extremely distasteful and a cause for much resentment.

Below the Mason-Dixon Line, the city of New Orleans, only a fourth as large as New York, was the most populous city in the South and fifth overall. Long an agrarian society, significant signs of industrialization had yet to gain a foothold in the South while slavery was flourishing more than ever, approaching a population of around 2 million strong. It was a coerced workforce driving a southern economy dependent on cotton, now the country's leading export. The political side of the South, seemingly always in a hostile and agitated state, was again carping over perceived ill treatment at the hands of iniquitous outsiders. Southern states, particularly South Carolina, were reeling under economic hardships they blamed on protective tariffs that were draining away their financial resources. And southern anger continued to boil as well over the steady stream of anti-slave literature that flooded the country, and of meddling sympathizers guiding fugitive slaves to the North. In the years ahead southern anger against the North would increase even more as radical anti-slave advocates like Bostonian William Lloyd Garrison instigated a whole new era of abolitionism.

Mindful of the intricate complexities inherent in a slave society, Jackson was also aware of the tenor of the South's recent wave of belligerent rhetoric. The southern states continued to feel more alienated than ever before as sectional disputes over the morality of slavery, the growing abolitionist movement, discriminatory protective tariffs, unfair banking laws, and the federal government's infringement on states' rights continued to grow increasingly hostile. The South was becoming more and more restless, its agents speaking of secession in terms considered treasonous in better times but somewhat politically correct during these more stressful years.

Jackson arrived in Washington, a dirty, smelly city of about 20,000, on

February 11, 1829. Staying at the new National Hotel, Jackson and his close advisors wiled away the time drafting the inaugural address and reviewing cabinet appointments. The most prestigious of them all, the secretary of state position, went to Van Buren, whom Jackson favored the most for his unwavering support and whom he preferred to succeed him in four years. Although the Washington insiders believed the Cabinet was mediocre at best, nearly all of them expressed strong opinions on states' rights, lower tariffs, and anti-banking sentiments, opinions of course consistent with those of the new president. And to the outrage of Virginians, for the first time in the nation's history no one from their state was appointed to the Cabinet, a payback for their loyalty to Adams four years earlier.

Meanwhile, preparations were finally completed for Jackson's inauguration. For the first time the swearing-in would be held outdoors on the East Portico to accommodate the enormous number of overjoyed Jacksonians expected that day. As inaugurations go, it would be the grandest spectacle the city ever experienced. The locals, however, looked on with open scorn as the enormous influx of unruly outsiders strained the resources of their fair city. They likened it to "the inundation of the northern barbarians into Rome, save that the tumultuous tide came in from a different point of the compass."

One portion of Jackson's speech, delivered on a beautiful and sunny March afternoon, illustrated his commitment to be fair on states' rights issues by reminding his audience, "In regard to the rights of the separate States I hope to be animated by a proper respect for those sovereign members of our Union, taking care not to confound the powers they have reserved to themselves with those they have granted to the Confederacy." On the sensitive issue of protectionist tariffs Jackson told the crowd, "It would seem to me that the spirit of equity, caution, and compromise ... requires that the great interests of agriculture, commerce, and manufactures should be equally favored [except for] any products of either of them that may be found essential to our national independence." He also expressed his desire to treat the Indian tribes in a humane way and with considerate attention to their rights and their wants, and foremost to "extinguish" the national debt. The most controversial statement in his address, however, was his intent to reform the government bureaucracy by purging the federal workforce of the incompetence and corruption so long entrenched in a seemingly life-long tenure. It required, he said, "the correction of those abuses that have brought the patronage of the Federal Government into conflict with the freedom of elections ... and have placed or continued power in unfaithful or incompetent hands."

At the conclusion of his speech Jackson bowed to the people, a symbolic salute of humility to his constituency. This gesture evidently aroused the thousands of spectators and the atmosphere grew decidedly more raucous as the multitude raised their voices in resounding approval. Breaking through the separating barrier, the crowd surged forward forcing Jackson and the other dignitaries back into the Capitol. At that point, the new president, now on horseback, began riding down Pennsylvania Avenue to the White House with his throng of admirers following behind.

Transformed into a screaming and unruly mob, the people stormed through the White House fighting over refreshments and destroying carpets, furniture, and china in the process. As noted by diarist Margaret B. Smith, the scene was "a rabble, a mob, of boys, negroes, women, children, scrambling, fighting, romping.... No arrangements had been made, no police officers placed on duty and the whole house had been inundated by the rabble mob.... The President after having been literally nearly pressed to death and almost suffocated and torn to pieces by the people in their eagerness to shake hands with Old Hickory, had retreated through the back way and had escaped to his lodgings at Gadsby's. Cut glass and china to the amount of several thousand dollars had been broken in the struggle to get the refreshments.... Ladies fainted, men were seen with bloody noses and such a scene of confusion took place as is impossible to describe—for those who got in could not get out by the door again but had to scramble out of windows." The removal of the unwanted visitors was tactfully accomplished by enticing them outside to the lawns where tubs of punch were placed and provided Jackson with the opportunity to surreptitiously slip out a rear window and away from the distracted mob. Unfortunately, in the eyes and minds of the Washington elitists, this unruly and noisy episode only confirmed their worst fears of a Jackson presidency.

To the dismay of many white collar workers who feared for their jobs in Washington, one of the first priorities for Jackson was to fulfill his inauguration pledge to reform the government by removing a number of corrupt or incompetent career federal bureaucrats from the civil service system. Jackson strongly opposed the life-long tenure many of these employees were enjoying and vowed to replace the "ins" with younger people that were more educated, more efficient, more effective, and most significantly, had demonstrated a loyalty to himself and the party. To allay the fears of many of his critics that he was merely cleaning house to employ his own people, Jackson told Congress, his actions were not to be construed as a firing, but as a "rotation" of deserving applicants into these positions. By the end of the year Jackson had rotated nearly one thousand federal office holders and in so doing had created a scandalous precedent. Even Calhoun, who remained in the vice president's office, but now under Jackson, condemned the practice of patronage "as an instrument to perpetuate power." Disregarding the outrage over his policy, Jackson's directive had for the first time invoked a system of party patronage and a policy of presidential appointees, a spoils system that has gained in scope ever since.

Given that Jackson's views on most of the political issues were unclear, one of the more divisive issues Washington politicos wondered about was how he would deal with the southern outcry over the Tariff of 1828, the so-called Tariff of Abominations. Although he clearly did not support protectionist tariffs since he thought they were unfair to the South, Jackson had also pledged during his campaign and in his inauguration address to eliminate the national debt during his term in office. As long as the monies from the tariffs were helping to pay off this debt, he had no plans to reduce the tariff from its present level.

Also of some concern was Jackson's position on the Bank. Over the years the Second Bank of the United States had generated much controversy over its policies and its organization and in turn had grown to be one of the primary sources of bitter sectional conflict. In fact, many people still shared the belief that the Bank should have been held accountable for its role in the depression a decade ago. Nevertheless, the northern section, those states north of the Ohio River, strongly supported the Bank as a vital partner working with the government for the benefit of the economic well-being of the country. At the same time, the southern opposition saw the institution as a large monopoly that took advantage of the working people for the benefit of the rich and powerful.

Over the preceding months, Washington insiders, the people moving within its political and social circles whom the capital is notorious for, had become abuzz with gossip and speculation over Jackson's resentment of the Bank and his opposition to renewing its charter. Although the Bank was not an immediate issue, the subject was broached by Jackson anyway in his first annual message to Congress on December 8.

Ignoring advice to avoid unnecessary controversy seven years before the Bank's charter expired, Jackson decided to clear the air over these annoying rumors and to state his position once and for all. First he questioned the legitimacy of the law that created the Bank in the first place, and clearly expressed his view that the Bank had failed to live up to its charter in "establishing a uniform and sound currency." He also expressed not only doubts over its constitutionality, despite the 1819 *McCulloch v. Maryland* case in which the Supreme Court ruled in the Bank's favor, but more significantly his desire to replace the institution. It was a position that shocked the Bank's president, Nicholas Biddle, and immediately placed the administration at odds with the Senate Finance Committee and the House Ways and Means Committee, which sided with the Bank. For the most part, however, with the exception of an occasional anti–Bank statement from Jackson and private comments on how he would change its rules, the conflict over the Bank during his term would remain muted until it resurfaced as a campaign issue in 1832.

With the growing chatter over state sovereignty and the loose talk of secession still resonating from the South over the tariff of 1828, the Jacksonian-controlled Twenty-first Congress convened on a chilly seventh of December in 1829. Taking their seats in the historic chambers, the latest crop of political leaders, along with the older veterans, waited eagerly to begin the nation's business. A number of important and interrelated proposals awaited congressional debate, several of which would be introduced in President Jackson's first annual message. Until this Congress adjourned in March 1831, these contentious issues reenergized the on-going sectional conflicts as representatives from each region attempted to gain an advantage to support their own political agendas.

Back on the congressional calendar were such concerns as additional tariff reforms, government policy for selling public lands, distributing surplus funds, and the states' rights issue of federal subsidies. With no legislative action required on banking issues at this time, congressional attention turned to the Tariff of 1828, the Tariff of Abominations, and how best to adjust its provisions to the satisfaction of everyone.

Despite an agreement in the House to fully discuss all southern objections and possible modifications to the tariff, southern leaders, most notably the South Carolinians, argued strenuously for repealing the tariff outright, a measure the House was not inclined to consider. Instead, in keeping with Jackson's pledge, the immediate position of the House Jacksonians was to keep the tariffs at their current level, at least until the national debt was paid off. Since a portion of the money from import duties was used to pay off the debt, (together with proceeds from the sale of public lands), they explained, there was little incentive to reduce the tariff until this debt was eliminated or at least reduced. What followed was the same bitter harangue from irate southern members complaining that they were being enslaved by Northern manufacturers. Notwithstanding their efforts, however, no action was taken on tariff reform in this Congress. Outraged and highly insulted over this most obvious snub to their section, the Southerners again reverted to their oft-repeated rhetoric for seceding from the Union. In fact, one popular dinner toast in southern circles was, "The tariff; a thing too detestable to have been contrived except by Yankees; to be enforced except by Kentuckians; or to be endured except by 'the submission men' of the South." Evidently, further discussions on tariff reform would have to wait until the next Congress was installed.

Following the War of 1812, with the country in dire financial straits, the Congress agreed to use the money from land sales to pay down the national debt, a figure estimated at the time to about $120 million. Using revenues of over $10 million per year from the land sales, plus a percentage of money from tariff revenues, President Jackson's campaign pledge to extinguish the national debt had assured the continuation of this policy. Since reducing tariffs was out of the question, the government's policy for selling public land remained a point of contention in Congress and one that inflamed bitter rhetoric and impassioned sectional conflict. This unsold land, some 72 million surveyed acres, was located not only within the remaining tracts of western lands that once constituted the Southwest Territory, land ceded by North Carolina and

Virginia in 1790, but also in the Alabama and Mississippi territories, specifically the land ceded from Georgia several years later. Included as well were government-owed property in the Louisiana Territory and the real estate in eastern Florida that was acquired in the Adams-Onís Treaty of 1819.

Since the formation of the young nation it was generally accepted that this land would be in a public trust for the benefit of the country as a whole. At the same time, however, the government's public land policy was not enthusiastically embraced by everybody as one addressing various sectional concerns.

For eastern entrepreneurs, particularly those in New England engaged in the growing experiment of private enterprise, the sale of this public land meant only increased westward migration. In turn, as more and more people moved away, needed resources of skills, money, and labor were drained away as well, a trend that region had already experienced for the past twenty years or so. Industrial growth, they complained, was being sacrificed for western development. Reflecting this dissatisfaction, nine eastern states went so far as to suggest distributing public lands to the states for educational and other purposes, a proposal rejected out of hand by Congress in 1822.

The advocates from the western section, on the other hand, were active in promoting their goal of reducing the price of the land, which sold at about a dollar an acre for a minimum of eighty acres. Making land more affordable, they reasoned, would increase the population of the western section and encourage further development. Senator Benton had led the fight for a new public land policy since 1824, one that demanded a program of low-priced land inducements to encourage westward expansion. Benton's proposal called for selling public lands at a lower price each year until a minimum of a few cents per acre was reached. Called the Graduation Plan, it was soundly defeated in Congress in 1828. Undeterred, other westerners called for the federal government to cede the public lands to the states in which they existed. Although debated, the idea was never acted upon.

Nevertheless, just before the Christmas recess of the Twenty-first Congress, another measure the die-hard westerners favored was also proposed in the Senate. This bill recommended preemption, a law that would forgive trespass charges on squatters occupying certain lands and allowed these settlers to purchase up to one hundred and sixty acres at $1.25 per acre. The opponents of this policy discredited the so-called settlers as nothing more than lawless rabble. Instead of industrious and hard-working people, they claimed, the so-called settlers were actually employees of land speculators taking part in a ploy to obtain the best lands for little money. The Jackson administration took a liking to the preemption bill, however, and after successfully pushing it through Congress, it became law in May of 1830. Written to last eight years, the bill would be readdressed in 1838.

As the national debt continued to diminish the question facing the administration was—what should be done with the projected surplus dollars in the

Treasury once the debt was cleared? Since the tariff money in this account was untouchable, most of the anticipated surplus would be the money from the sale of public lands.

Anticipating a loud outcry over having millions of dollars in surplus money in the government's coffers, Jackson was now prepared to revisit the recommendation he made to Congress in his first annual message. Therefore, Jackson declared that once the debt was retired the Treasury would distribute surplus funds from the land sales to the states for them to spend on internal improvements. Called his distribution plan, the amount of federal money the states received would be based on their congressional representation. To preclude inciting other issues in the process, a constitutional amendment may also be warranted, he suggested, in order to establish the legitimacy of its implementation.

The notion of dispersing federal funds to the states for internal improvements sparked yet another hotly debated issue that evoked political passions from each section of the country, pitting nationalist advocates against the proponents of states' rights.

Most northern states were generally supportive of the administration's funding proposal since it was consistent with elements of Clay's American System and it would still maintain the high protective tariffs. However, the western states resented Jackson's distribution plan. It was unfair, they complained, because the heavily populated eastern states would get the majority of the money. The South was also against the distribution plan. Federal funds given to the states for building roads, canals, and railroads in a systemic effort clashed head-on with their interpretation of the Constitution and their Jeffersonian doctrine of states' rights which disapproved of any federal intervention in local affairs. One southern congressman in particular, James K. Polk, thought federal subsidies for internal improvements only enhanced the power of the federal government over the states. Also quite significant, since the surplus funds in the Treasury could be used to replace the high tariffs, the South argued, why not simply reduce the import tariffs to the point where the combined revenues from tariff and land sales would finance the administration of the government? Finally, after considerable debate the Twenty-first Congress failed to take any action on Jackson's distribution proposal. By doing so, not only did Congress fail to answer the administration's question, but also brought up a second question to resolve as well—did the government have the right to use federal funds for state-authorized internal improvement projects?

Coincidently, also on the congressional agenda were a number of internal improvement projects. One of the bills sought to extend the National Road, the most ambitious road building project to date. Once completed the road would be the first land link between the east coast and the western frontier. Although contracts were initially issued in 1811, the War of 1812 prevented construction of the first segment until four years later. Originally called the

Cumberland Road, it was a stretch of macadam and gravel that ran from Cumberland, Maryland, to Wheeling, on the Ohio River. Largely through the efforts of Henry Clay, the National Road was continued westward through Ohio and Indiana to Vandalia, Illinois, and finally to St. Louis, Missouri, in the early 1830s. It was the nation's first interstate highway and eventually would extend across the country to California as U.S. Highway 40.

The bill that drew the most attention, however, was for the construction of the Maysville Road, a sixty-mile stretch from Maysville to Lexington, Kentucky. The supporters of this project, specifically proponents of internal improvements, envisioned the new road as a future connection to the National Road, a significant step toward improving the transportation system within their state.

Following its approval by both houses of Congress along sectional lines, the Maysville Bill was delivered to Jackson in May 1830. At this point Jackson found himself in a precarious position. Although his staunch western supporters, influential men like Senator Benton, strongly endorsed the idea of building the road, his southern states' rights wing was just as opposed to it and urged Jackson to use his veto power to reject it outright. Jackson understood full well that no matter what decision he made he risked provoking a division in his constituency.

In the end, after conferring with Van Buren, Jackson vetoed the Maysville bill. Southerners, of course, were elated that Jackson had sided with them on this important issue and for his apparent support for their states' rights doctrine. In an effort to strike a balance among his supporters, Jackson reminded them that his veto was not against federal funding for internal improvements in general, but only as it related to the Maysville road. Just as Monroe had done in 1818, he further explained that the government would indeed subsidize internal improvement projects but only those ventures considered "general, not local, national, not State." Since the $150,000 Maysville road project was a local initiative, it did not warrant federal support. The government lacked that right, he stated, because the power to fund internal improvements of a "purely local character" within any state was not specifically included in the Constitution and to do otherwise would be infringing on the sovereignty of that state. To resolve this matter once and for all and to appease the disgruntled westerners, he again recommended a constitutional amendment that would clearly enumerate this power.

In the days ahead an effort to override the veto failed and of the remaining bills for internal improvements, only two received a presidential approval for federal funding, one of which was for the National Road, the other a general survey bill. In 1833, the maintenance of the National Road was turned over to the states and from that time forward, to the opening days of the Civil War, no new national initiatives for internal improvements were considered.

With the population of southern slaves approaching two million, the problem of surplus slaves and how best to utilize their labor skills became an increasingly sensitive issue to southern planters. This was especially true for a number of slaveholders in the Deep South and it was therefore particularly gratifying when Jackson became interested in acquiring a relatively barren tract of land west of the Mississippi. This land was specifically the Mexican-owned area in present-day Texas where over 20,000 southern Americans and their slaves maintained a thriving farm community with the consent of the Mexican government. Under the guidance of Stephen F. Austin, they elected militia officers and justices of the peace, employed a civil and criminal code, and established an appellate court. Not surprisingly, Jackson's attempt to acquire this land was seen by southern politicians as a tremendous opportunity to not only relocate the surplus slaves but to also expand southern influence in national politics at the same time.

Therefore, while the Twenty-first Congress began its proceedings in December, the Jackson administration initiated a plan with the U.S. minister in Mexico City, Joel Poinsett, for buying this western territory. To the authorities in the U.S. the timing appeared to be right considering Mexico had just gained her independence from Spain. In order to take advantage of the resultant political upheaval, instructions were dispatched to Poinsett to immediately initiate the talks and to negotiate for a boundary at the Rio Grande. Furthermore, to entice their Mexican neighbor to the bargaining table, an offer of three million dollars was authorized for the deal even though the U.S. was willing to go as high as five million if necessary. At that point, President Vicente Guerrero became highly incensed, accused Poinsett and the U.S. of interfering in Mexico's internal affairs and demanded his immediate recall. As a result, relations between the U.S. and Mexico grew steadily worse and deteriorated to the point where the new minister, Anthony Butler, of Mississippi, put aside the Texas initiative and concerned himself primarily with negotiating claims for American citizens against the Mexican government. Following several failed attempts to restart the negotiations the procurement effort was called off.

With the nation evenly divided at twelve free and twelve slave states, the mere suggestion by the administration that it intended to buy Texas, with the possibility of spreading slavery into the western frontier, horrified most northerners. Reminiscent of the furor over admitting Missouri in 1818, they couldn't help but contemplate the appalling ramifications additional slave states would have on the political power structure in Washington. In fact, the dreadful likelihood that a number of slave states could also be formed in the lower section of the Louisiana Territory as well was enough to motivate a Connecticut senator, Samuel A. Foot, to introduce an inquiry into the government's policy for selling public lands. The New Englander called on the Committee on Public Lands to consider revising its policy to include his recommendations. Specifically, Foot suggested closing the surveyor general's office, deferring any further surveys, and to limit its land sales to only those tracts already surveyed.

To many political observers, however, if left unchallenged, Foot's recommendations would be detrimental to the future of western expansion. Therefore, it wasn't surprising that spokesmen from the West, leaders like Senator Benton from the slave state of Missouri, took every opportunity to pounce on this latest and outrageous attempt to inhibit westward migration and the resultant growth of the western section. Advocates of territorial expansion were already angry over the inhibiting factors inherent in the high price of public lands and now with Foot's recommendation on the floor of the Senate, tempers flared anew. New England, Benton said in January of 1830, wanted to "force poor people in the East to work as journeymen in the factories, instead of letting them go to new countries, acquire land and become independent freeholders." Furthermore, he said, the proposal was just another example of federal injustice exacted "to inflict unmixed, unmitigated evil upon the new States and territories."

Jumping into the fray to support Benton was states' rights advocate Robert Y. Hayne, the senior senator from South Carolina. Hayne became caught up in the passion of Benton's speech, but instead of continuing with the dialogue on public lands policy, the South Carolina senator seized this opportunity to lash out against the North and the federal government in language exemplifying the anger and deep sectional discord prevailing in the country. An alliance between southern and western interests was necessary, he claimed, to fight against the policies of the central government and its northern allies. The government's policies for revenue-producing tariffs and public land sales were a form of "parallel oppression," said Hayne, injurious to the South and the West alike. In so doing, his address became a shrill and fist-waving oratory that immediately skewed the debate away from public land policy into a sectional argument over the government's constitutional powers.

Hayne continued his venomous tirade by condemning the unfair tariff policies of the federal government and the resulting inequities to the interests of his state, and for that matter the entire South. He then went on to blame the disruptive influence of abolitionism on the "meddling statesmen" of the North and their malicious philosophies. And referring to the indiscriminate use of federal funds for internal improvements, Hayne insisted it was the northern states that benefited the most at the expense of the southern people who, in actuality, had no interest in having their money spent on canals or other such projects in Ohio or any other place in the North. These unreasonable policies, he argued, were designed "not to settle the country, and facilitate the formation of new states, but to fill our coffers by coining our lands into gold." Concluding his speech, a discourse steeped in sectional animosity, Hayne urged the two sections, the West and the South, to unite against the North and to fight against its attempt to increase the power of the federal government. Perhaps his defining moment came when he defended the right of any state to counter these unlawful practices by invoking the principle of nullification, a southern interpretation of states' rights that called for a state to simply ignore a federal statute it considered in violation of its rights.

Daniel Webster was extremely troubled not only because the public lands debate had taken on additional sectional arguments but also because of the southern senator's attack on the Constitution and particularly his cherished concept of one nation under an indissoluble union of states. And he was particularly outraged over the implication of Haynes' statement, "States may lawfully decide for themselves, whether, in a given case, the act of the general government transcends its power." It was unsettling to Webster that South Carolina believed, as many did in the South, in the doctrine of nullification, and that the sovereignty of the states gave it the right to secede from the Union.

Unable to sit idly by, over the next two days the New England senator, known for his superior oratorical and debating skills, delivered one of the most stirring and eloquent speeches ever presented on the floor of the U.S. Senate. In what has become known as the Webster-Hayne debate, Webster defended his position on slavery by insisting, "The domestic slavery of the Southern States I leave where I find it—in the hands of their own government. It is their affair, not mine." He also defended the preservation of the Union and the principles of the Constitution. The nation, he said, was not simply a compact of states, but a creation of the people, and the people endowed the Constitution and the government with complete sovereignty. Furthermore, if any state disagreed with a policy of the federal government, it had the right to challenge that policy in a court of law or to seek a constitutional amendment. Webster's speech reached its most poignant moment when, as part lecture and part reprimand, he forcefully and convincingly illustrated the philosophical differences between the two sections on recognizing the solidarity of the Union. Speaking before a Senate gallery packed with captivated spectators in an age where soaring political oratory was exhilarating entertainment, Webster explained, "Sir, if a railroad or canal beginning in South Carolina and ending in South Carolina, appeared to me to be of national importance ... [and] if I were to stand up here and ask, what interest has Massachusetts in a railroad in South Carolina? I should not be willing to face my constituents.... We look upon the States, not as separated, but as united. We love to dwell on that union and on the mutual happiness which it has so much promoted, and the common renown which it has so greatly contributed to acquire. In our contemplation Carolina and Ohio are parts of the same country; States united under the same general government, having interests, common, associated, intermingled. In whatever is within the proper sphere of the constitutional power of this government, we look upon the States as one; we do not impose geographical limits to our patriotic feeling or regard.... It is to that Union that we are chiefly indebted for whatever makes us most proud of our country.... Liberty and Union, now and for ever, one and inseparable."

Webster's speech had won the day and he was widely acclaimed as the consummate orator of all time. Such was the demand for his address that over one hundred thousand copies, printed in pamphlet form, were distributed throughout the United States.

Over the next several weeks Foot's recommendations were debated but were eventually tabled.

Meanwhile, on April 13, 1830, at a dinner honoring Jefferson's birthday, the South Carolinians devised a scheme to force Jackson to demonstrate his position on nullification which they suspected would be supportive to their section. The president, however, who was born in South Carolina, was warned beforehand by Van Buren that the customary round of toasts, by design, would be sympathetic to South Carolina's nullification point of view, and that he was being set up. Jackson attended the dinner well prepared to meet the ruse. Consequently, when his turn came and he was asked to propose a toast, the nullifiers were stunned when Jackson took an opposing view. Jackson arose from his chair, and with glass held high proclaimed in a strong and assertive voice, "Our Union. It must be preserved." As the polite applause subsided, Calhoun, a staunch advocate of nullification, was noticeably shaken. He immediately jumped to his feet and in his unique southern style immediately contradicted Jackson's toast with one of his own: "The Union; next to our liberties the most dear. May we all remember that it can only be preserved by respecting the rights of the States and distributing equally the benefits and burdens of the Union."

Although not as significant in terms of provoking a sectional conflict, it is worth noting that the southern quest for expanding its economic base was not confined exclusively to acquiring new territory in the Texas area, but was also pursued for land located right under the southerners' very noses. For this reason, southerners were also clamoring for the Jackson administration to do something about the thousands of Indians residing on millions of acres of choice territory in the Deep South, on fertile land they could use to cultivate cotton. The Cherokee tribe alone, for instance, resided on some seven million acres of land in Georgia. Southern hostility towards the Indians and their being obstacles to their economic progress became even more pronounced as cotton production expanded more and more into the Lower South and the Southwest.

Unfortunately, this was also tribal land to 60,000 Native Americans from five powerful Indian nations. These five tribes, the Cherokee, Creek, Choctaw, Chickasaw, and Seminole, were the so-called Five Civilized Tribes, a title derived from their successes in assimilating into the white man's culture.

Since the mid–18th century the white settlers viewed the presence of Indians in their midst not only as a degradation of their white society but also as an obstacle to their agricultural and economic progress. At first a policy of assimilation was attempted whereby government subsidized missionaries made an effort to educate the Indians in such subjects as Christianity and farming.

The government's position at the time was, "There is no place on earth to which they can migrate, and live in the savage and hunter state. The Indian tribes must, therefore, be progressively civilized, or successively perish."

Thomas Jefferson, however, recommended a different policy, one of removal. Policymakers in the U.S. during Jefferson's time never imagined the country would extend beyond the Mississippi and for that reason they considered moving the Indians completely out of the country and into this wide-open expanse of territory a better solution. It would be strictly voluntary and on their new western land, the government asserted, the resettled Indians could live in peace, free from harassment from white intruders, new diseases, and wars. Those choosing to remain behind would be subject to the laws of that state. It was purported to be a win-win situation for everyone.

Coincidentally, for years Old Hickory, a seasoned Indian fighter, was a staunch proponent of Indian removal. In fact, Jackson negotiated some nine treaties that relocated small numbers of the Creek and Seminole tribes between 1814 and 1824. As a result of these efforts, the United States gained control of over 20 million acres that included three-quarters of Alabama and Florida as well as parts of Kentucky, Mississippi, North Carolina, Georgia, and Tennessee.

Initially the Indians attempted to resist the government's removal plan by taking legal action. They claimed their treaties with the United States exempted them from the laws of the state in which they resided. In 1823, however, they received a severe blow when the U.S. Supreme Court ruled that although the Indians lived in the U.S. they could not hold title to the land because, in the court's opinion, the country's right of discovery took precedent over the Indians' right of occupancy.

Most of the furor over the government's attempt to remove the Indians came from the Christian evangelicals living with them. In defense of the Indians, they announced, "We view the Indian question, at present so much agitated in the United States, as being not merely of a political, but of a moral nature—inasmuch as it involves the maintenance or violation of the faith of our country—and as demanding, therefore, the most serious consideration of all American citizens, not only as patriots but as Christians." Opposition, as expected, also came from numerous towns throughout New England as well as from the northern press. In Boston, loud protestations from angry citizens were frequent occurrences. Since the Jackson administration casually dismissed Indian claims that treaties exempted them from laws of the states, meetings at Faneuil Hall gave northerners, particularly National Republicans, the opportunity to voice their displeasure, at times even calling for troops to invade the South.

At first, Jackson accepted the policy for both assimilation and removal. But by 1830 the Jackson administration settled exclusively on the policy of removal after the Supreme Court ruled that the state legislatures could not approve laws that conflicted with Indian treaties. Additionally, Chief Justice John Marshall opined that the federal government was obligated to prevent the incursion of white settlers onto tribal lands. Angry and frustrated over this judgment, it became apparent to Jackson that uprooting thousands of Indians from their ancestral lands would not be an easy task. And educating the Indians to coexist would take too much time, while in the interim the white man's world would overtake the Indians, a scenario likely to be more harmful to them than good. Even Vice President Calhoun agreed, saying, "They lose the lofty spirit and heroic courage of the savage state, without acquiring the virtues which belong to the civilized. Depressed in spirit, and debauched in morals, they dwindle away through a wretched existence, a nuisance to the surrounding country."

To gain the authority for this initiative, that same year, 1830, the administration muscled through Congress a piece of legislation called the Indian Removal Act. The provisions of the act gave the government the right to negotiate treaties with the Indians that would grant the tribes' large tracts of land in the West, on what was called Indian Territory mostly land of present-day Oklahoma, in exchange for their lands in the East. The goal of the negotiations was to convince the Indians that they would be better off to abandon their lands and to move west. Their agreement to relocate was still intended to be voluntary as long as the Indians acquiesced to U.S. demands. If not, they would be forced at gunpoint to leave. To the delight of the South, their frustrations over the Indian problem were now taken more seriously.

In his annual message to Congress in December of 1830 Jackson explained the merits of the Indian Removal Act. "It puts an end to all possible danger of collision between the authorities of the General and State Governments on account of the Indians," he said. "It will place a dense and civilized population in large tracts of country now occupied by a few savage hunters.... It will relieve the whole State of Mississippi and the western part of Alabama of Indian occupancy, and enable those States to advance rapidly in population, wealth, and power. It will separate the Indians from immediate contact with settlements of whites; free them from the power of the States; enable them to pursue happiness in their own way and under their own rude institutions; will retard the progress of decay, which is lessening their numbers, and perhaps cause them gradually, under the protection of the Government and through the influence of good counsels, to cast off their savage habits and become an interesting, civilized, and Christian community." To the Indians Jackson would further explain, "There your white brothers will not trouble you, they will have no claims to the lands, and you can live upon it, you and all your children, as long as the grass grows or the water runs, in peace and plenty. The land beyond the Mississippi belongs to the President and no one else, and he will give it to you forever." Under this rationale, Jackson thought he was doing the Indians a favor.

The promised land in the west, however, was definitely not of fertile soil and running rivers as the Indians were led to believe but an expanse of barren and dry desert wholly unsuitable for farming.

Despite the assurances they received, some tribes refused to voluntarily leave their tribal lands. Instead they preferred to wage war and fight to protect their ancient heritage as the Seminole tribe did in 1817 and again from 1835 to 1842 and 1855 to 1858.

The first to leave to avoid a hostile confrontation with the U.S. Army were the Choctaws, in September of 1830, followed by most of the Seminoles after the bloody Second Seminole War. The Creeks, cheated out of their lands by unscrupulous land speculators, were forced by the military to migrate west by 1837 without a removal treaty, as did the Chickasaws who were more or less forced to sign a treaty when unable to withstand the flood of white settlers trespassing onto their tribal lands. The Cherokee tribe, in contrast, refused to honor a removal agreement they considered bogus. When the U.S. Supreme Court denied their appeal U.S. troops were deployed in 1836 and forced the tribe to leave at bayonet point. In the ensuing march to the West, called the Trail of Tears, 4,000 Cherokee Indians died from hypothermia, starvation, and disease.

Although estimates vary, by 1837, fifty to eighty thousand Native Americans were removed from the eastern side of the Mississippi opening 25 million acres of new land to white settlement, cotton production, and more slavery.

The American Indians, on the other hand, despite the treaties which promised them security and freedom from the white man, were far from being settled. As the country continued to expand into the western territories, land that was once undesirable and given to the Indians was now highly sought after. To accommodate this increased expansion, thirteen years later, Congress passed the Indian Appropriations Act, a bill designed to relocate the Indians once again, this time to the confines of reservations.

Jackson's term in office was nearing the halfway point. With both Calhoun and Van Buren maneuvering for the next presidential bid, the predictable jealousies and rivalries had developed into intraparty bickering that pitted the vice president against the secretary of state. A dedicated loyalist, Van Buren was greatly admired by Jackson and enjoyed the fact that he had the president's ear. On the other hand, Vice President Calhoun's standing in the administration had fallen from grace. He was not looked upon as a team player and was suspected of conspiring against Jackson and Van Buren because of their close friendship. Calhoun's bruised ego was fairly apparent when he observed sarcastically to a friend that Van Buren was the "cock of the walk." And he was also miffed over Jackson's failure to include a South Carolinian in the Cabinet.

Jackson was extremely distraught as well over an on-going Washington social feud involving the wives and members of his Cabinet and the effect it was having on the working relationships of its members. The scandal was called the Eaton Affair because it revolved around the supposed infidelity of Peggy Eaton, the wife of John H. Eaton, the secretary of war. The backstabbing and lack of harmony over this incident had escalated to the point where it had become an unwanted distraction to Jackson's presidency. Old Hickory had long suspected that Calhoun and his wife, Floride, were the leading instigators in the feud by employing a conspiracy of false accusations and innuendo in an attempt to undermine the administration for their own selfish motives. But the final straw occurred when Jackson learned that Calhoun, while Monroe's secretary of war in 1817, had recommended Jackson's removal from his military command during a controversy over his attacks on Spanish ports in Florida. In fact, it was Calhoun's order for Jackson to take control of the Seminole Indians that sent Gen. Jackson into Spanish-held Florida in the first place. As it turned out, during that mission in 1818, Jackson executed two Englishmen suspected of being mercenaries, and had occupied Spanish provinces in Florida without congressional approval. To quell the growing furor, congressional hearings were held where Jackson was severely criticized by Clay for having exceeded his orders by invading a foreign province without authorization. In the end, however, Jackson was vindicated but from that time on he harbored a deep resentment for both Clay and Calhoun. And with these latest revelations, the personal animosity and the resultant rift between Calhoun and Jackson deepened.

Determined to rid his administration of Calhounites, by June of 1831, the entire Jackson Cabinet, with the exception of the postmaster general, was forced to resign. Also included in this shake-up was his loyal friend Van Buren who chose to resign as well to help Jackson persuade the rest of the Cabinet to follow suit.

To keep his closest confidant in the administration, Jackson nominated Van Buren to the post of ambassador to England. But in January 1832, when the vote in the Senate resulted in a tie, Calhoun saw his opportunity to exact his revenge. As prescribed under the Constitution, the vice president possessed the deciding vote. Accordingly, following a supposed collusion with Clay and other anti–Jackson forces, Calhoun applied his coup de grâce by denying Van Buren the ambassadorship. Calhoun's estrangement from the president was now complete.

When word of the vote reached Jackson, he angrily remarked, "I have no hesitation in saying that Calhoun is one of the most base, hypocritical and unprincipled villains in the United States. His course of secret session, and vote in the case of Mr. Van Buren had displayed a want of every sense of honor, justice, and magnanimity. His vote had dam'd him by all honest men in the Senate and when laid before the nation, and laid it will be, will not only dam him and his associates, but astonish the American people."

Although everyone in Washington understood that Jackson would serve only one term, they were sorely mistaken. One of Jackson's advisors, Major William B. Lewis, was quoted as saying the shift in political strategy occurred in an attempt to upset "the machinations of Mr. Calhoun and his friends, who were resolved on forcing General Jackson from the presidential chair after one term." Guided by this new revelation, the Jacksonians were prepared to nominate Jackson for a second run at the presidency in 1832 under the new banner of a Democratic Party with Van Buren as his vice-presidential running mate. Calhoun's prospects for gaining the presidency he so long desired had now dramatically diminished.

In December of 1831, the new Twenty-second Congress convened and taking his place within the marble opulence of the House of Representatives was former president John Quincy Adams. Following his campaign loss to Jackson, Adams returned to his home in Massachusetts where in November 1830 he was elected to Congress by his hometown supporters. Also taking his place in the new Congress was former House speaker and Adams's secretary of state Henry Clay, only recently elected to the Senate as well. With Senator Webster also taking his seat and Vice President Calhoun presiding, the Great Triumvirate appeared in the Senate together for the first time.

With the national debt nearly retired and the administration's distribution system for the Treasury's surplus funds seemingly unacceptable, there was still wide-spread concern that the enormous increase in the surplus was bound to have a highly corruptive influence in Washington. Therefore, to allay these fears, Jackson announced to the new Congress that the time had come to reduce tariff revenues. In making tariff reform one of his priorities, Jackson had wisely seized this opportunity to take a proactive position not only on the surplus issue, but also on tariff reform at the same time. He could kill two birds with one stone. Accordingly, a directive was issued to the Treasury Department to initiate a tariff reduction program. Southern partisans of nullification were, of course, overjoyed.

As chairman of the House Committee on Manufactures, former president Adams also decided to bring the tariff reform issue to a head as well. He began by conferring with Clay, now a member of the Senate manufactures committee, on the probability of reducing the high tariffs not only to appease the South but also in light of the looming potential for a large treasury surplus. Believing the administration was scheming to destroy his American System by reducing protective tariffs, Clay agreed to introduce such a measure but only to the extent that the reductions upheld the ideals of his American System. This meant maintaining the principles of protection for manufacturers at current or increased levels. He was fully prepared to submit a proposal to eliminate a number of duties, he told Adams, but only on those imports that did not require protection. Furthermore, he pointedly emphasized, he also had no qualms over raising duties on many of the protected goods as well, a move sure to inflame both the South and President Jackson. When Adams questioned Clay over the unreasonable and defiant stand he was taking, Clay's response was, "I do not care who it defies. To preserve, maintain, and strengthen the American System I would defy the South, the President, and the devil." That being said, Clay began to work on submitting his protectionist version of tariff reform.

In the meantime, another proposal was introduced by South Carolinian George McDuffie, chairman of the House Ways and Means Committee. His version, designed to the other extreme, favored the free-traders by cutting tariffs on protected goods to between 12 and 14 percent and eliminated duties on everything else. A chagrined Adams prepared for a certain clash between McDuffie's southern free-traders and the Clay protectionists.

A third alternative was submitted by Treasury Secretary Lewis McLane and represented the administration's version of a tariff reform bill. The McLane version proposed only modest cuts to most protected items but drastically slashed many of the duties on non-protected imports. More importantly, since the protective tariffs were relatively unscathed, to appease the South, the administration's bill substantially reduced the tariff on woolen cloth, the center of controversy and the South's principle complaint against the Tariff of Abominations. As a consequence, on average, the duty rates were reduced from 45 to about 33 percent.

That summer, Clay's bill went nowhere, as did McDuffie's, both unacceptable to southern sensibilities, South Carolina in particular. McLane's proposal, however, also called the McLane-Adams Tariff Bill, was accepted by Congress, again strictly along sectional lines, and on July 14, 1832, it was signed into law effective in March of the following year.

The unique feature of this reform bill was that it returned the current exorbitantly high tariff rates to the 1824 levels, to an average of some 33 percent. This was accomplished by the removal of a complex and fraudulent system of assessing valuations—a factor that helped to influence the high rates from the start, the reduction of the rates themselves, and the lowering of duties on unrefined woolen cloth used in slave clothing. The end result was a bill once suggested by the South that limited the amount of incoming tariff revenue so that when combined with the revenue from land sales, the total was deemed adequate to administer government operations. At the same time the bill provided for all the necessary economic protections and eliminated the concerns over the treasury surplus.

Despite the generosity of this bill, the South was still far from being satisfied. Unhappy that the protectionist tariff rates were not even lower, South Carolina once again described the bill as merely a federal conspiracy to reduce the surplus in order to save northern manufacturers. In the North, there were those who were unhappy as well. The McLane-Adams Tariff Bill was seen by textile manufacturers as the beginning of the end for the woolen industries, while the proponents of Clay's American System were incensed over this blatant concession to the southern free-trade radicals.

Although the new tariff legislation was now law, it remained a raw and festering boil in the southern psyche, fermenting even more sectional animosity as southern anti-government and anti–North sentiments deepened. In November of 1832, however, the boil would be lanced when the doctrine of nullification resurfaced once again.

In the meantime, the different sections, growing more and more aware of their unique and often conflicting economic interests, continued to muster the forces necessary to fight for the political power they each demanded. The southern states in particular continued to harbor a perception that the federal government was guilty of abusing its enormous power by dictating policies that transferred southern wealth into the pockets of northern manufacturers and bankers. These prejudicial policies, they claimed, blatantly disregarded the constitutional guarantee of equal protection under the law and effectively favored one section over another. In this light, the argument for states' rights was gaining momentum and would soon become a new rallying cry for the South in its attempt to galvanize its forces in the ever expanding sectional arguments. South Carolina, the principal instigator, began to take a closer look at nullification as a remedy to overcome the evils of a powerful central government and its discriminatory policies.

5

The Bank War and Southern Nullification (1832 to 1834)

By the fall of 1832, sectional disputes had become firmly entrenched in the daily exercise of political discourse. Seemingly blind to the ultimate consequences, these conflicts continued to divide the North and South. Derived from a growing awareness of unique political and economic needs and instigated by regional self-interests, a number of self-absorbed debates between the sections had become common occurrences in Washington for most of the past two decades.

Especially disconcerting to the South was a myriad of economic woes they blamed on unfair protective tariffs and corrupt national banking policies. The constitutionality of federal subsidies for internal improvements continued to be a troublesome issue for them, a policy thought to be in direct violation of their states' rights principles. Inciting conflict as well were the philosophical differences over the constitutional powers of the central government and its impact on the southern states, as was the on-going resistance in the North for returning fugitive slaves. Slavery, however, and the northern abolitionist movement to undermine it, were issues much too sensitive for a rational congressional debate. As stated earlier, these were issues Washington shunned on constitutional grounds, leaving them for the individual states to resolve.

In this highly volatile climate, two bitterly contested sectional issues resurfaced in the months leading up to the campaign of 1832. The Bank and protectionist tariff policies not only dominated the Washington political scene between the fall of 1831 and the spring of 1834, but to some degree helped to reelect Jackson to a second term, and to influence the beginnings of a new political party.

The Bank War and the Nullification Crisis were parallel challenges to the rule of law and the principles of the Constitution that severely tested the will of the president. Fought on the battlefields of Congress, each of these issues pitted the power of the executive office against the powers of the congressional and state legislatures.

In November of 1832, Andrew Jackson won his bid for reelection to a second term despite attempts by the opposition party to portray him as "King Andrew the First," and "the most absolute despot now at the head of any representative government on earth." This election was quite unique considering it was the first to nominate both major candidates at a national convention, and was also the first with a third-party candidate on the ballot. It was especially noteworthy that for the new and popular Democratic Party the victory was also its first. In fact, the Jackson–Van Buren ticket received an overwhelming 219 electoral votes as opposed to just 49 votes for their closest challenger, Henry Clay, and his running mate, John Sergeant, both candidates from the National Republican Party. Receiving seven votes was the Anti-Masonic Party candidate, William Wirt, of Maryland, who had served as attorney general in the two previous administrations. Keeping true to its nonconformist nature, South Carolina disregarded all the candidates. Instead, in a show of protest, the legislature gave its eleven electoral votes to a highly radical states' rights governor, John Floyd of Virginia.

To Jackson, the enormous mandate from his constituents, the ordinary people, was compelling proof that his supporters agreed with his continuing policies that reigned in the power of the rich elite and brought justice and fairness to the poor. With fifteen of the twenty-four states voting to keep the Democrats in office for another four years, the president was convinced more than ever that the Democratic Party was the party of the working man. Defeating Henry Clay so convincingly, one of the most powerful and distinguished statesmen in Washington, was particularly gratifying.

Clay's devastating loss in his bid for the presidency, his second successive trouncing for that high office, can be attributed to several factors but in some ways reflected the impact from the emergent Anti-Masonic Party. Organized only four years earlier as a simple movement to protest the existence of the secret Freemasonry organization, the new political party was concentrated mostly in the old Federalist strongholds of New England, Pennsylvania, and New York, states traditionally in the National Republican column. It was the disappearance and presumed murder of a Mason who threatened to expose the secret society and the subsequent cover-up that motivated the formation of the crusade against the brotherhood and the initial quest to defeat all Masons in public office. Mason leaders included such men as Thurlow Weed, a party organizer in the Adams campaign of 1824 and state senator William Seward, both from New York, as well as a radical abolitionist attorney, Thaddeus Stevens of Vermont, and Connecticut congressman Samuel A. Foot, instigator of the historic Webster-Hayne debate. It was widely believed that as the campaigning got underway the Anti-Masons and the National Republicans would merge. Doing so, political observers mused, would have been a strategic and clever political maneuver necessary to overcome the challenge from the Democratic administration. Even Clay thought it was inevitable "for the natural tendency of all divisions of the minority is to cohesion." Clay's refusal to condemn the Masons, however, and to renounce his own membership, prohibited such a union. Consequently, the popularity of the Anti-Masons as a rising political force undercut Clay's strength in the northern region.

Another blow to Clay's candidacy was his misguided campaign strategy to force Jackson's hand on re-chartering the Second Bank of the United States long before it was scheduled to expire in 1836. It was certainly no secret to Clay, or to anyone else, that Jackson was adamantly opposed to renewing the Bank charter. He made that point perfectly clear in his first annual message to Congress back in 1829. Jackson had always minimized the importance of the Bank and its vital influence on the nation's sound financial health. Instead he despised its seemingly corrupt power, a force bred, he thought, from its unholy alliances with greedy northern entrepreneurs, politicians, and land speculators. Jackson's distrust and fear of banks and their speculative financial schemes derived from his encounters with creditors in Tennessee as a young man. Involved in a land deal in 1795 that went awry, Jackson nearly went to prison for debts it took 15 years for him to pay off.

From the western section Senator Benton remained strongly critical of the Bank as one "having too much power over the people," as did the South, which also thought the Bank violated the states' rights principle of a weak national government. Most of the northern states, on the other hand, were in favor of re-chartering the Bank, mainly because it was an essential part of the American System.

Cognizant of the political ramifications this issue represented, Jackson was still unsure how he would institute his fight against the Bank, an institution he frequently referred to as the Monster.

Consequently, well before the candidates were selected, Clay's scheme was to make the Bank the central issue of his campaign. When the Twenty-second Congress first convened in December of 1831, he would use his unrivaled influence to drive through a re-chartering bill in order to force Jackson into a position where he had to either accept the charter or veto it. Clay and his advisors considered the timing for this tactic, coming before the election, was certain to alienate and further divide his coalition no matter which way he decided, a definite advantage for the National Republicans.

Unknown to Clay, however, that October, Secretary of the Treasury Louis McLane had met with Jackson to outline a series of initiatives he was planning to introduce to the upcoming Congress. During this meeting, McLane, a staunch proponent of the Bank, launched into a strong defense of the institution and ultimately recommended that Jackson reconsider his refusal to grant the Bank's charter, provided of course, that the charter was restructured to contain the necessary checks and balances. Extremely impressed with McLane's presentation, Jackson was unexpectedly persuaded not only to back off his attacks on the Bank but also to support the will of the Congress in this matter. At the end of the meeting, Jackson agreed to McLane's proposal, but with two very important caveats, the Bank charter would have to be restructured to his satisfaction and, he also strongly emphasized, under no circumstances would he tolerate any effort to introduce a bill to charter the Bank before the election. On October 19, McLane informed Biddle, the Bank's president, of Jackson's desire to go along with the decision of Congress, as well as the requirements for a revised charter and particularly the conditions to avoid a veto.

Learning of Jackson's apparent acquiescence to the wisdom of Congress, Clay was now certain that if push came to shove Jackson would not veto a banking bill before the election but would certainly do so if reelected. He also believed that no matter how Jackson decided, the dissidents would abandon the Democratic Party. At that point his own people would convince the disgruntled Jacksonians Democrats to join his campaign on the National Republican side.

Evidently the opportunity to gain a broader political following may have blinded Clay to the realities of a presidential veto, as was the case for Biddle as well, who thought the Bank was sacrosanct and was anxious to secure a new charter under any terms. So, despite the advice from McLane to wait until after the election, which was obviously overlooked, a petition for the charter was filed by Biddle in January of 1832 with the urging of Clay and with the support from Webster, the Bank's attorney.

Following months of adversary-inspired delays through multiple committees, caucus meetings, investigations, and time-consuming motions, in May, the bill for extending the Bank's charter for another fifteen years was finally brought before the Twenty-second Congress. Following two months of spirited debate in which Benton strenuously spoke in opposition, Webster in favor, and with extensive lobbying from the Bank on its own behalf, the final bill with a number of modifications was approved by both Houses. Not surprisingly, northern and southern Jacksonians failed to unite against the bill. Instead sectional partisanship overwhelmingly influenced the final outcome of their vote. Eighty percent of the northerners in the Senate voted for the Bank, while three-quarters of the southerners were opposed, reflecting a similar pattern in the House.

Predictably, on July 10, 1832, Jackson vetoed the bill he still considered unconstitutional and a monopoly to enrich the mostly foreign stockholders. When "his people" were unable to pay their debts, he often remarked, they lost everything they owned or were incarcerated in debtors' prison. But when banks were unable to pay their debts they merely suspended payment while the powerful directors and the rich foreign stockholders were free from accountability. Besides, Jackson was well aware that if the charter was renewed, these very stockholders would reap even more financial rewards on the increased value of the Bank's stock, money, he said, coming out of the pockets of the American people. In the accompanying message with his veto Jackson declared, "It is much regretted that the rich and powerful too often bend the acts of government to their selfish purposes" at the expense of "the humble members of society, the farmers, mechanics, and laborers, who have neither the time or the means of securing like favors to themselves...."

Within days one Democratic newspaper headline blared out praise for Jackson's stand against the corrupt and entrenched political-financial establishment, saying his veto demonstrated "the final decision of the President between the Aristocracy and the People—he stands by the People." Needless to say, advocates of the Bank, the National Republicans and northern financiers, were extremely disappointed over Jackson's veto. In fact, an opposing newspaper printed in large banner headlines just the opposite, "THE KING UPON THE THRONE: The People in the Dust!!!" It was unthinkable, the newspaper angrily exclaimed, that by a stroke of a pen an institution so vital to the nation in matters of currency, credit, and exchange could be so callously cast aside.

In the Senate, Webster spoke on behalf of the northern section and assailed Jackson's veto, expressing outrage over Jackson's absolute and flagrant disregard for the will of the Congress and for that matter the judgment of the Supreme Court on the Bank's constitutionality. Jackson, however, assuming equal rights with the Congress and the Supreme Court, would quickly retort, "The opinion of the judges has no more authority over Congress than the opinion of Congress has over the judges, and on that point the President is independent of both." He also added, "The authority of the Supreme Court must not, therefore, be permitted to control the Congress or the Executive." Although Jackson's message explaining his veto was applauded by most of his grassroots constituency, his blatant arrogance against Congress and the judiciary rankled many party leaders and even threatened to divide the Democratic Party. Following several emergency caucuses the Democrats were able to reach an amicable agreement over their differences that not only saved the party from further damage but also united them behind Jackson's veto.

Despite all the National Republican efforts to capitalize on this issue during the campaign, it had negligible effect on the outcome of the election. Ironically, it may have contributed to their defeat since Clay's attempt to smear Jackson for shutting down the Bank was overshadowed once again by the unwavering admiration of his loyal constituents. Old Hickory's extremely popular image as an enemy of political privilege and social elitism was much too strong for Clay to overcome.

Also taking some of the blame for Clay's loss was the National Republicans' consistent pandering to this very class of elitist Jacksonians fought against, coupled with the failure of Clay's campaign strategists to understand the sentiments of the ordinary people. Taken together, along with the party's lack of organization and campaigning skills, its run for the presidency resulted in a gross inability to attract alienated Jacksonians and other new voters, such as southern dissidents and Anti-Masons, to sign on to the National Republican ideology. In the end, Clay's campaign relied heavily, albeit erroneously, on the principles of his American System to carry the day.

As a political force to be reckoned with, the National Republicans were in dire straits. Severely beaten a second time, they desperately needed to establish a new party, acquire a new persona, and a new strategy for rallying the people to their cause.

Meanwhile, with his veto sustained by Congress, the banking issue was temporarily set aside as Jackson's attention was drawn away to growing problems in South Carolina.

Increasingly embittered over the outrageous misuse of federal power and the resultant plight of their state, the leaders of South Carolina, the perennial maverick of the plantation states, could no longer sit idly by as their economy continued to worsen. The federal government's imposition of protectionist tariffs was a long and festering irritant for the state legislators and one they had to address immediately.

South Carolina had tried once before, several months after the passage of the Tariff of Abominations in 1828, to outline their difficulties with protective tariffs. At the time, John C. Calhoun, one of South Carolina's favorite sons and a dedicated states' rights advocate, was persuaded by a radical legislative committee to write a paper outlining the ills that had befallen the state from these tariffs and what he thought would be the best remedy to combat them. Calhoun agreed to voice his opinion and recommendations on one condition. Since he was then the recently elected vice president and had plans to succeed Jackson to the higher office in four years, he was concerned that his views could possibly impact his political future. In that light, he insisted that his authorship remained secret. His completed thesis, however, called the South Carolina Exposition, was considered so extreme that even the radical state officials refused to sanction it. Instead they opted for another, much less inflammatory protest that was mildly provocative but yet remained indicative of South Carolina's resentment to the tariff of 1828.

Protective tariffs, in Calhoun's view, were siphoning wealth away from hard working southerners into the pockets of northern industrialists. Therefore, in his view, the powers of the federal government were callously being used to benefit one section over the other. In his dissertation, Calhoun insisted the tariff of 1828 was unconstitutional and called for nullification, a principle derived from an extreme belief in the doctrine of states' rights which permitted a state to simple nullify, or render as null and void, any federal law it considered unconstitutional.

Calhoun's opinion on nullification wasn't exactly new but one adapted from a so-called constructionist viewpoint first formulated by Jefferson and Madison in 1798. This view, under the concept of states' rights, insisted that the Union was a voluntary compact of states which had formed the Constitution itself and therefore possessed undivided sovereignty. At the same time, the federal government, which was delegated only limited powers by these very states, had no right to exercise powers not specifically assigned to it by the U.S. Constitution, which states, "The powers not delegated to the United States by the Constitution, nor prohibited by it to the States, are reserved to the States respectively, or to the people." Therefore, to the supporters of nullification, the power to nullify a federal law was one of those reserved powers. Many moderate southerners, however, were fearful that this interpretation and pursuit of states' rights principles could only lead to further sectional conflicts, and perhaps even secession. Consequently, the threat of nullification remained just that, at least for the moment.

Then, in January 1830, during the Webster-Hayne debate, the specter of nullification resurfaced once again when Senator Hayne, of South Carolina, bitterly remarked, "States may lawfully decide for themselves, whether, in a given case, the act of the general government transcends its power." Later, at the White House, Jackson penned a letter to the senator that in no uncertain terms explained the reasons why he didn't agree with the theory of nullification. "For the rights of the states, no one had a higher regard and respect than myself," Jackson said, but at the same time, he could not agree "that a state had the power to nulify [*sic*] the Legislative enactments of the General Government" or that President Jefferson ever had "such an opinion." Instead, he reminded Hayne that the United States government "depends on a will of the majority," and that "in all Republics the voice of a Majority must prevail."

In the summer of 1831, Calhoun addressed the doctrine of nullification anew. With his split from Jackson now a forgone conclusion and his quest for the presidency all but over, Calhoun spoke out openly in defense of nullification, the philosophy he believed would lead his beloved state down the path to salvation. This work, popularly known as the Fort Hill address, transformed what was once a nullification bullying tactic into one of political expediency. In his address he reiterated what most South Carolinians already knew, that protective tariffs had split the country into two opposing sections, and the unfortunate result was that "no two distinct nations ever entertained more opposite views of policy." He also reminded his people that in Congress the debates had become "an annual struggle between the two sections ... a struggle in which all the noble and generous feelings of patriotism are gradually subsiding into sectional and selfish attachments."

Soon after his address, efforts were underway in South Carolina by Calhoun, Sen. Hayne, Congressman McDuffie, Gov. James Hamilton, Jr. and other extreme states' rights advocates that would continue over the months ahead to garner statewide political support for the nullification movement. Their campaign proved to be a highly successful one, a campaign that ultimately united the low country merchants with the upcountry planters in a move they thought would save the economy of their state.

When briefed on the volatile situation in South Carolina, Jackson thought nullification was absurd and refused to discuss the matter. Instead, he blamed Calhoun and his fellow nullifiers for plotting a scheme to undermine him and his administration for their own selfish motives. Nevertheless, despite his outward rhetoric to the contrary, Jackson dispatched agents to Charleston to keep him abreast of the growing unrest.

In the South Carolina state elections of October 1832, it came as no surprise when the champions of nullification succeeded in gaining two-thirds control of the statehouse over the opposing Unionists, a faction that categorically rejected the doctrine of nullification. The new legislature promptly authorized a convention and the following month South Carolina delegates convened in Columbia to address their tariff difficulties with the federal government once and for all.

On their agenda the delegates were asked to consider Calhoun's political philosophy of nullification and to decide if it should be implemented on behalf of the most recent federally imposed protective tariffs. Although the outcome was certainly a foregone conclusion, on the 24th of November, the product of this at times raucous gathering, was a Nullification Ordinance that outlined several unequivocal points. First, the tariff of 1828, the infamous Tariff of Abominations and its alleged revision, the McLane-Adams Tariff Bill of 1832, were considered null and void and as a result the collection of import duties would cease effective the first day of February 1833. The nullifiers also forbade the state courts to pass judgment on the constitutionality of the ordinance or to direct appeals to the U.S. Supreme Court. An oath to uphold the ordinance was also required for all state officials except legislators. Finally, if the U.S. government chose to enforce the collection of duties within South Carolina the people would "thenceforth hold themselves absolved from all further obligation to maintain or preserve their political connection with the people of the other States; and will forthwith proceed to organize a separate government...." And to support their warning, Gov. Hamilton promptly called for the immediate recruitment of two thousand armed volunteers and for five times that number to be organized into the state militia.

The threat from South Carolina was crystal clear. Following approval of the proclamation from the state legislature, the doctrine of nullification would no longer be merely a controversial states' rights issue for political discussions but a state edict mandating its actual practice. And if that wasn't enough, South Carolina was prepared for armed resistance and to secede from the Union if its actions were challenged. Nullification, they argued, was the right and the means for any state to protect itself from the discriminatory powers of the U.S. government.

The reaction to the news of this ordinance was swift. Nullification was on everyone's lips, the predominant subject of gossip in the parlors, the shops throughout the cities and towns, the barbeques, and even at the slave auctions. Street violence and riots were common occurrences as gatherings of nullifiers, proudly sporting their blue and orange cockade of the States' Rights and Free Trade party, clashed repeatedly with the Unionists, each attempting to silence the opposing view.

Within this turmoil, on November 27, the South Carolina legislature reconvened to enact a series of laws to enforce the Nullification Ordinance, to raise an army, and to purchase arms. During this session they also cast the states' eleven electoral votes for John Floyd and named their senior senator, Robert Y. Hayne, to replace Hamilton as governor. Hamilton, in turn, would command the state's militia.

With the South Carolina legislature now in session and with the fate of the Union in its hands, an angry but resolute president finally reacted to the growing crisis by issuing his Nullification Proclamation. Although born in South Carolina and an ardent states' rights advocate, Jackson was now forced by this emergency to take on a more nationalist and hawkish perspective, a point of view that received mixed reactions from his supporters within the party.

In his proclamation to the state of South Carolina on December 10, Jackson warned the legislature that if it enacted the nullification ordinance a dangerous precedent would be established. It was evident, he said, "that to give the right of resisting laws ... coupled with the uncontrolled right to decide what laws deserve [to be resisted], is to give the power of resisting all laws." Nullification, he said, was illegal and that he considered "the power to annul a law of the United States ... incompatible with the existence of the Union, contradicted expressly by the letter of the Constitution, unauthorized by its spirit, inconsistent with every principle on which it was founded, and destructive of the great object for which it was formed." Jackson also reminded the southerners that although he was born a South Carolinian, as the "First Magistrate of our common country," he was authorized and duty-bound to protect the laws of the Constitution, and if necessary, even by force. On the threat to secede from the Union Jackson responded, "So obvious are the reasons which forbid this secession, that it is necessary only to allude to them. The Union was formed for the benefit of all. It was produced by mutual sacrifice of interest and opinions. Can those sacrifices be recalled? Can the States, who magnanimously surrendered their title to the territories of the West, recall the grant? Will the inhabitants of the inland States agree to pay the duties that may be imposed without their assent by those on the Atlantic or the Gulf, for their own benefit? Shall there be a free port in one State, and enormous duties in another? No one believes that any right exists in a single State to involve all the others in these and countless other evils, contrary to engagements solemnly made." Eloquently tempering his admonition was a promise to pursue legislation to modify the tariff, an offer of an olive branch that reflected Jackson's acknowledgment in his annual message to Congress six days earlier that he wanted to "relieve the people from unnecessary taxation" and that high tariffs contributed "in the minds of a large portion of our countrymen a spirit of discontent and jealousy dangerous to the stability of the Union."

In the likely event the Congress disregarded his attempt to compromise; Jackson had already called on the South Carolina Unionists to organize a civilian army to help support the U.S. troops against the state militia if and when the crisis warranted force. In fact, two hundred soldiers under the command of Gen. Winfield Scott had already been dispatched to garrison the forts in Charleston Harbor, and in Norfolk instructions from the War Department were also in place directing the naval commanders to ready the fleet for possible action against Charleston.

Governor Hayne, meanwhile, not to be outdone by Jackson's warlike conduct, reciprocated with bold and defiant rhetoric, vowing that he was prepared to enforce the will of the citizens of South Carolina in their fight against the unlawful power of the federal government. And to back up his pledge, in the final week of 1832 Governor Hayne called for additional volunteers to step forward to support their states' rights cause.

With the nullification crisis growing more and more intense, on December 28, nearly two months before his term expired, Calhoun resigned from his vice-presidency to fill the vacant senatorial seat left by Hayne. Back in the Senate, Calhoun vowed to continue the fight to uphold the principles of states' rights and the honor of his birthplace.

Although applauded by his nationalists backers for supporting the Constitution and the sovereignty of the Union, many Jacksonians in the South who supported states' rights as Jackson did looked unfavorably on Jackson's aggressive posturing. Ignoring the oath Jackson was sworn to uphold, they were aghast over his staunch adherence to the supremacy of the national government and his threat of military action to coerce his own constituency. These southern Democrats felt betrayed, not only over the implication and tone of Jackson's aggressive behavior towards the nullifiers, but also for his defiance of the Congress, the Supreme Court, and the law of the land during the banking crisis. As a result, beginning in 1833, a small minority of embittered Democrats from states throughout the South severed their ties with Jackson and the Democratic Party to establish their own states' rights factions in order to protest such blatant displays of tyranny. It was from these embryonic factions that the term Whig was first used.

In an effort to defuse the crisis, minimize the split in their party, appease the nullifiers, and to save the Union as well, congressional Democrats turned their attention to two proposals, one for tariff relief and another to enforce the collection of duties in South Carolina.

Given that sectional animosity was so deep, however, it was virtually impossible at the outset for the House, where all revenue bills must originate, to reach an amicable compromise on a scaled down tariff. When the Ways and Means Committee drew up a tariff reduction bill in January 1833, the Verplanck Bill, the same tired arguments resonated anew as northern protectionists clashed once again with southern free-traders, both parties complaining and arguing over how much the tariff should be cut. Agreeing to a compromise on tariff reform was always a very volatile issue in Congress and this was certainly no exception. Calhoun had once observed, "It is, in truth, hard to find a middle position where the principle of protection is asserted to be essential on one side, and fatal on the other. It involves not the question of concession, but surrender, on one side or the other." For this reason, although the Verplanck tariff bill was approved by the House, it was done so only grudgingly. The Senate was an entirely different matter.

Although the Constitution gave Jackson the authority to enforce national laws, Jackson believed in limited government and that most of the political power should reside in the states. Nevertheless, in mid–January, Jackson asked Congress to grant him the necessary powers for circumventing the efforts of the nullifiers. They included such tactics as using warships and revenue cutters as "floating custom houses," and new laws requiring that duties be paid only in cash. Jackson also wanted to use the federal court system in lieu of state courts to litigate tariff cases. And finally, pledging to use force only if the nullifiers struck first, Jackson requested permission to use federal troops and to call up the state militia without having to issue a proclamation. Jackson's bill was appropriately called the Force Bill.

If sectional disputes were inhibiting compromise on the Verplanck tariff bill, any remaining conciliatory air in the Congress quickly dissipated when debate over a bill to enforce the collection of duties began in the Senate

When debate opened in February, southern opposition to the Force Bill was immediate and manifested a vengeance completely alien for such a revered and historic chamber. Speaking on behalf of the bill was Massachusetts senator Daniel Webster, the preeminent orator who praised Jackson for his bold stance against the nullifiers. Webster's principal adversary on the Senate floor was none other than Senator John C. Calhoun, the ambassador of southern nullification. The South Carolinian, speaking in an almost inaudible, hoarse voice, explained the rationale behind his doctrine of nullification as a right of "interposition," the right for any state to interpose between a federal law it considered discriminatory or inequitable and the citizens of that state. Continuing with his rationale, Calhoun stressed once again that the real issue was a fundamental one that pitted the power of the larger and wealthier North against the liberty of the South, and if the South failed to resist this "steady encroachment of power, the severest and most debasing calamity and corruption will overspread the land." Webster, on the other hand, in his characteristic oratory, defended the Union for three hours and lashed out bitterly at Calhoun's revolutionary and destructive nullification doctrine. Nullification, he declared, was a path that would only lead to secession. The world will scarcely believe, he said, "that a single state should rush into conflict with all the rest ... and thus break up and destroy the world's last hope."

On February 20, as the Senate prepared to vote, Calhoun and his fourteen fellow nullifiers, knowing they lacked the ballots to win, abruptly left their seats and defiantly filed out of the chamber. When the final vote was tallied, the Force Bill was approved, 32 yeas, 1 nay, with 15 abstaining, the lone dissenter being John Tyler of Virginia.

Realistically, the radical nullifiers were a small minority in South Carolina and although they were a loud and vocal group they gained little support from the other southern states. With the threat of armed Unionists gathering throughout the state and federal military forces preparing for action, cooler heads began to prevail. This sentiment was expressed quite clearly when a meeting of leading nullifiers in Charleston declared that "all occasion for collision between the Federal and State authorities should be sedulously avoided on both sides." Jackson as well was having a change of heart. Reacting to the harsh criticism over his threatened use of force, Jackson decided to back off his inflammatory rhetoric, now expressing himself in more conciliatory tones.

In the meantime, both Clay and Calhoun wanted desperately to resolve the tariff impasse. Seeing the handwriting on the wall, Calhoun wanted something to appease his nullifiers without the perception of a retreat from their principles. Although Clay and Calhoun were extremely bitter rivals, they soon realized a compromise tariff bill would be impossible to negotiate with President Jackson, a common enemy to each of them. Accordingly, an unlikely alliance was formed between Clay and Calhoun that ultimately resulted in the approval of a new tariff bill. Speaking of his work to resolve the tariff impasse, Clay, the "Great Compromiser," remarked, "He who loves the Union must desire to see this agitating question brought to a termination." Called the Compromise Tariff of 1833, it failed to please everyone but since it was all they had to pacify the crisis, it was grudgingly approved by the House on February 26, as prearranged, less than a week before the Twenty-second Congress adjourned.

In its final form the bill proposed to "prevent the destruction of the political system, and to arrest civil war and restore peace and tranquility to the nation" by lowering the tariff rates, which at the time averaged about 33 percent, in small increments over a nine-year period. At that point the rates would be fixed at 1816 levels of about 20 percent. Although northern manufacturers objected to any reduction in tariffs, especially one as drastic as this, they were somewhat placated that the duties would now be based on the value of the goods at the port of entry, which in effect actually raised the tariff above the 20 percent level. Unable to gain support from the rest of the South for their cause, Calhoun and his nullifiers accepted the tariff bill as a means to back out of the crisis while saving face at the same time.

With time running out before Congress adjourned, the Compromise Tariff Bill was presented to the Senate while the Force Bill was promptly routed to the House for its consideration. Following three days of contentious debate in both chambers, the two bills were finally approved on March 1, one day before Congress adjourned and signed by Jackson the following day.

To demonstrate their intent to end the crisis as well, the nullifiers convened a convention in Columbia ten days later. There, in the closing hours of the meeting, the South Carolinians voted to repeal the Nullification Ordinance and the laws passed by the legislature, but yet, in a final show of defiance, voted to nullify the Force Bill as well.

Although debate still continues over whether it was Jackson or the Union, the nullifiers or states' rights that gained the most from this episode, it seems fairly reasonable that it was a compromise resolution in which nearly everyone benefited to some extent. Although the tariff was reduced to 1816 levels, the North had reason to be amenable considering protection would be guaranteed until 1842. And the South Carolina nullifiers, despite being isolated by the other southern states, managed to at least extract a significant reduction in the tariff from the federal government, a win of some sorts. Likewise, for the next nine years the Union was spared further sectional conflicts over protectionist tariffs, the calamity of an armed conflict, and perhaps secession. The states' rights doctrine, although somewhat weakened, remained intact for another day. By the same token, there were a few losers. The Democratic Party, for one, was damaged by the revolt of disgruntled Jacksonians who left the party over the president's actions, and Senator Calhoun as well was diminished after being forced to bargain with his enemies and to acquiescence to their demands.

President Jackson, however, was understandably elated over his victory, one he considered necessary to uphold the principles of the Constitution and to maintain the solidity of the Union. Exalting over his Nullification Proclamation in a letter to James Buchanan, his ambassador to Russia, Jackson wrote, "I met nullification at its threshold.... It opened the eyes of the people to the wicked designs of the nullifiers sided by the union of Clay, Calhoun, the Bank, and the corrupt of all parties. Not a modification of the tariff, but a separation of the Union by the Potomac was sought. Today advice informs us that South Carolina has repealed the ordinance of secession and all laws based upon it. Thus dies nullification and the doctrine of secession, never more to be heard of, only in holding up to scorn and indignation its projectors and abettors and handing their name to posterity as traitors to the best of governments."

With a compromise tariff finally in place until 1842 and the nullification crisis resolved at last, following his inauguration, Jackson turned his attention back to the Bank and specifically, the federal deposits residing there. Not satisfied with his veto to extend the Bank's charter nor to simply let it expire, Jackson was still determined to destroy the institution, declaring, "The bank is trying to kill me, but I will kill it!" Although his victim was severely wounded, he now set out to apply the coup de grâce.

Since the administration suspected the Bank was financially unsound, Jackson and his Cabinet discussed several questions concerning the government's future relations with the institution. One concern was the government deposits, some $10 million, and what to do with them. Certain that the government funds were unsafe, in March of '33, Jackson informed his Cabinet that he was willing to consider a new national bank, but only if it was located in Washington and under the jurisdiction of the federal government. Until then, he said, the government would gradually transfer all federal monies out of the current institution and into a number of selected state banks.

Listening intently to Jackson's objective, the Cabinet was far from unanimous in its approval. Vice President Van Buren wanted to delay the move until the new Twenty-third Congress could debate the question and authorize the withdrawal. Two other members were uncertain about such a drastic action, and McLane was flatly opposed, as were three others. Only the attorney general, Roger B. Taney, was wholeheartedly in agreement with Jackson and vowed to support his efforts. At the Bank, meanwhile, a besieged Biddle, a man whose life revolved around the institution he loved so dearly, vowed to fight Jackson's intent to transfer the funds, writing, "If they are withdrawn, it is a declaration of war." Later he repeated his position, forcefully reiterating his opposition to Jackson's move and insisting that Jackson, despite having "scalped Indians and imprisoned Judges," would not "have his way with the Bank." Meanwhile, Senator Webster, the Bank's counsel, tried desperately to prevent Jackson's planned action. But it was to no avail. It was now a battle between Biddle's pride and arrogance and Jackson's determination and will.

That spring, in a previously-planned shuffle, Secretary of the Treasury McLane was named to replace the secretary of state, Edward Livingston, and William J. Duane, an anti–Bank ally, was appointed to fill the vacant Treasury position. The new treasury secretary, however, to whom the law gave custody of the deposits, refused to take part in such a venture. Evidently, Duane was fully aware of a clause in the Bank's charter which specifically forbade the removal of funds unless Congress approved the withdrawal and only after congressional committees confirmed they were unsafe. He was also aware that recent congressional investigations had demonstrated just the reverse. What followed, of course, was a period of angry and somewhat animated exchanges between Jackson and Duane resulting in Duane's removal in September, when he was replaced with Jackson's chief advocate for removing the deposits, Roger B. Taney.

Despite the legal verbiage in the charter, the lack of support from his Cabinet, and the growing hostility within the party, two days later, on September 25, 1833, the order to remove the funds was issued effective on the first day of October.

The presidential order called for Taney to transfer the $10 million in U.S. funds from the Bank into a number of state banks, mostly those in the Northeast considered more loyal to the administration's fiscal policies. These deposit banks, also referred to as "pet banks," included such institutions as the Bank of America, and the Manhattan Bank, in New York City, and the Commonwealth and Merchants banks of Boston.

As a result of Jackson's order to withdraw government funds, in retaliation Biddle rebelliously called in all of its loans. "My own course is decided," he pointedly declared, "all the other banks and all the merchants may break, but the Bank of the United States shall not break." Smaller banks now became short on cash, credit was curtailed resulting in higher interest rates and prices shot upward across the country. Soon there was a financial panic on Wall Street where the value of stocks plummeted, sending many investors into bankruptcy, real estate values decreased, and unemployment began to rise. Many investors, irate over their enormous financial losses, at times highly exaggerated, blamed Jackson and his recent removal policy. Jackson, in turn, blamed Biddle and unscrupulous stockbrokers and Biddle blamed the administration. When he heard complaints that his constituents, the working-class people, were the victims of this new crisis, the president vehemently bellowed, "The people! The people, sir, are with me. I have undergone much peril for the liberties of this people, and Andrew Jackson yet lives to put his foot upon the head of the monster, and crush him to dust...."

As the Twenty-third Congress convened in December of 1833, thousands of petitions began to flood both houses urgently appealing for relief from Jackson's shameful actions. Pressure groups as well, protesting the widespread bankruptcies, diminishing property values, and other ruinous results of the panic, gathered outside the White House demanding to meet with Jackson. Highly agitated by their unruly and brash attempt at intimidation, Jackson had scant patience with their criticism and was not hesitant to express his views. "Relief, sir!" he scolded one group, "Come not to me for relief; go to the monster."

With the new Congress now in session, the Jackson administration prepared for the inevitable hearings and debates over the withdrawal and transfer of the funds. Since the question would be debated in the House, where the Democratic Party held a slight majority, and specifically in the Ways and Means Committee, they proceeded to stack the committee with a solid six to three majority and chose James K. Polk, a loyal thirty-six-year-old Democratic congressman from Tennessee, to be its chairman. Likewise, in the Senate, where the Democrats were in the minority, the National Republicans had the advantage. Of the forty-eight senators, twenty were National Republicans, six were anti–Jackson states' righters, and two were South Carolina nullifiers. With the Jacksonians outnumbered 28 to 20, Senator Clay took the lead on behalf of the Bank and in his inimitable fashion delivered a powerful and scathing four-day assault on the president. His tirade wasn't on the removal of funds, which at this point was "kept to the rear," but on Jackson's unlawful behavior for assuming "authority and power not conferred by the Constitution and laws, but in derogation of both."

At the end of his exhausting tirade, Clay introduced two startling resolutions, one rejecting Secretary Taney's justification for removing the funds, the other a call for the censure of the president for not only his usurpation of the Congress by removing the funds without their authorization, but also for dismissing a Cabinet member, Secretary Duane, without gaining permission from the Senate, an act some considered undermining the Senate's power of confirmation. Quickly jumping to Jackson's defense, Senator Benton berated the actions of the Bank for creating the financial crisis in the first place and angrily reminded his colleagues that the Senate lacked the authority to impose this sanction on Jackson. Impeachment, he bellowed, was a decision the Constitution reserved only for the House of Representatives. On the other hand, to Calhoun, the fiery southern spokesman, the issue was not entirely over the Bank, which he totally abhorred and preferred to "divorce the government entirely from the banking system." Although he was willing to restore the funds, to Calhoun the issue was actually a matter of power, the exercise of legislative versus executive power.

Finally, after three months of heated debate and repeated demands for Jackson to return the funds, on March 28, 1834, the Senate voted 26 to 20 for censure. Although Jackson would issue a protest to the Senate over the censure, he later acknowledged that Congress had "the power and right of the legislative department to provide by law for the custody, safe-keeping, and disposition of the public money and property of the United States."

Seven days after the censure was approved and following nearly a month of negotiations, party spokesman Rep. James K. Polk brought four measures to a vote in the House, all of which were endorsed by Jackson and the Democratic Party. They included a vote against renewing the Bank's charter, against restoring funds to the Bank, to continue the deposits in the state banks, and to hold another investigation of the Bank. Ultimately, they were all approved.

The western and southern sections were elated over these remarkable events, as was Jackson. Upon learning of the vote, Jackson jubilantly declared, "The overthrow of the opposition ... was a triumphant one, and puts to death, that mammoth of corruption and power, the Bank of the United States." As for Secretary Taney, he was rewarded shortly after by being appointed chief justice of the Supreme Court.

The mortally wounded Bank, severely diminished in its influence and power, would continue for two more years at which time it was re-chartered as a state bank, the Bank of the United States of Pennsylvania. Meanwhile, the adversarial confrontation over both the Bank and the nullification crisis left the North and the South even more estranged than ever as the political bonds between them continued to weaken.

6

The Turbulent Years (1834 to 1836)

Over the preceding decades sectional animosity between the North and South was an ever-growing fact of life and one that ultimately divided the country along the Mason-Dixon Line. This sectional resentment derived from such controversial issues as slavery, the Fugitive Slave Law, and abolitionism. The widening schism between the "two countries" was further exacerbated by bitter disputes over powers the Constitution did or did not provide to the Congress or the states, and over the political influence the North exerted in legislating what the South defined as discriminatory laws and White House policies detrimental to the South and the southern people. These laws instituted protective tariffs, budgetary and banking policies, as well as measures that impacted states' rights, political parity, and dissemination of public lands.

Although the North-South rift remained as intense as ever, during the years from 1834 to 1836 significant sectional disputes were relatively minor. Instead, during these turbulent years the Washington bureaucrats were occupied primarily with solving a common problem, namely the severe fiscal difficulties confronting the country as a whole. These difficulties included recognizing the causes of the economic downturn, the impact those problems were having not only on the people but also on a fragile and deteriorating national economy, and galvanizing the political acumen for applying the necessary corrective actions. Also on the agenda during this time was the unwanted prospect of debating slavery in the hallowed halls of Congress, a matter quite distasteful to the elected officials in Washington. The divisions within the Democratic Party and the repercussions the fracture would have in the upcoming presidential election were also of great concern.

In the spring of 1834, as the repercussions of the Bank War waned, signs of a reemerging prosperity were becoming more evident. Deposit banks began to experience huge increases in foreign capital which, in turn, triggered an enormous demand for credit to finance the swelling escalation of land sale transactions. In fact, land sales would increase from 2 million acres in 1830 to over 12 million by 1835. Appeasing the speculators at an unprecedented rate, scores of bank loans rapidly fueled the rising economy. Increased foreign demands for cotton exports and other goods, as well as booming profits in the manufacturing sector, also contributed to the good economic times. At the same time, the steady growth in northern manufacturing created a windfall of new jobs not only in the factories and mills but also to satisfy the demand for thousands of miles of new rail lines to help transport the abundance of products and produce to ever-expanding markets. As the economy grew, foreign investment capital continued to flood the banks. With jobs plentiful, thousands upon thousands of poor Irish and German immigrants were lured to the bustling cities of the North to take part in what would become known as the "American Dream."

But the boom would be short-lived.

By the end of the year, the prospect of a promising future became a devastating loss to many of those very workers as the unrestrained growth began to create problems of its own. State debt began to increase from a proliferation of internal improvement projects, and consumer prices rose dramatically compounded by a corresponding decrease in wages. Soon, northern workers were outraged over the merciless attacks on their already meager standard of living. Having to get by on poor wages or struggle for jobs with unwanted competition from free blacks and newly arrived immigrants, northern laborers, such as railroad and canal workers and longshoremen, lashed out in an outbreak of labor strikes and violent riots.

As the Senate attempted to come to grips with the latest economic downturn, Clay brazenly took out the nation's frustrations by directing his speech to Vice President Van Buren listening attentively from his lofty perch in the chamber. "Go and tell him [the president] ... the actual condition of this bleeding country," he implored. "Depict to him, if you can find the language to portray, the heartrending wretchedness of thousands of the working-classes out of employment. Tell him of the tears of helpless widows ... and of unclad and unfed orphans." Van Buren, meanwhile, remained stoic and unmoved.

Over the next several years frequent and widespread rioting became commonplace in many northeastern states. Angry and unruly protesters vented their frustrations by demonstrating not only against the current economic downturn but also against the renewed abolitionist movement inspired by Garrison's *Liberator* and against the free blacks who were now the unfortunate scapegoats of many unemployed white laborers. In Baltimore, rioters violently reacted to the suspension of services by the Bank of Maryland by destroying not only the bank but also the house of the mayor. Street fighting between the hostile mobs and militia troops continued for three days, but unable to contain the brutality after scores of people were killed and wounded, the troops withdrew leaving the hooligans to their own devices. Rioting was particularly rampant in New York City where overcrowding and poor living conditions bred an environment of civil unrest and unchecked crime that was growing out of control. A group of local citizens, for example, clashed with a mob of Irish immigrants during the municipal elections. So severe was the fighting the mayor and the police were unable to quell the disorder. Angry mobs broke into the city's flour warehouse, and a riot by the local stonecutters occurred when the city decided to use prison convicts to cut the marble for a new building in the New York University complex. New York gangs, consisting of young ruffians in their teens and early twenties, constantly roamed the Bowery and the waterfront alleys engaging in numerous stabbings and robberies. And brawls at the scores of local bars had become quite commonplace. Arson was a weekly occurrence in the crime-ridden city, the most notable occurring in December 1835 when hundreds of shops and millions of dollars in merchandise were reduced to ashes.

A high point in the violence occurred on January 30, 1835, when Jackson was nearly assassinated as he emerged onto the East Portico of the Capitol. Jackson's life was spared when both guns of the unemployed painter failed to fire.

One of Jackson's primary initiatives in his second term, therefore, was to delve into the chaotic financial instability that was severely impeding the economic health of the country. Continuing his attack on the U.S. banking system, he now focused on establishing new banking laws that would provide the government with more control over its assets. The deposit banks must not continue to receive federal funds, particularly the millions of dollars in land revenues, without proper government oversight, he declared to Congress in his annual message. There were twenty-two deposit banks in 1834 with holdings of some $9 million in federal deposits. And if the present trend continued to the end of his term, that amount could rise to approximately $30 million by 1836.

Recognizing the power and influence the deposit banks would have over the banking industry with so much government revenue in its grasp, and to head off any potential calamity as a result, he strongly urged Congress to enact laws that enabled the government to increase its regulation over the daily transactions of these federal funds. To supplement the banking policies already established by former Treasury Secretary Taney and continued by his successor, Levi Woodbury, the government must assume stricter oversight authority, he insisted, just as the Bank of the United States had earlier. These initiatives, as expected, exposed Jackson to much criticism from his critics who charged he was now attempting to practice exactly what he fought against with Biddle.

In addition to the need for controls on government deposits, the administration also wanted to eliminate paper bank notes from circulation. To replace the bank notes, Democratic leaders considered the present crisis an excellent opportunity to compel the banks to transact their business with gold and silver or hard money. The use of hard-money, they opined, would further restrain economic growth and provide the country with a more stable currency.

The previous congressional session had taken no action on the administration's banking reform bill; therefore, in February 1835, Tennessee congressman James K. Polk introduced it once again. As presented, the measure simply prohibited U.S. banks holding federal deposits from accepting $5 paper notes from other banks. The administration was fairly confident that with this restriction, the exchange of gold and silver coin would ultimately drive higher value paper notes out of circulation as well. A second element of the bill required the deposit banks to maintain a hard-money reserve equal to one-quarter of their paper notes in circulation.

The Democratic majority in Congress, however, was unable to reach an agreement on this proposal. They were hopelessly split between the hard-money people who wanted stability, more regulation and fewer banks, and the paper-money advocates who argued for stability and regulation as well but persisted in their demands for more deposit banks. Consequently, in March, Congress adjourned with no action taken on the banking bill for a second time.

It wasn't until the new Twenty-fourth Congress gaveled into session in December 1835 that urgent calls were made for a compromise bill to resolve the issues in the administration's banking proposal, specifically those between the hard and paper-money advocates. Finally heeding the need for stronger banking regulations, the Deposit-Distribution Act was introduced by a Senate select committee that improved the regulation of federal deposits and restricted the use of small bank notes of $5 or less. A significant element of the compromise directed that no deposit bank would continue to hold government funds if that bank suspended specie payments. Included in the bill, as well, were provisions for increasing the number of deposit banks holding government funds to over eighty, and a requirement to distribute any surplus funds in excess of $5 million from the deposit banks to the state treasuries. The surplus funds would be distributed to the states in four installments three months apart beginning in January 1837 and would be based on the population of the respective state. In lieu of distributing the money outright to the states for internal improvements, an infringement on their states' rights, the compromise bill identified the installments as loans to be used by the states as they wished.

The compromise wound its way through both Houses and was on Jackson's desk in June 1836. Although Jackson received the banking regulations he wanted, as well as the limits on small bank notes, he wasn't overly enthusiastic about accepting the bill as it was written because of the distribution provision and the increase in the quantity of banks. But not wanting to relive the many fights he endured in the past over the Bank, he half-heartedly acquiesced to the language of the bill and since his treasury secretary would select the new banks, many of those with Democratic connections, he was somewhat appeased. In this light Jackson reluctantly signed the bill.

Satisfied with the provisions of the new banking bill, the Jackson administration now turned its attention to curbing the frenzy in public lands speculation.

As mentioned previously, adding fuel to the raging economy was the enormous explosion in public land sales. The financial climate that instigated these land sales was initiated by a heavy influx of foreign investments attracted by the improving economy. This flood of available capital inflated bank reserves and created an enormous market for speculative loans. Most of these loans were given to people from all walks of life hoping to buy land on credit and then resell it at a profit to the hordes of settlers moving west. The receipts from the groundswell of land speculation overburdened the Treasury by contributing half of the nearly $50 million in surplus funds, money that only taxed the administration's efforts to slow the economy. Therefore, a month after the Deposit-Distribution Act was signed into law, Secretary Woodbury, at the behest of the president, issued a treasury order that instituted a new fiscal program designed to hinder the availability of loans to profit-seeking opportunists. Known as the Specie Circular, the order prohibited all government land-office personnel from finalizing public land sales unless the purchases were made in gold or silver. The administration's restrictive change to a hard-money policy not only accomplished its intended goal of decreasing land sales but in the process also aggravated the crisis by causing a corresponding reduction in the treasury surplus, money mandated by the Deposit-Distribution Act for distribution to the states.

At the time it was customary for the House to receive petitions from their constituents seeking action on any number of public issues. Ordinarily they would be accepted for debate but whenever petitions on slavery were received the southern members simply refused to acknowledge their existence. They were concerned that bringing them to the floor for debate would only encourage a flood of such petitions on an issue they were not inclined to discuss in that forum. This rationale was more or less the norm since slavery was considered by many Washington politicians to be a state issue rather than a federal one. Therefore, occasionally, when the divisive issue of slavery was brought to the floor for debate in either chamber, the matter was usually tabled. Congress had no jurisdiction over slavery in the states, lawmakers declared. It was a states' rights issue beyond the reach of federal law. And furthermore, in their view, state governments addressed more matters that influenced people's everyday lives than did Congress.

The District of Columbia, however, was one exception the southerners could not dispute. Washington, D.C., did not meet the strict definition of a state and it was a place where slave auctions were a thriving and abhorrent business, an enterprise that consistently motivated a flood of petitions for Congress to shut down.

The issue came to a head in December 1835 when James Hammond, a young congressman from South Carolina, filed a motion for the House to refuse accepting any petitions dealing with slavery. At this point former president John Quincy Adams, a staunch advocate against slavery, saw his opportunity to introduce some three hundred petitions during the first week of the New Year in a defiant challenge to Hammond's motion. These appeals from constituents in Massachusetts sought to abolish slavery and the slave trade in Washington.

To address Hammond's motion on the receipt of these slavery petitions, a House select committee was formed and chaired by South Carolina congressman Henry L. Pinckney. Basically, one side of the issue argued that although the guarantee of the right of petition was being upheld, it was not a legitimate one if the petition was not being addressed. The opposing view pointed out that if slavery petitions were addressed on the House floor where would it lead? "Here the subject of abolition would be agitated session after session," they argued, "and from hence the assaults on the property and institutions of the people of the slaveholding States would be disseminated ... over the whole Union."

In May 1836, the committee published its report which stated that all petitions on the issue of slavery "shall, without being either printed or referred, be laid upon the table, and that no further action whatever shall be had thereon." The final report of the committee, know as the Gag Rule, was approved 117 to 68 with nearly 80 percent of northern Democrats voting yea, a reflection of the administration's strong opposition to abolitionism.

The Gag Rule immediately ignited a firestorm of controversy in the House over its constitutionality, specifically its infringement on the First Amendment right to free speech and the right to petition elected representatives. In a demonstration of protest, the American Anti-Slavery Society defiantly flooded the House with nearly a half million petitions in the first two years after the Gag Rule was in force. Classified as a House procedural rule, however, it was nevertheless adopted annually until 1844.

While the administration and the Twenty-fourth Congress wrestled with stabilizing the economy, establishing new banking policies, and the Gag Rule, in Texas a different and equally significant battle was also playing itself out at the same time.

After Mexico obtained its final independence from Spain in 1821, chaos there was hardly anything new during these tumultuous years. Even when

President Jackson attempted to purchase land there in 1829, land that encompassed the state of Coahuila-Texas, government unrest was nearly a way of life. Since that time President Vicente Guerrero had been overthrown by Anastasio Bustamante who in turn was overthrown by the hero of Mexico's fight for independence, General Antonio López de Santa Anna. In one of his first acts as president, Santa Anna replaced the Mexican Constitution and abolished all legislatures in the existing states of Mexico, replacing them with military governors. To the Americans living in Coahuila-Texas (referred to as Texans), this development was especially bad news. Guerrero had previously outlawed slavery in Mexico in 1829 but never enforced the emancipation edict in Coahuila-Texas. Now, Santa Anna was not only going to enforce that law but was also planning to drive out the Texans as well.

The outraged Texans decided to take matters into their own hands. It was a clear message to President Santa Anna that they were willing to fight to the last man for the freedom of their community. To increase the strength of their rebel forces, the Texans offered parcels of land to all those willing to join in their cause. Soon, hundreds of volunteers poured into Texas, arriving mostly from the bordering states of the South. As the movement gained in strength and resources, in December of 1835, some 400 Texans went on to capture the Mexican military headquarters in San Antonio after forcing the evacuation of the Mexican troops garrisoned there.

So angered was Santa Anna over the attack on San Antonio that he organized an army of some six thousand men and marched northward to crush the revolt and the Texans once and for all. While Santa Anna's forces made their way across the Rio Grande, the Texans thought it prudent under the circumstances to withdraw from San Antonio. But not everyone agreed to evacuate. Instead, 155 of the Texans, along with 32 reinforcements, moved into an old Franciscan mission called the Alamo to make their stand not only to defend the city but to also defend their honor.

Following a twelve day siege, Santa Anna's army struck on March 6, 1836. The assault took only three hours. When it was over all but a few of the Americans were killed and the few that survived were immediately executed. The bodies of all 187 men were then stacked and burned. Two weeks later, at Goliad, another group of Texans surrendered to Santa Anna after he agreed to treat them as prisoners of war. Following their surrender, however, Santa Anna had a change of heart and ordered the 350 Texans shot.

Meanwhile, on March 2, a six-member delegation called the convention of 1836 met in Washington-on-the-Brazos and proclaimed Texas's independence from Mexico. Following this historic proclamation, Sam Houston, the ex-governor of Tennessee and one of the members of the convention, was chosen to command the ragtag but dedicated Texas army.

Finally, on April 21, 1836, as morale began to wane, Houston and his 800 mounted Texans surprised Santa Anna's army of about 1,500 troops near the

San Jacinto River, close to present-day Houston. With newfound energy, the Texans immediately charged into the camp of the sleeping soldiers. Shouting "Remember the Alamo," they overran the camp, defeated the Mexican forces and captured Santa Anna the following day. After spending two months in chains Santa Anna was persuaded to sign the so-called Treaty of Velasco which officially granted Texas her independence and Santa Anna his freedom.

Within months, overtures were made for the possible annexation of Texas into the Union as a slave state. As this movement gathered momentum the opponents of slavery expansion reacted in sheer horror once again at the thought of slavery being extended into the West, just as they had done in 1818 when Missouri applied for statehood and again in 1829 when Jackson was attempting to purchase Coahuila-Texas.

By this time, however, northern opposition to slavery and the spread of forced servitude into the territories had become so intense and so controversial a sectional issue that by the end of the congressional session further debate on annexation for Texas was postponed indefinitely. Instead, to avoid provoking a war with Mexico as well as an unwanted congressional debate over Texas's annexation, and with it the unwanted repercussions over slavery and its extension into the West, Congress thought it prudent to simply do what it does best—compromise.

In the final days of the Jackson administration, therefore, both houses approved resolutions that merely recognized the Republic of Texas, and on March 3, 1837, his last day in office, Jackson appointed the U.S. chargé d'affaires, one of his final acts as president.

In the meantime, the state of Arkansas was admitted to the Union as a slave state in June 1836, and to maintain Senate parity, the free state of Michigan was also granted statehood seven months later. The United States now consisted of twenty-six states evenly divided between free and slave.

While Congress grappled with the issues facing the country and the Texans fought for their freedom from Mexican rule, another struggle was also taking place as the campaign season for the 1836 presidential election rapidly approached.

By that time, the political opponents of Jackson's flagrant usurpation of congressional and judicial authority during the Bank war and nullification crisis had redefined their political loyalties by coalescing into a new political fraternity they called the Whig Party. It was a name the Founding Fathers had borrowed from the Brits during the Revolution to symbolize their own fight against King George III for independence, a goal the embittered Jackson enemies believed they were fighting for against "King Andrew." The Whigs were a political entity that Clay, its principal leader, described as one acting "to rescue the Government and public liberty, from the impending dangers, which Jacksonism has created."

The remaining members of the National Republicans made up the bulk of the Whig Party along with most of the Anti-Masons, the exception being those Anti-Masons residing in Pennsylvania and a number of New England states which chose to remain loyal to their own organization. Disgruntled northern Democrats joined the ranks of the Whigs as well to protest the president's transfer of the Bank deposits and other unlawful monetary policies, as did a contingent of reformers within the abolitionist movement, upset over the Jacksonians stated aversion to their cause. Also signing on were a group of embittered southern Democrats fed up with Jackson's aggressive behavior during the nullification crisis. For that reason, even John C. Calhoun lent his support along with scores of southern nullifiers, at least for the short term. Calhoun and his followers would eventually rejoin the Democratic Party in 1837. The perception of this new alignment, at least to the insiders of the Washington political scene, was that the Whigs were merely a coalition of anti–Jackson malcontents. Or as the future publisher of the *New York Tribune*, Horace Greeley, remarked, the Whigs were but "undisciplined opponents of a great party."

The principal issues the Whigs were counting on to gain some traction in the upcoming presidential election were Jackson's monetary policies. But it became quite evident to party leaders following the disappointing results of the 1835 state elections that the Whigs had to seriously reconsider their political strategy. The results clearly demonstrated that resentment against the Democrats and their handling of the economy had declined and also confirmed that the party had to campaign on the newer issues that concerned the voters the most instead of relying solely on their anti–Jackson rhetoric. "The Whigs as a party are without plan, purpose or principle," a saddened Whig wrote. "Their unskillfulness and imbecility deters the young and ambitious from joining them."

Instead of organizing a national convention, as the Democrats would do in May 1835 to nominate Van Buren, the Whigs relied on the old-style state legislative caucuses to submit the name of a presidential nominee. Under their anti-party ideology, the Whigs felt political conventions transferred the choice of the nation's leaders from the people to the politicians and under that arrangement a politician's free will would always be undermined by his subservience to party discipline. But here was the rub. Because the Whigs were a coalition of National Republicans, abolitionists, former northern and southern Democrats, Anti-Masons, and southern nullifiers, they were unable to agree on any single candidate that satisfied their own particular agendas. As a result, when the dust finally settled, three candidates emerged from this seemingly chaotic process which only further weakened their run for the presidency.

There was also the perception at the time of a so-called Whig strategy, a scheme that developed because the Whigs knew they could not succeed against Van Buren with a single candidate. Therefore, the Whigs were said to have intentionally selected multiple candidates to ensure that no nominee would receive the required number of electoral votes. The election would then be decided in the House of Representatives where they felt they had more of a fighting chance to win the election.

Be that as it may, in January 1835, Massachusetts Whigs nominated Daniel Webster as the northern candidate. Despite his political experience and oratory skills, however, he was still unable to gain a significant degree of support from the party outside of his home state. Evidently, his close association with Biddle and the Bank were considered by party leaders as a liability and would become much too controversial during the campaign.

A second nominee was agreed upon in December by the northern Anti-Masons meeting in Pennsylvania. A Virginian reared in the Midwest, he was a relatively new face on the Washington scene named William H. Harrison. His only claim to anything approaching notoriety occurred at Tippecanoe, Indiana, in 1811 when as a general in the regular army he put down a Shawnee uprising, and for a time saw duty in Canada during the War of 1812. Although he later represented Ohio in the House and Senate, supported Clay's American System and the Bank, many of his critics thought his résumé lacked the high level of political expertise to be successful in an election against a well-seasoned politician like Van Buren. Harrison's backers, however, such as the editors of a Cincinnati newspaper, vigorously stressed that his attributes as an Indian fighter and war hero would make him a very attractive candidate to the voters, a strategy, they reminded their readers, that proved quite successful for the Democrats in 1829.

The southern Whigs also had a candidate in mind that on the surface appeared rather out of step with the rest of the party. He was Senator Hugh L. White. What made White somewhat different from the rest of the pack was that he was a staunch Jacksonian Democrat. Although a fellow Tennessean, a close friend of the president, and a loyal supporter of Jackson's Force Bill and anti–Bank ideology, there was one caveat. The same level of dedication that he afforded to Jackson was now shifted to his opposition to Van Buren and his run for the White House. It was for that reason he agreed to run as a Whig. But also, and perhaps more importantly, he was a southern slaveholder that vowed to defend the peculiar institution against the invasion of northern propaganda.

In the present climate many southern Whigs were fearful that a northern president, particularly Van Buren, who was instrumental in gaining approval for the Tariff of Abominations, would not be receptive to their fight against northern anti-slavery forces. "I think our interests imperatively require a Slave holding President," said one Louisiana senator. "Vote for a Northern President from a free state," cried out the headlines of a Virginia newspaper, "and when the test comes, he will support the abolitionists." It was an unfair portrayal of Van Buren, however, and one that finally injected the issue of slavery into a presidential campaign.

Democrats across the country were enraged over this insult to Van Buren and lashed back, declaring the southern branch of the Whig Party was making every "effort to excite Southern prejudice," and that "the effort to make a southern sectional party out of the abolition question has been most eagerly pressed by the enemies of the administration." To maintain his southern supporters, therefore, Van Buren had to remind the Whigs that he was also once a slaveholder, that he was against abolitionism, and to reiterate his position that slavery should never be abolished in the capital city.

Also stung by this harsh criticism against the office of the president, the administration would soon enter into the abolitionist controversy as well.

In reality, the administration feared the continued abolitionist movement could provoke the South into seceding from the Union. There was also much concern that supporting the movement would only alienate the southern wing of the party, a faction the Democrats needed to preserve. But most of all, as the 1836 presidential campaigns began to take on steam, the Democrats wanted to dispel the notion that they were an uncaring party and to demonstrate the party was indeed a friend of the South despite the inflammatory campaign rhetoric to the contrary. To help provide this impression the administration, in a self-serving gesture, assured the South that an order of the postmaster general would be issued prohibiting the delivery of all abolitionist-inspired material to the South.

As the presidential campaigns rolled into action, the Whigs continued to run primarily on an anti–Jacksonian theme. It was one that consistently conveyed the dangers of an executive tyranny that threatened the autonomy and power of Congress. They also embraced the American System, chartering of more banks, circulation of paper bank notes, and more federal subsidies for internal improvements. As for Van Buren, besides the charge that he was Jackson's hand-picked successor, the Whigs also insisted Van Buren was a mere puppet who had accomplished very little on his own. He was entirely dependent on Jackson, they said, and the president was now striving to continue his dictatorial policies of the past eight years through Van Buren. Viewed as effeminate by many Whigs, Van Buren was frequently the butt of political caricatures because of his partiality for tightly laced corsets, gaudy jewelry, and dainty slippers.

The Democratic Party, on the other hand, seeking to avoid debate on such controversial issues as the economy, slavery, abolitionism, and the Texas petition for annexation, presented no endorsed party platform for Van Buren and his running mate, Richard M. Johnson, to run on. Instead, not willing to trade personal attacks with the opposition, their strategy was to simply ignore the criticism and the issues and to present their position in a published party statement. In their message the Democrats stressed the important role of and their commitment to party politics as one that ensured loyalties, attracted the best and most gifted men, and prevented "attempts at the usurpation of power, and thereby preserve the rights of the People."

Although this strategy may have played a small role in the Democratic victory, it was the inability of the Whigs to unite behind one solid candidate that became a major factor in their defeat. When the election returns were finally tabulated in November, Van Buren won eight northern states and seven slave states for 170 electoral votes. In fact, the Democrats captured 65 percent of their electoral votes from the top four vote-rich states of New York, Pennsylvania, Virginia, and North Carolina. The Whigs won five northern states and only six of the thirteen slave states. Of the Whig candidates, Harrison won seven states for 73 votes, White gained 26 votes from two states, his home state of Tennessee and from Georgia, and fourteen votes went to Webster from his local constituency in Massachusetts. The maverick legislature in South Carolina refused to vote for White because he had supported Jackson's Force Bill. Instead, they cast their entire eleven electoral votes for a Whig senator from North Carolina, Willie P. Mangum. The Democrats also won the edge in both houses of the upcoming Twenty-fifth Congress. There were 33 Democrats in the Senate and only 19 Whigs, and in the House of Representatives, 125 Democrats had seats compared to 116 Whigs. This election was also a significant milestone in U.S. political history because it marked the beginning of the second two-party system. For the first time in over forty years two distinct parties would emerge, each with substantially different positions on the issues. In Illinois, meanwhile, a young and promising Whig named Abraham Lincoln was elected to a term in the state legislature.

With this loss the Whigs found themselves back to square one. This time, however, without Jackson in power to rally against, they had to find new issues to keep their coalition intact. The problem, the Whigs were shocked to discover, was that most of the country seemed receptive to Van Buren's vow to continue Jackson's policies.

To explain his position on slavery and to put it to rest once and for all, in his inauguration address Van Buren reminded everyone how as a "happy and flourishing people we stand without a parallel in the world" and that "we present an aggregate of human prosperity surely not elsewhere to be found." But of all the dangers lurking, he said, "perhaps the greatest ... was the institution of domestic slavery." Continuing with his speech before the throng gathered at the Capitol, he also reminded his listeners that "Our forefathers were deeply impressed with the delicacy of this subject, and they treated it with a forbearance ... that it never until the present period disturbed the tranquility of our common country." Trying to stifle the growing anxiety over slavery he went on to implore the people to take heed of that forbearance which had proved "to be humane, patriotic, expedient, honorable, and just." Van Buren declared as president he would be an "inflexible and uncompromising opponent of every attempt on the part of Congress to abolish slavery in the District of Columbia against the wishes of the slaveholding States, and also with a determination equally resolute to resist the slightest interference with it in the States where it exists."

As the new Democratic administration took over the reins of power, the acrimonious issue of Texas statehood still reverberated within the halls of Congress. The daunting issue of slavery and the northern efforts to contain it within its borders also began to creep into the political arena for the first time. But with the new Congress and the new president continuing to struggle over the economy, sectional conflicts would continue to be either avoided or diluted for another four years as the country grappled with the ever present and more pressing fiscal problems.

7

The Panic and Sub-Treasuries (1837 to 1840)

In May of 1837, with Van Buren now residing on Pennsylvania Avenue, news arrived at the White House that deposit banks in New York City were suspending their specie payments in direct violation of the new federal banking laws. From New York to New Orleans, like the proverbial falling dominoes, other deposit banks followed suit and soon numerous banks, unable to collect payment on their loans, were forced to close their doors. Without financial backing, businesses closed, unemployment began to rise anew, and stocks and property fell to a fraction of their true value. "The immense fortunes which we heard so much about in the days of speculation have melted away like the snows before an April sun," remarked one observer. And the New York diarist George Templeton Strong observed, "So they go—smash, crash.... Near two hundred and fifty failures thus far."

It was called the Panic of 1837.

The Whigs, of course, including Clay, Calhoun, and Webster, blamed Jackson and Van Buren for initiating the crisis. Jackson's anti-banking policies, they claimed, particularly the destruction of the Bank of the United States and the transfer of funds to the so-called deposit banks, had destroyed the restraining mechanisms that were already in place. Also, the Whigs gleefully noted, the administration's pursuit of a hard-money standard via the Specie Circular had undermined confidence in paper notes and was instrumental in moving large quantities of gold and silver coin from the east to the western banks where the land sales were financed. It was a move, they claimed, that only exacerbated the shortage of specie even more and ultimately forced the eastern banks to implement steps to safeguard their own reserves. When questioned about the nation's grim financial condition and what could be done about it, Calhoun remarked bitterly, "It is too late. You cannot prevent the catastrophe.... The times are as unsound as the currency, and the excitement of party are little calculated to qualify us for the emergency."

Van Buren, however, would shrug off all these claims. The fault belonged with the bankers, the president responded. It was the banks not the government, he emphasized, that encouraged the excessive use of unstable paper notes and it was they who instigated the policies of loose credit which in turn created a frenzy of over-speculation. Also contributing to the crisis, Van Buren continued, was the extravagant lifestyle of many Americans, or as he described it, "the rapid growth among all classes, and especially in our great commercial towns, of luxurious habits founded too often on merely fancied wealth, detrimental alike to the industry, the resources, and the morals of the people." In turn, he opined, this fancied lifestyle was a factor that contributed to the heavy debt owed to English merchants and English banks.

Most Whigs, however, presumed the Specie Circular was the real culprit behind the country's economic problems and numerous appeals were made to Van Buren to rescind the treasury order, a move he was sorely tempted to carry out. But after listening to the views of his Cabinet and his close advisors, who were hopelessly divided, and even his predecessor, who thought his hard-money edict was still "popular with the people," Van Buren, after much uncertainty and a hesitancy to lose favor with Jackson, decided to preserve the Specie Circular as it was. A few well-meaning politicians within the party even asked Van Buren to consider re-chartering the Bank of the United States, a suggestion he rejected out of hand by adhering to the Jacksonian philosophy that the Bank "was a concentration of power dangerous to [voters'] liberties."

While the claims of both parties contained some elements of truth, there were other factors as well that triggered the Panic of 1837, factors derived from foreign sources that proved to be even more significant in bringing about the financial downturn.

Beginning in the latter half of 1836, the Bank of England feared it could suffer a loss of its specie reserves if proper precautionary steps were not taken immediately. In a strictly defensive maneuver, therefore, the bank increased its interest rates and eliminated the availability of credit to English merchants who were operating in the American import-export business. Strapped with these new financial burdens, the English merchants were forced not only to cut off credit to their U.S. counterparts but also to demand immediate payment in specie for all outstanding accounts. As a result, eastern banks began to experience a heavy demand for specie from their local merchants to ship to England. At the same time, to support land offices doing business under the provisions of the Specie Circular, much of their hard-money had also gone to the western banks as well. In a protectionist move similar to that taken by the Bank of England, the deposit banks in New York City suspended specie payments also in order to preclude the loss of their own reserves.

Furthermore, without the availability of credit, English merchants were unable to pay for future shipments of cotton. With British demands for cotton reduced and imports drastically curtailed, government revenue from import duties plummeted. When this loss was added to the lost income already being experienced from reduced land sales, the Treasury Department predicted it could soon be operating from a deficit instead of a surplus. And with surplus funds rapidly dwindling, the Treasury would be hard pressed to make the fourth and final installment due to the states under the Deposit-Distribution Act.

Faced with a seemingly Herculean problem to resolve, Van Buren knew that with the nation's economic health in a tailspin and its citizens suffering immensely, he had to respond to this latest crisis very quickly. Particularly disconcerting was that no matter what decision he made he could worsen the ideological division within the Democratic Party, where the radical anti-banking wing advocated a hard-money policy while the conservative pro-banking Democrats supported a paper-money scenario. Compounding these problems, Treasury Secretary Levi Woodbury also pointed out that one provision of the Deposit-Distribution Act of 1836 had specifically mandated that no deposit bank could hold government funds if it withheld specie payments. And according to Woodbury nearly all of the deposit banks had done just that. Therefore, to enforce the Specie Circular's prohibition against such suspensions, Van Buren now wrestled with how to withdraw federal deposits from the government accounts without making matters worse, and also what to do with these funds and any new incoming revenues.

Finally, after much soul searching, in the summer of 1837, Van Buren chose to side with the hard-money faction of the party. By continuing to maintain the anti-banking and anti-paper position of his predecessor, Van Buren knew full well his actions threatened to drive the conservative wing into the waiting arms of the Whigs. To communicate his proposals and to get a jump start on confronting these economic problems he called for a special session of Congress to meet in September.

Van Buren's efforts to revive the economy were briefly interrupted in August by a visit from Memucan Hunt, a representative from the Republic of Texas. In Washington to lobby for Texas statehood, Hunt surmised that the economic woes of the United States would in all likelihood encourage Van Buren to consider Texas annexation as a means to capture the South for the next presidential election. The Texan even assumed he had the backing of three southerners in the Cabinet to help him persuade the president. Bursting with confidence, Hunt wrote a letter to Secretary of State John Forsyth asking for immediate statehood or else he would negotiate commercial treaties with other foreign countries to the further detriment of the United States economy. Annoyed by Hunt's threat and his blatant arrogance, the administration dismissed the application on the grounds that "while Texas was at war with Mexico the United States could not agree to annexation because it would involve the country in the war." Besides, Van Buren was also aware of the growing anti-annexation movement in the North to prevent the spread of slavery and wanted to maintain a relative peace and unity within the party.

By the time the Twenty-fifth Congress met in special session it was quite clear that the actions by Great Britain were the catalyst for the Panic of 1837, or in Van Buren's words, "the measures adopted by the foreign creditors ... to reduce their debts and to withdraw from the United States a large portion of our specie." To avoid an immediate and potentially catastrophic shortfall in the surplus, in his message to Congress that September, Van Buren requested a postponement of the government's final installment to the states due in October. He also reminded Congress that both the Bank of the U.S. and the deposit banks had their opportunity to succeed and that both had failed. And now, because these so-called pet banks were in violation of the law, all government deposits must cease immediately and the funds now residing in their vaults placed under direct control of the federal government. To accomplish this, he requested Congress authorize the transfer of these funds into a number of government-owned repositories or sub-treasuries scattered throughout the country to be supervised by assistant treasurers accountable to the secretary of the Treasury. He called this new government policy the Independent Treasury system. In the meantime Secretary Woodbury would deposit all new government monies in the vaults of various federal institutions of his choice.

Reaction to Van Buren's proposal was mixed. While he was praised for his "moral courage" by James Buchanan, and his message applauded by the administration's newspaper, the *Globe,* as "the boldest and highest stand ever taken by a chief magistrate," opposition to the proposal came quickly as well, especially from the deposit banks and Democratic conservatives who claimed the system of sub-treasuries was an attack on the entire system of credit and would ultimately destroy the banks, a scenario, they claimed, much too terrible to contemplate.

In preparation for the debate on Van Buren's sub-treasuries, in the House the Democrats wisely installed James K. Polk as speaker, who in turn made sure a sympathetic Democrat chaired the all-important Ways and Means Committee. The Senate Finance Committee was also appropriately aligned to support Van Buren's five proposals, four of which were promptly approved by both chambers. These four included measures to postpone the last installment to the states; to grant approval for the treasury secretary to withdraw all government funds from the deposit banks; to grant a delay to merchants for payment of custom house bonds; and for the issuance of ten million dollars in Treasury notes to pay for government expenses. The fifth item up for debate, Van Buren's Independent Treasury system, was much more controversial and required much more scrutiny.

As expected, Clay and Webster spoke out forcefully against Van Buren's sub-treasuries, preferring instead to re-charter a new Bank of the United States, and understandably, both delivered impassioned speeches praising the merits of the current state banking system over the one the administration proposed. One of Van Buren's newest supporters, however, was his old archrival from South Carolina who had returned to the Democratic fold along with his fellow nullifiers. Calhoun agreed with the concept of the sub-treasuries but in so doing attached an amendment to the bill that required the Treasury to accept only gold or silver from the state banks after 1840. Senator Benton, for one, was especially pleased with Calhoun's amendment. A dedicated hard-money man, the Missouri senator carried the moniker "Old Bullion" for his past attempts to institute a monetary system of government minted gold and silver coin. Now with Calhoun's proposal on the table, Benton vowed to see his long cherished initiative come to fruition. Finally, after many hours of ingratiating speeches and embellished blustering, in October, the Senate's Independent Treasury Bill, including Calhoun's amendment, was accepted strictly along party lines.

With the Democratic majority in the House somewhat fragile, however, winning approval there would be much more difficult. Holding the balance of power was a block of pro-bank conservatives who opposed the independent treasuries with a vengeance. To improve the bill's chances for passage, therefore, on October 14, two days before the special session ended, a motion was made and approved to postpone debate on the bill until the first regular session began in December.

The objections to Van Buren's economic recovery strategy, particularly the Independent Treasury Bill, became quite obvious following the fall state elections. It seems the issues resulting from the Panic of 1837 gave birth to a revitalized Whig Party. The downward spiral in the economy and the chaotic banking situation provided issues the Whigs were looking for to replace obsolete anti–Jacksonian rhetoric, new issues they could rally around, as well as a new image to politicize its philosophy for economic recovery and a new hope for the nation without anarchy and corruption. On the basis of their new-found political fodder, the election results showed substantial gains for the Whigs in New York, Maine, Massachusetts, and Rhode Island, as well as Ohio, Illinois, and North Carolina where the Whigs were now the majority party. In New York, gala dinners were held where Whig speakers, such as John Bell of Tennessee and Daniel Webster, mesmerized enraptured diners for hours amid endless toasts to the success of their party. "Never before," said an ecstatic reveler at one such affair, "had there been such an assemblage of Whigs. A band of union and good-fellowship has been formed which will extend far and wide, and the delegates will go home ... filled with confident hopes of a return of a national prosperity, and with a determination to restore the government of the Constitution and the laws."

With the exception of the Democratic strongholds of Alabama and Mississippi, the Whigs were gaining more and more strength in the South as well, especially in the loyal Democratic state of Virginia, where voters were show-ing signs of abandoning Van Buren over his sub-treasury system. Concerned that the Independent Treasury Bill and the continuation of the Specie Circu-lar would stifle the economy, deny credit for the country's expansion, and threaten state banks, the voters sent a clear message that Van Buren and his Democratic Party could possibly be fighting an uphill battle not only over his economic programs but also for a future second term. Nevertheless, Van Buren still remained detached from the furor surrounding his proposals. He spoke with unwavering optimism that his economic plans were, in fact, gaining momentum and once approved would serve the country well.

As the end of 1837 approached the dreaded issue of slavery entered the halls of Congress once again. Voter petitions to abolish slavery in the District of Columbia were introduced once more in the House by John Quincy Adams and other northerners over a three-day period. In another effort to stifle addi-tional petitions, a resolution to renew the Gag Rule was introduced in the House by a congressman from Virginia. More specific than the one passed in 1836, it stated, "No petitions relating to slavery or the trade in slaves in any State, District or Territory of the United States shall be read, printed, com-mitted, or in any manner acted upon by the House." There was relatively lit-tle debate on the resolution, except perhaps when Adams declared the Gag Rule unconstitutional. But he set off an even fiercer storm of protest when he introduced a petition from a group of slaves asking for a debate over ending slavery in the District. The southern members were aghast over Adams' inso-lence and disrespect. Imagine, they complained, petitions from slaves being pre-sented to this august body. They were highly insulted and demanded Adams be censured. Ultimately, the Gag Rule was reinstated for another year by an overwhelming vote of 122 to 74. In the Senate that December, similar peti-tions against slavery in the District were also tabled without being debated by a vote of 25 to 20. Interestingly enough, the Senate Democrats were still demonstrating their allegiance to the cause of slavery. Of the 25 approving votes, 23 were from Democrats.

Still intensely opposed to discussing slavery in the Senate, Calhoun main-tained his belief that "if a single step was yield, the fanatical spirit would be reanimated." The encouraging vote for tabling the petitions compelled Cal-houn to go one step further. He wanted to put the Senate on record as sup-porting slavery once and for all and to accomplish this Calhoun introduced a number of resolutions. They included his consistent view that the states alone had jurisdiction over their own domestic institutions, namely slavery. Another was for the Senate to declare that the federal government had an obligation "not to interfere with the stability and security [of these] domestic institu-tions" and that any interference with slavery in the District or in the territo-ries was "a direct and dangerous attack on the institutions of all the slaveholding States." Also, and more significant was for the Senate to declare that any refusal to annex new slave territory (meaning Texas) was unconstitutional and discriminatory toward the South. With a few modifications from Clay and a nod of approval from Van Buren, the Senate dutifully approved Calhoun's resolutions the following month by a wide margin. It was quite telling that the Democratic votes for the majority on both the Gag Rule and for Calhoun's resolutions firmly cemented the administration's endorsement of slavery.

Besides the sub-treasury bill, also on the congressional agenda was the renewal of the preemption bill. Originally signed in May of 1830, the measure granted squatters on public lands the right to purchase 160 acres at the low price of $1.25 per acre before the property was submitted for sale to the general public. Senator Robert J. Walker of Mississippi, in voicing support for the bill, thought it would give "the worthy and enterprising [settler] preference [over the] cold and heartless speculator...." In addition, the bill would ensure that "the honest and hardy cultivator [was not] driven from his property that he had toiled so hard to secure." Designed primarily to appease the West, the bill easily passed the Senate on January 30, 1838, and was approved by the House in June.

The following day Van Buren's Independent Treasury Bill was resubmitted in the Senate by Silas Wright of New York. It was the moment of reckoning for Van Buren, who staked his leadership and his reelection bid on getting this measure through Congress. In arguing for the bill, Wright cited the overriding need for withdrawing the millions of federal dollars from the deposit banks. And to illustrate the urgency of this move, he had only to remind them of the many risky speculative loans handed out under the present system. "The whole splendid public domain, that rich inheritance from our fathers of the Republic," Wright pointed out, had been "exchanged [for] bank rags." In addition to Calhoun's specie amendment to appease the hard-money crowd, a second modification was also included hopefully to win over the conservatives. The bill would retain the deposit banks in the system but only in a limited role for special federal deposits.

Again, hostile reaction to Wright's speech came mostly from the Democratic conservatives who wanted nothing to do with sub-treasuries but instead demanded the system of deposit banks remain as it was. Van Buren's policy was wrong for the country, they said, it would be too expensive, inhibit credit, and increase executive patronage as well. The Whigs also reiterated their long professed objections to the bill as bad for the banks and by extension even worse for the economy. Removing the deposits would reduce their reserves on which loans were based, they argued, and with smaller reserves the amount of cash available would create higher prices during a time when the opposite ought to be the goal. The Great Triumvirate was also at their oratorical best as Calhoun, in defense of supporting Van Buren, eloquently fought off personal attacks by the combined forces of Clay and Webster. Debate continued for several days, sometimes congenial, most times filled with harsh and mean spirited accusations. One such confrontation between two House members, Jonathan Cilley, a Maine Democrat, and James W. Webb, a Whig from Kentucky, ended in a rifle duel. After Cilley was killed further debate was delayed until mid–March.

When the Senate vote was finally taken on March 26, the Independent Treasury Bill was narrowly accepted 27 to 25. Surprisingly, one of the nay votes came from a principal advocate of the bill, John C. Calhoun, who withdrew his support in protest when his specie clause was removed from the measure in the final hours of debate.

In the House a somewhat different version of the Senate's bill was introduced. Unlike the Senate bill, this one included Calhoun's specie clause and quite understandably was the measure the administration favored, as well as Calhoun. Although Van Buren was pleased that his bill squeaked through the Senate, he knew from past experience that with Calhoun's specie amendment still attached to the House version, the bill would have a tougher road to travel.

And if that wasn't enough to concern the administration, elimination of the Specie Circular itself was now being vigorously pursued as well by both Webster and Clay, a combination Van Buren knew would only prolong the fight over his treasury bill. Therefore, growing weary of defending Jackson's pet initiative, Van Buren finally relented and the resolution for repealing the circular was approved by the Senate on May 26 and the House four days later. The Specie Circular, long an irritant to its detractors, was finally history.

When House debate on the sub-treasuries commenced in June, it became fairly apparent to the administration that the conservatives were beginning to waver. In sheer desperation, Van Buren ordered Calhoun's specie clause struck from the bill to encourage their further support. And again, without the specie amendment, Calhoun's supporters switched their allegiance and voted against the bill. Even the administration's support of the preemption bill failed to sway western votes. To no one's surprise, two weeks before Congress was set to adjourn, Van Buren came up short once again when on June 25, 1838, the House voted to reject the independent treasuries. Although the Calhounites voted against the Treasury bill, much of the blame for the bill's demise was attributed to the bloc of Democrats who controlled the balance of power in the House and postponed it the year before.

With the defeat of his Independent Treasury Bill and the repeal of the Specie Circular, Van Buren was disconsolate. Not only had he lost the battle in Congress but the Democratic Party was also being deserted by a growing number of its members from the conservative wing. The realignment of these conservatives, who were particularly strong in Virginia and New York, were expected to play an enormous role in the state and congressional elections and were now giving Van Buren and his supporters anxious moments as they looked towards 1840. In Van Buren's home state of New York, for instance, a key state for any political candidate, the Whigs swept the slate in the fall elections and replaced the Democratic governor with a Whig named William H. Seward. In Virginia, paper-money conservatives weakened the party's strength there by splitting the party's vote when they ran their own candidates against the hard-money Democrats. As a result, the Whigs gained additional seats in the legislature.

In 1838, in spite of the country's difficulties, the financial outlook began to improve following a shipment of specie from England to the deposit banks in New York. And with the repeal of Jackson's Specie Circular back in May, the country appeared to be on the road to recovery. Unfortunately, the upturn in the nation's economic health was brief once again. In October 1839 the British banks renewed their restrictive credit policies which again forced American banks to reinstate their suspension of specie payments. In large cities bread lines returned, numerous soup kitchens flourished, and because many coal mines closed donations of fuel were requested to help the poor get through the winter. In New York, business setbacks reduced traffic on the canals which in turn caused a steep decline in toll revenue. Scores of factories throughout New England and the major cities of the East had little choice but to shut their doors, driving hundreds of workers back into unemployment and further despair. In the South, many planters went bankrupt, their slaves sold off for a fraction of their previous value. Internal improvement projects such as new railroad lines, canals, and roads were halted, forcing additional increases in unemployment and investment losses. As George Templeton Strong described it, the people were "out of kash, out of kredit, out of karacter and out of klothes." This time the road back would be a long and painful experience, one which continued well into the mid–1840's.

In March of 1839 the second regular session of Congress adjourned without any further effort to revive Van Buren's Independent Treasury Bill. With little accomplished to ease the economic crisis, Van Buren and the Democrats looked ahead hoping the last half of his presidential term would prove more fruitful than the first. "The past year [had] not been one of unalloyed prosperity" Van Buren mused. "Serious embarrassments yet derange the trade of many of our cities."

The Twenty-sixth Congress convened on December 2, 1839, a session that would last until the following July. The makeup of the Congress had not changed to any great degree with two significant exceptions. The balance of power in the House was no longer vested in the Democratic conservatives since all but four had moved on to join the ranks of the Whig Party and speaker James K. Polk resigned to make a run for governor in Tennessee. In the Senate, the Democrats still held on to a commanding majority.

On January 6, 1840, Silas Wright brought the Independent Treasury Bill to the floor of the Senate for a third time. This latest version identified specific repositories and vaults for deposit of government funds, including the United States Mint and the branch mint at New Orleans, in addition to the identities of the four receivers general, at New York, Boston, Charleston, and St. Louis. The bill also contained provisions for additional government regulation of state banks, and to gain support of the Calhounites, a specie clause was also included. This clause required all payments to or by the government to be exclusively in gold or silver after June 30, 1843, a move that prompted Calhoun's pledge to assure the bill's passage. The combination of greater regulation and hard money evidently satisfied the other members of the Senate as well, who approved the bill on January 23 by a vote of 24 to 18.

In the House the bill was introduced on March 11, and almost immediately became stalled in the Ways and Means Committee. After many delays, parliamentary actions and speeches, Van Buren's bill was finally voted on in late June passing 124 to 107. In the final tally, only the four Democratic conservatives voted against it. Van Buren had succeeded at last. Government funds which had resided in the Bank, then been transferred to the deposit banks, were now going to sub-treasuries. He was ecstatic over the passage of the Treasury bill as was Senator Benton, who called it "the distinguishing glory of the Twenty-sixth Congress, and the 'crowning mercy' of Mr. Van Buren's administration." Van Buren signed the bill on the Fourth of July 1840 so that the people could celebrate two grand moments in American history on the same day.

To the chagrin of the Whig opponents, the sub-treasury system proved to have no damaging effects on the state banks or upon the business world at large. In addition, it failed to increase political patronage or presidential power over commercial interests as many had feared. But it wouldn't be long before the Whigs struck back.

8

John Tyler and Texas Too (1840 to 1845)

Assembling in Baltimore, the Democratic Party held its presidential convention on May 5 and 6, 1840, and to no one's surprise, Van Buren was nominated for a second term. Still shackled with an economic depression, however, and opposed by a united Whig Party, the Democrats were in a quandary and knew the race would be extremely difficult to win. Even the possible loss of the big prize, Van Buren's home base of New York with forty-two electoral votes, was growing more likely and only added to their insecurity.

Another problem confronting the Democrats was the new Liberty Party, a collection of political abolitionists using the electorate forum as a means to further their abolitionist cause. As you recall, the Liberty Party was an offspring of the northern abolitionist movement which had been growing more divisive since the early thirties. At that time William Lloyd Garrison introduced his radical anti-slave journal, the *Liberator,* and founded the American Anti-Slave Society. But in 1839 a more conservative faction split away from Garrison and it was this group that ultimately formed the Liberty Party, a federation threatening to steal northern votes away from the Democrats. It certainly was no secret that Van Buren opposed the abolitionist movement. He made this quite clear in his campaign of 1836 and by his support of Calhoun's resolutions in 1838. Consequently, although abolition was a very sensitive issue to the party and one they didn't want to confront during the campaign, the combination of the abolitionist movement, threats of expanding slavery into the western territories, and the possibility of Texas becoming a new slave state had placed the issue of slavery squarely on the minds of thousands of voters.

Yet, looking ahead to the upcoming struggle, the party was somewhat consoled knowing its political base was still primarily the working people, the immigrants, Irish Catholics, Dutch and German farmers, and all those who detested the patronizing superiority of those people the Democratic workers compartmentalized as Whigs. And it was, after all, the Whigs that legislated temperance laws, a political move they adamantly refused to support.

The Whigs had gathered in Harrisburg that previous December for their very first national convention. It was an enormous and raucous affair, as one could expect with an attendance of some 3,000 delegates. Contending for the nomination was Gen. Winfield Scott, who was making his first bid for the presidency. A veteran of the War of 1812 and the commander of U.S. forces in the nullification crisis of 1833, Scott was always attired in full military regalia. The 6-foot 5-inch general was an impressive sight and his military presence was undeniable. Also in the running was William H. Harrison, one of the three Whig candidates in the election four years earlier. Henry Clay, the Whig congressional leader and the perennial front-runner, was also in the pack. The Kentucky senator was eager to make another run for the executive mansion and was quite optimistic about his chances.

But these were different times and Clay was one of its victims. As a member of a political party that saw northern Whigs espousing radical views against slavery, Clay's standing as a southern slaveholder endorsing the institution played a large role in his losing the Whig endorsement. When the final gavel was struck at this seemingly chaotic event, Harrison was chosen as the Whig candidate for president and John Tyler as his running mate.

Occasionally, at conventions of this sort, the nominee selected isn't always the best, but is instead the least controversial. And Harrison was all that—a political nonentity. But more importantly he was a military hero and for obvious political reasons just the kind of person Whig leaders favored for their candidate. However, on the downside, despite the notoriety gained as the Hero of Tippecanoe, Harrison wasn't able to stir up the same patriotic emotions as Old Hickory was able to do. On the other hand, he had no enemies, no significant standing, and no real position on the issues. In short, he wouldn't offend any of the voters within the various factions that constituted the Whig Party, and that was just fine with the party leaders. Besides, among the three Whigs that ran in the last election, Harrison was the biggest vote getter and he still had his personal charisma, a trait the Whigs were sure to exploit. With the party now united behind one candidate, the Whigs were more than confident in the outcome.

On the Whig campaign trail there were improvised log cabins and barrels of hard cider everywhere, symbolic of Harrison's frontier roots. In cities from Boston and New York to Dayton, throngs of enthusiastic crowds gathered chanting the Whig slogan "Tippecanoe and Tyler too" and colorful banners proclaimed "Every breeze says change! The cry, the universal cry is for a change" and "With Tip and Tyler/ We'll burst Van's biler." It was a campaign of theatrics, a campaign that entertained with torchlight parades and makeshift floats. There were well-organized mass rallies with the usual off-pitch bands, songs and merriment, bonfires, barbeques, and endless speeches on Harrison's behalf while avoiding as much as possible the hot-button issues that were dividing the country.

Instead, the Whig strategy was to concentrate mostly on delivering the party message for improving the economy. They would promote economic development and stability through programs that expanded instead of stifled credit, as sub-treasuries were purported to do, through greater economic diversification and subsidies to the states.

And as the nation's economic difficulties worsened in 1840, the Whigs grew more and more confident that their message was being heard. This self-assurance was motivated to a great extent by the encouraging state election returns from across the country, particularly in the key states of New York, Pennsylvania, North Carolina, and Ohio. The Whig message was especially appealing to the majority of rich southern planters, the aristocracy, as well as northern entrepreneurs, professionals, merchants and manufacturers. The Whigs' strategy had accomplished its intended goal.

As the Whig Party predicted, its win was overwhelming. Of the 26 states in the Union, Harrison captured 19 of them for 234 electoral votes, an unqualified thrashing of Van Buren's collection of only 60 votes. To make the victory even sweeter, the Whigs also controlled both houses of Congress. They held a 30 to 22 majority in the Senate and a decided edge in the House by winning a total of 133 seats to 102, a clear signal that the party would marshal all of its forces to accomplish its primary objective for energizing its economic program—a new Bank of the United States. What was particularly encouraging to the Whigs was that of the fifteen states that voted Democratic in the 1836 election, nine of them switched to the Whig column in 1840. Even Van Buren's beloved state of New York had abandoned its favorite son and the Democratic Party. With the Liberty Party gaining only one-half of 1 percent of the popular vote, Democratic concerns over the damage they would do to Van Buren in the North never quite materialized. Instead, it was most likely Van Buren's handling of the economy and his pandering to southern slaveholders that had alienated most of the northern voters.

In Washington the weather for Inauguration Day was not fit for man or beast. Despite the extremely cold temperature, Harrison stepped to the podium and delivered the longest inauguration speech of any president—one hour and forty minutes. The new president, however, the first Whig to reach the White House, never got his chance to implement the party's economic recovery programs. One month to the day after his inauguration the sixty-eight-year-old died of pneumonia, a condition supposedly caused by the prolonged exposure to the frigid temperatures on that fateful day in March.

John Tyler, Harrison's fifty-one-year-old vice president, was sworn in two days later, on April 6, 1841. This change in command marked the first time in the nation's history that a vice president would ascend to the presidency after the death of the incumbent.

Tyler's difficulties began almost immediately. At first he was considered by his detractors as an acting president and was dubbed "His Accidency," a moniker arising over the question of his legitimacy for occupying the office without being elected. This assertion was put to rest after Congress affirmed that he indeed had the full powers and privileges of the office. But aside from that, Tyler carried some unwanted baggage into office that concerned the leaders of the Whig Party immensely.

Since his earlier days in the House of Representatives (1817–21) and in the Senate (1827–36) the Virginian's political ideology was fiercely independent, a character trait that called his party loyalty into question. As a maverick Democrat at the time, Tyler was a strict disciple of states' rights and as such held firm to the belief that federal powers were limited to only those granted in the Constitution. On this and other controversial issues he voted his own conscience despite the position of his party.

During his tenure in both houses, for example, Tyler remained faithful to the Democratic Party line on several issues. These included a vote against Clay's American System, supporting Jackson's veto on renewing the charter for the Second Bank of the United States, his stance against federal funding for internal improvements, and the president's rejection of nullification and protective tariffs. Nevertheless, living up to his nonpartisan proclivities, he also ignored party loyalty when he defended Clay during the corrupt bargain scandal and went against Jackson by voting to reject the Force Bill of 1833. Even more damaging to his party loyalty was when he voted for censure of President Jackson for attempting to remove federal deposits from the Bank, and then his refusal to reverse his position by voting to expunge the Senate censure when directed by the Democratic legislature in Virginia. Instead, Tyler resigned his Democratic seat in protest and joined the states' rights southerners in the Whig Party, becoming their vice-presidential candidate on Hugh L. White's losing ticket.

Now as president, and still as independent as always, Tyler was on a collision course with the Whig congressional caucus and Senator Clay in particular over several economic reforms he intended to propose for the next Congress.

That spring, at a meeting with Clay and other Whig congressional leaders, Tyler outlined the priorities he was prepared to pursue. They included the repeal of the independent treasuries, a new policy for surplus-revenue distributions to help the states strapped with debts, particularly in the South and West, new tariffs to pump needed money into the treasury coffers to help offset the distributions, and to avoid a deficit, he called for an additional bond issue. When he concluded, Tyler issued a stern warning to all those present. Since it would hinder his plans to balance the budget, he would reject any new tariffs if they increased the rate over the 20 percent already scheduled to occur in July of 1842 under the Compromise Tariff of 1833. And while gazing at Clay who was planning to submit a bill for a national bank, Tyler reminded the group that he opposed a national bank and would, without hesitation, veto any bank bill as unconstitutional.

Clay was stunned over Tyler's assertiveness, especially to the bank bill, a pet initiative he and others party members favored and one he was determined to champion. Clay always believed that only a national bank could hold sufficient funds to provide the loans necessary to lure investors. Encouraging more credit, he insisted, would be the means to help fuel an economic recovery. Long the leader of his party, Clay was furious over Tyler's condescending attitude and refused to be dictated to in such a manner. Not to be outwitted by the president, Clay exploited all the political influence he had amassed over the years and maneuvered himself into the chairmanship position of the Senate Finance Committee. By initiating conspiratorial arrangements with several other House and Senate committees, Clay and his allies moved to challenge Tyler on the bank bill in the special session of the Twenty-seventh Congress set to begin on May 31, 1841.

The special session of Congress was called to help solve the problems brought on by the weakened economy. The economic development program the administration pursued was a package vital for relieving the current fiscal crisis and one the voters had mandated by their votes in the last election. Clay's own economic reforms would, in most respects, agree with Tyler's on such proposals as a $12 million bond issue, a policy for distributing land sale revenue to the states, and particularly repealing the sub-treasury law. Clay's plans even promoted a new revenue tariff to Tyler's specifications. Added to Clay's list, however, was a bill that would pit the powerful senator against the President of the United States. This measure, called the Fiscal Bank Bill, would create a new Bank of the United States in the nation's capital.

With Clay consistently attacked for his dictatorial and overbearing ways, the expected power struggle between executive tyranny and legislative arrogance would soon take center stage. As Clay painfully admitted to a friend, "We are in a crisis as a party. Mr. Tyler's opinions about a Bank are giving us great trouble. Indeed, they not only threaten a defeat on that measure, but endanger the permanency, and the ascendancy of the Whig cause."

One of the first measures Clay pushed through Congress was a bill to repeal Van Buren's independent treasuries, an action essential before his new banking bill could be considered. Signed into law only the previous July, it was determined by the majority of partisan Whig lawmakers that the sub-treasury program did little to help the financial situation while at the same time it had a negative effect on the bank credit structure across the country. Since the Whigs controlled Congress the measure easily sailed through both houses. Despite three years of hard work by the Van Buren administration to get the Independent Treasury Bill passed, all was lost in June when Tyler signed its repeal into law effective August 13, 1841.

After considerable wrangling and arm twisting to incorporate policy changes for state branches, the compromised version of Clay's Fiscal Bank Bill meandered its way through the House and Senate mostly along party-line votes. On August 16, as predicted, Tyler rejected the bill on constitutional grounds, objecting mostly to the power given to the bank's branches to discount loans or promissory notes without authorization from the states. Obviously, the Democrats were publicly siding with Tyler's decision, hoping they could help assure a breach between the president and his party for their own political purposes. Sectional repercussions were, of course, also predicable depending on the side of the issue one supported. In some parts of the country Tyler was soundly castigated or burned in effigy, while in other areas his veto was praised.

On learning the news of Tyler's veto, Clay angrily remarked, "Tyler is on his way to the Democratic camp. They will give him lodgings in some outhouse, but they will never trust him. He will stand here, like [Benedict] Arnold in England, a monument of his own perfidy and disgrace."

Shortly after the veto, several Whig congressmen and a few members of the Cabinet gave proponents of the Bank bill the impression that Tyler would agree to sign banking legislature if it contained specific modifications that, among other things, established the Bank as a fiscal agent of the government. In fact, at one of these meetings Tyler reportedly exclaimed, "Now if you will send me this bill I will sign it in twenty-four hours." The backers of the bill, although not fully supportive of Tyler's recommendations, were so committed on getting a new Bank of the United States that they agreed to incorporate all of the modifications. Under those conditions the measure was rewritten to satisfy the wishes of the president. Even the word "bank" was dropped from the name of the bill to remove the stigma associated with that term and was now identified as the Fiscal Corporation Bill. Clay grudgingly went along with the changes because, "Though but half the loaf, it is still better than no bread."

Tyler, meanwhile, was incensed over the verbal and written abuse he was subjected to from members of his own party over his veto, particularly from Clay. He was being accused, along with his Virginian supporters, of intentionally creating conditions to break up the Whigs in order to form a new party, one that suited his own philosophy. Therefore, to avoid another veto at this time, Tyler asked for a postponement of the modified banking bill until it could be taken up at the first regular session of Congress to convene in December 1841.

Angered over the president's request to postpone a bill tailored exactly to his specifications, the Whigs were determined more than ever to force it upon him. After all, they argued, didn't he say he would sign it in twenty-four hours? Disregarding Tyler's appeal, Clay's bill was introduced for debate and one month before the special session adjourned it was approved by Congress and forwarded to the White House. On September 9, Tyler defiantly rejected the Bank bill once again.

Meanwhile, a $12 million loan to help finance the expected government deficit was passed, as was a bankruptcy law to ease the burden on entrepreneurs and creditors, a measure designed to appease the East. A comprehensive tariff and distribution program was postponed until it could be studied more fully in the first regular session. Nevertheless, Tyler's veto was a bitter pill for the Whigs to swallow. It struck at the heart and soul of their economic recovery agenda and they vowed he was going to pay.

To protest Tyler's intransigence, two days after his second veto the entire Tyler Cabinet resigned, with the exception of Daniel Webster, Tyler's secretary of state. Sensing Tyler's declining popularity, Webster continued to serve in the administration but only to further his own presidential ambitions. And to voice their displeasure and outrage, Whig congressmen assembled outside the Capitol and in a series of denigrating speeches Tyler's executive tyranny was not only compared to Jackson's, but he was also called "a man destitute of intellect and integrity...." To close the matter the Whigs expunged the president from the Whig Party.

Standing alone in his office, Tyler was now a president without a party and the Whigs a party without a president. To drive their point home, congressional actions were stalled and Tyler found it increasingly difficult to gain approval for his appointments and legislative proposals. He was rejected by the Whigs and the Democrats refused to acknowledge him as president.

In his first annual message to Congress that December of 1841, Tyler reiterated the need for action to resolve the terrible financial problems confronting the country. Of urgent concern, he warned, was the government's need for more money to cover the enormous shortfall expected when the tariff rates begin to decline in January. As you recall, under the provisions of the Compromise Tariff of 1833, the rates were scheduled to drop dramatically on January 1, 1842, and then again in July to a 20 percent level. Over the following months, however, Tyler was forced to amend his original demands for new income when he realized the impracticality of maintaining the government with the tariffs at a 20 percent levy. Instead he now demanded all distributions to the states from the surplus be stopped, a demand contrary to the desires of congressional Whigs.

When the first regular session of Congress met, the most critical debate on the Senate floor addressed the government's need for increased revenue. Grasping this opportunity to sever all ties with Tyler and to restrict the power of the presidency, the Whigs, under the leadership of Henry Clay, sought to implement measures that were completely at odds with Tyler's wishes. Clay's proposal not only called for a higher tariff than the 20 percent but also for an increase in distributions to further assist the states struggling with excessive debt. In March, confident that his economic recovery plan was in the capable hands of the Whig leadership, Clay retired to his estate in Kentucky, supposedly to allow a more affable relationship between the legislative and executive branches and to tend to personal affairs. Realistically however, Clay went home to await his nomination to the presidency. Until then he still continued to influence the direction of the party.

With such a bold agenda that ran contrary to Tyler's wishes, the Whigs suspected the president was sure to wield his veto once again. To prevent that from happening, their scheme was to prolong the debate until the financial crisis became so unbearable that Tyler would be forced to approve Clay's bill. If he didn't, Tyler could be blamed for impeding the work expended by Congress to resolve the government's financial difficulties. Even if the Democrats voted to uphold the veto, as they were expected to do, they would also be accountable to the voters as well. Either way Tyler chose to go, it was a win for the Whigs.

In the meantime, before Clay's proposal was acted upon, Millard Fillmore, the Whig chairman of the House and Ways Committee, introduced a bill in June that postponed the final July tariff cuts for one month. Included in the same bill was a passage that also delayed distributions for a month as well. Called the "little tariff," its purpose was to preclude further deficits by gaining a little extra revenue for the government while Congress was engaged in these debates. Without hesitation, on June 29, 1842, Tyler vetoed that bill as well.

The Whigs were outraged at yet another example of Tyler's blatant and repeated insults to the legislative branch. John J. Crittenden, also of Kentucky and Clay's replacement in the Senate, couldn't resist venting his anger to a friend, writing, "My wish is to see the Whig party rid of him—rid of the nuisance."

The Whigs soon rationalized that Tyler's vetoes guaranteed not only his downfall in the voters' eyes but ensured Clay's election in 1844. "Tyler is one of your best friends," Sen. Crittenden remarked to Clay. "His last veto has served us all well." Clay, of course, still resting at home, was in total agreement.

With a taste for blood, the Whigs schemed to apply the coup de grace. By this time Clay's proposal had wound its way through both houses and was now on the president's desk—a new tariff and distribution bill the Whigs were certain Tyler would reject. Called the Tariff of 1842, the bill greatly increased the tariff rates above the 20 percent level and in effect took the rates back up to the 30 percent levels of 1833. It greatly benefited the northern manufacturing sector with more protection and gave the government the extra revenue it sorely needed. The bill also authorized the continuance of revenue distribution and as expected, on August 9, Tyler vetoed it, but only over the distribution provisions.

Even though the Whigs had made their point, they soon realized that as the majority party, accomplishing nothing in this session might create a backlash against them at the polls in the next election. To avoid the appearance of being uncompromising, the Whigs decided to change their tactics. Both measures would be submitted to Tyler but in two separate bills. Quickly rushed back to the White House, Tyler agreed the need for additional revenue was paramount and reluctantly signed the tariff bill one day before Congress adjourned on the thirty-first, but renewed his veto of the distribution bill.

Angered over the new protective tariff, the South was again preaching its victimization and secession rhetoric but by now these antics had grown weak and stale and the demonstrations were to no avail. After years of unrelenting bickering over the discriminatory nature of tariffs, the South would soon accept the fact that tariffs were one of the tools necessary for preserving a sound national economy. Besides, with the possible annexation of Texas on the horizon, the South was certain there would be new issues for them to challenge their enemies in both the North and the federal government.

As the breach widened between the Whigs and the president, Tyler struck back by stacking his administration with more and more of his Democratic supporters to fill the many vacancies from deaths, resignations, and internal reshufflings. Widespread replacement of Whigs with Tyler loyalists was soon quite evident in such federal departments as custom houses and the judiciary. One Massachusetts legislator wrote, "Corruption and Tyler, and Tyler and Corruption, will stick together as long as Cataline and treason. The name of Tyler will stink in the nostrils of the people; for the history of our Government affords no such palpable example of the prostitution of the executive patronage to the wicked purpose of bribery."

Although the Whigs had clearly demonstrated to the voters the weaknesses of Tyler's character, the actions taken by the Whigs to help correct the economic condition of the country were far from what the people were led to believe. With the promises made by the Whigs still resonating in their ears, the voters expected their living standards to improve much more rapidly. With the Independent Treasury Bill scrapped and no new banking directives to replace it, all government funds would now be managed at the discretion of the treasury secretary. On that note, many voters questioned the wisdom of repealing the Treasury Bill without first instituting new fiscal directives to guide the treasury secretary. The business community was also upset because the $12 million bond issue never fulfilled the Whigs' intent. Since the government was bankrupt very few wanted to subscribe to the bonds. And certainly with higher tariffs the Whigs could not claim they created a stabilized economy. That became abundantly clear in 1842 and 1843 when the results from state legislative and gubernatorial elections began rolling in with the Whigs losing in a big way. For example, when the present Congress convened in 1841 following Harrison's election, the Whigs controlled the Senate 30 to 22 and in the House they ruled as well. By the time the Twenty-eighth Congress was seated two years later, their Senate majority was 27 to 25 and in the House the Whigs were now the minority party with only 79 members as opposed to 142 for the

Democrats. This was a sure sign the economy was still the primary issue and that the voters now blamed the Whigs for a stimulus package that was slow to revitalize the economy and their own lives. Strangely enough, Tyler, a Democrat turned Whig, but yet speaking as a Democrat, was exhilarated over this turn of events. He thought the Democratic gains were "the greatest political victory ever won within my recollection ... achieved entirely upon the vetoes of the Bank bills presented to me at the special session."

While the economy drew much attention in Congress and the 1843 election campaigns prepared for action, new sectional rumblings were stirring once again.

Ever since gaining their independence, the Texans expressed a willingness to join the Union to gain a degree of protection against the growing threats from Mexico. The drive for annexation, however, never quite materialized and now the Texas question had become so pervasive it threatened to be a major issue in the upcoming presidential campaign.

In the South, statehood for Texas was already a major political issue. Once Texas was brought into their federation, southerners agreed, they could extend slavery into the West, perhaps create and populate new slave states, gain more congressional representation and with it the resultant power to determine not only the fate of the South but also the destiny of the country. Over the years ahead, this scenario of southern expansion and domination would be perceived in the North as the "slave-power conspiracy."

While southerners became more persistent in calling for statehood, the North bristled in combative protestations against it. It was quite obvious that northerners wanted to prohibit the extension of slavery for exactly the same reasons the South embraced it. "Will we extend slavery or will we promote Liberty & Freedom?" asked Rep. Joshua R. Giddings of Ohio. "To give the south the preponderance of political power would be itself a surrender of our Tariff, our internal improvements, our distribution of the proceeds of public lands, ... it would be a transfer of our political power to the slaveholders. And a base and degrading surrender of our selves to the power & protection of slavery. It is the most abominable proposition with which a free people were ever insulted."

The growing tensions over Texas statehood became even more intense beginning in 1842 when northern abolitionists heard reports that Great Britain was showing an unusual amount of interest in the new republic. At the time there were indications that the British government was growing increasingly concerned over disappointing production figures from its widely scattered sugar and cotton plantations. The British believed their free-labor colonies were unable to compete with the same products produced by slave-labor enterprises. Therefore, as a defensive measure to protect their interests, they sought methods to simply eliminate the competition. Texas, it appeared, may have posed a potential threat to Great Britian's East Indies cotton plantations.

Recognizing the British concerns as a great opportunity to thwart southern efforts to promote the spread of slavery, the abolitionists sent an emissary to persuade the anti-slavery Brits to join in their efforts to purchase freedom for the slaves in Texas. If this maneuver could be pulled off, they reasoned, Texas could have an opportunity to be the fourteenth free state and effectively block further expansion of southern slavery to the West at the same time.

In January 1843 the Tyler administration first heard of the British-Texas connection from a letter published by Virginian congressman Thomas W. Gilmer, and learned later that the British were prepared to offer a large loan to the abolitionists. When confronted by the American minister, the British government scoffed at these ridiculous assertions and told the administration they had no plans "to acquire any dominate influence in Texas, or to have any kind of connection with her except the fair and open trade and commerce which she has with all other nations." Tyler, however, as a southerner and proslavery advocate wasn't convinced by the British statement, believing the denial was a ruse and that the British government was actually scheming to force abolition on Texas.

Many influential southerners in and around Washington were also following this developing drama with great interest and immediately recognized the consequences of losing Texas, a vital component in any plan that might arise for their economic growth and social expansion. To circumvent the British and also to head off any future attempts for the abolitionists to spread their activities into Texas, pro-annexation southerners demanded the administration resume the stalled discussions with Texas on this most critical issue. Whether southern demands played any role is unclear, but secret negotiations resumed in September 1843 between Secretary of State Abel P. Upshur and Texas President Sam Houston. One of the outspoken southerners was Henry Wise, a future governor of Virginia, who declared "that unless by a treaty with Mexico the South can add more weight to her end of the lever of national power ... the balance of interest is gone, and the safeguard of American property, thin air."

Mexico, however, had other ideas. Since Mexico never recognized the independence of Texas, they warned Tyler in no uncertain terms that the annexation of Texas was certain to lead to war. But Tyler, for his own political motives, ignored their warning and instructed Congress to disregard the Mexican threat. Looking ahead to the upcoming nominating convention, Tyler began to outline his strategy for influencing the annexation of Texas before the presidential campaigning got underway.

With Tyler's nomination in doubt many in Congress were suspicious of his sudden interest in Texas. Some thought the administration was exaggerating the British connection as part of an enormous plot to create a new issue, one that would assure Tyler's nomination. Senator Benton, in a speech on the Senate floor called Tyler's assertion of a British takeover a "cry of wolf where there was no wolf." Other Washington politicos took Tyler at his word and thought he was truly trying to save Texas from falling under the influence of the British government. But, since Tyler had fractured the Whig Party and had lost many of his supporters over his economic vetoes, some historians point out that it was primarily a move to create a new issue to exploit for his own presidential ambitions. Under that scenario, Tyler could take advantage of the growing territorial expansion sentiment sweeping the country, while at the same time enhance his popularity with the pro-annexationists. Furthermore, contemplating his reelection bid, Tyler seized this opportunity to advance his own chances for a second term. Granting statehood to Texas, he mused, would halt the feuding within the party over economic matters, accomplish something of significance in an otherwise mediocre term, and would reinvigorate a new constituent loyalty toward his own nomination bid.

Clay was again the most likely choice for the Whigs while the Democratic hopes were with Van Buren, also making another bid for the White House. Annexation, an issue neither of the frontrunners particularly wanted in the campaign, was a losing proposition no matter how it was supported. Statehood for Texas, both adamantly proclaimed, could institute war with Mexico, a conflict the country must avoid. Conversely, with northern resentment against the extension of slavery growing more intense, if annexation was again denied the prospect for disunion by the South was also a real possibility.

Van Buren had already voiced his opposition to annexation. The former president was concerned that since the Mexican government believed Texas was still under its jurisdiction, granting statehood to Texas would be seen as a belligerent act against Mexico, a confrontation he preferred to avoid. He would soon discover, however, that many of his supporters did not agree with that position and it would cost him dearly.

As the legislative leader of the Whig Party, Clay's views on granting statehood to Texas were spelled out in a letter written to the *National Intelligencer*. In it he remarked that "annexation and war with Mexico are identical.... I consider the annexation of Texas at this time, without the assent of Mexico, as a measure compromising the national character, involving us certainly in war with Mexico, probably with foreign powers, dangerous to the integrity of the Union, inexpedient in the present financial condition of the country, and not called for by any general expression of public opinion." Incredibly, both frontrunners were in agreement politically on this very troublesome issue—statehood for Texas should not be granted at this time.

With Clay and Van Buren both coming out against annexation, if the president hoped to get the nomination he would have to align himself with the southern annexationists from both parties. His plan to accomplish this required an immediate and aggressive pro-active policy toward bringing Texas into the Union as a slave state. He said as much to Upshur, who became secretary of state when intense pressure from the Whigs forced Webster to resign.

Texas, he said, was "the only matter that will take sufficient hold of the feelings of the South to rally it on a southern candidate and weaken Clay & Van Buren so much there as to bring the election into the House." Evidently, Tyler believed that if the election was sent to the House he would be presented as a third party compromise candidate and his southern supporters would assure his victory.

Coincidentally, at the end of February 1844, Upshur, along with Thomas W. Gilmer, now the secretary of the Navy, were killed when a new gun, the Peacemaker, exploded during a demonstration aboard the U.S.S. *Princeton*. Following this dreadful accident Tyler took advantage of an enormous opportunity to enhance his efforts to secure Texas. To replace Upshur as secretary of state, he appointed the man who was arguably the most outspoken advocate for slavery and its expansion, John C. Calhoun. This shameful and aggressive political maneuver to influence his goal for immediate annexation and the extension of slavery was, of course, contrary to the published positions of both his Whig and the Democratic opponents and was sure to create waves within the political campaigns.

Moving into his State Department office on April 1, one of the first foreign policy initiatives on Calhoun's agenda was to complete the final negotiations with Texas that Upshur had started. Eleven days later Calhoun delivered the signed annexation agreement to Tyler who eagerly forwarded the documents to the Senate on April 22 for ratification. Still, Tyler knew this matter was far from being a done deal. Considering the two opposing front-runners had already reached an agreement against immediate annexation and the Whigs in Congress had refused to work with him, it appeared to Tyler that their opponents were planning to isolate both Calhoun and himself and to leave them high and dry on the Texas question.

On May 1, the Whigs met in Baltimore at the Universalist church in what could be called the greatest tribute to one of their own. The convention hall was festooned with Clay banners and ribbons, Clay hats, Clay portraits, badges and sashes, and even live raccoons, mascots symbolizing the man of the hour. Clay was routinely and unanimously voted the Whig nominee on a platform that extolled the grand principles of the party, on instituting the long cherished doctrine of the American System, on renewing their pledge for economic reforms and to fight against executive usurpation. Interestingly enough, never once did the platform mention the ongoing efforts for and against the annexation of Texas.

In the Democratic camp, harmony was not so apparent. Van Buren's opposition to annexation completely disregarded the intense pressure he was under from highly influential and powerful pro-slavery and pro-annexationist party leaders, men such as Andrew Jackson and Calhoun. Unfortunately, Van Buren's single-mindedness would ultimately seal his fate at the May 27 nominating convention also held in Baltimore. The new enemies of Van Buren, primarily from the southern wing of his own party, wanted dearly to include Texas in the southern family of states. However, Van Buren's anti-annexation declaration terribly disappointed the southerners and frustrated them to the point where they searched for an opportunity to strike back.

This opportunity soon presented itself at the convention when an impassioned debate ensued over whether a majority vote would determine the party's nominee or the current two-thirds rule. Knowing that Van Buren could not possibly win the nomination if the two-thirds vote requirement was retained, it was fairly obvious that Van Buren's opponents would insist on retaining the current format. So persuasive was their argument, however, that following an acrimonious convention battle they were able to convince the delegates to keep the two-thirds vote rule intact.

To no one's surprise, the two leading Democratic candidates, Van Buren and Lewis Cass, a former U.S. minister to France, were unable to gain the necessary two-thirds of the delegates following three days and eight ballots. Following numerous caucuses by various state delegations, it was finally agreed that the name of another candidate had to be submitted for consideration. The candidate they selected behind the scenes was the former congressman from Tennessee, James K. Polk, who had been mentioned earlier as a possible Van Buren running mate. Although Polk served as speaker of the House from 1835 to 1839 he was not particularly well known outside the party. But he was a southern man, and his views on expansionist issues, such as the annexation of Texas and negotiating for the Oregon territory, put him in good stead in the present political climate. More significantly, Polk also won an endorsement from former President Andrew Jackson, a certain clincher to win the nomination. On the next ballot, assisted by strong lobbying efforts from Polk supporters working the convention delegates, Polk gained the necessary votes and became the first dark horse presidential candidate in U.S. history. Striving to benefit from the growing expansionist interests, the Democratic platform pledged the party would strive for "the reoccupation of Oregon and the reannexation of Texas, at the earliest practicable period...."

Calhoun and his followers from across the South were ecstatic not only over Polk's nomination but also over the Democratic platform regarding Texas. They were extremely delighted that at last a southern slaveholder and an advocate for Texas statehood was the leader of their party.

Even the Whigs, as the opposition party, were overjoyed over the results of the Democratic convention. They couldn't believe their good fortune that Polk, who was thought to have scant political credentials and who had recently lost two consecutive bids for governor of Tennessee (1841 and 1843), was now nominated for President of the United States. Brimming with optimism, the Whigs truly saw their presidency on the horizon and looked forward to an exceptionally easy victory. One Georgian Whig, unable to restrain his enthusiasm, exclaimed, "We will literally crush the ticket. We consider it here as giving up the game." And a Georgia newspaper article asked, "Polk! Who is he? What has he done to give him prominence over Buchanan, Van Buren, Johnson, Cass, Calhoun?"

The Van Buren Democrats in the North, in contrast, were outraged that their candidate was jettisoned by such unethical parliamentary maneuvers for the likes of Polk. On June the eighth they evened the score when the treaty for Texas statehood was brought to the Senate floor of the Twenty-eighth Congress for ratification. When the final vote was tallied the Democratic Van Burenites threw in with 27 of the 30 Whigs to reject the treaty 35 to 16.

Tyler, meanwhile, was nominated by a small contingent of supporters on a platform supporting Texas annexation. Convened at Calvert Hall in Baltimore on May 27 as well, his nomination was a fitting gift for the 55-year-old who was married two weeks later.

In the House the treaty received even more scrutiny than it received in the Senate. A major sticking point was the unresolved dispute between Texas and Mexico over the 2,000 mile southern border. Texas authorities had vehemently insisted for years that the Rio Grande was the southernmost line separating the two adversaries. Mexico was adamant as well in its insistence that the border with the U.S. extended along the Nueces River northward, which effectively cut Texas in two. For that reason, the 150-mile wide land area in between these two claims was appropriately called the Disputed Territory. The treaty, however, conveniently avoided the border dispute by including a provision for the United States to negotiate the issue with Mexico, but only after the treaty was ratified.

Another matter of significant concern, especially to the northerners, was the question of slavery in Texas. Would Texas be brought into the Union as a free state or a slave state? Evidently the northerners had a plausible reason to be troubled about this critical question. There waiting in the wings, also primed and ready to accept statehood was Florida, another Deep South slave state. This concern was particularly acute to the southern power brokers as well. With the number of slave and free states evenly divided at the time, this was an enormous opportunity for the South to gain additional political clout.

But once again the result was a defeat for Tyler's efforts and once again Texas statehood was put on hold.

Southern hostility to the treaty's rejection was immediate. Again, the cry of nullification and calls for secession could be heard as angry agitators added to the growing turmoil. Whether it came from the halls of Congress, the statehouses, a town meeting, or a newspaper editorial, the desire to separate from the Union was growing more palatable following the recent loss of the annexation bill.

In an attempt to reinforce the sagging spirits of the southern Democrats, party leaders called for party unity and reminded them that the most noteworthy plank of the Democratic platform read, "Our title to the whole of the

Territory of Oregon is clear and unquestionable ... and that the reoccupation of Oregon and the reannexation of Texas, at the earliest practicable period, are great American measures...." Polk, they insisted, was the right man at the right time to ensure these measures were accomplished.

Tyler, meanwhile, recognizing the reality of his diminishing support, withdrew his candidacy in August and in his parting speech urged all those supporting Texas statehood to rally behind Polk. "The Pres. Is ready to go for Polk tooth & nail," the Boston customs collector remarked, if "Texas should be backed up strongly. This is true policy & no time is to be lost."

As the campaigns got underway they illustrated the sharp differences between the two candidates and their parties. While both candidates were southern slaveholders, Polk was opposed to protective tariffs and distribution of federal funds to the states while Clay promoted these measures as part of his American System. On annexation, Polk's position was well established and the Democratic platform was committed to Texas statehood. Clay, on the other hand, opposed it and for that reason most anti-annexation Whigs in the North would remain loyal to Clay, as ironically, would much of the southern Whig planter aristocracy. These were the large cotton planters, those experiencing low production yields from worn out soil conditions, who feared the potential competition from Texas. Clay would also retain support from southern Whigs that remained loyal to their party's principles that the annexation of Texas was very wrong. These Whig voters disregarded the sectional controversy but held firm to the party line that the annexation of Texas was an immoral land grab of Mexican soil by greedy speculators and would only lead to war as Clay had reminded them in his letter to the *National Intelligencer*. In fact, Clay's early campaign strategy was to convince southern mothers that if Polk was elected their young sons would be fighting and losing their lives in the barren wastelands of Texas.

During the heat of the campaign, however, Polk was gaining the upper hand by driving home his cause for annexation. And with the anti-annexation Liberty Party in the mix and still gaining strength in the North, Clay was now forced to make a risky adjustment to his political ideology by softening his position on Texas. To a southern newspaper he wrote, "I have ... no hesitation in saying that, far from having any personal objection to the annexation of Texas, I should be glad to see it, without dishonor, without war, with the common consent of the Union, and upon just and fair terms." In Clay's message the spread of slavery was now a "temporary institution," rationalizing the supposition that over time the country would become "overwhelmingly populated with white citizens" and certainly no reason to refuse annexation. Although anti-annexation Whigs in the North had been loyal to Clay in the past, this political flip-flop alienated many of his supporters, especially in the key state of New York, and placed Clay in a very difficult position. He still had to somehow appease his southern loyalist constituency, while at the same time prevent his northern supporters from moving over to the Liberty Party. If he failed, it could cost him the presidency.

But, in the end, the outcome of the election was bad news for the Whigs and even worse for Clay. For the fourth time his aspirations to hold the highest office in the land had eluded him. His role in not providing the voters the economic stability he had promised and his wavering position over Texas alienated many of his constituents. Although his outward demeanor cloaked his inner disappointment, this loss must have been a terrible blow to Clay, knowing that his years of public service had gone unrewarded yet again. Longtime supporters of Clay, the seasoned political veteran, were shocked over his loss to Polk. After all, the Whigs lamented, Clay was the better candidate, was more eloquent, more intelligent, and was so much more experienced. One disbelieving southern voter complained, "The malcontents of these United States have given the greatest blow to elective government that was ever given," while Millard Fillmore lamented, "May God save the country, for it is evident the people will not."

Of the 26 states, Clay won only the eleven predominant Whig states for 105 electoral votes. Three were from the South—Tennessee, North Carolina, and Kentucky—while the other eight were the northern states of Ohio, Maryland, Delaware, New Jersey, Vermont, Massachusetts, Connecticut and Rhode Island. Polk, on the other hand, captured all the rest for 170 votes. As historians point out, however, the race was much closer than the electoral vote totals indicated. The most significant factor in the results, many claim, was the surprising strength of the Liberty Party in New York where it had siphoned away roughly five thousand of Clay's supporters. The popular vote was so close in New York (Clay lost by about 1 percent of the vote) that if only a portion of those five thousand had stayed with Clay he could have won the state's thirty-six electoral votes, enough to give him the presidency instead of Polk. Soon after his devastating loss, Clay, now greatly depressed and nearly sixty-seven years of age, retired to Ashland, his estate in Kentucky.

Following the election, the issue over Texas statehood was still at a fever pitch. The lame duck Tyler and congressional annexationists interpreted Polk's election as a southern mandate for bringing Texas into the Union. As expected, in December 1844, as the second congressional session got underway, an annexation measure was reintroduced in the House. During the course of the debates the Tyler-endorsed plan, which, besides granting statehood, would have required the U.S. to pay for all Texas' debts, was replaced by a Whig plan designed to be more appealing to the southern section. It was called the Brown plan, after Milton H. Brown of Tennessee, the coalition leader of the southern Whigs presenting this idea. Brown's resolution would bring Texas into the Union with the state responsible for paying its own debts while the federal government would be responsible for the negotiations with Mexico over the border. The real clincher, however, was a provision to allow Texas the right to divide into four additional slave states in the future as long as the new states were formed below the 36°30' line of the Missouri Compromise of 1820. With the potential for ten more senators to bolster its political power this provision practically guaranteed its passage in the House.

But in the Whig controlled Senate the battle lines were more sharply at odds. Northern Whigs were still fiercely opposed to Texas statehood largely over the unresolved border dispute as well as the slavery issue and, of course, the impact additional states would have on the balance of power. They were simply outraged that the subject of annexation was even being considered without any resolutions on these matters and because there was no precedent for annexing an independent country. Debates were particularly heated over whether Texas would come in as a territory or as one or more slave or free states. Finally, to break the impasse, Senator Benton offered an amendment that postponed the debates until after a new round of peaceful negotiations were held between the United States and Texas that would answer all these questions once and for all.

As the quarreling continued and tempers became more frayed, many northern Whigs grew testier than ever, pointing out that annexation for Texas was a complete sham. Southerners, they pointed out, were in fact quite reluctant to live among the people of mixed races, as they have always been. Except for extending slavery into Texas and to the country further west, they opined, southerners were rather lukewarm to the notion of expansion. In Texas, they suggested, the southerners merely wanted the land, but not the people. Southern Whigs were extremely livid over these insensitive accusations and responded rather bluntly that we "can never unite with the northern Whigs and do any good. The northern Whigs are the most cold-hearted-bigoted-selfish & incorrigible people upon earth.... They are the abolition party of the U. States. They have no common feelings with us whatever."

After assessing the potential vote count on the new Brown plan it was feared by the bill's proponents that their Senate majority would fall short. So in order to avoid this unwanted outcome, a compromise amendment was introduced whereby both the Brown plan for immediate annexation and the Benton amendment for more treaty negotiations would be submitted to the president as a joint resolution and he alone would have to decide. By a vote of 27 to 25, on February 27, 1845, the Benton-Brown compromise was carried. (The requirement for passage of the amended joint resolution is only by a simple majority of members present in each house.) Subsequently passed by the House, it was delivered to the White House.

The president to decide this question, at least to the members of the Congress as a gesture of courtesy, would be the recently elected James K. Polk. But, evidently, Tyler had his own agenda and decided, notwithstanding Congress' intent, that he had some unfinished business to attend to before he left office, business he hoped would leave something noteworthy for history to judge his tenure. After reviewing the proposal before him, to no one's surprise, Tyler selected the Brown plan for immediate annexation. Two days later, on March 3, his last full day in power, Tyler ordered his charge d'affaires in Texas to prepare the necessary documents offering statehood. For good measure, Tyler also signed a bill earlier that day that brought Florida into the Union as the twenty-seventh state and the fourteenth supporting the institution of slavery.

The significance of Tyler's actions on Texas, although not apparent to some people at the time, was that it added more impetus to a popular and growing national movement called expansionism.

9

The Expansionist Agenda (1845 to 1846)

Moving quickly from the crowded lobby of the Coleman Hotel, the new president-elect gingerly entered the open carriage for the short ride to the capitol. In a torrential rainstorm, the presidential entourage, escorted by a mercilessly drenched contingent of soldiers, sloshed their way down a muddy Pennsylvania Avenue. It was mid-morning of March 4, 1845, and despite the inclement weather, several thousand sodden spectators had gathered to witness James K. Polk, who, like the ten before him, would soon take the oath of office.

Speaking to a sea of umbrellas, Polk, in his inauguration address, soon reaffirmed his position on the latest sectional issue of the times—immediate statehood for Texas. It was a proposal adamantly opposed by Mexico, who still considered the Texas region under its jurisdiction, and by the antislavery groups in the North who shuddered over the consequences of such a move. Polk had unceasingly pledged during the presidential campaign to work hard toward this goal. It was the issue that got him elected, and now was the time to reinforce that commitment.

As Polk explained, "The Republic of Texas has made known her desire to come into our Union, to form a part of our Confederacy and enjoy with us the blessings of liberty secured and guaranteed by our Constitution. Texas was once a part of our country—was unwisely ceded away to a foreign power—is now independent, and possesses an undoubted right to dispose of a part or the whole of her territory and to merge her sovereignty as a separate and independent state in ours.... To Texas the reunion is important, because the strong protecting arm of our Government would be extended over her, and the vast resources of her fertile soil and genial climate would be speedily developed, while the safety of New Orleans and of our whole southwestern frontier against

135

hostile aggression, as well as the interests of the whole Union, would be promoted by it." Continuing on with his address the new president assured the people that he would "endeavor by all constitutional, honorable, and appropriate means to consummate the expressed will of the people and Government of the United States by the reannexation of Texas to our Union at the earliest practicable period."

Polk also touched on a second campaign pledge, one purposely designed to counter-balance northern objections and the political ramifications over granting statehood to Texas. Specifically, it was the question of the proposed border in the Oregon wilderness where the slogan "Fifty-four Forty or Fight" had purportedly become the rallying cry of his presidential campaign. The country at the time was composed of fourteen slave states and thirteen free states; not exactly the ratio northerners were accustomed to. Keeping in mind the highly sensitive nature of maintaining Senate parity, therefore, the inclusion of the Oregon issue into the campaign, a free territory, was a wisely designed maneuver to offset the growing sectional criticism from northern expansionists and anti-slave factions over the issue of granting statehood to Texas, a potential fifteenth slave enclave.

Since 1818, the United States and Great Britain shared the occupation of the Oregon territory, but with a steady stream of American pioneers settling there, the time was long overdue for the United States to stake a claim to this land for herself. "Our title to the country of Oregon," Polk pointedly gestured, "is clear and unquestionable ... our people, increasing to many millions, have filled the eastern valley of the Mississippi, adventurously ascended the Missouri to its headsprings, and are already engaged in establishing the blessings of self-government in valleys of which the rivers flow to the Pacific.... To us belongs the duty of protecting them adequately wherever they may be upon our soil. The increasing facilities of intercourse will easily bring the States, of which the formation in that part of our territory can not be long delayed, within the sphere of our federative Union. In the meantime every obligation imposed by treaty or conventional stipulation should be sacredly respected."

Scanning the drenched onlookers from a newly constructed platform over the East Portico, Polk understood full well that the opinions he expressed today would set off a firestorm of controversy. And in all likelihood he was about to face war with either Mexico or Great Britain—or both.

The 49-year-old president, the first of 10 children, was born on a farm in Mecklenburg County, North Carolina. Reared in one of the wealthiest families in the region, most of the family fortune came from the elder Polk's farming, surveying, and land speculation ventures following their move to Tennessee. Polk returned to his native state in 1815 and graduated at the head of his class from the University of North Carolina three years later. While gainfully employed in a thriving law practice in Nashville, he married into the equally powerful and influential Democratic family of Sarah Childress, an

James K. Polk. During his single term in office the 11th president nearly doubled the size of the country in fulfilling his expansionist agenda. Reproduction of a daguerreotype circa 1845–49. Courtesy of the Library of Congress.

asset which contributed heavily to the success of his political ambitions. Following a two-year stint in the state legislature and then fourteen years in the U.S. House of Representatives, an ambitious and highly motivated Polk retired from Congress in 1839 to serve one four-year term as the governor of Tennessee.

Not only was a new president of the United States inaugurated that day but also a new era in American territorial ambitions. Although Polk had firmly set his sights on acquiring both Texas and the Oregon Territory, he also coveted California as well and would do most anything to get it. For Polk was now the leader of a recent wave of political sentiment, a movement that envisioned an America whose borders were limited only by the natural boundaries of the Atlantic and Pacific oceans, and to some of its proponents, even beyond.

It was a movement called expansionism. And together with the potential extension of slavery and Polk's aggressive agenda to fulfill his expansionist goals, a whole new round of sectional tensions would intensify like never before. It was unavoidable that as the old sectional conflicts over tariffs, banks, and public land sales, among other policies, became less and less troublesome, new political goals of expansionism would widen the breech between the northern and southern states even more.

Unquestionably, to the throng of listeners and to the thousands more that would read his words in the days ahead, Polk's message left little doubt about his own expansionist convictions and of his desire to pursue these continental objectives. "As our population has expanded, the Union has been cemented and strengthened. As our boundaries have been enlarged and our agricultural population has been spread over a large surface, our federative system has acquired additional strength and security.... It is confidently believed that our system may be safely extended to the utmost bounds of our territorial limits, and that as it shall be extended the bonds of our Union, so far from being weakened, will become stronger."

The primary message of the expansionist movement was the advantages of an ever expanding nation. In the Northeast, immigrants by the hundreds of thousands, mostly Catholics, inundated the larger cities of New York, Boston, and Philadelphia. Over the previous fifteen years, since 1830, over one and a half million newcomers had arrived on the eastern shores. Jobs were scarce, the cities were overcrowded and living conditions were appalling for the shiploads of mostly Irish and German immigrants flooding the East Coast. The country needed to expand, for settlers to farm the millions of acres of rich, fertile land and to tap the vast reservoir of natural resources. Not only would it enrich the people, but it would also benefit the nation's economy, productivity, prosperity, and strength. Expansionism was a philosophy that envisioned populating new territories with American pioneers, native and foreign born. Ensconced on their newly chosen territory they would form local governments and eventually, when the local or territorial bureaucracy demonstrated a readiness for it, they would be encouraged to apply for statehood. The United States, the expansionists argued, by annexing more states, would become a stronger nation by sharing the benefits of its democratic system of government. In return, these new states would not only reap the benefits of a free and equal self-governing entity protected by the doctrine of states' rights, but also share in the rewards of a politically, economically, and socially viable central government. There was a second tenet in their philosophy, and perhaps to some, a more sincere motive than the desire to extend the blessings of American democracy. This was to reaffirm the ideology of the Monroe Doctrine, a position that would keep foreign nations, chiefly Great Britain, from establishing footholds in the open territories of the American landscape. And yet to others, those with different political ambitions, expansionism may have been a convenient cover for legitimately extending the reach of slavery into the western territories.

One of the principal sponsors of expansionism at the time was Democrat John L. O'Sullivan, a 31-year-old lawyer and editor living in New York City. Born in Europe to American parents, O'Sullivan received his education from Columbia College and was the co-founder of the *Democratic Review* and the *New York Morning News*. Probably the most vocal public advocate of expansionism, he used his newspapers to communicate this philosophy on a daily basis, chiefly in New York where his two publications were located. However, O'Sullivan was far from being the only voice preaching the doctrine of expansionism. From New York to the Mississippi, many other Democratic newspapers also supported the cause, stirring up enormous amounts of public debate in New England, Ohio, Indiana, Illinois, and other middle-western states. But O'Sullivan dealt merely in the theoretical rhetoric and on the merits of expansionism. Although his ideas fed the growth of the movement, he had little actual input into the establishment of concrete U.S. policy towards reaching these goals.

The editorial drumbeat of expansionism also reflected the philosophy and principle force behind the movement in Washington, John Quincy Adams. As secretary of state in the Monroe administration, Adams demonstrated his expansionist inclinations when he tirelessly worked toward obtaining the joint occupation of the Oregon Territory with Britain in 1818. His imperialistic ideals also enabled the United States to gain concessions from Spain a year later in the Adams-Onís Treaty. That pact not only ceded the territory of eastern Florida to the United States but also transferred all Spanish claims to the Pacific Northwest to the U.S. as well, (territory north of present-day California). In return, however, the U.S. relinquished all claims to Texas, a trade-off perceived by many as a horrible mistake. And as the chief architect for prohibiting European colonization in the western hemisphere, Adams's expansionist ideology was skillfully reflected in the text of the Monroe Doctrine of 1823. In Congress over the succeeding years, the expansionist movement dominated the political debate. In turn, it created a vicious circle of acrimonious and sectional hostility between its supporters and its detractors, transformed conflicting and hotly contested oratory into government policy, and finally policy into more dissention.

Polk entered his presidential office for the first time on March 4 and although not bound by Tyler's Texas decision of the previous day, he believed the final determination on this very sensitive issue should have been his. Therefore, finding it only prudent to confide in his Cabinet, a hand-picked body sure to be partial to his expansionist philosophy, one of his first orders was to delay the Texas proceedings until all the Cabinet appointments were filled.

On March 10, 1845, the full contingent of Cabinet secretaries assembled in Polk's office at the White House to discuss the Texas situation. Following hours of careful deliberations, and after evaluating the advice from such capable and talented individuals as James Buchanan, the new secretary of state, and Robert J. Walker of Mississippi, Polk's closest friend and secretary of the Treasury, Polk agreed with Tyler's decision and renewed the offer of immediate statehood to Texas. This momentous decision, as popular as it was to expansionists, lit the fuse for the explosion that was sure to follow in the years ahead.

While the administration was evaluating Tyler's decision, the President of the Republic of Texas, Anson Jones, in collaboration with his predecessor, Sam Houston, also conferred over the annexation issue as well. In the course of their discussions, Jones and Houston agreed that the proposal for immediate annexation was not in the best interest of Texas. Instead, they preferred the amendment suggested by Senator Benton that called for additional negotiations between the two countries which they believed would have offered Texans better terms. In a desperate attempt to sidetrack statehood, later that March, Jones sent a startling letter to the Mexican president, José Joaquín de

Herrera, telling him that Texas would not "annex herself or become subject to any country whatsoever" if he agreed to recognize Texas independence, a position Mexican authorities had vigorously opposed for years. Incredibly, two months later the Mexican government consented to the Jones offer. They would recognize the independence of Texas but only if Jones was true to his word and refused annexation. It was an enormous concession indeed—but it was not to be. In June the Texas Congress unanimously approved annexation and the Texas Convention followed up on July 4 by also endorsing statehood. And to finally put the matter to rest, a popular referendum agreed overwhelmingly. All that remained was for ratification by the Twenty-ninth Congress set to convene on December the first.

In the meantime, about three weeks after Polk was inaugurated, Gen. Juan N. Almonte, the Mexican minister to the U.S., packed his bags and stormed out of Washington outraged over the decision to offer statehood to Texas. This reaction was hardly a surprise to the Polk administration since they knew full well the Mexican government, representing a proud, nationalistic people, always considered Texas as their own despite their loss at the Battle of San Jacinto in 1836.

As you recall it was at San Jacinto that Sam Houston and his small army defeated the much larger Mexican infantry, captured the president and general, Antonio López de Santa Anna, and held him in chains for two months. The Texans finally persuaded Santa Anna to sign the Treaty of Velasco which granted Texas her independence and Santa Anna his freedom. The Mexican government, quite predictably, called this tactic patently illegal and refused to recognize the legitimacy of the treaty. The Mexican authorities claimed that Santa Anna, while being held captive, was coerced into signing the pact as a stipulation for his release. In this context, therefore, they considered the treaty and the so-called independence a sham.

With the Mexican minister abandoning his post and the United States about to "steal" Texas, diplomatic relations between the two countries was effectively severed and the likelihood of war were glaringly predicted in the national press. To compound the sense of an impending crisis, since early spring thousands of Mexican troops were seen setting up gun batteries along the Mexican edge of the Rio Grande near Matamoros. Well aware of the growing presence of Mexican troops, officials in Texas began to be concerned about the safety of their people.

Not only was Polk facing imminent hostilities with Mexico, but negotiations with the British over settling the border dispute in the Oregon territory were also teetering menacingly towards a conflict. Two schools of thought now circulated the political landscape over what to do about the region, both diametrically opposed and hotly contested. Should the United States take a protracted approach towards Oregon by slowly occupying the territory and at some future date peacefully addressing the annexation question? The opposing view and the more aggressive position called for an immediate confrontation with Britain now rather than later. Proponents of the first alternative wanted to handle the situation peacefully; the other side feared that eventually clashes between the British and American inhabitants during this period would lead to violence and bloodshed anyway. The time for action was now before this happened. Calhoun, on the other hand, preferred to wait. "There is only one means by which it can be done," he said, "but that, fortunately, is the most powerful of all—time. All we want to effect our object in this case, is a wise and masterly inactivity."

Jointly occupied by both Great Britain and the United States since the Convention of 1818, the area consisted of present-day Washington, Oregon, including Vancouver Island, Idaho, and parts of Montana and Wyoming. British fur traders were mostly confined to the north of the Columbia River, American pioneers to the south. The thousands of pioneers who had settled in this wilderness had formed their own local governments and were now seeking security for their own democratic processes. But first the on-going dispute over the boundary between the United States and the British colony of Canada had to be settled.

Evidently the two countries failed to accurately locate the boundary in a 1793 treaty and after years of bickering the two sides finally decided to make the correction. They met again in 1818 and this time agreed upon 49°, the line previously established for the northern boundary of the Louisiana Purchase which ran from Minnesota west to the Rocky Mountains. Furthermore, while negotiations were being conducted during the final days of the Tyler administration, an agreement was also reached to continue this long-established line of 49° all the way to the Pacific.

But now that was a problem. Polk's campaign promise to the northerners in 1844 committed him to establish a new line farther north, one designated at 54° 40', the southern border of present-day Alaska. During the course of the new negotiations Polk realized this pledge was totally unrealistic. Consequently, despite the political repercussions sure to follow, a concession was offered to the British by U.S. envoy Louis McLane, the former Treasury secretary in the Jackson administration, that instead of insisting on the 54° 40' line, Polk would now accept the originally established line of 49°. The only impediment remaining now was the disposition of Vancouver Island. But, learning that several of the comments made in his inauguration address upset the British, Polk, in order to soothe their ruffled sensitivities, ordered McLane to modify the U.S. position once again by also conceding Vancouver Island.

To the utter amazement of everyone concerned, the British Minister to Washington, when informed of the U.S. proposal by Secretary of State James Buchanan, rejected the offer. When the shocking report of the minister's refusal reached the British authorities in London they immediately renounced his decision and sought to reopen the negotiations fully prepared to accept Polk's offer. But it was too late.

Following the British minister's rejection of his offer, Polk met with his Cabinet on August 26, 1845. At this meeting the president, still infuriated over the snub of his liberal proposal, insisted that since no counteroffer was presented from the British he was withdrawing his concession and reverting to his original policy. In this tone, he directed Buchanan to "assert and enforce our right to the whole Oregon territory from the 49° to 54° 40' north latitude"

To further emphasize his position, in his first annual message to Congress in December, Polk submitted a request for the termination of the 27-year-old agreement with Britain on the joint occupation of the Oregon Territory, and asked Congress to extend the protection of United States laws to the Americans residing there. In his message Polk said, "Oregon is part of the North American continent, to which, it is confidently affirmed, the title of the United States is the best now in existence.... The British proposition of compromise ... can never for a moment be entertained by the United States." Polk's bold stance was somewhat bolstered by Jackson's advice to stand firm with Britain: "No temporizing with Britain now.... England with all her boast dare not go to war."

In addition to the annexation of Texas and for acquiring the Oregon Territory from the British, in the course of his message Polk also outlined the other initiatives he would pursue during his only term as president. Since Van Buren's sub-treasuries died a quick death during Tyler's Whig administration, he was determined to revive the law in order to keep the people's money out of the state banks and safe in the security of federal vaults.

And on the subject of tariffs, Polk believed protection was of secondary consideration, one incidental to the principal goal of providing financial income for the government to operate. In his words, "The largest portion of our people are agriculturists. Others are employed in manufactures, commerce, navigation, and the mechanic arts. They are all engaged in their respective pursuits and their joint labors constitute the national or home industry. To tax one branch of this home industry for the benefit of another would be unjust. No one of these interests can rightfully claim an advantage over the others, or to be enriched by impoverishing the others. All are equally entitled to the fostering care and protection of the Government." Although it took years in coming, these were sweet words to southern ears. Both of these initiatives would be taken up in the coming spring and summer.

On December 29, 1845, the Texas statehood question was finally settled. The Twenty-ninth Congress formally accepted Texas into the Union as the twenty-eighth state and, as history would dictate, the fifteenth and last slave state admitted to the southern fraternity. Although the antislavery contingent in Congress could have defeated the annexation treaty, Polk's promise of the

Oregon territory was still enough to guarantee their acquiescence. Polk now set his sights on California.

With statehood for Texas approved a new expansionism philosophy came to the forefront, a doctrine that would further influence Polk's political agenda. Without firing a shot, only a stroke of a pen, thousands of square miles of western territory were added to the United States. As a result, this taste of expansionism unleashed a new and highly vociferous wave of enthusiasm across the country to extend American democracy even farther. In Washington it focused Polk's expansionist gaze not only to the Mexican provinces of California and New Mexico, but also toward Mexico herself. Americans were on the move, said the expansionists, looking to strike out on their own, to carve out their own future in new frontiers just waiting for them and the thousands to follow. One Democratic congressman explained it this way. In his opinion, God had not "designed that the original States should be the only abode of liberty on earth. On the contrary, He only designed them as the great center from which civilization, religion, and liberty should radiate and radiate until the whole continent shall bask in their blessing."

This new doctrine was called Manifest Destiny, a term coined by O'Sullivan in 1845 to gain additional public and political support for the expansionist movement. Rallying to this latest surge of interest on the heels of the annexation of Texas and the possible settlement of the Oregon issue, O'Sullivan exclaimed, "Yes, more, more, more...! till the whole boundless continent is ours."

The new ideology carried expansionism to yet another level. Manifest Destiny put forth the notion that the U.S. was not merely endowed with the absolute right to expand. She was also divinely ordained to extend her borders and her ideals of freedom and prosperity from coast to coast and even to the far reaches of the continent. Furthermore, the U.S. was obligated to open her system to all wanting to share in her freedoms. O'Sullivan expressed his vision of Manifest Destiny as "a right such as that of the tree to the space of air and earth suitable for the full expansion of its principle and destiny of growth" and "of the stream to the channel required for the still accumulating volume of its flow." Indeed, some followers were so obsessed with the concept of Manifest Destiny and their divine right to extend U.S. borders to other lands that they predicted it would happen whether the Spanish inhabitants or for that matter, the Indians, the Canadians, or the Mexicans wanted it or not.

Indeed, this was a far cry from the Jefferson years when many in the government were opposed to further statehood. Additional states, they argued, would be too remote, their seats of government too far from Washington for the proper conduct of business. Instead, the far western lands would be better served as independent countries.

But the proponents of Manifest Destiny thought Jefferson's vision in 1801, that there would be "room enough for our descendants to the thousandth and ten thousandth generation" in an America extending only to the Mississippi, was now quite unrealistic as the country slowly edged towards the mid-century mark. Despite the dangers, hardships, and risks to their lives from diseases and Indian attacks, under this new doctrine Americans were motivated more than ever to migrate to the Far West.

Manifest Destiny, however, in spite of all the patriotic rhetoric and flag-waving, was not entirely accepted by either section. A huge degree of resistance came from the North, primarily from the fear of extending slavery into these very territories. In the South the apprehension came from introducing the inferior mixed-race people of Mexico into white southern society, and yet from others it was still the notion that the country would be too large to govern efficiently if allowed to expand. Critics, such as Horace Greeley, the editor of the *New York Tribune*, expounded his own ideology that the country would be better served if it took care of its own problems first when he wrote, "A nation cannot simultaneously devote its energies to the absorption of others' territories and the improvement of its own."

Although it was principally a Democratic initiative, Whigs were not generally opposed to Manifest Destiny and its basic concept of extending American democracy to others, but were adamantly against expansion, in any form, if it was to be accomplished by force. The coercion of others to satisfy one's self-interests alarmed the Whigs immensely and had the effect of sharply delineating party lines not only at the national level but also in state legislatures. This in turn greatly reinforced party loyalty among the rank and file, but in the eyes of the Whig Party, Polk's new expansionist agenda towards the Mexican provinces in the Far West had all the hallmarks of what they opposed.

As the Texas annexation issue was playing itself out in Washington, Mexico continued to move its troops northward. With thousands of soldiers and artillery assembling along the Rio Grande, the Texas government hastily submitted an urgent request to Washington for military protection largely from fears of possible Mexican incursions from Matamoros. From that point on the expansionist inclinations within the administration kicked into high gear and as a result, the Mexican situation dominated Polk's entire term in office.

In response to the appeal President Polk immediately issued orders to Gen. Zachary Taylor at Fort Jesup, Louisiana, to assemble 2,000 troops and to stand by for further instructions. Secretary of War William L. Marcy sent the orders on May 28, 1845, and specifically told the general that once the Texans accepted annexation they would be "entitled from this government to defense and protection from foreign invasion and Indian incursons [*sic*]" and that his troops should be "placed and kept in readiness to perform this duty." The army, however, was not to set foot in Texas until Taylor received word that the Texans had accepted annexation.

A 60-year-old veteran of the War of 1812 as well as the Black Hawk and

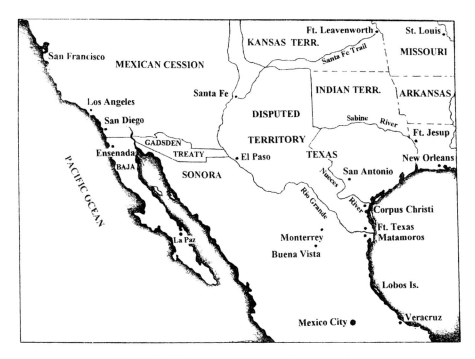

The United States and Mexico (1848–1854).

Seminole wars, Taylor was born in Virginia and raised on his father's large plantation in Kentucky. As the third son in a family of six boys and three girls, growing up in the wild frontier provided Taylor little in the way of formal education except for occasional studies under local tutors. Captivated by his father's stories and heroic tales of the American Revolution, the young lad was drawn into a life in the military. Now, after nearly forty years in the army, he was called "Old Zack" by his admiring troops. His weathered expression and heavily creased features were a badge of honor and a testament to his many years of enduring the hardships of frontier life and fighting Indians for the military. Other than his love for the army, Old Zack was a farmer at heart. Like his father before him, Taylor relished the pleasures of a planter's life. Indeed, he owned two plantations in the South, one in Mississippi and the other in Louisiana, and a number of slaves to work the fields. Despite his years of military service, however, Taylor was relatively unknown to the Washington bureaucracy, as were his political ambitions. And to Polk, these factors weighed significantly toward Taylor's being selected for this important assignment at the Mexican border.

Responding to news of imminent Texas annexation, in mid–June of 1845, Taylor's army departed Fort Jesup, delivered by several transports down the Sabine River to New Orleans. After conferring with other government officials there, and satisfied that the Texas Congress had indeed assured her statehood, Taylor promptly ordered his two infantry regiments to sail to Corpus Christi, a small Mexican town on the southern side of the Nueces River. A third regiment of 300 dragoons (mounted infantrymen formed as a cavalry) was also dispatched to Corpus Christi, traveling overland via San Antonio. By the end of August, Taylor had his entire command in place inside the disputed territory, the area between the Nueces River and the Rio Grande. Camped roughly 150 miles north of the Rio Grande, the recognized American border, Taylor was well aware of the implications his invasion would have on the Mexican government and the risks he faced from Mexican lancers that would assuredly be sent out to intercept him.

While Taylor's army began setting up camp in August, a relative calm once again prevailed in Washington. With cooler heads also evident in Mexico City, an offer was made to reestablish ties with the United States government, a move immediately seized upon by Polk as an excellent opportunity to play his expansionist trump card. To take advantage of Mexico's bid for diplomatic relations, Polk recommended that Congress appropriate a cash payment, as high as $40 million, for the purchase of California and New Mexico. In addition to selling the land the Mexican government would also have to agree to the Rio Grande border which, under this agreement, would extend westward straight to the Pacific. Polk was now exercising his expansionist agenda with fervor, pushing the Mexican government even harder to give up California, a territory he wanted very badly before, he feared, it was taken by the English Crown. With little debate, Congress quickly agreed.

To negotiate this deal on behalf of the United States, in November, Polk selected John Slidell as his envoy. A New Yorker by birth, he was a man of limitless ambition surpassed perhaps by his enormous ego, a craving he seemingly never quite satisfied. In the years ahead he would become an adopted southerner and take on strong Confederate allegiances. In fact, as the Confederate commissioner to France, he would gain a bit of notoriety for his role in the Trent Affair scandal in November of 1861. Also an ardent expansionist himself, Slidell was soon dispatched to Mexico City arriving via Veracruz on December 6.

Slidell was well aware that in 1840 Mexico had been ordered by a commission to pay millions of dollars to American citizens to settle damage claims from years of revolution. He also knew the government was unable to pay this debt because the Mexican treasury went bankrupt four years later. Using this knowledge as a bargaining chip, Slidell's instructions were to pick up the tab for these damage claims, approximately $3 million, if Mexico agreed to recognize the Rio Grande border. Employing a second ploy, Slidell also planned to offer an additional $5 million if Mexico agreed to relinquish New Mexico. And to sweeten the pot even more, if Mexico agreed to extend the boundary to include San Francisco Bay, an additional $20 million would be provided or even $25 million for all of California.

Slidell's mission, however, could not have come at a worse time. The Mexican government was going through a crisis not only with powerful political interest groups but also with a maverick portion of the Mexican army. Extremely powerful and fanatical factions, those who refused to accept the fact that Texas had won its independence from Mexico, adamantly opposed the U.S. annexation of Texas and, for that matter, any government dialogue with the United States. They angrily denounced the Herrera government and protested any further dealings with the United States over what they perceived as their territory. At the same time, in Mexico City, Gen. Mariano Paredes and a large body of loyal troops were creating further unrest over the government's handling of the Texas debacle and saw this incident as an excellent opportunity to challenge the power of the Herrera government. In this context, when Slidell arrived in Mexico City representing the U.S., he was roundly harassed by the Mexican officials who challenged his credentials and refused to recognize his authority. Unable to carry out his mission, Slidell was ordered to leave Mexico City and to wait in Veracruz for further instructions from Washington.

On January 12, 1846, Polk received the news of Slidell's treatment at the hands of the Mexican government and its refusal to consider his proposal. Outraged over this lack of civility and good faith, the next day Polk issued new orders to General Taylor, through Secretary of War Marcy, designed to demonstrate the seriousness of American resolve. The new directive instructed Taylor to advance his army southward from Corpus Christi to the banks of the Rio Grande. In addition, Taylor was told, "It is not designed, in our present relations with Mexico, that you should treat her as an enemy; but should she assume that character by a declaration of war, or any open act of hostility toward us, you will not act merely on the defensive, if your relative means enable you to act otherwise...."

Eager for action after nearly seven months of waiting, in March Taylor's army broke camp and filed out of Corpus Christi. Now reinforced to six regiments, the nearly 3,600 troops on this expedition consisted mostly of regulars who were tough and well disciplined, a character trait instinctively gained over years of fighting hostile Plains Indians.

The 150 mile trek was a grueling measure of stamina and fortitude for Taylor and his army. Plodding southward for days in the blistering heat, the men somehow endured through the many hardships. Going without water, at times for days on end, the dehydrated and scorched army finally arrived near the Rio Grande on March 24 and shortly thereafter marched downriver opposite the Mexican town of Matamoros. Once encamped, Taylor unlimbered a light artillery battery that clearly threatened the peace of the city and the Mexican army camp located just across the river. A ramshackle defensive fortification was also erected called Fort Texas. Here with the Rio Grande separating them, both armies postured in a show of force.

The Mexicans deeply resented the presence of U.S. troops at the Rio Grande. It reflected a blatant demonstration of American arrogance, an arrogance that belittled the modest might of a poorer nation. Their pride, their honor, and their esteem were profoundly offended and for this reason the culpable invaders had to be repulsed at any cost.

In the last week of April the Mexicans made the first move when they ordered some 1,600 cavalrymen across the Rio Grande a few miles from Taylor's camp at Fort Texas. Receiving reports of the Mexican incursion, Taylor dispatched a reconnaissance force of 63 dragoons under Capt. Seth B. Thornton to the vicinity to investigate. In a surprise attack the following day, the dragoons were surrounded and captured after a brief firefight in which 16 Americans were killed or wounded.

To the War Department Taylor immediately reported, "Hostilities may now be considered as commenced." In the Mexican camp meanwhile, General Mariano Arista was reported to have gleefully remarked, "I had the pleasure of being the first to start the war."

It should be noted here that many historians believe this one relatively minor attack on Thornton's troops, in itself, was not the sole cause of the war, but was merely the immediate catalyst that set if off. Also to be considered, they opined, was the fact that many Americans, particularly those living in the southern states, harbored an extreme hatred towards Mexico. This was particularly true for those who remembered the Alamo and the merciless slaughter of its entire garrison by General Antonio López de Santa Anna's troops, the senseless massacre of over 300 Texans at Goliad only weeks later, and the wanton murder of scores of Texas prisoners in 1842. By the same token, many Mexicans were hostile to America and its citizens, a resentment created by the death and destruction from American's aggressive and unrelenting quest for Mexican land since 1836. In any event, the combination of several factors, including mutual animosity, political instability, unending border clashes, the annexation of Texas, and the goals of Manifest Destiny, had all contributed to this bad blood and to the resultant hostilities.

Word of the Mexican invasion, the attack on Captain Thornton's men, and the 16 American casualties reached the White House on the evening of May 9, 1846. The president immediately called in his Cabinet to discuss the shocking news. The Cabinet, which previously displayed some hesitation over declaring war with Mexico, was now unanimously in favor of announcing a state of hostilities.

In a message to Congress two days later, Polk did not hesitate to show where the blame belonged when he asked Congress to declare war. Mexico, he said, "has passed the boundary of the United States, has invaded our territory and shed American blood upon American soil."

In Congress, however, there were those who were not so convinced. To be sure, the expansionists were quite pleased with these recent events, but the opponents of a war, a small group of both Whigs and Democrats alike, were unhappy with the way Polk's bill was worded. They vehemently opposed Polk's blaming of Mexico for creating this crisis when, they argued, the attack occurred not in the U.S. but in the unresolved disputed territory, and what's more, Taylor's not so subtle actions were quite aggressive in themselves and more than likely could have provoked the incident. Even Lincoln, a freshman congressman from Illinois, voiced opposition to Polk's rationale for war. In fact he called for a "spot resolution," a demand for Polk to identify the exact spot where American blood was shed. Back home, however, since Illinoisans supported Polk and his move to the Rio Grande, Lincoln was severely criticized by his constituents over his demands with one article referring to Lincoln as the "Benedict Arnold of our district."

Since the Democratic leadership in the House wanted to act on Polk's declaration of war bill without delay, rules were established that severely limited the time for debate. The only discourse occurred when the Whigs, through manipulation of parliamentary rules, were able to criticize this Democratic ploy to ram the bill through. In the Senate as well, the Democrats set aside only one day for debate. And again it fell upon the Whigs to object to the hostile acts of both Polk and Taylor, acts they insisted, that only inflamed the circumstances and incited the attack. Notwithstanding these opposing views, Polk's recommendation to declare war was overwhelmingly passed by both the House and the Senate.

At first blush, the margin of victory in the congressional vote was somewhat misleading. Many who voted for the bill did so reluctantly, still morally opposed to the wording, "Whereas, by the act of the Republic of Mexico, a state of war exists between the United States and that Republic," while others disagreed with Polk's provocative orders to Taylor. And there were those, primarily Whigs, who abstained entirely, disagreeing with the shameless way the proceedings were being conducted, refusing to lend legitimacy to Polk's misrepresentation of the facts as they understood them. Northerners, both Whigs and Democrats in Congress, especially New Englanders, firmly believed Polk's motives for the war were part of a much broader southern scheme, a part of what they called the slave-power conspiracy. Under the guise of expansionism, they claimed, the Polk administration was specifically intending to expand slavery into the territories, on land Polk was seeking to steal from Mexico. But despite one's objections on going to war or the bitterness over the manner in which the war was invoked, Congress knew this was a time for solidarity and support for the fighting men in the American army. Consequently, when the congressional balloting concluded on May 13, 1846, war was declared against Mexico. And with the full consent of Congress $10 million was appropriated as was authorization to recruit up to 50,000 volunteers.

As the conflict in Mexico began to escalate, Polk found himself in somewhat of a quandary over the Oregon border dispute. His reneging on the generous concessions inflamed the Brits, whose saber-rattling was becoming noticeably more hostile. Not eager to engage in a fight with Great Britain at the same time he was waging a war with Mexico, he felt the time had come to resolve this matter once and for all. Therefore, Polk notified the British authorities that he was inclined to resume negotiations and that he would agree to return to his original terms. The boundary between the United States and Canada would be established at 49° (the northern border of present-day Washington) and Vancouver Island would be granted to the British. The Oregon Treaty, signed on June 15, 1846, secured for the U.S. land now occupied by Oregon, Washington and parts of Idaho, Montana, and Wyoming. More importantly, it also averted the unwelcome prospect of a war with Britain. Three days later the Senate agreed to ratify the treaty.

The Senate vote, although significant by averting two concurrent wars, was also historic in one other respect. The northern Democrats had supported Polk in everything he asked for in his quest to annex the slave state of Texas. At the same time they believed he would show the same tireless energy in obtaining all of the free territory in Oregon that they wanted and that he had campaigned for. But, the northern Democrats complained, when the Oregon issue came to the table, Polk suddenly backed away from his campaign promise of "Fifty-four Forty or Fight" and had settled for much less. The northern Democrats, therefore, bitter over Polk's perceived betrayal, severed their party loyalty and rebelled against the president. Twelve of them voted against the treaty while only three voted to approve. The treaty was ratified only because every Senate Whig voted for it.

More revealing, perhaps, was that for the first time, northern Democrats in the Senate openly and defiantly split with the president, a move that portended a new and dramatic shift in the mood of the country. Unwittingly, it was also a preview to a more volatile phase of sectional conflicts looming just over the horizon.

By the fall of 1846 the war with Mexico had developed into a full blown conflict as troops began to mobilize on several different fronts. In addition to Taylor's drive into northern Mexico, the American battle lines were also drawn across the Mexican provinces west of the Mississippi.

Along this front Col. Stephen W. Kearny was directed to lead 1,600 Missourians out of Fort Leavenworth, a major army post in the Kansas Territory. Following a march down the Santa Fe Trail, he was to challenge Mexican forces in New Mexico.

Mostly desolate and dry, New Mexico was considered for years as too remote, too neglected, and too inhospitable by the United States to be taken seriously. Similarly, its relative isolation from Mexico City was also quite significant and did much to explain the quasi-independence of New Mexico, where at times the law was something one interpreted for one. But times had changed, especially for those with expansionist inclinations who now saw New Mexico in a different light.

Kearny entered Santa Fe unopposed on August 18, established an occupational government, and ultimately advanced his men to San Diego, California, where he assisted U.S. naval forces in the occupation of Los Angeles.

Polk's interest in the Mexican province of California was particularly acute and, to some of his critics, the real gleam in his eye. The province was sparsely populated in 1846 with an estimated 25,000 inhabitants. Of that number less than half were white settlers, the rest being Mexicans, Indians, and native-born Californians called Californios, who were in every other respect Mexican.

California, like New Mexico, was largely a desolate and lawless region. Its government was managed superficially by a civil governor residing in its capital, Los Angeles, or in the Spanish vernacular, Ciudad de Los Angeles. As a result of these inherent weaknesses, California was a frequent victim of violent revolutionary forces. But despite these and many other detractions, followers of Manifest Destiny had long assumed California would at some point join the Union under peaceful conditions as Texas had done in 1845. Except these were volatile times and evolving events were rapidly altering that prospect.

These wide-ranging movements of U.S. forces reflected the government's initial strategy in dealing with her southern neighbor. That strategy, simply stated, was to equip a sufficient number of troops to restrain the Mexican army and to occupy only the northern provinces. Exposed to this level of military duress, Polk predicted, would soon force the Mexican government to the bargaining table where it would readily accept a land settlement consistent with his expansionist demands.

Despite Polk's assurances of a quick victory, however, toward the end of 1846 public support for the war was beginning to wane. Reports of American brutality against Mexican civilians, desecration of their Catholic churches by American troops, and disease ridden conditions for our boys were causing much consternation in the press. In the White House, it was also becoming apparent to Polk and to his Cabinet that the progress of the war was not living up to their expectations as well. Polk wanted to fight a brief war, a war that would bring Mexico quickly to her knees begging for a negotiated peace. And during these negotiations California and New Mexico would be put on the table, and perhaps even more, as a prerequisite for a peaceful settlement. The Mexicans, he now assessed, were a proud and determined people and not about to concede easily. Therefore a different strategy had to be employed to put this matter to rest because the current program of a limited war in the northern provinces wasn't working as planned. The problem, the administration concluded, was that the army was only hitting Mexico's extremities, not her soul. As a consequence, following weeks of deliberations, Polk recommended a concentrated drive on the very heart of Mexico itself—Mexico City. But there was one problem: who would lead the way?

Following numerous discussions with his Cabinet and with close advisors from the Congress over this very question, only two viable candidates stood out from all the rest, Zachary Taylor and Polk's military advisor and general-in-chief, Winfield Scott. And that's where Polk was in a bind. It seems both of these generals were members of the opposing political party and both were gaining support for political office whether they wanted it or not. There were other generals considered, to be sure, but they were either too old, lacked the background and experience for this campaign, their personalities made them unsuitable to work with, or they were needed somewhere else. In the end, Polk rejected them all.

Perhaps closer to the truth was that having committed himself to only one term, the president, a loyal and incorrigible Democrat, reckoned that the Whig Party would be significantly strengthened by Taylor's sudden rise in stature and would therefore be a potential threat in the next presidential election. It seems Taylor's popularity was soaring higher than ever. In fact, such was the elation and pride over Taylor's victory at Monterrey in September that he was now approaching the level of a national hero and was even mentioned as a possible presidential candidate. "Taylor for President" banners were now being seen everywhere while political rhetoric castigated both Polk and his general-in-chief for their escalation of the conflict.

In contrast, although Scott was Polk's military advisor and a national hero from his exploits in the War of 1812, Polk's affection for the general was somewhat strained. Polk always felt that Scott was an overbearing egotist. And by virtue of his military stature, the general always tried to impress on Polk that he was the wiser of the two, that he was the one in control of the situation and the person with all the answers. Also, as it was with Taylor, Polk's hesitation was also based to a large degree on his suspicions of Scott's presidential ambitions.

Finally persuaded that his general-in-chief was not a serious political threat and the right man for the job, the choice was made. Accordingly, on November 19, 1846, Polk reluctantly selected Scott as the commander to lead U.S. forces into Mexico City.

Nevertheless, President Polk remained quite apprehensive over Taylor's rising political appeal and with growing concern was keenly following the movement with interest.

10

Territorial Sectionalism (1846 to 1847)

Shortly after the U.S. declared war with Mexico, a new round of political bickering surfaced almost immediately between the northern and southern sections of the country. Undeniably, in those chaotic antebellum years regional conflicts were hardly anything new. To be sure, most of these earlier quarrels derived from a long and painful history of social, economic, and cultural differences between the two sections. Differences such as slave labor versus wage labor, relative economic inequities of an agricultural society to a growing industrialized one, opposing perceptions over policies on protective tariffs, states' rights, abolitionism, nullification, banking laws, and over numerous other disparities, all interrelated and all derived from conflicting values and ideology.

While slavery was arguably the common thread throughout the history of these sectional conflicts, now a more divisive and contemptuous element, namely the right to extend slavery into any newly acquired territory, was also added to the mix. It was the most disruptive issue in the fifteen years leading up to the Civil War; it was also the issue that drove the deepest wedge between the North and the South since it guaranteed the permanency of slavery and threatened to drastically upset the long cherished political power balance in favor of the slave states. The focus in the North now began to shift away from emancipation of the southern slaves to a new free-soil movement designed to keep slavery out of the territories. And as a result, the split between the two political rivals widened even more and triggered the emergence of a political debate I call territorial sectionalism.

With the ink on the congressional declaration of war barely dry and the acquisition of new territory hardly discerned, the battle for its spoils was already forming in the back rooms of Congress. Faced with the prospect of sharing huge tracts of new federal land and the implications of that eventuality, sectional discord took on a whole new dimension with the federal government now, and for the first time, becoming a central player in the slavery question.

Considering all the potential Mexican territory at stake, sectional conflicts were ratcheted up into a vicious and ignoble political struggle, both sides acting like voracious family members bickering over a potential inheritance from a dying relative's will.

On one hand, although many southern politicians could support territorial expansion for political gains, they preferred not to acquire this new land because, in their opinion, it was unsuitable for profitable cultivation and therefore unsuitable for slavery. Furthermore, Mexican laws already prohibited slavery in their provinces as did the laws of Mother Nature. Even Calhoun, who had returned to the Senate following Polk's election, thought slavery would never succeed in the harsh conditions of the Mexican territories. Calhoun, for his part, disapproved of acquiring all this Mexican territory, concerned over the impact it would have on the South. "Mexico is to us the forbidden fruit," he said, "the penalty of eating it [is] to subject our institutions to political death."

However, the proponents of expansionism from both sections, those faithfully committed to the doctrine of Manifest Destiny, salivated over the opportunities and advantages the country would inherit by acquiring the Mexican territories.

Within that group were the fanatical southern expansionists who saw the possible acquisition of new territory as an ideal chance for them to fulfill their political, economic, and social goals. Simply put, they would populate the new lands with southern families and their slaves, intensify their cash crop economy, and augment their existing slave society financially, culturally, and politically. In time they would gain a number of statehoods and increase their congressional representation, which in turn would enhance their political power in Washington and insure the survival of their slave society and their way of life. This position was eloquently revealed when a Georgia newspaper printed that bringing slavery into the territories would "secure to the South the balance of power in the Confederacy, and, for all coming time ... give her the control in the operation of the Government."

Obviously, in the North the so-called free-soilers were enraged over this prospect and considered the southern rhetoric highly inflammatory. Although slavery was always at the root of most sectional conflicts, just the prospect of forced servitude migrating into the territories hit a raw nerve in the North and added a whole new meaning to their argument. Northerners believed that slavery was such an intolerable moral evil that it could not be allowed to expand and thus perpetuate itself in the process. And most important to the political savvy in Washington, the extension of slavery would significantly increase the political power of the South in the national political arena, a political arrogance the North was determined to resist at all costs. Furthermore, the North believed its economic growth depended a great deal on its own continued expansion into the new territories. If planters and their slaves were allowed to settle there, the farmers from the North, who adamantly opposed competing against slave labor, would not. Moreover, and perhaps just as significant, the goals of the southern expansionists fueled even more northern condemnation of the Mexican War. Northerners interpreted these goals as part of a slave-power conspiracy designed by Polk, along with southern planters and political leaders, to acquire more territory not only to extend the institution of slavery but also to take control of the central government at the expense of their personal and civil liberties. Therefore, by challenging this so-called slave power and by preventing the extension of slavery the North ensured its own economic and political growth and at the same time slavery would be confined within its present borders where it belonged.

In reply to his critics Polk defended his war policy and further explained that any terms for peace would naturally include Mexican territory but only as a means to "indemnify our claimants on Mexico and to defray the expenses of the war."

One of the administration's supporters, John L. O'Sullivan, although a principal proponent of territorial expansion, was convinced the war was not being waged to conquer Mexican land and attempted to discount the opposing rhetoric. In his *New York Morning News* he wrote, "It by no means follows when we invade our enemy's country that we are bound or intend to keep it; nor have we seen even the slightest evidence of any intention on the part of the administration, to acquire by conquest and hold permanently by virtue of such conquest, a single foot of Mexican territory.... The attempt would be as monstrous as it would be new in our history and short-lived, indeed, would be the power and influence of those who should undertake it. They would be looked upon as the worst of traitors...."

In addition to the talk of war and its potential spoils, there were several other measures recommended by President Polk in his annual message that were approved. One of these bills was Polk's attempt to revive Van Buren's sub-treasuries system, a measure repealed during the Tyler years. Now called the Constitutional Treasury Act, the bill easily wound its way through the Democratic controlled Congress and became law in August of 1846. Under this law, all government funds would now be placed in federal vaults. Arguably Polk's greatest economic achievement of his presidency, the new treasury act was so successful it remained in force until 1913 when it was replaced by the Federal Reserve System.

A new tariff was also debated. Like most Democrats traditionally opposed to protective tariffs, Polk believed the levy of duties should be fair to all. At the urging of the president, therefore, Secretary Walker sought to lower the 1842 rates to a minimum on most domestically manufactured goods and essential items, a welcomed relief for the consumers, while at the same time increasing the rates on many materials imported by manufacturers. Obviously, this proposal brought on the wrath of the northern industrialist elites who lobbied strenuously to defeat Polk's lower tariff bill, even with attempts at bribery. Northern Democrats were also angry, particularly in Pennsylvania where party leaders had campaigned for Polk on a pledge that tariffs would not be reduced. But this time the western interests prevailed. The new tariff was calculated to stimulate more trade which, in turn, would add much needed revenue into the Treasury coffers. Also, with their growing number of farmlands, the West was willing to trade off a degree of protection for the chance to widen their foreign markets for selling surplus grain. Called the Walker Tariff of 1846, it was accepted by Congress in July and for the next fifteen years or so, despite the South's aversion to tariffs, the issue would remain somewhat dormant as more important events took over the political center ring.

Seeds of the new sectional conflict were sown two days before the end of the first congressional session. It was August 8, 1846, when President Polk introduced a unique $2 million appropriation bill. Also submitted at the same time was his recommendation to organize Oregon as a territory, a prerequisite for the settlers there to form a legitimate government. Still anticipating a quick end to the hostilities, he explained that the purpose of the funds was to support the negotiations with the Mexican government, an advance "earnest payment" in any future treaty by which the United States would not only acquire a peaceful solution of the war but acquire additional territory as well. The president had originally requested, rather haughtily, that his appropriations bill be debated and voted upon in executive session so as to keep his objectives secret. As expected, however, his desire to conceal his motives from the public was immediately rejected by the Senate Whigs. They were outraged that Polk was so blatantly conspiratorial and were also quick to point out that Polk's request finally exposed his true intent and substantiated what they knew all along. They were now convinced that Polk was pursuing a war with Mexico not simply over a border dispute but as a pretext for gaining more territory to widen the practice of slavery, particularly California and New Mexico. The appropriations, the Whigs suspected, were to bribe Mexican officials into an agreement to end the war for that purpose.

Acquiescing to Whig demands for disclosure, in the oppressive heat of that August day, debate began on Polk's appropriations bill. Still furious over Polk's boldness, northern Whigs in the House quickly assailed the Democratic president's political motives for the war and angrily challenged their Democratic colleagues to amend the bill so as to forbid slavery in any territory that might be gained from Mexico.

Out of the chaos of this tumultuous debate, a first-term and relatively obscure Democrat did just that. From Pennsylvania, David Wilmot, heretofore a staunch party supporter, was recognized by the chair and fired the first volley from the recently formed free-soil faction. Wilmot was one of many northern Democrats who were fearful that backing Polk's bill would stigmatize them as acquiescing to a southern-inspired scheme to extend slavery. In response to these northern fears of a slave-power conspiracy and his belief that Congress did in fact have the power to regulate slavery by virtue of the Ordinance of 1787, Wilmot offered an amendment to the appropriations bill, called the Wilmot Proviso. His amendment that hot August night not only stunned the congressional body, but would also permanently alter the way the country dealt with the question of extending slavery outside of its present borders.

The Wilmot Proviso provided "that, as an express and fundamental condition to the acquisition of any territory from the Republic of Mexico ... neither slavery or involuntary servitude shall ever exist in any part of said territory."

As mentioned earlier, there were many opposing issues in the past that contributed to frequent North-South conflicts but the animosity between the sections was demonstrated most dramatically and more disruptively in a political sense with the Wilmot Proviso. Wilmot brought to the table an issue that provoked many unanswered questions over the extent of constitutional powers, the future of slavery, and sectional political domination. The ramifications of its intent set off a firestorm of bitter debate, emotional confrontation, and political strife that threatened to undermine the country.

Why would a young first-term Democrat suggest such a measure in clear opposition to his president and his party? Wilmot explained his motives this way: "The negro race already occupy enough of this fair continent ... I would preserve for free white labor a fair country ... where the sons of toil, of my own race and own color, can live without the disgrace which association with negro slavery brings upon free labor." Continuing with his explanation against extending slavery to the Mexican territories, Wilmot said, "God forbid that we should be the means of planting this institution upon it."

But evidently, besides the sincerity of his free-soil views, Wilmot was also part of a growing group of northern Democrats sending a message to Polk that they were fed up with the southern domination of their party. They still harbored bitterness over the refusal of the southern wing of the Democratic Party to endorse Martin Van Buren for the presidency in 1844. This flagrant denial, the northern Democrats asserted, was a clear move to disrupt the legitimacy of the nominating process and amounted to nothing less than another exercise in slave power. A further example of Polk's alienation of his northern constituents was his acquiescence to Britain in the Oregon border dispute. Polk knew the northerners wanted all of Oregon right up to the Alaskan border and they felt betrayed by Polk's disregard for their position. Northern manufacturers were also furious when Polk pushed through the Walker tariff bill, a measure submitted by Treasury Secretary Robert J. Walker in July that reduced domestic tariffs. Again, although its success was proven not only when it provided much needed revenue to the U.S. Treasury, stimulated trade, and improved relations with Britain that had degraded since the Oregon border dispute, it was a measure sternly opposed by northerners and narrowly passed by southern votes. These were some of the many grievances which exacerbated sectional tensions within the party and prompted one northern Democrat to exclaim, "The administration is Southern, Southern, Southern...! Since the South have fixed boundaries for free territories, let the North fix boundaries for slave territories."

Aware of the growing anxiety in Congress and the divisive tone of the arguments over territorial and slavery expansion, the *Boston Whig* recognized the signs of a changing political alignment. "As if by magic," they observed, "it brought to a head the great question which is to divide the American people."

In the North the political ramifications of the proviso shifted the loyalties of both opposing parties so that in matters relating to the spread of slavery, they were now united. The northern Democrats and the northern Whigs, the free-soilers, wholeheartedly supported the proviso as an instrument to keep the territories free of the peculiar institution.

In stark contrast, however, southerners of both parties vigorously opposed the blatant discrimination of the Wilmot Proviso. They resented the proviso mostly because it implied that they were inferior, not equal to the northerners and therefore not permitted to take their property into the new territories. It was a denial of their equal rights, they claimed, and an insult to the sacred honor of their citizens. On this issue both parties were united in their determination to defeat any attempt to impose the proviso on the southern people. Furthermore, the southerners argued, since the South was furnishing most of the fighting men in the Mexican campaigns and would suffer most of the casualties for this new land, southern families should be able to enjoy the benefits of their sacrifices by having the same rights afforded to everyone else.

In arguing against the Wilmot Proviso, James Hammond of South Carolina probably summed it up best in describing the expansionist rationale. He warned his southern brethren that by enacting the proviso, ten free states would eventually be admitted into the Union. And in Congress, the North would then "ride over us rough shod ... proclaim freedom or something equivalent to it to our slaves and reduce us to the condition of Hayti.... Our only safety is in equality of power. If we do not act now, we deliberately consign our children, not our posterity, but our children to the flames." Calls for secession were renewed as more and more southerners began to vent their pent-up anger.

In the White House, Polk called the proviso "a mischievous and foolish amendment. If persisted in it will be attended with terrible consequences to the country, and cannot fail to destroy the Democratic Party, if it does not ultimately threaten the Union itself. Slavery was one of the questions adjusted in the compromises of the Constitution. It has, and can have, no legitimate connection with the war with Mexico."

Following several hours of a carefully controlled debate, including a motion that failed to table the bill, Polk's appropriations bill with Wilmot's amendment attached, passed the House by a vote of 85 to 80. The most striking footnote to this vote was that it, with a few exceptions, reflected a North-South sectional bias in lieu of party-line discipline. Northern Whigs and northern Democrats voted for it, southern Whigs and southern Democrats voted against it.

Since the southerners were the majority section in the Senate, their administration-supported strategy on August 10, the last day before adjournment, was to offer a motion to strike the proviso from the House bill in the final hour of the congressional session and thereby force the House to accept the returned bill, sans the proviso, without time for further debate. The northern Whigs, on the other hand, countered this move with a filibuster. By implementing this legislative tactic, they hoped the delay would force a Senate vote on the original House version, with the proviso still included, before this session of Congress closed. However, the bill never reached a vote. It seems the clock on the House wall was set some eight to ten minutes faster than that in the Senate. Therefore, the House had already adjourned during the last moments of the prolonged filibuster and to the chagrin of the Whigs, had closed the congressional session. As a result, no action was taken on organizing Oregon and a disappointed president was denied his $2 million bargaining fund. And the question of territorial slavery remained just that—a question.

Party loyalty had always been an unwritten rule in Congress so it was particularly striking that again, as in the Oregon Treaty vote, congressional support for the Wilmot Proviso was not entirely along party lines but along sectional lines. Wilmot's amendment had now divided the Congress into two factions—northern free-soilers supporting the proviso against southern expansionists opposed to the proviso. The repercussions of a divided Congress would be felt over the years ahead as sectional conflicts over Manifest Destiny and the extension of slavery reshaped political ideology into national policy.

Within all the scandalous rhetoric swirling over Manifest Destiny and the spread of slavery, one dynamic of territorial sectionalism was abundantly clear. For both sections of the country, the real struggle at the root of this new conflict was the quest for political power, pure and simple, free states versus slave states, North against South, free-soilers against expansionists.

Shortly after the annexation of Texas in 1845, northern Whigs and Democrats alike feared the tenuous balance of political power in Washington was being threatened like never before. Over the years Congress had made a point of carefully maintaining this balance by admitting states into the Union in pairs—one free, one slave. This was true since 1816 and 1817 when Indiana and Mississippi joined the Union as the tenth free state and tenth slave state. Congress continued this practice for the next twenty years at which point the country was evenly divided at thirteen. But the harsh reality, the North complained, was that in just 1845 alone, the fourteenth and fifteenth slave states, Florida and Texas, were both admitted to the Union and tipped the power balance in favor of the South, a trend they were indeed alarmed over. And with the push for southern expansion into the Mexican territories coupled with the growing support for taking all of Mexico, northerners were poised to challenge any effort by the South to carry out their expansionist goals for more political power.

Many northerners considered these political maneuvers further evidence of the South's continuing efforts to carry out the slave-power conspiracy, to spread slavery and increase southern political influence in Washington. Power in the hands of the South, they claimed, was an abuse of power, while power in the hands of the North was the model of republicanism. Therefore the best way to prevent this shift in power was to simply deny southern access to the territories.

The Northern fear of slavepower was effectively reflected by Wilmot when he wrote, "So dangerous do I believe the spirit and demands of the Slave Power, so insufferable its arrogance, if I saw the way open to strike an effectual and decisive blow against its domination at this time, I would do so, even at the temporary loss of other principles."

While the North feared the Mexican territory could enhance southern political power, at the same time the South was growing extremely anxious over the increasing population of the North for the same reason. Immigrants, mostly Irish and German, were flooding the northeastern section of the country by the hundreds of thousands. The waves of newcomers continued unabated, flowing westward into the heartland and then to the Pacific. From their perspective, southerners feared that over time, as territorial governments formed, a large number of free states would be incorporated into the Union. This, they countered, would upset the balance of power in favor of the North and, quite conceivably, jeopardize the very existence of their unique way of life.

These two scenarios then, more land for the South, and more population growth in the North, were interpreted as the means for one side or the other to gain more political power and was the crux of the new sectional conflict.

As the New Year began President Polk gazed out across the frozen White House landscape and felt somewhat pleased that his first two years in office had been successful ones. In the Far Northwest a war with Britain was averted and thousands of square miles of new territory were now part of the United States. What remained was to get this new acquisition organized into the Oregon Territory so that when the local government expressed a desire, application for statehood could be considered. He was also quite pleased that Iowa, the fourteenth free state, was recently annexed in December. It was a move that put the North a bit closer to parity although not particularly helpful in reducing the ongoing sectional strife. In addition, in the Far West, New

Mexico was now under federal jurisdiction and with his behind-the-scenes efforts in California, Polk was certain she would follow as well. Also, south of the border, the war in Mexico was progressing quite well. General Taylor, whose soaring popularity had made him a potential presidential candidate, had recently captured Monterrey while the pompous general-in-chief, Winfield Scott, was preparing to launch an ambitious campaign to occupy Mexico City itself. Although most of his annual message to Congress in December of '46 attempted to explain the origins of the war, i.e., the Mexican incursion into American territory, the Whigs were not convinced. The opposition party insisted he was the real aggressor, a charge Polk abhorred. All in all, however, Polk was quite satisfied that his expansionist ambitions were indeed off to a very good start.

Still attempting to reach an agreement to end the standoff on the Mexican territories, one that both sides could agree upon, in January 1847, an earlier proposal to apportion the prospective territories was resurrected by Secretary of State Buchanan. This proposal, besides the Wilmot Proviso, represented the second of at least six attempts to find an amiable solution to this potential territorial problem. It was initially suggested by Rep. William W. Wick, an Indiana Democrat, during the debate over Wilmot's proviso last August. Wick reminded his colleagues that Congress already established a boundary line between free states and slave states in the Louisiana Purchase when it passed the Missouri Compromise of 1820. This line, Wick explained, was set at 36° 30'. Why not simply extend that line all the way to the Pacific? Although no action was taken at the time, Buchanan revisited Wick's boundary-extension idea with the thought of applying it in this situation. President Polk, as well as his Cabinet, was thoroughly briefed on this initiative and they fully agreed with the principle of this proposal and Buchanan's attempt to derail further sectional conflict. For 25 years, they opined, this demarcation line was accepted without question, without problems, and had kept the peace. Henceforth, under Buchanan's bill, any territory gained from the war with Mexico would be divided roughly into two halves at this line, free to the North, slave to the South.

Unfortunately, Buchanan's bill never came up for debate. Before he could act on his resolution Congress adjourned. Therefore, along with Wilmot's proviso, Buchanan's proposal to resolve the territorial issue was also put off for another day.

The following month, Polk's appropriation bill was brought to the House floor once again. Now increased from two to three million dollars, the measure also included the highly controversial Wilmot Proviso, added a second time with every affirmative vote coming from the North. Quite predictably, the bill easily passed the House thanks to the support of the northern vote, both Democrat and Whig alike.

Two weeks later the measure came before the Senate and was approved there as well, but again, not before southern votes had struck the proviso from the bill. The modified measure was returned to the House where it was accepted on March 3, the last day of the Twenty-ninth congressional session. The bill's acceptance in the House became possible this time, even without the proviso, when a number of northern congressmen, called doughfaces, were tactfully persuaded by administration arm-twisting to join the southerners to insure its passage. It was premature to consider extending slavery into the territories at this time, they insisted; better to wait until the territories were actually acquired. Consequently, despite all the heated arguments, the fracture in party unity, threats and counter-threats, Congress continued to avoid the contentious issue of slavery as well as its expansion into the territories. Nevertheless, Polk finally had his three million dollars.

Still debated along with the appropriation bill, as it was in August of 1846, was the bill to organize the Oregon Territory. Tucked within the measure was the authority to grant free status to the new territory by simply applying the provisions of the old Northwest Ordinance of 1787, an agreement that prohibited slavery north of the Ohio River. Characteristically, in the Senate the South refused to approve any provision that granted a free status to a northern territory without a counterbalancing slave status to a southern territory. As a result, southern votes in committee scratched the free status provision from the bill. Preferring not to vote for the amended version, the northerners eventually tabled the bill in retaliation. The American settlers in Oregon, meanwhile, eager to legitimize their local governments, would have to wait until August 1848.

Over the preceding several months, dissention between the two sections noticeably grew, both sides engaging in more of the same old and tired accusations, aggressive threats and counter-threats. On the one hand the North would angrily admonish the South over its deplorable conditions, a result from maintaining the curse of slavery, while the South, resentful of being stigmatized as an unequal, would threaten to secede if their rights were not protected.

Be that as it may, during all this clamor and upheaval, one point was gradually taking hold. Although the federal government would take possession of all the unorganized Mexican land, if it was indeed part of a negotiated peace settlement, one larger question remained unanswered: did the Constitution grant Congress the right or the authority to permit or deny slavery on this land? Depending on their political agendas, some thought it did while others thought it didn't. But, if Congress didn't have that authority, who did?

For those northerners who held the opinion that Congress was already vested with that authority, they only had to point to instances where Congress did in fact deal with slavery in the territories. For one, the first Congress under the Constitution excluded slavery in the Northwest Territory under the Ordinance of 1787, but obviously at the time there was little sectional opposition to hinder such a decision. Another example occurred in 1790 and again in 1802 when Congress accepted the conditions imposed by North Carolina and Georgia respectively to permit slavery on land the two states ceded to the federal government. This land was ultimately organized into the Southwest Territory and the Mississippi Territory. And Congress admitted Kentucky into the Union in 1792 as a slave state without ever being a territory as it did with Texas in 1845, as well as accepting Missouri as a slave state in 1820 under specific congressional boundary limits.

Representing the southern point of view was Senator John C. Calhoun. Sixty-four years old and in failing health, Calhoun was the epitome of a southern states' rights radical. Even his expression, as he gazed out through deeply intense and burning eyes, warned of a fiery persona stoked by many years of fighting for a cause he sincerely considered just. His political experience in national affairs spanned some 39 years through three terms in the House and serving as secretary of war under Monroe, vice president in both the Adams and the Jackson administrations, secretary of state under Tyler and sixteen years as a senator from South Carolina. With these credentials it was no wonder Calhoun was revered in the South as their chief spokesman.

Calhoun opined that his position not only addressed the constitutional question but was also a way to resolve the territorial issue as well. Since Congress did not have the constitutional authority to deny slavery in any of the existing states, Calhoun reasoned, it could not deny slavery in the territories either, especially on land that was common to all the sovereign states. This point of view was unequivocal and steadfast. Many of Calhoun's followers in the South were convinced that not only was this common land open to everyone, but also that Congress could not prevent a slave owner from taking his human property into the territories just as he could a horse or a mule.

In the North, as well, there were those who insisted the Constitution granted no jurisdiction to Congress in the territories because while the land was in the United States, it was not, in actuality, part of the United States. As with Buchanan's border extension, no action was ever taken on Calhoun's resolution, but when all was said and done, it was becoming more and more apparent to both sides that the Constitution left Congress extremely limited in its ability to address the question of slavery.

By August 1847 Buchanan was so convinced that his idea to extend the Missouri Compromise line would resolve the territorial question that he chose to champion this effort in his upcoming bid for the Democratic nomination for president. The details of Buchanan's proposal were picked up by the Democratic newspapers and published that fall. The coverage was intense and consistently urged the public to support his cause.

Buchanan's critics, of course, were quick to castigate his views, especially in the whig press where his proposal was soundly ridiculed. Why, Whig newspapers sarcastically asked, was Buchanan proposing to allow slavery in the territories now when in 1819 he was against slavery in Missouri or any other territory?

Nevertheless, although his proposal on its merits had little to argue against, especially since many thought slavery would never take root in these territories anyway, the northern Whigs envisioned quite a different scenario. Many northerners had reached the conclusion that merely fixing a boundary between slave states and free states at 36° 30' was only opening a Pandora's box. If Buchanan's idea was accepted, they explained, the South would then strive to include all of Mexico, and perhaps even Central America and Cuba as some were suggesting, into a final settlement of the war with Mexico. Under that scenario, the South would dominate not only the United States but also the entire American hemisphere, a thought much too repulsive for the North to even contemplate.

In the White House meanwhile, as the likelihood of Mexico's surrender grew, ongoing discussions were being held on what the administration considered a final solution to the Mexican issue—the acquisition of all of Mexico. It would be accomplished over a period of time, California and New Mexico would be acquired first, as partial compensation, while the rest of Mexico remained under military occupation until future conditions, such as the will of the Mexican people, warranted annexation. Northern expansionists, like John L. O'Sullivan, were enormously excited over this prospect as were several northern newspapers. The *Philadelphia Public Ledger*, for one, justified its support for taking the whole of Mexico by writing it would "remove a hostile neighbor in itself; to prevent it becoming a neighbor both hostile and dangerous in European hands; to enable us to command the Pacific and the Gulf of Mexico...; to redeem the Mexican people from anarchy..., to facilitate the entire removal of those rivals [the British] from the continent; to open Mexico, as an extensive market to our manufacturers...; to prevent monarchy from gaining any additional ground on the American continent, North or South, and thus to facilitate its entire removal."

Others expressed support for taking all of Mexico as a way to redress wrongs perpetrated on the United States over the years. In their view, to withdraw the army without obtaining this reparation was wrong and would make the country's war efforts meaningless and the U.S. the laughingstock of the world. Many Democratic expansionists relished the all Mexico scenario as a just means for obtaining a lasting peace and for satisfying the desires of the Mexican people who wanted to enjoy the fruits of freedom.

While these opinions came principally from the expansionist press, the northern Whigs, who resented any acquisition by force, some Democrats, and much of the public at large, did not hold this point of view for three reasons. Their hostility stemmed from a disdain for such a massive land grab over a weaker neighbor as taking all of Mexico would be, the cost of a prolonged occupation which was deemed unreasonable, and the incorporation of millions of people of colored and mixed breeds into the U.S., a prospect looked upon quite unfavorably to most people, especially in the South. In time, however, most northern Whigs came to accept the notion of accepting only California and New Mexico when they were persuaded that it was fair indemnity for U.S. losses.

In his December 1847 message to the new Congress, however, Polk insisted no policy was planned for acquiring all of Mexico but reiterated his desire for a just and full indemnity. And he stressed, the country would be occupied as long as necessary to obtain those ends.

Later that month, the fourth proposal to unravel the territorial question was submitted by Sen. Lewis Cass of Michigan, another candidate for the Democratic presidential nomination and a supporter for taking all of Mexico as a last resort for a permanent peace. Recognizing the lack of definitive legislative power the Constitution gave to Congress over the territories, Cass revived a proposal first suggested by Polk's vice president, George Dallas. The question of slavery in any new lands, Cass opined, should be addressed solely by the local governments of the territories, and that "the people of a territory have, in all that appertains to their internal condition, the same sovereign rights as the people of a state." It was called popular sovereignty and, in effect, would leave the Wilmot Proviso moot. Many in Washington thought popular sovereignty was worth looking into since it left the sticky problem of slavery up to the people in that particular territory. It was the only fair thing to do and since Mexico had outlawed slavery years ago Cass was certain which way the people would decide. The problem was Cass failed to delineate when the local governments of the territories would exert this control—in the territorial stage or at the point they were applying for statehood.

At any rate the response to the idea of popular sovereignty was swift and deadly. If Congress didn't have the power under the Constitution to restrict slavery in the territories, how could the territories themselves have that power?

Again, the country remained divided not only by sectional considerations over the extension of slavery, but also over the powers Congress possessed to legislate for or against slavery in the territories.

11

A Time to Compromise (1847 to 1850)

Following his win at Monterrey, Gen. Taylor's forces went on to defeat Santa Anna at the Battle of Buena Vista in February of 1847. This was the end of Taylor's command in Mexico and with his popularity at home continuing to gain momentum, Old Zack returned to the U.S. to contemplate a run for the presidency.

With General Scott taking up the gauntlet, over the next seven months his army sailed from Lobos Island, captured Veracruz, and after occupying a string of smaller Mexican towns, he and his bedraggled warriors triumphantly marched into Mexico City on September 14, 1847. Five months later, on February 2, 1848, the Treaty of Guadalupe Hidalgo was signed. To the relief of the anti-war advocates, the battle with Mexico was finally over. But in Congress, the territorial battles raged on.

Senate Whigs who were opposed to "Mr. Polk's War" from the beginning and were equally against taking the territorial spoils of that war now found themselves in a Catch-22. If they voted against ratifying the treaty they would be voting for extending the war. Similarly, if they voted for the treaty they would be unwilling participants to the land grab they totally abhorred. The frenzied and salivating hawks in the administration, however, all expansionists in their own right, were clamoring for even more territory. Mexico was on the verge of collapse, they argued, a perfect time to take the entire republic, a scenario Polk was inclined to agree with. Nevertheless, he knew the people were fed up with the war and wanted it to end. Besides, he mused, if the treaty was rejected to push for more concessions Mexico would not concede, Congress would not support the continued fighting of his army, and without funding for war supplies the army would have to be withdrawn, all with nothing gained. Consequently, following an intense and spirited debate, the Treaty of

Guadalupe Hidalgo was ratified on March 10 by a vote of 38 to 14. The Mexican Senate subsequently approved the treaty two months later.

Under the provisions of the treaty, Mexico agreed to recognize the Rio Grande as the U.S. border with Texas and to cede her northern territory to the United States. To appease the Whigs who were against an American land grab, Polk agreed to pay the Mexicans $15 million for the ceded land and $3 million for American damage claims against Mexico. In monetary terms the cost of the war was an estimated $97,000,000. In human terms the U.S. lost about 14,000 lives out of some 105,000 who served, 11,000 from disease and exposure alone. This is reputed to be the highest death rate of any war in our history. Only about 1,700 died in actual combat.

When Polk took office in 1845 the United States had not been enlarged for 25 years. With the victory over Mexico two years later, some 525,000 square miles were added, land consisting of present-day California, Nevada and Utah, most of New Mexico and Arizona, and parts of Colorado and Wyoming. Added to the area gained from the annexation of Texas and the Oregon Territory treaty, the U.S., under Polk, had grown by 1.2 million square miles, nearly double its previous size.

In political terms the war was a victory for the proponents of expansionism to be sure. But in the greater scheme of things it triggered an enormous period of internal strife, social and political divisions, and brought to the forefront a new and bitter phase of territorial sectionalism.

The United States Senate had just ratified the Treaty of Guadalupe Hidalgo and the vision of thousands upon thousands of square miles of new territory had gone from a hypothetical debate to one of harsh reality. And with that reality sectional dissention in Congress and in the press got its second wind as the country struggled not only with how to divvy up the territories and whether to expand slavery into them, but also what to do with all the people already living there. In this context, it wasn't long before the ugly head of racism was also added to the mix.

Particularly problematic were the some 8 million Mexicans living in the territories that were looked upon by some whites as inferior and considered to be aboriginal Indians, descendants of tribes from the time of Cortez. It was unthinkable and somewhat repulsive for these individuals to accept the notion that lazy and uneducated Mexican peasants living in mud-brick houses and in grinding poverty could ever assimilate into the American society and culture.

Some held the opinion that the process of assimilation would be fairly rapid, like Sen. Sidney Breeze of Illinois, who thought that with the infusion of Europeans into their population and with proper education over a decade; there would be a gradual but steady improvement in their "manners, customs, and language." On the other hand, there were lawmakers who thought the whole sordid affair was deplorable and took great comfort in believing that if assimilation was indeed possible at all it would never happen in their lifetime. Extreme racists and anti-expansionists, of course, maintained that it could never happen.

Not only was the assimilation of indigent Mexicans looked upon as an enormous and unwanted social problem but also the thousands of Indians that ranged across the western plains. The Native Americans belonged to such tribes as the warlike Apache, a people primarily inhabiting the mountains and plains of southern Arizona and New Mexico. Like most of the western Indian tribes the Apache were principally nomads hunting buffalo for subsistence, a way of life forced upon them because of unsuitable farming conditions in much of the arid lands. Led by leaders such as Geronimo and Cochise, the Apache were notorious for their cruelty and daring raids on settlers taking part in the American westward movement. Other tribes scattered throughout the western territories included the Comanche, in the Texas-Oklahoma area, and the Pawnee in Nebraska. The Sioux or Lakota tribe, ruled by Chief Sitting Bull, ranged far and wide throughout the northern plains of the present day Dakotas, Nebraska, Iowa, Montana, and Minnesota. The Navaho, Cherokee, and Blackfoot were several other tribes that also inhabited the western territories.

Of much concern as well was the introduction of mixed breeds into American society, the inevitable blend of Indians, Mexicans, and blacks. With the free blacks and southern slaves also added into the equation, the white citizenry was in an enormous quandary. Mixed races were considered, at least by those embracing the philosophy of Swiss scholar Johann J. von Tschudi, "as generally inferior to the pure races, and as members of society they were the worst class of citizens."

Southerners in particular felt quite strongly about the new Americans and were solidly united in expressing their views against them. Calhoun, their chief spokesman, made a point of addressing the Congress with several questions for the members to consider on their way home for supper that evening. "Ours, sir, is the Government of a white race. The greatest misfortunes of Spanish America are to be traced to the fatal error of placing these colored races on an equality with the white race. That error destroyed the social arrangement which formed the basis of society.... Are they fit for self-government and for governing you? Are you, any of you, willing that your States should be governed by these twenty-odd Mexican States, with a population of about only one million of your blood, and two or three millions of mixed blood better informed—all the rest pure Indians, a mixed blood equally ignorant and unfit for liberty, impure races, not as good as the Cherokees or Choctaws?" The *New York Evening Post* even questioned how the United States could "by one stroke of a secretary's pen, reconsign this beautiful country to the custody of the ignorant cowards, and profligate ruffians who have ruled it for the last twenty-five years?"

Whig senator Waddy Thompson, also from South Carolina, was greatly distressed over the recent acquisition of Mexican territory and lamented that the country "will add a large population, aliens to us in feeling, education, race, and religion—a people unaccustomed to work, and accustomed to insubordination and resistance to law, the expense of governing whom will be ten times as great as the revenues derived from them."

From both sections of the country many politicians in Congress were inclined to resist territorial expansion for these reasons and never hesitated to voice their opposition to the unsavory inheritance of unclean aliens into the American culture. At the same time, however, an equally persuasive argument was made by proponents of Manifest Destiny who articulated the many benefits the U.S., and the southern section in particular, could realize from this windfall of territorial growth. Meanwhile, within the Washington crowd, other, more pragmatic, leaders shrugged off the entire problem as simply one that came with the territory.

As we know, in the East a quasi solution for partitioning the races was previously legislated by Congress and enforced by President Jackson when it was decided to simply round up the Indians and confine them all to reservations. But this time the situation was somewhat different. It was a problem of monumental propositions. Particularly frustrating was that a divided nation, now faced with inheriting millions of Mexicans and scores of marauding Indian tribes, was still attempting, without success, to reconcile its own existing social and political differences and prejudices.

The problem of what to do with the new territories and the even more complex questions of whether slavery could ever be extended into all this land, and by whose authority, continued to fester in the Congress. The harried lawmakers wrestled for a compromise solution, one that hopefully could satisfy both sections. But with neither side willing to yield to the other, they came up with little to show for their efforts.

Southern votes had set aside the Wilmot Proviso, and Buchanan's proposal to extend the Missouri Compromise line of 36° 30' to the western shores was tabled back in March 1847 without so much as a debate, as was Calhoun's. The fourth proposal for resolving the territorial problem was submitted by Sen. Cass. Called popular sovereignty, it reached a similar fate as well.

In the midst of all this turmoil and doubt, in July of 1848, a fifth proposal was put on the table which illustrated the uncertainty and lack of consensus between the two sections in the Congress. Called the Clayton Compromise after Sen. John M. Clayton, the measure shifted the responsibility from the Congress and the people in the territory to the judiciary. The proposal not only prohibited Congress from imposing restrictions on slavery but also denied the right for territorial governments in California and New Mexico to make any laws dealing with slavery within their borders. Yet, Clayton continued, a slave brought into that territory could petition the federal courts to rule on the status of slavery in that area. Although passed by the Senate, in the House the bill was tabled as well, the vote mostly along sectional lines.

As congressional squabbles continued over the new territories, the expansion of slavery, and constitutional authority, that May of 1848, the Democratic National Convention convened in Baltimore.

The major candidates in the running were Secretary Buchanan and Senator Cass, each relying on the appeal of their territorial resolutions to capture the majority of votes for nomination. As the delegates arrived to take their places a commotion attracted the attention of the organizers. It was discovered that the state of New York was represented by two delegations, each attempting to gain entrance into the Universalist Church. One group supported the nomination of Cass, the overweight senator from Michigan noted for his shoddy red wig. They were called Hunkers, a name they earned because of their unshakable hankering for public office and the notoriety they would derive from it at the expense of their principles. The other delegates, the Barnburners, were an assemblage of New York extremists and staunch anti-slave radicals who gained the reputation as a group likely to burn down the barn to get rid of the "Polk-rats." They came with their own agenda and were pursuing the nomination of their own candidate to implement it, namely ex–Democratic president Martin Van Buren. After much confusion it was decided to seat both factions in the convention hall but to split the New York vote between them. Although both delegations strenuously objected to this ruling, the Barnburners became highly indignant over not being recognized as the sole New York delegation and stormed out of the convention vowing to run their candidate under a new political banner. With their departure, the remaining Hunkers were allowed into the convention but could not vote.

Following the fourth ballot popular sovereignty won the day when Lewis Cass was selected as the Democratic presidential candidate. Not wanting to upset party unity between the two sections, however, the Democrats chose to avoid endorsing popular sovereignty in their platform or for that matter to take any public position for or against slavery in the territories. Even campaign literature on Cass was published in two versions, one for northern consumption, the other distributed throughout the South.

For the Whigs, however, matters were a little more complicated. When the Senate approved the Treaty of Guadalupe Hidalgo in March, the Whigs realized they no longer had the central issue they counted on to win the election, namely running against the war. Despite the obvious token payment of $15 million, the stealing of thousands of square miles of Mexican territory was an issue the victorious Democrats could now gloat over. "It is doubtful whether we can beat the scoundrels next Pres. Election," wrote one Indiana editor. "The war will have been ended and an immense acquisition of Land will be pointed to as the result of Democracy—the Land stealing, even among our best Christian, is popular."

In light of their dilemma, General Zachary Taylor, the hero of the Mexican War, became more appealing than ever as a likely candidate to head the Whig ticket. It was a proven winning strategy for the Whigs in 1840 when General Harrison was overwhelmingly elected and the Whigs were confident Taylor would do the same. Considering his rising popularity after his celebrated triumphs at Monterrey and Buena Vista, Old Zack had wide appeal across party lines which made him an easy choice for the nomination. Although Taylor had no political credentials to speak of, no platform to run on, no profound political views, and was lacking in oratorical skills, he was well-liked, void of political baggage, and pledged to support whatever Congress decided on the territorial issue.

It was enough to win 62 percent of the southern delegates and 39 percent of the northerners and enabled Taylor to defeat his rivals, one of which was none other than fellow general Winfield Scott, who evidently suffered from too much baggage. To illustrate the influence the war heroes had on the delegates, the two generals easily outpaced the civilian political veterans in the race, Clay and Webster, by capturing over 80 percent of the votes between them.

As a southerner who employed over a hundred slaves on his cotton and sugar plantations, Taylor's candidacy absolutely delighted many Dixie Whigs who relished the idea of having "kinfolk" in the White House. Senator Robert Toombs of Georgia probably summed it up the best when he said Taylor was a "Southern man, a slaveholder, a cotton planter" identified "from birth, association, and conviction ... with the South."

Many Whigs in the North, however, were not pleased. There were those northern anti-slavery doves who voiced concern that nominating a popular war hero like Taylor was actually an act of desperation. Taylor's nomination, they complained, only acknowledged the party's inability to win on the critical issues of the times and resembled Jacksonian opportunism, something they passionately opposed. In reality, northern Whigs were fearful of the encroachment of slavery and had preferred someone other than the two southern candidates. Many had voiced the opinion that "we must have a Northern man for our candidate." Indeed, the northern Whigs were so incensed over Taylor's nomination that one Massachusetts delegate, visibly anguished, screamed to the assembled body, "We have nominated a gentleman ... who is anything but a Whig, and, sir, I will go home, and so help me God, I will do all I can to defeat the election of that candidate." The fact that Taylor never voted, had no sincere party affiliation, and refused to take a public position on Whig domestic policies concerned many northern Whigs. They were growing more and more dissatisfied with Taylor's apparent disregard for Whig principles. Moreover, many northern Whigs resented the nomination of Taylor not only because he was a southern slaveholder but also over the control the southern wing boldly exerted in his selection. Reminiscent of the disdain northern

Democrats displayed over southern domination of their party two years earlier, the Whigs were livid over the actions of the southern delegates. In fact, one New England Whig expressed the rage most of his party members felt when he exclaimed bitterly that southerners "have trampled on the rights and just claims of the North sufficiently long and have fairly shit upon all our Northern statesmen and are now trying to rub it in." The North must "take a stand" to bring "the South to their proper level."

In response to this criticism Taylor explained that his desire to remain nonpartisan and to subscribe to a "No Party" philosophy was elemental. His election, he said, would result from the wide support he would receive from across the spectrum of voters, not simply those from the Whig Party.

Losing out as well that June was Taylor's principal rival for the nomination, Henry Clay. Considering Taylor's lack of background in national politics or for that matter any public office and the damage this could cause the country, Clay was persuaded that he must enter the race for the good of the Whig Party and the nation. Idolized by his supporters, the retired 70-year-old Whig leader agreed to leave his Kentucky estate, Ashland, to make another run for the White House.

For years Clay had aspirations to lead the country and would occasionally remark to friends with a wry grin, "Is there, frankly, anyone better qualified to be president? I have yet to meet the gentleman who is my superior." A well respected statesman of immense political savvy, Clay, along with Calhoun and Webster, was one of the primary driving forces in Congress for decades. Dominating the political-power machine, it was Clay and Webster, the compromiser and debater extraordinaire on one side of the arguments, Calhoun, the unwavering champion of southern equality and southern rights on the other.

This was Clay's fifth try for the White House and it must have been a sad realization for the aged statesman that it would be his last. He failed to win the nomination in 1840 and was a presidential candidate in 1824, 1832, and in 1844, his most disappointing loss of all. At that time his failure to support the annexation of Texas had cost him the southern vote. Apparently this time Clay's public opposition to both slavery and the Mexican War had alienated southern Whigs and the fact that he received only one-quarter of the northern vote also contributed to his loss.

Following the fourth and final ballot, Clay ended up with an embarrassing 35 votes to Taylor's 171 but he may have been comforted by the notion that strong congressional leaders like Calhoun, Webster, and himself, had little chance of ever winning the presidency. Their enormous resume of political experience, gained from a lifetime of public service also, ironically, secured a host of political enemies, all quite determined to block their path to the White House.

Before the convention adjourned Millard Fillmore was chosen as Taylor's running mate.

The nomination of Taylor sent shock waves throughout the North, and antislavery Whigs, especially the staunch free-soil opponents of slavery extension, vowed to defect. The growing dissention within their ranks, they grimly predicted, would result in the ultimate demise of the Whig Party. Furthermore, the desire to abandon their party gave additional impetus for the formation of a new coalition more in tune with their antislavery principles.

As a result, scores of northern Whigs and Democrats, all sharing a free-soil persuasion, joined forces with the New York contingent of Barnburners, the same mavericks that left the Whig convention in May. Assembling with several other splinter groups at Utica, New York, on June 21, they formed the Free Soil Party. These splinter groups included the Liberty Party, the group of anti-slavery abolitionists who had twice previously run James G. Birney for the presidency in the early 1840s, and another faction of the northern anti-slavery Whigs called the Conscience Whigs, a bloc that also rejected the notion of slavery in the territories.

Two months later, the Free Soil Party met in Buffalo where its members nominated Van Buren as their candidate on a platform that advocated the principles and adoption of the Wilmot Proviso. It was a clear challenge to Taylor, who refused to take a position for or against the extension of slavery, and to Cass, who promised he would veto the proviso.

Although not a serious threat to either of the two major parties, the mere introduction of the Free Soil Party into the presidential race and its threat to bring the territorial issues into the campaign, forced them both to modify their campaign strategy. Since the Free Soil Party came out loudly advocating Wilmot's no slavery in the territories proviso, the Democrats and Whigs could no longer simply ignore the issue. The free-soilers, in no uncertain terms, were publicly vowing to "fight on, and fight for ever" for "free soil, free speech, free labor, and free men." Therefore, prudently moving to publicly advocate a position on slavery in the territories, the Democrats now lauded Cass's popular sovereignty to the northerners as the best way to keep slavery out of the territories while at the same time appeasing southerners by pledging to veto the Wilmot Proviso.

This form of political two-face was possible during an age when most rank and file voters received their information on controversial issues from what their local politicians and partisan newspapers told them, information that invariably came direct from the party's campaign headquarters. And just as the Democratic campaign officials had done on behalf of their candidate, Taylor's men also forwarded one collection of campaign material to the North that exaggerated Taylor's appeal to the Yankees while at the same time sending different material to the South that made Taylor just as favorable there.

In the election of 1848 the voters could for the first time cast their ballots for president and vice president on the same day. By winning eight of the fifteen slave states and seven of the fifteen free states, General Zachary Taylor captured 163 of the 290 electoral votes and was later inaugurated as the twelfth president of the U.S. In the process, however, the congressional balance of power had shifted away from the Whigs, who lost their majority, and as a result the Democrats now ruled in both chambers.

As the final months of his presidency ticked away, Polk decided to initiate a final drive to satisfy his expansionist proclivities. Statehood for California and New Mexico had been a four-year quest for Polk, even to the point where many of his detractors in Congress and in the press were convinced the Mexican conflict was his way of carrying out a slave-power conspiracy. To launch his expansionist goals, Polk sent two recommendations to the lame-duck Congress. First, he called for the formation of territorial governments in both California and New Mexico. In addition, as an advocate for Buchanan's resolution to settle the territorial slavery question, he recommended reviving the proposal to extend the Missouri Compromise line to the Pacific, a direct contradiction to the party's support of popular sovereignty. Polk's plea, however, fell on deaf ears.

The second session of the Thirtieth Congress began in December and ran its course until March 1849. During those four months a mood of anger and bitterness resonated throughout its time-honored and historic chambers as debate on the Mexican Cession resumed and quickly raised the passions of both sections. As fast as the northerners in the House were to pass a sweeping territorial bill that excluded slavery, the southerners in the Senate, infuriated over this blatant insult to their intelligence, were just as quick to squash it amid fist fights and threats of secession. Still lacking a meeting of the minds on the territorial problems, various alternatives were proposed to the assembled body. Sen. Stephen Douglas of Illinois, for example, suggested a sixth resolution. He suggested bypassing the territorial stage altogether for the entire Mexican acquisition. This proposition, extreme as it appeared, would grant immediate statehood to all of the Mexican territory. As one enormous state the citizens would then decide the slavery question for themselves under a form of popular sovereignty. A bill was also introduced to apply an older resolution, the Wilmot Proviso, but this time only to California and New Mexico. Despite the sincerity of both sides, none of these proposals satisfied the deeply divided Congress.

It was in this climate of uncertainty and hostility, particularly instigated by the continuous threat of the Wilmot Proviso and the calls for abolishing slavery in Washington, that a southern caucus was convened that December of 1848. In an attempt to fulfill a long-standing goal, Sen. Calhoun thought the time had come to unite the southerners in Congress under the flag of a new political party. Called the Southern Rights Party, it would provide an integrated front to fight the North; a common voice to address southern grievances, and hopefully, lead to a new two-party system based upon sectional considerations—free-soilers versus pro-slavery expansionists. Sixty-nine southern members from both parties agreed to attend. At this hastily called meeting Calhoun was asked to write a position paper to the southern people that addressed their long-standing concerns. In the Address of the Southern Delegates in Congress to Their Constituents, Calhoun reiterated all the old and oft-stated injustices that northerners and northern legislators had imposed on the rights of their section. It was particularly insulting, he exclaimed, for southerners to be excluded from the new territories merely because they owned slaves and called on all southerners to unite against this common enemy so determined to force them into a "subordinate and dependent condition." Continuing, Calhoun insisted that the southern people were justified, even obligated, to defend slavery by any means, even secession, because their "property, prosperity, equality, liberty, and safety" were at stake. Two months later, however, when it came time for the southern lawmakers to sign the document in a clear expression of unanimity, only 48 of the 121 congressmen signed, a clear defeat for Calhoun's hope for a new, united South. Not surprisingly, included in the 73 who refused to go along with the caucus were 46 of the 48 southern Whigs who remained confident in their hearts that Taylor, whom they overwhelmingly supported, would carry out his pledge to settle the sectional crisis.

Meanwhile, Congress remained in a quagmire, both parties growing more divided, both finding it more difficult to gain majority votes when the voting was almost always influenced by sectional considerations. As the end of the session neared, sectional alignment remained firm, Whigs and Democrats in the North against Whigs and Democrats in the South. In March, as a result of their intransigence, the lame-duck congressional session concluded without passing a single piece of territorial legislation.

To the trepidation of both southern Whigs and Democrats, by April of 1849 Taylor's true colors were beginning to show when he dispatched an envoy to California's leaders to encourage them to apply for immediate statehood. Even more disconcerting to the South, especially to the southern Whigs who had strongly supported Taylor, was his address to a Pennsylvania audience in which he remarked, "The people of the North need have no apprehension of the further extension of slavery." At the same time, when one of his loyal southern supporters, seeking to be reassured that Taylor would veto Wilmot's Proviso if passed by Congress, was told, "If Congress sees fit to pass it [the Wilmot Proviso], I will not veto it."

All doubts over Taylor's true position were painfully eliminated in December when he sent his first annual message to the new Congress that outlined his plan to resolve the sectional difficulties. In his message Taylor confirmed his desire for immediate statehood for both California and New Mexico as free states without going through the territorial stage first. Bypassing the territorial stage was extremely worrisome to the South because the basis for acceptance or denial of slavery in that stage had yet to be determined, but as a state, slavery could easily be prohibited outright by legislative action. The new president was convinced that his policy was sound and would eliminate the vexing and long-standing sectional tensions. It was quite obvious to Taylor that eliminating the territorial stage made sense because in his opinion it would simply avoid the dispute over slavery and render the highly controversial Wilmot Proviso moot. And to drive that point home, Taylor dispatched several of his representatives to New Mexico and California to help jump-start their annexation process.

Many southerners in the new Congress, Whig and Democrat alike, were quite angry with Taylor. They believed he should have made an effort to work with them first on ways to settle the territorial problems instead of pursuing this policy unilaterally. Although it was generally assumed by most people in the South that California and New Mexico would, in time, apply for and gain approval for statehood as free states, southerners of both parties were particularly outraged that their man was now blatantly siding with the North to the point where some were calling him a traitor to his people and his southern heritage.

This notion that California and New Mexico would eventually be admitted as free states was virtually accepted for three reasons. One, the residents of both territories were all non-slaveholders under prior Mexican laws that prohibited slavery. Two, because the people living there were convinced the institution was immoral and a curse they would not tolerate, and finally because many considered the poor soil and arid Southwest climate as too inhospitable for growing the celebrated cash crops the southern economy depended on. Even though many southerners accepted this notion as well, the South felt betrayed and angry over Taylor's decision on California and New Mexico because they were getting nothing in exchange for their support and they allowed themselves to be drawn into accepting the perception of Taylor's loyalty to them and their cause.

It came as no surprise, therefore, that again the halls of Congress reverberated with southern threats to secede if their equal rights were not upheld and they were not allowed to take their slaves to the newly acquired territories. Even Jefferson Davis, who was once Taylor's son-in-law until his wife died, and fought under him in the Mexican War, became so upset during a heated debate over the president's maneuver that at one point he even challenged an Illinois congressman to a duel.

The Dixie politicians appealed to Taylor to reconsider his insult to the southern voters who believed in him and had supported his candidacy. But the president held firm, telling them that he already had agents in Monterey and Santa Fe to get the mechanics of annexation started. Evidently, California had already begun the annexation process after establishing a constitution and electing a governor and legislature. New Mexico, on the other hand, would not continue the process until its border dispute with Texas was resolved.

When Texas became an independent republic the government had fixed the upper Rio Grande as the western boundary with New Mexico. Under this arrangement Texas laid claim to over half of the land constituting present-day New Mexico. The dispute was clearly defined by Lincoln some years later when he described it this way, "She [Texas] was a slave state, and consequently the farther west the slavery men could push her border, the more slave country they secured; and the farther east the slavery opponents could thrust the boundary back, the less slave ground was secured. Thus this was just as clearly a slavery question as any of the others."

Meanwhile, parallel to the ongoing territorial debates over California and New Mexico, the Wilmot Proviso, popular sovereignty, extending the 36° 30' line, judicial litigation on slavery, immediate annexation of the Mexican Cession as one huge state, and all the other attempts to resolve the sectional questions over the territories, the South began to realize another serious problem was right before their unseeing eyes and they appeared to be in a no-win situation: specifically, their political power in Congress.

With the acceptance of Wisconsin back in May of 1848, the senatorial balance of power was now even at 15 slave states and 15 free states. Nevertheless, it became quite apparent to the South that its on-going struggle to gain political dominance in the Senate was being lost. The reason for the apprehension was that while all the remaining territory in the Louisiana Purchase north of the 36° 30' line was considered open for free states as was the Oregon Territory, there was no slave territory waiting to apply for statehood. The only remaining real estate left open for the further growth of the South was the unorganized territory of present-day Oklahoma, presently an Indian enclave and extremely unlikely to interest southern expansionists, and the land of the Mexican Cession, land Taylor was beginning to parcel out in favor of the free states.

Also weighing heavily on the southern psyche was their population growth, which had been stagnant for a number of years while in the North it was steadily increasing. When all these factors were taken together, it portended a future of steadily decreasing voting power in Congress and a growing threat to the future survival of the South and the southern slave society. With this revelation dawning on the South, a very serious issue began to take hold. The South had to do something now to preserve its way of life and to do it decisively.

The choice facing the southerners was doing nothing and face extinction or to make a stand either for a guaranteed congressionally protected slave society or for disunion. Either way, they must preserve their slave-oriented culture.

By the end of 1849 the unrelenting and heated rhetoric from the southern press over southern ills and threats of secession had inflamed the southern people to near hysteria. But despite the unmistakable signs of southern disaffection and of a southern resolve to abandon the Union, the president was still unwavering in his decision and offered no concessions and no apologies to the southern states contemplating such an action. The mood in Washington had suddenly shifted away from a territorial and slavery crisis to one of disunion. One Illinois congressman, sensing the dire mood in Washington, remarked, "There is a bad state of things here. I fear this Union is in danger."

Concerned over the mounting and obvious dangers of disunion, several members of Congress urgently called for a compromise in this most perilous of times. Fortunately, there was one person who still continued to search for a middle ground that would avoid secession and save the Union.

Taking on this initiative was Henry Clay, who was returned to the Senate by the Kentucky legislature after several years of retirement. Keenly aware of southern dissatisfaction over Taylor's declaration and their dire threats of secession, Clay decided to return to Congress in order to contribute his conciliatory skills toward reaching a comprehensive compromise between the two sides. Known as the "Great Compromiser" for his ability to resolve bitter disputes, as he had done several times earlier, Clay formulated a plan designed to provide an alternative to Taylor's proposal and one he considered fair enough to break the impasse. Whether his plan or Taylor's could meet the challenge remained to be seen, but following assurances of support from his Senate rival, Daniel Webster, and with his characteristic confidence in his reputation, Clay prepared to present his ideas to the Congress.

Once again, the "Great Triumvirate" was together in Washington. While Clay took up residence in several rooms at the National Hotel, Calhoun, extremely ill and feeble, resided closer to the Capitol, at the old Hill's boardinghouse where the Supreme Court is now located. And the Websters were still living at Vine Cottage, on Louisiana Avenue, also in close proximity to the Senate.

On January 29, 1850, with news of Clay's upcoming presentation the talk of Washington, the U.S. Capitol was inundated with excited spectators drawn to the scene like fans to a modern-day sporting event. They overflowed into the aisles, the corridors and even into the adjoining library. The ornate Senate chamber, resplendent in plush crimson and gold carpeting, and columns of variegated marble, was uncharacteristically muted as the senior senator began to speak. The learned assemblage, sitting attentive at their mahogany desks, strained to hear every word from the master compromiser. During four hours of reverberating oratory, Clay introduced a series of resolutions crafted to reconcile the political differences then dividing the nation, or to cure the "five wounds," as he would later describe them. It was essentially a plan to save the Union.

Clay's proposal contained three pairs of concessions. In addition there were two resolutions that clearly favored the South. Basically, the plan asked the North to accept more concessions than the South because the North was "numerically more powerful than the slave States" and because the North's egregious behavior towards slavery was a "sentiment without sacrifice, a sentiment without danger, a sentiment without hazard, without peril, without loss." But, in reality, in its final form most of the concessions went to the North.

First, Clay's plan admitted California as a free state and as a concession to the South he created two territorial governments from the remaining Mexican Cession, the Utah Territory and the New Mexico Territory, and recommended they be formed without any restrictions for or against slavery. Clay had no qualms about recommending no restrictions on slavery in these territories; since slavery had been abolished by Mexican law, he believed the prohibitions would continue until some future territorial legislature changed them.

Secondly, he would abolish the slave trade in the nation's capital. At the same time, Clay chose to maintain the institution in Maryland unless both the District and Maryland mutually agreed to abolish it there as well.

And finally, the plan would settle the New Mexico–Texas border dispute by having Texas surrender her border claims, thereby leaving New Mexico intact. In return, Texas would be compensated by the U.S. assumption of the debt incurred by Texas bondholders while an independent republic.

The other two points were obviously written to benefit the South. The first would deny congressional power over the interstate slave trade. The second responded to years of complaints by the South over the weaknesses of the Fugitive Slave Act of 1793. Clay's proposal would replace the old federal statute with a new and even stronger law designed to return runaway slaves to their rightful owners.

Over the next six months, beginning on February 5, the intensive debate on Clay's bill reflected the contrasting extremes of institutionalized ideology the lawmakers had to overcome. Many in Congress were still opposed to any form of compromise and northern criticism of Clay's ideas was just as cutting as that from the South. William H. Seward called Clay's proposal "magnificent humbug," and Joshua R. Giddings of Ohio predicted it would "fall stillborn," while Jefferson Davis remarked, "The South gets nothing while the North gets everything." Southern Democrats also fumed that Clay's plan would prohibit slaveholders from taking their slaves into any of the Mexican Cession because of his insistence that Mexican law against slavery still prevailed. On the issue of slavery in the District, Georgian Robert Toombs made his point extremely clear when he exclaimed before the House, "The South is prepared to teach the North that she is in earnest. If any bill is passed by this Congress abolishing slavery in the District of Columbia, or incorporating the Wilmot Proviso in any form, I will introduce a resolution in this House declaring that this Union be dissolved."

During the course of this historic debate the southern point of view on this matter was presented by Sen. John C. Calhoun. Calhoun being too ill to stand before the assembly, however, it was delivered on March 4, 1850, by Sen. James M. Mason and portrayed an image of doom and gloom for southern society. In his speech Calhoun blamed "the current crisis" on highly biased congressional legislation of the past, such as the Northwest Ordinance of 1787 and the Missouri Compromise of 1820, for prohibiting slavery in vast areas of the country. He also blamed the Wilmot Proviso and the directives of the "new Executive Proviso of General Taylor, which arrogantly usurp the sovereignty of the states over the territories, all had or have but one purpose: to give the North absolute control over the Federal Government, with a view to the final abolition of slavery in the southern states." He also called the insidious and continuing attacks on their institution the mechanism designed by the northern abolitionists to divide the two sections into warring factions over slavery. Continuing on, Calhoun characterized the bonds between the states as "cords." Although many and of varied nature, he wrote, over time the ongoing stress over slavery and other sectional conflicts had broken many of them and was now in the process of breaking the political ones as well. And once all the cords are broken, disunion would be inevitable. Finally, Calhoun offered five ways to save the Union. The North must stop its attacks on slavery, agree to restore California to a territorial status, return runaway slaves to their owners, grant the South equal access to the territories, and agree to a constitutional amendment that would "restore to the South..., the power she possessed of protecting herself before the equilibrium between the two sections was destroyed by the action of this government."

Calhoun's speech pointed out the deep discontent in the South, but more significantly, his address added a stronger voice to the many warnings from others that secession was looming just ahead.

All this talk about disunion troubled Clay, a slave owner himself. Speaking before the Senate following Calhoun's speech, the old lawmaker scolded its southern members by reminding them, "We slaveholders allow ourselves to speak too frequently, and with too much levity, of a separation of this Union. I cannot believe," he continued, "that it is prudent or wise to be so often alluding to it. We ought not to be perpetually exclaiming wolf, wolf, wolf."

A week later, Sen. William H. Seward, a leading anti-slavery Whig and advisor to the president, offered his opposing views that in a large degree represented not only his own opinion but also that of most northern Americans. Rejecting Calhoun's diatribe out of hand and not parsing words in an oratorical style long lost in modern politics, Seward reminded his audience, "You cannot roll back the tide of social progress." Slavery was wrong, he said, and will eventually cease to exist. But his principal point was that "there is a higher law than the Constitution." In addition to the constitutional powers vested in Congress to prohibit slavery from the territories, he lectured his audience, there was the law of God in which all men are seen as equal. Southerners and the southern press ridiculed Seward's speech as "monstrous and diabolical."

Not reflecting the administration's position, even President Taylor sought to distance himself from the address and the resulting furor.

In a rather poignant and extremely prophetic letter to Mason, Calhoun voiced his concern for the Union. "The Union is doomed to dissolution," he lamented. "There is no mistaking the signs. I am satisfied in my judgment even were the questions which now agitate Congress settled to the satisfaction and concurrence of the Southern States, it would not avert, or materially delay, the catastrophe. I fix its probable occurrence within twelve years or three Presidential terms. You and others of your age will probably live to see it; I shall not. The mode by which it will be is not so clear; it may be brought about in a manner that none now foresee. But the probability is it will explode in a Presidential election."

On March 31, 1850, the voice of the southern opposition, John C. Calhoun, died at the age of 68. Taking his place was Senator Jefferson Davis, the Mexican War hero from the state of Mississippi and like Calhoun a fanatical champion of southern rights.

Over the past several years Calhoun had championed a valiant struggle to organize a fight for southern rights. To accomplish this goal the South Carolina senator endeavored to organize a southern political confederation called the Southern Rights Party. By bringing the southerners together he had hoped to unite the South into a single voice to fight against the evils of the Wilmot Proviso and the myriad of other northern transgressions where strength in numbers would hopefully prevail. But although the southern states had common problems, their failing was the lack of a common solution; they were hopelessly divided. On one hand were the "fire-eaters," people like Calhoun, William L. Yancey, of Alabama, Virginian Edmund Ruffin, and R. B. Rhett, the editor of the *Charleston Mercury*. They were among the extreme fanatics who were fed up with the repetitive and tired rhetoric and wanted drastic action, many calling for the South to leave the Union immediately. On the other hand, the moderates or Unionists, saw abandoning the Union as disloyalty in the extreme. Instead, they sought a way to mend the fences between the two sections. These opposing views within the South led to distrust, animosity, and impotence in arriving at a common southern strategy.

To address the onslaught of criticism over Clay's recommendations, a Select Committee of Thirteen (7 Whigs and 6 Democrats from 7 slave states and 8 free states), which Senator Clay chaired, reexamined, re-debated, dissected, and rewrote the compromise, now called the Omnibus Bill. In April the five new proposals were lumped together in one all inclusive bill, making it impossible for one section to approve one proposal while rejecting another. In that light, Clay was fairly confident that the compromisers were in the majority and would approve his bill, accepting those proposals they didn't like in order to get the ones they wanted.

The following month Senate debate on Clay's Omnibus Bill showed sure signs of the measure's imminent defeat when no clear majority for approval became evident. In an attempt to drum up support for his bill, Clay stood before his Senate colleagues and delivered a clear-cut comparison of his plan and Taylor's. "Here are five wounds," he said, "bleeding and threatening the well-being, if not the existence of the body politic. What is the plan of the president? Is it to treat all the wounds? No such thing. It is only to heal one of the five, and to leave the other four to bleed more profusely than ever, by the sole admission of California, even if it should produce death itself."

On Pennsylvania Avenue, however, Taylor was convinced his plan to grant immediate statehood to California was the best one for the country and even planned to veto Clay's compromise if it came to his desk. And over the weeks ahead it became increasingly apparent that the administration was pushing hard to ensure the president's plan would succeed at all cost. Senator Webster recognized the poor prospects for the Omnibus Bill writing on July the Fourth: "Many, many members do not wish to vote against the President's plan. He seems to have more feeling on the subject than I can well account for, & I believe some members of his Administration take a good deal of pains to defeat the compromise."

Coincidentally, that same night Taylor suffered from severe abdominal pains following Independence Day festivities at the unfinished Washington Monument. Five days later he died. His untimely death at sixty-five was attributed by some to an infection in his digestive system from his overindulgence of the celebratory refreshments.

Moving unexpectedly into the White House was Taylor's vice president, 50-year-old Millard Fillmore, an anti-slave Whig from New York. Prior to joining Taylor on the winning presidential ticket, Fillmore's only worthy achievement of some note was his stint as the chairman of the House Ways and Means Committee between 1833 and 1835. Now free to carry out his own agenda, within days of taking office Fillmore began to shake up his predecessor's administration by accepting the resignation of Taylor's entire Cabinet, taking on Senator Webster as his secretary of state, throwing out New Mexico's bid for statehood, and contrary to Taylor's position, placing his wholehearted support behind the Omnibus Bill. After learning of Webster's appointment, Senator Seward soberly remarked, "The government is in the hands of Mr. Webster, and Mr. Clay is its organ in Congress."

Despite the new administration's support of Clay's compromise, on the day of reckoning, July 31, the measure was defeated. It was a victim of a southern coalition of secessionists, free soilers, several northern Whigs, and a contingent of Taylor supporters still determined to carry out his policy. Illinois senator Stephen A. Douglas, not one to mince words, gave his opinion on the bill's defeat by observing, "If Mr. Clay's name had not been associated with the bills, they would have passed long ago. The administration was jealous of him and hated him and some Democrats were weak enough to fear that the success of his bill would make him President."

Following the roll call, Senator Clay, who had championed the bill with some 70 presentations before Congress, left Washington for the beaches of Newport, Rhode Island, to recover from an illness, exhaustion and more disappointment.

Although temporarily sidetracked, Clay's proposal was down but not out. With Calhoun deceased and Clay recuperating at Newport, a new generation of advocates stepped up to the podium to renew the effort towards a lasting compromise. They were legislators such as Jefferson Davis, selected to fill Calhoun's massive shoes, and Sen. William H. Seward, an anti-slave radical from New York. One of these new leaders also was the young Stephen A. Douglas, a diminutive senator from Illinois who was now recognized as the new driving force behind the compromise measure.

Five feet, four inches tall, Douglas was the chairman of the Senate Committee on Territories whose capacity for hard work was inversely proportional to his size and earned him the sobriquet "Little Giant." Never a believer in the Omnibus Bill as written, Douglas undertook a new strategy. He broke out each of the five components of the bill separately and with a little help from Fillmore managed to gather the necessary number of supporters from each section to insure passage of each component.

Proponents of this strategy were convinced it was worth the effort considering the alternative. Secession had always been a frequent southern threat and was looked upon with ever growing suspicion, but nevertheless it was a threat very few wanted to challenge.

On August 9, the separate components of the compromise bill began to wind their way through Senate and House debates, each undergoing congressional fine tuning over the following five weeks. Immediately delivered to the White House, Fillmore signed each of them as they came to his desk, the last on September 17.

The Compromise of 1850, as the bill became popularly known, although similar in some respects to Clay's original plan was also somewhat different. It paved the way for the annexation of California as the thirty-first state in December 1850, while dividing most of the remaining Mexican Cession into two territories. One was the Utah Territory, land now comprising the states of Nevada and Utah, and the other was the New Mexico Territory, the area of present-day Arizona and New Mexico. While California would be a free state, the slave status of the new territories was established under a form of popular sovereignty. The Compromise directed their formation "with or without slavery, as their constitutions may prescribe." Also, the terrible specter of slave auctions was banished forever from the streets of the nation's capital. To settle the Texas–New Mexico border dispute, Texas grew by some 33,000 square miles to the east while relinquishing her claim to the disputed border with New Mexico. In return, Texas would be compensated with $10 million, half of which would go directly to Texas bondholders. And lastly, a stronger

Fugitive Slave Act was enacted that established stronger guidelines for the apprehension and return of runaway slaves.

To call this a compromise bill, however, is somewhat of a misnomer. Although the bill gave up something for both sections, upon closer examination of the roll calls, historians have concluded that the majority of the votes for each component were in fact strictly along sectional lines with little compromising at all. As they pointed out, the northern vote in the House and Senate was enough to accept both the admission of California as a free state and the abolishment of the slave trade in Washington, while the majority of southern votes ensured the passage of the Fugitive Slave Act and the territorial status of Utah and New Mexico without slavery restrictions. Of the total, the Texas–New Mexico border dispute was perhaps the only one requiring compromise and concession.

Nevertheless, the mood in Washington was one of sheer elation and relief. The congressional assemblage was overjoyed that at last their long and arduous struggle was finally over. Ecstatic with finally settling the most troubling problem of their time, the celebrations now began. "The Union is saved," the tipsy lawmakers exclaimed as equally boisterous crowds gathered in the downtown streets. To many of the celebrants the combined provisions of the Missouri Compromise and the Compromise of 1850 ensured that sectional tensions over slavery expansion were indeed over. So optimistic were the lawmakers that Senator Douglas vowed "never to make another speech upon the slavery question in the Halls of Congress." Even an elated President Fillmore remarked that the Compromise was "a final settlement" of all sectional problems. Most of those within earshot of Fillmore's comment probably agreed with him. Most, that is, except Sen. Salmon P. Chase of Ohio, who remarked after hearing the president's speech, "The question of slavery in the territories has been avoided. It has not been settled."

In the end, the perception of a reasonable legislative solution allayed the hostile tensions over the expansion of slavery and toned down the threat of secession, at least for a while. With the Compromise of 1850 now law, however, a new and equally troubling period for both sections still lay ahead.

12

Sectional Politics (1850 to 1853)

Over the days and months ahead the majority of Congress, both northern and southern, both Democrats and Whigs, continued to express unswerving support for the Compromise of 1850. It would save the Union, they happily exclaimed, reveling in their perceived success in resolving this latest sectional crisis. Despite their elation, if the goal of the compromise measure was to lessen the sectional agitation over slavery, it was certainly a questionable effort considering it contained a built-in contradiction that seemingly made that goal nearly impossible to achieve.

That contradiction was the new Fugitive Slave Act, a measure that equaled the derisiveness and emotional passion of even the Wilmot Proviso itself. Overwhelmingly endorsed by the Southern elite, the new law passed mostly along sectional lines in both the House and Senate. The appeal of this law was that it superseded and strengthened the older 1793 edict as a means to recover runaway slaves that had taken refuge in the North. While the new and improved law intended to give assurances to the slave owners that their slaves would be apprehended and returned, continued opposition in many northern cities still made enforcement very difficult and once again stirred up bitter resentment between the sections over the institution of slavery.

As deplorable as the Fugitive Slave Act appeared to the North, the law was mandated under the U.S. Constitution which specifically directed that any "person held to service or labor in one state" who flees to another state, "shall be delivered up on claim of the party to whom such service or labor shall be due."

Unlike the previous law, however, the provisions of the new measure directed that exclusive authority for tracking down slaves for the owners was now under the jurisdiction of a federal marshal and his deputies. The statute also instructed the marshal to cooperate fully with the slave owners or be fined $1000. In turn, he was empowered to demand the assistance and cooperation of the local police and citizens in the capture of the fugitive, a proviso the citizens were loath to obey. For those who refused to cooperate, the law specified a penalty of heavy fines and six month imprisonment.

Once apprehended, the suspected runaway was brought before a court appointed commissioner for a hearing based solely on the affidavit of anyone claiming to be the owner, and with absolutely no rights to a defense of a jury trial. The commissioner was then paid $5 if in his judgment the suspect was not the person so claimed in the affidavit and was set free, or $10 if he ruled in favor of the slave owner. Obviously, it was much more lucrative for an unsavory commissioner to opt on the side of the slave owner which glaringly pointed out the obscenity in the whole process.

The majority of blacks brought before the court were nearly always transported to their southern owner to spend their lives in the shadow of the overseer's whip. The length of time a fugitive was missing was of no consequence because the law did not contain a statute of limitations. Many of these fugitives, both men and women, were gainfully employed in the North for many years where they married and had children of their own. It mattered little to the authorities that these families were now crushed over a loss of a parent, at times simply snatched from his own bed in the middle of the night. In fact, in some cases, the slave owner was granted title to the entire family.

Furthermore, under the new law it was still possible for any free black to be a potential target for kidnapping despite the personal liberty laws enacted by some states to counteract this possibility. In many instances free blacks were simply picked up randomly off the street or as victims of mistaken identity. Once in custody they found themselves powerless to correct such a terrible injustice. Consequently, the escalating apprehension and panic that pervaded the black communities quickly motivated the abolitionists to endorse the continued resistance to this "hateful statute of kidnappers," as the law was described by Boston preacher Theodore Parker. Even the black leader Frederick Douglass, once a pacifist, was now declaring, "Slave-holders ... tyrants and despots have no right to live. The only way to make the fugitive slave law a dead letter is to make half a dozen or more dead kidnappers." In some instances the blacks themselves took matters into their own hands by storming the courthouse or even the jail to rescue the imprisoned fugitive, or overpowering a slave's captors at an enormous risk to their own safety. The fugitive was then given sanctuary and secretly transported out of harm's way.

To abolitionists in New York, Philadelphia, Harrisburg, and particularly those in Boston, the center of antislavery sentiments, the notion of enforcing this law was interpreted as a travesty of justice and immoral in every conceivable way. To voice their opposition, the word went out during Sunday sermons and in the daily newspapers denouncing the law and the people empowered to enforce it. To illustrate the lengths some northern officials impeded enforcement of the law, one anti-slave handbill posted in Boston in 1851 warned,

"CAUTION!! COLORED PEOPLE OF BOSTON, ONE & ALL, You are hereby respectfully CAUTIONED and advised, to avoid conversing with the Watchmen and Police Officers of Boston, For since the recent ORDER OF THE MAYOR & ALDERMEN, they are empowered to act as KIDNAP-PERS AND SLAVE CATCHERS, And they have already been actually employed in KIDNAPPING, CATCHING, AND KEEPING SLAVES. Therefore, if you value your LIBERTY, and the Welfare of the Fugitives among you, shun them in every possible manner, as so many HOUNDS on the track of the most unfortunate of your race. Keep a Sharp Look Out for KIDNAP-PERS, and have TOP EYE open."

The abolitionists were quite aware that Washington never hesitated to send large contingents of troops wherever they were needed to keep the peace or to spare no expense if called upon to insure a captured runaway slave was returned to the South. For this reason, Secretary of State Daniel Webster, an advocate of the law, was especially criticized, as well as President Fillmore, also one of its principal supporters.

To help reduce the growing anxiety among his constituents, Webster visited Boston to explain the rationale involved behind enacting the Compromise. Although highly exuberant rallies were frequently held in Faneuil Hall to denounce the new statute, Webster attempted to persuade the people to accept its rules no matter how perverted they appeared to be. "No man is at liberty to set up, or affect to set up, his own conscience as above the law, in a matter which respects the rights of others, and the obligations, civil, social, and political due to others from him. Such a pretense," he said, "saps the foundation of all government.... There must be no flinching, no doubt, nor hesitation."

In the South, however, the Fugitive Slave Act was something more significant than merely capturing a wayward slave; it was a matter of upholding southern rights and supporting the principle of southern pride and southern honor. Some historians today even suggest the South, by virtue of its unrelenting desire for this unreasonable and wicked law, really wanted to use the law as a weapon of aggression against the North. It was, they claim, a means to inflict grief and suffering on those particularly offended by it and not as a realistic means for catching the relatively small number of runaway slaves. One estimate claims that out of the tens of thousands of runaway slaves over the ten year period since passage of the 1850 Fugitive Slave Act, only about three hundred fugitives were actually recovered. In this regard, not only was its effectiveness as a deterrent proven to be unfounded but also its effectiveness as a means to apprehend fugitives.

As barbaric as the Fugitive Slave Act was perceived in some northern circles, most northerners were willing to acquiesce to its principles to further the cause of peace and stability. In Washington, as well, there was little official sentiment to alter any elements of the Compromise. As an ardent supporter of the Compromise, and the Fugitive Slave Act in particular, President Fillmore told Congress in December of 1850 that he thought the Compromise was "in its character final and irrevocable." Yet many anti–Compromise northern Whigs, especially in Boston and New York, were embarrassed and outraged over their president's acquiescence to the southern section. Simply ignoring the tired threat of secession, they called out for a repeal of all pro–South concessions, particularly the Fugitive Slave Act, to save the Whig Party from ridicule and scorn.

Congress was inclined to agree with Fillmore that the Compromise was indeed the final word on the slavery problem and that the measure should stand as written. They shamelessly confirmed that point when Sen. Charles Sumner of Massachusetts made an attempt to repeal the Fugitive Slave Act. His bill failed in the Senate when it received only four votes. Obviously, Senator Douglas, the force behind the Compromise, also considered the conflict over slavery in the territories a dead issue. "Let us cease agitating," he implored his fellow senators, "stop the debate, and drop the subject."

As 1851 rolled in, Fillmore was faced with yet another problem. Ever since the Wilmot Proviso was introduced neither sectional nor party lines remained clearly delineated. This time the basis for the breakdown occurred when the northern and southern wings of both parties failed to unite and vote as one voice to either accept or reject each element of the Compromise. Instead, the northern wing of the Whig Party joined forces with the southern wing of the Democratic Party and the southern wing of the Whig Party did the same with the northern Democrats. This crossing of party lines, therefore, eliminated any distinctive party differences many voters needed to remain loyal to one party or the other.

As a result of the split in Whig Party unity and the fracture of loyal party discipline, a number of northern Whigs from both houses of Congress spoke of abandoning the party altogether. They, and like-minded southern Democrats, would establish a Unionist coalition in a quest for a more partisan political alignment. Even Henry Clay, despite being a staunch disciple of Whig principles, announced that he could endorse the new party, especially if the northern Whigs continued to oppose the Compromise and if by their actions also included abolitionism into Whig dogma. He declared, "From that moment I renounce the party and cease to be a Whig."

To help soothe northern sensibilities and to prevent the further weakening of the Whig Party, Fillmore was forced to defend his position in an attempt to unify the Whigs. This was especially true for his support of the Fugitive Slave Act. Northern Whigs, Fillmore responded, did "not fully appreciate the dangers to which we are exposed from the South, and the infinite importance of setting an example of maintaining the Constitution in all its parts." In essence, Fillmore was explaining that he had to sign the Fugitive Slave Act because instead of limiting his judgment strictly to maintain the party's electoral competitiveness, he had to consider the welfare of the country as a whole. Secession, he said, was a threat he took seriously and would, if necessary, "bring the whole force of the government" to bear on any state to ensure the Fugitive Slave Act was obeyed to thwart that threat. He was convinced the Compromise had resolved the slavery and the Mexican Cession issues and, in turn, would ultimately save the Union.

Despite the administration's approval of the Compromise and its growing, albeit reluctant, acceptance in the North, many southern radicals, like Jefferson Davis, were convinced the benefits to the South were extremely limited. For this reason they stubbornly clung to the notion that secession was still inevitable. Although the Fugitive Slave Act had passed, they opined, little was actually gained because the law was already mandated by the Constitution. In addition, besides losing the slave trade in Washington, they also lost a great deal of slave territory to New Mexico in the border resolution with Texas. And even worse, the extremists complained, California would be admitted as a free state with no offsetting concession to the South, an action that upset the political balance in the Senate. By virtue of these conclusions and of the continuing efforts by abolitionists in parts of the North to resist supporting the Fugitive Slave Act, southern rights activists, slaveholders, and many other southern aristocrats were reenergized with even more resentment and hostility which only reinforced their desire to secede from the Union. Indeed, Georgia, Mississippi, Alabama, and South Carolina, the four southern states where the Democratic extreme fringe advocating secession was the strongest, were determined to bring the issue of disunion to a head. To rationalize their behavior, these southern extremists blamed the Compromise of 1850 for sowing the new seeds of secession.

As a result, governors in all four states called on their legislators to elect or consider electing delegates to meet and debate the issue of seceding from the Union. Georgia's delegates were the first to meet in convention on December 10, 1850, and the outcome clearly demonstrated the wide range of political and moral convictions still present in the South over leaving the Union. At the convention the stage was set for a confrontation between the two adversaries. On one side of the debate were the pro-secessionists, specifically the Southern Rights coalition made up of Democrats and a smattering of Whigs. On the other side were their antagonists, the Unionists, a coalition that understood the ramifications of secession and would fight to oppose it. Virtually all of the Georgian Whigs and nearly half of the Democrats supported the Unionist philosophy.

Besides the obvious clash of principles between the secessionists and the Unionists, there was also a division among the secessionists themselves. One faction, called actionists, wanted Georgia to secede immediately even if it meant taking this drastic action alone. On the other side of the argument were the cooperationists, sometimes called submissionists, who preferred to cooperate with all the other southern states and if secession was agreed to, they would act in concert with them in a show of unity. Consequently, instead of the secessionists being united in a political battle against the Unionists, the battle wound up being fought among the secessionists themselves, between actionists and cooperationists. Not surprisingly, when the voting was completed the Unionists prevailed overwhelmingly.

To save face with the other southern states, at the conclusion of the convention it was clearly pointed out in the so-called Georgia Platform that even though Georgia did "not wholly approve" of the Compromise, it accepted the measure "as a permanent adjustment of this sectional controversy" and Georgia's position on secession was conditional upon the full compliance of the North, most especially the satisfactory enforcement of the Fugitive Slave Act. With this declaration the North was on notice that secession, at least in the minds of the Georgians, was still considered a viable means to remedy their grievances but only if their conditions were not adhered to.

Although the delegates failed to agree on secession, the Unionists determined the fate of the current secessionist movement by the sheer power of their numbers. Noting the lack of unity in Georgia and its reluctance to leave the Union, the remaining three states came to the conclusion that it was now too late for them to gain any consensus for abandoning the Union in this current climate. Secession may have been a priority for southern aristocracy, but as far as the grass-roots voters were concerned, leaving the Union was "utterly unsanctioned by the Federal Constitution." This point was driven home in the fall of 1851 when Unionists governors were elected in Georgia and Mississippi.

It was increasingly clear to most northerners that despite the years of heated rhetoric and threats of secession, when push came to shove, the South had not yet come to terms with such a dramatic action. At the present time a great majority of southerners still held to the belief that secession was tantamount to treason and was certainly not a move that would solve their problems. This lack of unity and resolve, therefore, only reinforced the opinion in the North that the ongoing demands for leaving the Union had always been and still were nothing more than calculated threats from a loud and vocal minority to obtain concessions from the federal government. The *New York Times* even noted, "The peril of disunion, always exaggerated, has ceased to be even a scarecrow."

If the threat of secession was looked upon by some as superficial, the ever-expanding rift between the North and South was not. Diarist Philip Hone, shortly before his death in 1851 wrote, "The dreadful question of slavery, which has cast an inextinguishable brand of discord between the North and the South of this hitherto happy land has taken a tangible and definite shape on the question of the admission of the new State of California into the Union.... The flame is no longer smothered; the fanatics of the North and the disunionists of the South have made a gulf so deep that no friendly foot can pass it; enmity so fierce that reason cannot allay it; unconquerable, sectional jealousy, the most bitter personal hostility.... Passion rules the deliberations of the people's representatives to a degree which, from present appearances, will prevent the dispatch of public business of any kind.... The South stands ready to retire from the Union, and bloody wars will be the fatal consequences. White men will cut each other throats, and servile insurrections will render the fertile fields of the South a deserted monument of the madness of man. On the other hand the Abolitionists of the North will listen to no terms of compromise ... they profess to hold it of no value unless the power is conceded to them of restraining the extension of the great moral evil which overshadows the land."

Daniel Webster was also anxious over the loose talk of secession. "Peaceful secession!" he inquired, "What would be the results? Where is the line to be drawn? What states are to secede? What is to remain an American? What am I to be? An American no longer. Am I to become a sectional man, a local man, a separatist, with no country in common with the gentlemen who sit around me here...? Heaven forbid! Where is the flag of the republic to remain...? Shall the man of the Yellowstone and the Platte be connected, in the new republic, with the man who lives on the Southern extremity of the Cape of Florida? Sir, I am ashamed to pursue this line of remark.... I would rather hear of natural blasts and mildews, war, pestilence, and famine, than to hear gentlemen talk of secession. To break up this great government! To dismember this glorious country...! No, Sir! There will be no secession!"

In regard to the Fugitive Slave Act, pockets of resistance continued to fester in many parts of the North over enforcing the law, but after all was said and done, by 1852 northern support for the Compromise had taken hold, albeit tenuously, and the furor over the Fugitive Slave Act gradually began to subside over the following decade. Then, with thousands upon thousands of blacks abandoning their masters to follow the victorious Union forces, the law was finally repealed on June 28, 1864.

Barely audible over the carnival-like atmosphere in the hall, on June 1, 1852, the Democratic nominating convention was gaveled into session. As the delegates meandered within the assemblage one could sense the supreme confidence in their demeanor. They were still flush from their smashing victories in the mid-term elections two years earlier, an accomplishment influenced to a great degree by their unification following the Compromise of 1850. Always an economic windfall, the convention created a boom for the hotels, boarding houses, saloons, and brothels as some six hundred Democratic delegates swarmed into Baltimore.

Vying for their party's presidential nomination were the three leaders of the conservative northern wing: Lewis Cass, of Michigan, the principal force behind popular sovereignty, who many surmised was running to redeem his disappointing loss in 1848, and two contenders from the Polk administration.

They were Polk's secretary of war, William L. Marcy, of New York, the long shot, and from Pennsylvania, Polk's secretary of state, James Buchanan, the candidate of choice for the southern Democrats. Despite being a northerner, in the South Buchanan was favored because he had "Southern principles" and would be more conducive to their needs. Running as well was the 39-year-old upcoming political star, Sen. Stephen A. Douglas of Illinois. It seems the Little Giant's newfound notoriety from his efforts on the Compromise bill had whetted his appetite for a more lofty position from which to carry out his political and personal agenda. Douglas was the leader of the so-called Young Americans, a group dedicated to the doctrine of Manifest Destiny. Attempting to exploit their candidate's youthful persona in an otherwise aged assemblage, his Young American constituency published one campaign article in the *Democratic Review* extolling the reasons why Douglas should represent the party. He would not be a man "trammeled with ideas belonging to an anterior era," they wrote, "or a man of merely local fame and local affections, but a statesman who can bring young blood, young ideas, and young hearts to the councils of the Republic. He must not be a mere general, a mere lawyer, a mere wire-puller."

As the speeches droned on and the infighting for the highly prized undecided votes continued, the tenor of the convention was anything but congenial. Despite the many back room deals, trade-offs, and arm twisting, none of the candidates was able to satisfy the necessary two-thirds rule required for nomination, the same rule invoked in 1844 to withhold the nomination from Van Buren. After three days and 48 ballots and deadlocked without a nominee, all sides finally rallied around the dark horse candidate prearranged and groomed for such an occurrence, Franklin Pierce, a relatively unknown figure to the public at large. On learning that Pierce was selected, George Templeton Strong remarked, "Nobody knows much of Franklin Pierce, except that he is a decent sort of man in private life. Very possibly he may run all the better, as Polk did, for his insignificance." The fact that Pierce was a strong supporter of the Compromise, which of course included the Fugitive Slave Act, made his candidacy quite palatable to many southerners and in the end was one of the most significant factors that won him the nomination. Unlike the Whigs, however, who would experience dissension over their platform, the Democrats had wide party support for their so-called "southern platform," one that reaffirmed the legitimacy of federal intervention in enforcing the Fugitive Slave Act and the advocacy of Cass's doctrine of popular sovereignty in the territories.

Although the two-thirds rule was the primary factor in the loss for all the candidates, the real coup de grace for Senator Douglas, as a relative newcomer, was when one of his young backers wrote an article that attacked the other candidates in a stinging tirade, calling them "Old Fogies." Highly insulted, the Little Giant's rivals united in a conspiracy to defeat him.

The Whigs also held their national convention in Baltimore about two weeks later with the Compromise bill also playing a key role in their nominating process. Being considered for the nomination were three candidates, Fillmore, General Scott, and Webster.

Fillmore threw his hat into the ring fully convinced that not only his signing and support for the Compromise bill, which he considered his greatest achievement, but also his vigorous efforts to enforce the capture of runaway slaves would help him carry the day. The president's struggle on their behalf obviously pleased the southern Whigs tremendously but at the same time severely alienated the northern Whigs.

Challenging the direction the president was taking their party, the northern Whigs were convinced their interpretation of Whig principles was the right one, principles they believed reflected anti-slavery and a non-extension philosophy. Accordingly, the northern Whigs agreed their best choice for the presidency was the aging general and only remaining war hero, old "Fuss and Feathers," Winfield Scott, whose support for the Compromise was lukewarm at best. Reflecting on Scott's candidacy many southerners agreed with one Tennessee congressmen who concluded that Scott was only being used as a tool by his northern backers because he was "not publicly identified with ... the compromise in such a way as to make it impossible for that large portion of the Northern Whigs to support him, who are hostile to those measures, and who maintain their local political position by fomenting the prejudices of the North against the South."

It was quite ironic that at a time when sectional identity had taken on such significance, the southern faction of the party was endorsing a northerner from New York, while the northern wing was endorsing a candidate from Virginia.

Also in the hunt was Secretary of State Daniel Webster. Seventy-two years old and in failing health, despite the concerned advice from his friends to forgo the stress of the nominating process, he entered his name into the race as well. Like Clay and Calhoun, Webster always yearned for the high office, a yearning consistently rebuffed by his own party. Although Webster could count on support from his New England constituency, he knew his prospects were still poor against the likes of Fillmore, who had substantial support already pledged to him from both the North and South.

During the course of the convention this glaring sectional rivalry became so disruptive that the divided delegates were unable to give any of the three candidates the winning majority after fifty-two chaotic ballots. Finally, on the following roll call enough fence-sitting southerners switched their votes away from Fillmore to win the nomination for General Scott.

Since they were in the majority, the pro–Compromise Whigs, primarily the Fillmore and Webster supporters, were instrumental in determining the construction of the Whig platform, a move that instigated much intra-party squabbling. The platform, for example, advocated the finality of the Compromise and the party's commitment to enforcing the Fugitive Slave Act, a clear indication of the administration's strong influence in adopting the Whig position. Despite the objections and the refusal of the Scott people to accept this platform, however, enough northern moderates switched their votes to gain its final passage. This switch enabled the party to agree, at least in principle, that the Compromise was a settlement to the territorial questions. Adding to the problems over the platform were the remaining free-soil Whigs in the party. Disappointed that the platform did not reject the Fugitive Slave Act outright, they defected to the Free Soil Party to nominate their own candidate and to adopt their own platform. Consequently, in August, at the Free Soil convention at Boston's Faneuil Hall, they selected Sen. John P. Hale of New Hampshire.

With the party in disarray and on the verge of collapse, the Whigs were now faced with initiating efforts to attract new voters to their weakening base. In desperation, they turned their attention to the feasibility of gaining voter support from the millions of immigrants inundating the northern states and migrating west. These newcomers, mostly Irish and Germans, flowed onto U.S. shores at an unprecedented rate and had placed the Whigs in a massive predicament. Historically attracted to the Democratic Party and with a five-year residency requirement for naturalization satisfied, many were now eligible to vote. Under this scenario, the Whigs feared the Democrats were assured of hundreds of thousands of new votes in the upcoming election, votes the Whigs dearly needed. Exacerbating their predicament as well was that most of the immigrants were Roman Catholic. Not only was the heavy influx of foreigners into the country upsetting to a sizeable number of Americans, but their religious affiliation was extremely offensive to anti–Catholic Protestant-Americans, including those within the Whig Party. This bigotry derived from their fear of papal control of the United States government, a condition originating with the teachings of the Protestant church. Their sermons claimed allegiance to the Pope was synonymous with allegiance to a foreign prince who, the preachers stated, was allegedly waiting to politically overpower the U.S. government through the continuous influx of his followers. Called Nativists, they harbored a fanatical opposition not only to all foreign-born immigrants holding public office, but even to all Catholics, preferring to elect native-born Protestants instead.

The roots of the Nativist movement, or the Know-Nothings as they were generally called, extended back to 1849. At the time secret fraternities were formed, such as the Order of the Star Spangled Banner in New York and the Order of the United Sons of America in Pennsylvania, consisting entirely of native-born Protestants. Resembling the degree-oriented structure of the Masons, their goal was to prevent Catholics and immigrants from participating in the political process. And whenever questions were posed from non-members about the secret organization, their standard reply would always be "I know nothing." Hence the name Know-Nothings.

The motivating factor at the foundation of these secret fraternities was the hundreds of thousands of immigrants coming into the United States since the '30s and '40s. Mostly indigent Irish and German, the Irish newcomers preferred to remain in the Northeast where they lived in the gritty squalor of congested neighborhoods and crowded tenements. Without a meaningful education and unable to speak fluent English, most suffered the indignities of long term unemployment and as a result, in the larger cities like New York, Boston, Philadelphia, and St. Louis, crime soared, public drunkenness was chronic and to the exasperation of the local taxpayers, expenditures for public assistance steadily grew. While the Irish accounted for approximately half of the population of Boston and New York by the 1850s, most of the Germans traveled to the farms of the Midwest where they reestablished a lifestyle incorporating their old-country heritage and customs with some aspects of American traditions.

The newcomers spoke a different language, dressed differently, ate different foods, worshiped in a different church, and were in many other ways culturally out of step with the American way. As a consequence, many Americans feared the U.S. was being overtaken by the dregs of Europe, who they pointed out were filling American prisons, poorhouses, and saloons and were even blamed for rising rents and food prices. And, they also complained, the immigrants who did work accepted very low wages which only undermined the vitality of the labor system.

The resentment and friction between the general population and foreign immigrants continued to evolve even as a by-product of the enormous railroad construction projects in the early 1850s. As construction workers, many of whom were immigrants, built an ever expanding web of track, scores of American-born laborers employed by shipping enterprises along rivers and canals now found themselves out of work. They were the unfortunate victims of technological growth, of businesses lost to the more rapid, more efficient, and cheaper mode of transporting goods, people, and materials. And in the cities and towns where the railroads stopped, various industries sprang up and competition suddenly grew between manufacturing firms in the Midwest and those in the East. Invariably this explosive boom in the local economies often resulted in a benefit to the consumer who could now obtain more goods and at lower prices. At the same time it promoted layoffs, lower wages and fewer jobs for many native-born Americans. The net result was that thousands of these frustrated workers, unable to find jobs or unwilling to accept lower wages, lashed out at the immigrants as the cause of all their grief.

Despite this background of hostility toward Catholics and all foreigners in particular, following endless caucuses the decision was finally made by the Whig leaders to make an exception to their traditional party position and to direct their campaign efforts toward winning over the huge potential support of the Catholic immigrants. Not everyone in the party agreed, however, and the decision to pursue the immigrant vote threatened to aggravate the Whig difficulties even further. With this significant change in Whig philosophy, the Nativists within the party also vowed to leave as well. Nevertheless, Whig leaders thought it was much more important to prevent the Democrats from benefiting from the immigrant votes than to lose the relatively smaller number of Nativists. After all, they opined, Scott had two daughters brought up as Catholic in Catholic convents, a sure-fire public relations tactic to exploit during the campaign.

By now the Whigs were more divided than ever and on the brink of disaster. Not only couldn't they agree on the Compromise, but also the southern wing rejected Scott as the presidential nominee, while the northern wing rejected Fillmore and the party platform. Furthermore, the free-soilers within the party disapproved of the platform and both candidates and nominated their own candidate under a new party banner in the process. At the same time, the Nativists within the party resented the political decision to embrace foreigners and Catholics and were threatening to walk out on the party too. By virtue of this deep schism within the Whig Party, the Democrats were, for all intents and purposes, assured of victory in the upcoming presidential election.

But similar to the Whigs, the Democrats also found themselves in a quandary over the immigrant vote. As mentioned earlier, one highly visible and alarming effect from the enormous influx of foreigners was the appalling poverty, which in turn triggered dreadful slums, a high incidence of drunkenness, and escalating crime. In fact, the perception of wide-spread and seemingly unrestrained drunkenness was so pervasive that highly organized temperance movements were formed in most major cities of the North. These movements, designed to encourage the people to accept some degree of self-restraint in the consumption of alcoholic beverages, went largely ignored by the immigrants, who often patronized the local pubs as their principal form of social interaction. Although the laws resulting from the temperance movement, called Maine laws because the movement gained its first success in Maine, were largely unenforceable, the notoriety over the temperance movement itself served to reinforce the Nativist bigotry and stereotype of the foreigners invading U.S. shores.

The outcry from an irate citizenry for stiff temperance laws to curb this growing threat to American society placed the Democrats in a bind. To publicly endorse prohibition laws, which they favored, would mean offending the immigrants, who were solidly against anyone tampering with their social proclivities. The Democrats, therefore, in a form of mid–18th century political correctness, were quite reluctant to speak out against temperance laws so as to avoid the risk of losing their enormous immigrant constituency.

In November 1852, to no one's great surprise, even in some corners of the

Whig camp, Franklin Pierce easily won the presidential election claiming 27 of the 31 states as well as capturing Democratic control of the new Congress by large margins. In the electoral vote his tally was a smashing 254 to 42, the largest margin of victory since Monroe's 231 to 1 landslide win in 1820. The only four states captured by General Scott were Massachusetts, Vermont, Kentucky, and Tennessee. In fact, the Whigs lost votes in every state but Virginia. Viewed as inept and untrustworthy, Scott lost primarily because he was considered an unfriendly foe of the Compromise at a time when both parties were moving to embrace the measure. And the Whigs miscalculated Scott's appeal to the immigrants when they discovered the Democrats had published letters Scott had written years earlier. In these letters Scott insisted on a longer waiting period for naturalization of foreigners, something more in line with the twenty-five years espoused by the Nativists, a tactic that put the immigrant voters solidly behind the Democrats.

Although the Know-Nothings had little impact on this election, their popularity would steadily grow. By 1854, under the banner of the American Party, they would be a force to be reckoned with.

One significant aspect of this election was the extraordinary lack of voter turnout for both parties. Still suffering from a lack of clear party distinctions and relevant issues, one editor remarked, "Party ties are measurably weakened, and partially broken. Indifference and apathy have taken possession of the public mind." It was becoming increasingly clear that the political times were changing and with it, the end of the Second Party System.

During the interval between the nominating conventions and the election the nation lost the last two statesmen of the Great Triumvirate. On June 29, 1852, seventy-five-year-old Henry Clay, the "Prince of the Senate," died. Too ill to leave his bed, Clay spent the last months of his life confined to his room at the National Hotel in Washington unable to be with his beloved and ailing wife in his final moments. The flood of glowing tributes and eulogies that followed, from congressmen and senators, Democrats and Whigs, although dignified and moving, could not truly capture the essence of his character, his oratorical genius, or his patriotism. Drawn by a team of gray horses, his funeral procession proceeded up Pennsylvania Avenue to the Capitol where Clay had the signal honor of being the first American to lie in state in the grandeur of the Capitol Rotunda.

While Clay's cortege journeyed to his final resting place in Lexington, Kentucky, Daniel Webster became much too ill to remain in the administration. He returned to Boston where he was honored with a grand parade, a lavish dinner, and endless speeches. Webster continued on to his home in Marshfield where over the next several months his condition continued to deteriorate. In the waning hours of October 23, with his family, several relatives, friends, and servants by his bedside, the seventy-year-old gave his parting farewells to each of them in turn. Shortly after two o'clock the following morning, the great orator was dead. At the memorial services in Faneuil Hall, attended by three thousand mourners, a speaker remarked how "everyone looked as if he had been at the funeral of his own father." Following a simple funeral, Webster was interred at the family cemetery in Marshfield.

The new 48-year-old president, a graduate of Bowdoin College, practiced law for a number of years before trying his hand in politics in the New Hampshire legislature. Elected to the U.S. Senate in 1837, Pierce left Washington five years later when the combination of politics and liquor began to threaten his marriage to a temperance-minded wife. He returned to New Hampshire where he maintained a political leadership role until the war with Mexico was declared. Following his enlistment as a private, Pierce was rapidly advanced to colonel. Later, as a general, he served under Scott from the battle of Veracruz to the capture of Mexico City. Pierce returned to his law practice following the war and four years later was sent to the Democratic National Convention as New Hampshire's favorite son.

Taking the oath of office in a driving March snowstorm, the new president was not only the youngest man to that date so elected, but Pierce was and still is the only president to chose the words "to affirm" in taking his presidential oath instead of "to swear," a choice he made on religious grounds and fully sanctioned by the U.S. Constitution.

To drive home his position on the Compromise, in his inauguration speech Pierce reminded the snow covered crowd, "I hold that the laws of 1850, commonly called the compromise measures, are strictly constitutional and to be unhesitatingly carried into effect." He also clearly outlined his position on territorial expansion by saying, "The apprehension of dangers from extended territory, multiplied States, accumulated wealth, and augmented population has proved to be unfounded. The stars upon your banner have become nearly threefold their original number; your densely populated possessions skirt the shores of the two great oceans; and yet this vast increase in people and territory has not only shown itself compatible with the harmonious action of the States and Federal Government in their respective constitutional spheres, but has afforded an additional guaranty of the strength and integrity of both.... The policy of my administration will not be controlled by any timid forebodings of evil from expansion ... our attitude as a nation and our position on the globe render[s] the acquisition of certain possessions not within our jurisdiction eminently important for our protection, if not in the future essential for the preservation of the rights of commerce and the peace of the world."

13

Filibusters (1849 to 1860)

During the Polk administration expansionism was a national goal, a drive to extend the borders of the United States from the Atlantic to the Pacific. But since Polk's expansionist goals were virtually fulfilled, that fervent and near fanaticism had diminished during the Whig administrations of Taylor and Fillmore. Expansionism now became more of a sectional priority, principally in the South, where the unrelenting desire to extend that culture to other quarters remained just as strong. And now that Pierce had promised his administration would not be timid in its expansionist agenda, the South felt reassured that better days were indeed ahead. With all the Mexican Cession parceled out under the Compromise of 1850, and the remaining territories north of 36° 30' seemingly accounted for under the Compromise of 1820 and the Oregon Treaty, southern aims were merely directed elsewhere—southward to Cuba.

The desire for Cuba, an island under Spanish control and with over a half million slaves, was hardly a recent love affair for the South. President Polk first expressed an interest in buying the "Pearl of the West Indies" in 1848. "I am decidedly in favour of purchasing Cuba," he reassured the expansionists, "and making it one of the States of [the] Union." Polk's message was refreshing news to the planters of the Deep South since they were convinced slavery in the western territories was highly improbable. It was generally accepted that the people there were against it and the soil and climate was certainly unsuitable for growing the cash crops bankrolling their economy. For many planters, therefore, expansion westward was not that critical a factor as expansion to the South, to Cuba and perhaps even beyond.

Unfortunately for the South, Polk's attempt to purchase Cuba was a dismal failure. Implausible as it may be, the administration's representative in Spain was a man unable to speak Spanish, supposedly a necessary prerequisite for that post. Consequently, his attempt to communicate Polk's offer wasn't taken all that seriously and as a result the $100 million bid was soundly rejected. Dismissing the offer out of hand, Spanish officials countered that sooner then sell Cuba to the United States, Spain would "prefer seeing it sunk in the ocean."

Southern congressional leaders were outraged over this fiasco to say the least. With the possibility of increasing their representation in Congress by as many as fifteen, they refused to simply shrug it off. On the contrary, they were more determined than ever to acquire the island. This was especially true of Jefferson Davis. Extremely frustrated over Polk's incompetent effort, he forcefully reminded his fellow planters in the Senate of their objective. "Cuba must be ours to increase the number of slaveholding constituencies," he demanded. Since diplomacy had failed to gain their objective, he said, perhaps a stronger form of dialogue was necessary. And that they agreed was armed intervention.

In September 1849, a ragtag army of several hundred men was recruited for an invasion of Cuba under the command of a Cuban revolutionary named Narciso López. This motley crew of adventurers, renegades, and mercenaries were called filibusters, a Spanish word meaning pirate or specifically one who engages in unauthorized warfare against a country with which his own country is at peace. After both Jefferson Davis and Robert E. Lee turned down offers to lead the filibusters, López decided to take on the role himself. To reinforce the manpower needed for the expedition, López was convinced that when his men launched their attack, enough Cuban revolutionaries would rise up against the government and join forces in the overthrow of Havana. But it was not to be. By that time the new president was Zachary Taylor, and upon learning of the planned attack Taylor immediately confiscated their ships, effectively ending the expedition before it began.

Not to be deterred, López traveled to Mississippi and met with Gov. John Quitman, a former general who served under Scott in the capture of Mexico City. The purpose of the meeting was to outline the details of a new invasion plan and to persuade Quitman to command the expedition. Citing his responsibilities as governor as his first priority, Quitman politely refused but offered whatever help he could provide, particularly in financing the expedition.

In May 1850, with a new army of some 600 armed and eager volunteers and several make-shift transports, López sailed out of New Orleans for the beaches of northern Cuba. Following the uneventful crossing of the Gulf, the filibusters secured the beachhead, stormed into the interior, and quickly captured the town of Cárdenas. Up to this point everything had gone as planned, but soon it occurred to López that he was in serious trouble. The expected Cuban revolutionaries never appeared and without those reinforcements López knew it would be suicide for his men to challenge the larger and more experienced Spanish army. López, therefore, had little choice but to abort the operation and return to New Orleans.

Although the South treated López as a hero for a valiant effort, the Taylor administration was not amused over this escapade against a foreign government and indicted him for being in violation of the neutrality laws. Also charged was one of his principal sponsors, Governor Quitman, but when three trials failed to reach a verdict on just one of the relatively minor defendants, the charges were dropped.

Over the months ahead, López traveled across the South in an attempt to encourage support for yet another filibuster expedition. Although his luster had tarnished somewhat, from time to time he was wined and dined by local officials and in the process managed to assemble some 400 new followers. Benefactors of López and his cause, like Mississippi Senator Albert G. Brown, toasted the brash young man exclaiming, "I want Cuba, and I know that sooner or later we must have it."

In 1851, a determined López and his motley group of filibusters sailed out of New Orleans on August 3 in a third attempt to capture Havana. This time they were in for a big surprise because news of López and his proposed expedition had reached Cuban officials and, needless to say, Spanish troops were patiently waiting for them to arrive. As a result, in the ensuing battle some 200 filibusters were killed and of those captured over 100 were sent to a prison in Spain. And, to close this matter once and for all, before a cheering crowd in Havana, López was garroted and the remaining 51 Americans were lined up and shot.

Although anti–Spanish sentiment ran high throughout New Orleans with cries for revenge, President Fillmore took no direct action against Spain over this incident except to gain the release of the American prisoners.

In 1853, with a new administration in Washington, President Pierce appeared ready to deliver on his promise to deal with the southern interest in Cuba. In fact, ex–Governor John Quitman, now free to follow his own expansionist urgings, had met with officials in Washington on at least one occasion to discuss his role in leading yet another expedition to the island. And because news of the proposed expedition to Cuba had surfaced, it gained much greater financial support from the Cuban junta in New York City and politically from several contacts within the Pierce administration, such as Secretary of War Jefferson Davis, and several prominent southern state leaders as well. To avoid any legal or political problems, there was even a move to repeal the neutrality laws to insure Quitman would not be restricted in carrying out this scheme. In addition, the Cuban junta vested Quitman with all the powers necessary to achieve his objective and if he succeeded in installing a pro-slavery government in Havana, he would receive one million dollars, certainly a generous compensation package in the mid–nineteenth century.

It seems Quitman's concept of military intelligence and the value of maintaining clandestine expeditions classified was not well considered. The Spanish government in Madrid became fully aware of this latest and most publicized venture and immediately set up countermeasures to combat this blatant attempt to invade their little island once again. Following deliberations at the highest level, in September, a new Spanish envoy was quickly dispatched to Cuba to implement stronger security measures. One of his first acts as the new Cuban administrator was to issue a decree that not only put an end to the slave trade but also freed many of the slaves on the island. If that wasn't unsettling enough to the stunned planters, the freed slaves were then recruited into an armed militia to challenge Quitman's filibusters, and the government would detain any planter found supporting the American venture. But in June of 1854, as Quitman was in the process of gathering his 3,000 men, an armed warship, and $300,000 in expense money, he learned the Pierce administration suddenly revised its strategy for acquiring Cuba. The filibuster campaign was now ruled out and a second attempt to purchase the island was adopted instead.

Historically there were two suppositions for this change in direction. For one, it would be much easier to simply buy the island than to lose lives fighting for it and was a move many northern expansionists favored. However, many historians believe a more compelling reason was the enormous negative backlash expected from the North against the Democratic Party over a perceived scheme against Cuba designed to benefit the proslavery advocates. Acquiescing to the advice from his advisors, Pierce agreed that a filibuster expedition to Cuba would appear too aggressive and too pro-slave at this time. Instead it would be more prudent, at least for now, to tone down his position on expansionism.

In line with the administration's new Cuban policy, on April 3, 1854, Secretary of State William L. Marcy authorized his minister to Spain, Pierre Soulé, to offer the Spanish government up to $130 million for Cuba. Furthermore, a second caveat to the order dealt with the alternative if the Spanish officials refused to accept the deal. The order to Soulé specified, "You will then direct your effort to the next desirable object, which is to detach that island from the Spanish dominion and from all dependence on any European power." As expected, the Spanish government refused to sell.

As a follow-up to the Spanish government's refusal to do business, in the fall, Soulé met with two of the other European U.S. ministers at Ostend, Belgium. The meeting of the three ministers was ordered by Secretary Marcy to discuss the entire Cuban situation and to issue a memorandum to the State Department outlining the details of their conclusions. Attending this meeting, in addition to Soulé, were James Buchanan and John Y. Mason, the ministers to Britain and France respectively.

After three days of discussions the ministers drew up a declaration on October 18, 1854, which clearly stated that "Cuba is as necessary to the North American republic as any of its present members, and that it belongs naturally to that great family of states of which the Union is the Providential Nursery." Furthermore, if the United States determined that Spain's refusal to sell Cuba would "seriously endanger our internal peace" then "by every law, human and Divine, we shall be justified in wresting it from Spain if we possess the power." This was called the Ostend Manifesto. To the embarrassment of all parties concerned, it was leaked to the press and in November published in the *New York Herald* amid cries from outraged anti-slave proponents. Stung by the avalanche of criticism over this entire fiasco, Pierce not only revoked his order to Soulé, who was forced to resign, but also stopped any effort to repeal the neutrality laws and abandoned any further efforts to obtain Cuba.

Other attempts at territorial acquisition through filibustering campaigns were clearly in vogue during the mid–1850s. In addition to López and Quitman and their quest to take over Cuba, on the west coast another self-appointed redeemer was also creating havoc and drawing the wrath of the Pierce administration.

He was William Walker, a lean young man carrying less than 125 pounds on a little five-foot, five-inch frame. A unique Tennessean of enormous ambition and boundless energy, Walker completed college at the tender age of fourteen and then went on to the University of Pennsylvania where he received a degree in medicine at nineteen. In 1853, following brief periods as a doctor, lawyer, and journalist, his restless and unfulfilled spirit brought him to San Francisco. Unlike the thousands of others streaming into the area, Walker's interest was not to prospect for gold but to engage in more adventurous endeavors.

The 29-year-old, in a clear contradiction to his obvious diminutive appearance, chartered a ship and three weeks later led a gang of some fifty tough filibusters in a scheme to take over the territories of Baja California and Sonora, in northern Mexico. Being a pro-slavery southerner and an expansionist, his ultimate goal was to capture this land and annex it to the United States as slave territory so the South could acquire a degree of political balance with the North.

Walker and his small army embarked at San Francisco in October 1853 and about three weeks later landed at La Paz, the capital of Baja, where he took on an additional two hundred volunteers. In the course of their bold expedition, Walker captured La Paz, declared its independence, and renamed the territory the Republic of Lower California. Moving his forces on to Ensenada, where he established his headquarters, Walker issued a proclamation that not only annexed Sonora to his growing empire but also named the combined territory the Republic of Sonora. Walker then brazenly installed himself as president.

Walker's popularity in the South soared as news of his exploits became known and hundreds of sympathizers, eager to join his campaign, flocked to support his cause. San Francisco newspapers applauded his exploits, writing, "The term filibuster no longer means a pirate.... It means the compassing of the weak by the strong.... The term filibuster is now identical with the pioneer of progress...."

But soon the volunteers found conditions not as they had expected. Food was scarce and many supplies had already been depleted. Discontent began to infect the filibusters, causing many to desert the expedition. Nevertheless, emboldened by his initial success, Walker went on to invade Sonora with his remaining troops and at this point confronted his first taste of serious resistance. In the face of heavy fighting more than half of Walker's remaining filibusters also deserted while the others fled from the fight, leaving the bodies of dead comrades strewn across the fields. With less than forty of his surviving men, Walker fled back across the border to San Diego in May where he surrendered to authorities. Hailed as a hero, he was granted a parole and later acquitted of violating the neutrality laws in a trial in San Francisco.

With filibustering now in his blood, Walker saw another opportunity to fulfill his new craving for power. This time he would go to Nicaragua. A tropical country with an abundance of blistering heat and fertile soil for growing cotton, sugar, and coffee, it was an ideal setting for southern entrepreneurs to expand their cash crop interests. Unfortunately, with southern attention still concentrated on Cuba, serious interest in Nicaragua had not yet developed. Even more inviting, particularly to American shipping moguls, was the possibility of building a canal through Nicaragua to the Pacific. Although it would be a Herculean effort in labor and costs, the proposed canal would literally take weeks off the travel time between the east and west coasts of the United States.

Walker's interest did not lie with either the potential for enormous profits in farm produce or in building the canal. Instead his ambitions were motivated by the power and prestige inherent with overthrowing the Nicaraguan government, an unstable entity ostensibly in endless revolutions. In fact, a revolution was currently in progress that pitted the British-backed Nicaraguans against the Leonese. Being the weaker of the two adversaries, the Leonese rebels sought Walker's assistance, a request he could not pass up.

Casting his lot with the rebels, in May of 1855, his advance force of approximately fifty filibusters set sail from San Francisco for the jungles of Nicaragua. Meanwhile, since the American and British governments were experiencing less than amiable relations at the time, the illegality of filibuster campaigns was conveniently overlooked by U.S. authorities.

Walker's expedition was not exactly a compulsive one but was well planned, well equipped, and well financed by millionaire shipping tycoon Cornelius Vanderbilt, who undoubtedly had an ulterior motive for his generosity. His investment ultimately paid off when the Nicaraguan soldiers proved to be no match for the highly motivated band of rebels and filibusters. To cap off his latest victory, Walker proudly appointed himself the commander in chief of the Nicaraguan army, or generalissimo. It was indeed a far cry from his journalism days.

Southern newspapers were elated over this turn of events and began to praise Walker for fighting for a cause he believed was just. In Washington, Walker's escapade was also received quite favorably and confirmed a year later when Pierce dispatched an envoy to the Nicaraguan capital to signal U.S. diplomatic recognition. At the same time the North was calling him a pirate, a renegade, and a disgrace to his country.

It wasn't until mid–1856, as southern planters streamed into Nicaragua, that the South fully recognized the latent potential of this Central American country. Although slavery was abolished some ten years earlier, the Southern elitists simply shrugged it off, confident they would re-establish the institution there at the appropriate time.

The events in Nicaragua, however, had not gone unnoticed by other Central American countries. Concerned over the steady flow of Americans into their neck of the world, Guatemala, San Salvador, and Costa Rica formed a coalition to overthrow this new government and its brash gringo general.

In July of 1856 the situation began to turn ugly when the Nicaraguan president defected and Walker appointed himself the new leader of the country. As the new Nicaraguan President, Walker immediately began exercising his executive powers. In the fickle world of politics where you never quite know who your enemy is, Walker began by revoking the franchise which the Vanderbilt Steamship Company held for transporting passengers through the proposed canal. Instead, the right of transit was now granted to Vanderbilt's competitor. Needless to say, Vanderbilt was so outraged over Walker's betrayal that he threw in with the South American coalition and promised to finance its efforts to overthrow the brash American. President Pierce, as well, was so angered by Walker's audacity that he immediately recalled his representative and rescinded U.S. diplomatic recognition.

With Vanderbilt now supporting the coalition's offensive and relations with the United States severed, Walker found his revolution in dire straits. He desperately needed someone to shore up his crumbling empire with more troops and more money. And that's when Walker turned to the South, where he was still celebrated as a hero of the southern expansionist cause. To clinch the relationship with his benefactor, in September, Walker shocked the little nation when he reversed the anti-slavery laws that were in force for thirty-two years. It was an unprecedented move, and one that obviously thrilled the southern elites. And to add an exclamation point, his message to the southern planters was conveyed by the Nicaraguan press. "In the name of the white race, [Walker] now offers Nicaragua to you and your slaves, at a time when you have not a friend on the face of the earth." But it was all too late. The Central American coalition struck in force and the vanquished Walker, fearing for his life, was forced out of Nicaragua. Returning to New Orleans, Walker, as always, was given a rousing reception, paraded through the streets and praised for his selfless fight for southern honor.

But yet again, his unrelenting desire to expand southern influence compelled him to try anew. Consequently, with the backing of southern money, men, and equipment, Walker made several more attempts to reach Nicaragua.

On the second expedition in November 1857 the U.S. Navy stopped his ship and he was returned to New Orleans to stand trial. Again he was acquitted of violating the neutrality law. His third expedition over a year later ended when his ship hit a reef and sank off the Central American coast. Rescued by a passing British ship, Walker and his men were unceremoniously transported to Mobile.

Unfortunately, while in Honduras to gather support for his fourth expedition, the news of Walker's presence inflamed the local citizens. Before the situation worsened, Walker and his men escaped from the hostile crowd and boarded a British ship moored nearby. Instead of being taken back to the U.S., however, the British captain turned Walker over to the Hondurans. Imprisoned, tried by court-martial, and convicted, Walker was shot by a Nicaraguan firing squad on September 12, 1860. Walker's filibustering days were over, and so too was the southern quest to fulfill a Manifest Destiny.

14

The Kansas-Nebraska Act (1852 to 1854)

Although Congress made every attempt to avoid legislative conflicts over slavery since the passage of the Compromise of 1850, sectional feuding still remained an active component of antebellum politics. This time the two sides clashed over a highly desired western link for a transcontinental railroad line, which in turn triggered further disputes over partitioning the remaining territory of the Louisiana Purchase. These equally divisive issues not only continued to exacerbate sectional tensions but also to further agitate the controversial issues of slavery in the territories, political superiority, and economic expansion.

While the popularity of Manifest Destiny raged throughout the nation in the middle 1840s, an ancillary interest quickly developed for building a transcontinental rail line. Steam locomotion had by now proven itself not only as an economical and speedy method to transport goods and travelers but also as a vital link for encouraging the further growth of the country. This realization provided the widespread impetus for discussions on possible rail lines connecting the West coast to both the North and the South. Talk was free and easy in the mid–1840s and scores of visionaries soon predicted the inevitable growth of cities and markets as the new railroad lines snaked their way across the country. U.S. commerce, the economy, the standard of living, and increasing prosperity, they said, all embraced in a huge web of rail and rolling stock would make the United States a world power. Other technological advances, such as instant communications by telegraph, also encouraged the growing acceptance and the feasibility of managing a vast country and challenged the objections of some that the country would be too large to govern effectively.

Asa Whitney, a locomotive designer and builder who was also a distant cousin of Eli Whitney, proposed building a railroad line from Lake Michigan to the Pacific: "[It] would bring all our immensely wide-spread population together as one vast city; the moral and social effects of which must harmonize all together as one family, with but one interest—the general good of all." The catch to Whitney's proposal was the government had to agree to sell him a 60-mile wide strip along the entire route for only ten cents an acre. It would be a self-financing project, he claimed. Money for financing the construction of the line, which the government would ultimately own, would come from the revenue taken in by Whitney as he sold his land. Although Whitney's idea of a railroad linking the two coasts was well received in Washington, and was consistently debated in both chambers of Congress, it never gained the political traction it may have deserved and as a result was never acted upon.

Nevertheless, the allure for constructing a rail line from an eastern city to the West Coast was indeed intriguing and its potential benefits to the nation became quite apparent to more than a few forward-thinking individuals. It would be a monumental financial and engineering project, one that required the support of the U.S. government, a prospect very few people considered as forthcoming. But at the same time it was also a speculative venture, notwithstanding the fact that it was steadily growing in popularity. The thought of miles upon miles of iron track stretching across the barren land of the Far West captured the imagination of people from all walks of life. From the ordinary farmers searching for wider markets to the railroad tycoons who saw an enormous opportunity to increase their wealth and their prestige, the financial benefits of the railroad were extremely appealing. Even a few politicians, always alert not only for prospects that would benefit the country but also for their own jobs and financial security, began to take a more avid interest in the railroad.

Over time, railroad barons, land speculators, and scores of various city and state officials, individuals from both sections with entrepreneurial interests or expansionist inclinations, combined forces to advocate construction of the railroad. Their efforts in this initiative, although exploitive to the extreme, were certain to satisfy their self-serving agendas. As these powerful special interests groups became more aware of the benefits of a transcontinental railroad, lobbying campaigns in Washington were stepped up to urge the government to demonstrate more concrete action in adopting a comprehensive railroad construction program.

Stephen A. Douglas, then a young 32-year-old congressman, was one politician struck early on by the potential of such a venture. Caught up in the spirit of the movement, within months of Whitney's published proposal, the Little Giant decided to fine tune the idea with one of his own. Instead of connecting Lake Michigan to the Columbia River, as Whitney proposed, the Illinois congressman suggested building the railroad from Chicago to San Francisco, "if that country could be annexed in time." And instead of depending on land sales to drive the construction, which could take many years, he preferred to lay the tracks immediately in order to attract the settlers to the railroad which, in turn, would encourage them to purchase land in the territories. But, here too there was another hitch. Since the land west of Iowa over which the road would pass had yet to be surveyed for land distribution, Douglas had to first submit a bill to organize that vast region, an expanse of open wilderness called the Nebraska Territory. The bill Douglas submitted, however, failed to sway his fellow members in the House of Representatives and it went nowhere. Nevertheless, far from being discouraged, Douglas had staked his claim for a transcontinental railroad and vowed to continue his pursuit of this initiative.

When the second session of the Thirty-second Congress opened in December 1852 the issue of a railroad connection to California was again on the agenda. The immediate issue facing debate was not the question of the railroad, per se, for the concept was pretty

Stephen A. Douglas around 1858. The "Little Giant" championed the Compromise of 1850 and the Kansas-Nebraska Act of 1854, two of the most divisive pieces of legislation of the antebellum period. Courtesy of the Library of Congress.

much accepted. Instead the issue developed into a sectional feud over which city would be the easternmost terminal. Would the rail line originate from the South or from a city in the North?

Particularly interested in being near a rail line were the remote cities and towns west of the Mississippi whose only access to eastern markets was the nearby rivers and canals. The railroad would provide a much needed boost for their economy. With this prospect in mind, they eagerly anticipated the arrival of an army of railroad workers to their fair cities as well as hordes of telegraph workers to string up miles of communication lines to the far reaches of the

East Coast. This sudden influx of technology, they hoped, would bring with it all the makings of an economic boom for them and the surrounding area through increased industrialization, commercial agriculture, and entrepreneurial opportunities.

Since the South was far behind the North in rail mileage to begin with, it only seemed fair to extend the line from the southern section. Obviously, this rationale sounded reasonable enough to southern planters who lobbied strenuously for a southern route as an excellent opportunity to expand their markets. At the same time, southern politicians were keenly aware that northern interests demanded a more central route to encourage further growth of their own economy and to expand their own political base, something the South would vigorously fight to prevent. As a consequence, the warring sections created a competitive atmosphere reminiscent of rival cities today vying for an Olympic venue.

The most popularly expressed locations were either Chicago or St. Louis, and in the South it was New Orleans, Charleston, or Memphis. In these key cities many elected officials eagerly jumped on the railroad bandwagon hoping to capture a piece of the action, aware of the enormous impact bringing the railroad to their constituents would have on their political careers, personal wealth and their reputation. Chicago, for example, was relying on Douglas to bring home the prize, especially after the legislature elected him to the U.S. Senate in 1847. In fact, city leaders had already built a connector link to Galena, Illinois, two years later so confident were they on being selected. Lobbying to get the eastern terminal at St. Louis was Senator Thomas H. Benton, while at the same time, Sen. Pierre Soulé of Louisiana was vying for a route from New Orleans to the California coast favoring a route via the Gila River area, a strip of land across today's southern New Mexico and Arizona.

Lawmakers in every session of Congress filed rival bills for the railroad, each one hoping to resolve this contentious question. But with both sides demanding more consideration for a line originating in their section, agreements were impossible to reach. Since a single line appeared to be out of the question, an attempt was made to satisfy both sections by recommending a main line across northern Texas, New Mexico, and to the West Coast, with branches going to the Gulf of Mexico, the Pacific Northwest, and north to Iowa. The idea was proposed by Sen. William M. Gwin of California, who supported a southern route because the territories there were already organized. In Congress, the plan was considered much too grandiose and was defeated.

Soon it became quite apparent that a vote for any railroad route would never succeed because of fierce opposition from those in the rival section. To break this deadlock, a Senate amendment was introduced which gave President Fillmore the right to award a $20 million contract through a competitive bidding process, to decide the location of the route, and the location of the terminals as well. Sensing the administration may favor a southern route, Democratic senator James A. Shields of Illinois, after conferring with Douglas and Senator Cass, brought up the issue concerning the constitutionality of spending federal funds within a sovereign state. As a countermeasure to Gwin's proposal, Shields offered his own amendment that limited federal funding only to a road being constructed through a territory but not "a road within the limits of any existing state of the Union." Since any southern route would obviously pass through the enormous expanses of Texas, it appeared highly unlikely that, based solely on those constitutional considerations, Congress would agree to a southern route when a northern path would simply cut across the open and still unorganized Nebraska territory. Obviously the southern bloc refused to support such a measure and the entire matter never came up for vote.

In March of 1853, just before the congressional session adjourned, Douglas made a second attempt to organize the Nebraska Territory to accommodate the northern route. The timing for introducing this bill could not have been better because pressure had been steadily mounting on Congress to open up this region to westward expansion. Thousands of settlers, anxious to start a new life on its fertile soil, were unable to purchase land in Nebraska since it had yet to be surveyed by the government. There was also pressure from those whose interests were motivated by the opportunity to exploit the hidden riches of the untapped natural resources. And the railroad barons were still salivating over the prospect of lucrative profits, as were the many potential entrepreneurs of peripheral industries that would spring up from this venture. These and many others lobbied tirelessly for the route through Nebraska and without the slightest regard to the rights of the Indians residing there.

Senator Douglas was chairman of the Committee on Territories in the Senate at the time and although his bill easily passed muster in the House, again the Senate was another matter. A flamboyant frontier-style politician, Douglas was once described as short, "broad-shouldered and big-chested" with "a stout, strong neck ... a square jaw and broad chin; a rather large, firm-set mouth ... quick piercing eyes with a deep, dark, scowling, menacing horizontal wrinkle between them; a broad forehead and an abundance of dark hair which ... he wore rather long and which, when in excitement, he shook and tossed about defiantly like a lion's mane ... the very incarnation of forceful combativeness."

Under the senator's plan, the program to organize Nebraska took advantage of three enormous opportunities. It laid the groundwork for constructing the railroad, created a common issue for the Democratic Party to rally around, and it greatly benefited the development of the West. Being a political leader of some influence and stature, a run for the presidency was also on his mind as well. In the South, however, Douglas's motives were looked upon with growing suspicion.

After a contentious and bitter debate, the Illinois senator's bill had little chance of success. To get revenge for the support the northerners gave to the Shields amendment, the southern senators voted to table the measure. They also claimed it would violate the rights of the Indians inhabiting the territory, but perhaps more realistically, the South refused to pass any bill that was favorable to northern efforts towards building a railroad to the Pacific, a move that, in effect, was counterproductive to their own efforts as well. Consequently, Congress again failed to pass a single piece of legislation that advanced the cause for either Nebraska or the railroad.

The Little Giant's motives for pursuing a route from Chicago were varied, but like most of the railroad advocates it was partly self-serving. By the early fifties he had amassed a sizable fortune from real estate deals in Illinois and was also heavily invested in Superior City, Michigan. Douglas was well aware that the price of land through which the Central Illinois railroad passed had reportedly increased from a mere sixteen cents an acre in the 1830s to thirty dollars an acre over the following fifteen years. Consequently, if he succeeded in routing the proposed railroad through this area, his holdings would increase tremendously.

Aside from his personal affairs, he was also convinced that connecting with the Far West was in the best interest of the country. His interest in that part of the country was a product of the Young America doctrine which believed in making America "an ocean-bound republic, [without] disputes about boundaries, or red-lines upon maps." In fact, he clearly illustrated his commitment to this region when he remarked in the Senate, "There is a power in this nation greater than either the North or the South—a growing, increasing, swelling power.... That power is the country known as the Great West.... There, Sir, is the hope of this nation—the resting place of the power that is not only to control, but to save the Union."

Although Douglas favored a rail line from Chicago and certainly made no secret of it, he had little authority in the actual mechanics of locating the route. Like many powerful people in Washington, he had picked up a few enemies among the more senior Democrats and was, in all likelihood, snubbed by President Pierce in his allocation of patronage. Hence, the responsibility for conducting the surveys went to Jefferson Davis, the new secretary of war. Eager to quickly establish a line to his liking, Davis had already dispatched surveyors to investigate several potential southern routes, including his choice from Charleston, through El Paso and the Gila River area to Monterey. Of course having the president's ear was a distinct advantage as well, considering the influence Davis could have in lobbying for support of his southern route.

Particularly disheartening to Douglas was that his anxieties over the role Davis could play in this political drama may not have been unfounded. President Pierce soon issued a directive to his new minister to Mexico, James Gadsden to negotiate for a 250,000 square mile parcel of land in the vicinity of the

Gila River to accommodate the southern route. Furthermore, Pierce insisted the new acquisition must include all of Lower California and contain a port on the Gulf of California. A South Carolinian and railroad executive in civilian life, Gadsden was authorized to offer up to $50 million to close a deal. Mexican president Santa Anna, however, was not persuaded to sell off such a large tract of his shrinking country. But since Santa Anna was always hard up for cash his counteroffer was a much smaller parcel of land, about 55,000 square miles without Lower California and the Gulf port for only $15 million. Like Davis, Gadsden was also a big supporter of the Gila River route and found he had little choice but to accept Santa Anna's deal or walk away with nothing. In December of 1853, therefore, the treaty was signed and the following month the U.S. Senate received the treaty for discussion.

Not surprisingly, the treaty was immediately opposed by northern antislave senators who were against acquiring more land where slavery could be introduced. The southern contingent was clearly enthusiastic over the entire treaty but sensed its imminent defeat if concessions were not made. To save Gadsden's deal, following a round of political maneuvers that frequently occur in the backrooms of Washington, the southerners agreed to accept an amendment that reduced the purchase by about 9,000 square miles and the payment to $10 million. Even then, it took the support from a solid coalition of twenty-one southern senators to carry the day. On April 25, 1854, the treaty was finally accepted and the proposed southern route for the railroad was now in place.

In the meantime, as the debate over the Gadsden treaty played itself out, Senator Douglas had not given up on his goal to organize the Nebraska Territory, land that would provide the northern right-of-way for the railroad he so dearly wanted. But first he had to overcome one more obstacle—how was he going to get the southern support he needed to carry this off? Being north of the 36° 30' line the territory would fall under the provisions of the Missouri Compromise of 1820. This meant slavery was "forever prohibited" above that line so any future states cut from this territory would have to be free. And, obviously, the South wanted no part in increasing the number of free states with the resultant increase in northern political power without a measure that provided comparable benefits to them. This placed Douglas in somewhat of a dilemma. He knew there would be an uproar from free-soilers if he attempted to repeal the no-slavery provision of the Missouri Compromise. But at the same time, since the no-slavery restriction was the main obstacle preventing southern support for his bill, he knew he had to be extremely creative to win the backing of both sections.

To overcome this obstacle, Douglas decided to form a cabal with the four most powerful southern proslavery Democrats in the Senate, no less than the chairmen of the finance, foreign relations, and judiciary committees, and the president pro tempore. They were Robert M.T. Hunter and James M. Mason of Virginia, Andrew P. Butler of South Carolina, and David P. Atchison of

Missouri, respectively, who called themselves the "F Street Mess" because they all resided at the same boarding house on F Street.

According to their reasoning, because Congress refused to extend the time-honored no-slavery restriction of the Missouri Compromise to the Utah–New Mexico issue, this learned body must have inferred that the popular sovereignty provision invoked by the 1850 Compromise simply superceded the exclusionary restriction of the older Missouri Compromise of 1820. During the course of their meetings Douglas was under heavy pressure from the southern senators to rewrite his bill using this very loose interpretation. Eventually, he reluctantly consented to their demands when they insisted their rendition of the government's motives would make the bill more palatable to the southerners.

Although this self-serving rationale was somewhat of a stretch, in January of 1854, Douglas brought forward a draft copy of his revised bill. Under this new version, the same principles of popular sovereignty would be invoked for the Nebraska Territory as expressed in the Utah–New Mexico clause of the Compromise; specifically, the territory would come into the Union "with or without slavery, as their constitutions may prescribe at the time of their admission." It was indeed a clever attempt to circumvent the no-slavery restriction of 1820 with one of popular sovereignty. And all the while ignoring any mention of the Missouri Compromise itself.

Nevertheless, pointed out several southern congressmen, despite the crafty phraseology of the bill, they believed that although the basic rules of popular sovereignty allowed the people the right to rule on the slavery question, this judgment had to be carried out *after* the territorial stage. Furthermore, since the Compromise of 1820 prohibited slavery north of 36°30', no slaves were presently in the Nebraska Territory. And without slaves in the territory, the proslavery advocates would be hard pressed to establish a plausible reason for imposing slavery at the time of admission. Therefore the bill in its present format was considered unworkable and still unacceptable to the South.

The political implications of Douglas's veiled repeal of the no-slavery rule were quite obvious to a number of Whigs who saw an opportunity to gain some political points from the South by beating Douglas to the punch. Senator Archibald Dixon of Kentucky understood full well that the Compromise of 1820 was still the operative law in Nebraska and he also knew that even if the no-slavery provision was deleted in its entirety, the South would not be able to justify slavery in Nebraska. At the urging of Seward, therefore, Dixon offered an amendment to the Democratic bill that repealed the slavery ban outright. In this way the Whigs hoped to shore up their fractured party for the upcoming elections by presenting southern Whigs as better advocates of southern rights than southern Democrats. In addition, since the bill was inspired by the Democrats, the Whigs hoped to capitalize on the negative repercussions sure to come from northern voters.

Not to be outmaneuvered by the Whigs, following a quickly arranged meeting with party leaders Douglas was again persuaded to revise his bill a second time by simply claiming the Missouri Compromise was superceded by the recent Compromise of 1850 and was therefore considered "inoperative and void." Senator Atchison, one of the most fanatical supporters of southern rights, was extremely distressed over the prospect of seeing his state surrounded by free territory. He was particularly adamant in calling for the repeal of the Missouri Compromise, vowing to see Nebraska "sink in hell" if the territory was not open to slavery. Characterizing his bold changes to the bill, Douglas remarked, "I know it will raise a hell of a storm."

Douglas also presented another feature in his bill that was of enormous significance. After working together with Rep. William A. Richardson, Douglas's counterpart in the territorial committee on the House side, the bill was written to organize the entire Nebraska region into not one but two territories, a Kansas Territory and a Nebraska Territory. It was anticipated that ultimately one would be a free state and the other slave, thought to be Kansas since it would lie directly west of Missouri. Although the compromise was designed to appease northern voters, it was a move that would surely enrage the free-soilers even more but at the same time gain the necessary support from the South. When the revisions were completed, the new bill was called the Kansas-Nebraska Act.

Make no mistake about it, this was a big deal. For over 30 years the Missouri Compromise had guaranteed slave-free status to an enormous amount of northern territory. Even the mere suggestion of a repeal of its slavery prohibition brought stunned and incredulous reactions from the North and warned of an inevitable political war.

Except for two southerners, Jefferson Davis and Secretary of the Navy James Dobbin, the Cabinet steadfastly refused to support the bill. In light of the expected furor that would come from the White House, the Senate Committee on Territories thought it would be in its best interest to send a delegation to ascertain the president's position first hand before the bill was submitted and, if necessary, to gain his support on this very controversial and explosive issue.

Accordingly, on January 22, 1854, a delegation of congressional leaders from both houses, led by Douglas and Senator Atchison, went to the White House and met with Pierce. Following a spirited discourse on the matter, Pierce was pointedly advised he could lose the South if he failed to back the bill, especially the southern support he needed for his proposed Cuban initiative with John Quitman. After a silent period of contemplation, President Pierce agreed to support the Douglas bill. Thrilled by this success and wanting to capture the president's agreement in writing, within moments Douglas had the foresight to persuade Pierce to document in his own hand that the Missouri Compromise was "superseded by the principles of the legislation of

1850, commonly called the compromise measures and is hereby declared inoperative and void."

In Congress, the northern Whigs were livid and solidly against the Douglas bill. The same was true in the northern states where the repercussions over the White House deal were extremely vile and swift in coming. People vehemently opposed to the bill, especially in New England, hanged Douglas in effigy in many towns to demonstrate their revulsion to this latest political demonstration of the slave-power conspiracy.

All this backroom maneuvering was not going unnoticed by the northern free-soil coalitions. Aghast over the possibility their sacred Missouri Compromise could soon be scrapped; one northern free-soiler was heard to declare, "Despite corruption, bribery, and treachery, Nebraska, the heart of our continent, shall forever continue free." A coalition of twenty dedicated northern free-soil Democrats, led by the likes of Senators Salmon P. Chase and Charles Sumner, published a rebuke to the recent White House meeting in an antislave newspaper in Washington on January 24. Titled the Appeal of the Independent Democrats in Congress to the People of the United States, it laid out for all to read the bare facts as they perceived them. It angrily denounced Douglas for sacrificing the harmony of the country for his own political aspirations and his efforts to make Nebraska a "dreary region of despotism, inhabited by masters and slaves" and denigrated the Kansas-Nebraska bill as "a gross violation of a sacred pledge; as a criminal betrayal of precious rights; as part and parcel of an atrocious plot to exclude from a vast unoccupied region immigrants from the Old World and free laborers from our own State."

The intensity of the uproar over the article stunned the supporters of the proposed Kansas-Nebraska Act. Since they knew the "Appeal" was purposely written to arouse the emotions of the northern public, they fully anticipated a relatively small degree of criticism of Douglas's bill. But to their surprise they severely underestimated the scope and the passion of the outcry from the northern free-soilers. Especially affected were the free-soilers planning to sell their current property and resettle in the Nebraska Territory. They were absolutely livid over the prospect of this land falling under the laws of a slave society. The article clearly demonstrated the fierce public opposition to Douglas's Kansas-Nebraska Act and in effect gave notice that an intense sectional battle was looming.

On January 30, the Kansas-Nebraska Act took center stage in the Senate chamber and for five weeks the tumultuous debate and seemingly endless speeches droned on. Douglas, the star performer, was in his element. As he had done once before in 1850, by using his immense repertoire of oratory and debating skills, honed to perfection from years of personal and political confrontations, the senator from Illinois would meet the challenge of his foes head on.

What Douglas and his southern cabal had schemed was treasonous, his detractors said, and Douglas was the consummate traitor guilty of a sacrilege against the very Democratic principles he championed for so many years. His northern opponents, particularly Chase and Sumner, contended that the Missouri Compromise was a solemn pact approved in good faith by both sides and therefore unalterable by the Compromise of 1850.

Douglas chided the legitimacy of this argument, pointing out that the North had, by a large margin in fact, voted against the Missouri Compromise and even against Missouri statehood. They had, he insisted, always refused to support the very principle they now defended as sacred. In his trademark booming and gesticulating outbursts, arms swinging in wide sweeping motions for emphasis, hair whipping wildly in the process, Douglas also recounted his long history of advocating the principle of popular sovereignty. Indeed, so overwhelming was the force of Douglas's argument that the principal author of the "Appeal" was forced to apologize for his derogatory personal attacks on Douglas in the newspaper article.

Finally, after all the heated rhetoric was exhausted and after a marathon six hour performance that kept his audience transfixed in their seats, on March the third the Little Giant took his bows. His eloquence, his power of persuasion, and his contagious sense of morality had left its mark and by a roll call vote of 41 to 17, the Senate approved his bill. As they promised from the beginning, however, every northern Whig in the Senate voted against it, as did five of the twenty free-soil Democrats.

Having passed the Senate, the Kansas-Nebraska bill was delivered to the House, where on March 21, instead of going directly to the Committee on Territories, it was buried under a stack of other bills in the Committee of the Whole. This was a clear indication that the newly arrived bill was in serious trouble. Over the next two months effective application of pressure by Richardson managed to build a majority for passage. And by skillfully utilizing parliamentary procedures, each of the bills ahead of the Kansas-Nebraska measure was tabled. In May, Douglas's bill was finally brought to the floor for consideration. After 15 days of legislative mayhem the bill was approved on May 22 and as they had done in the Senate, every northern Whig voted against its passage. Eight days later, on May 30, 1854, President Pierce signed it into law.

Officially called "An Act to Organize the Territories of Nebraska and Kansas," this single piece of legislation was arguably the most controversial measure passed by Congress. It would fan the flames of turmoil in Kansas, further fracture the Democratic Party, dismember the Whigs, initiate the beginnings of a new national party, and launch a Springfield lawyer into political prominence.

(As for the transcontinental railroad, it was finally authorized by the Pacific Railway Act of 1862 and stretched from Omaha, Nebraska, to Sacramento, California. The Central Pacific Railroad moved westward while the

Union Pacific Railroad moved east, the two lines connecting at Promontory Summit, Utah, on May 10, 1869.)

Although Douglas had fulfilled his long sought after goal, before the debates began he was torn by a conflicting sense of guilt. He remarked to a friend how concerned he was over the effect his bill would have on the country and how he tried to persuade the others of his party that it was an unwise move. But he was always overruled by the party hierarchy, namely the F Street Mess, and ironically, in the end he was the one appointed to see it through. As if to relieve his tormented conscience, Douglas continued to expose his inner soul. "All my public life I have been among party men" and "for nearly twenty years I have been fighting for a place among the leaders of the party which seems to me most likely to promote the peace and prosperity of my country, and I have won it." Despite its grave error, he said, the party's decision was made and "I must either champion the policy the party has adopted or forfeit forever all that I have fought for—must throw away my whole life and not only cease to be a leader but sink into a nobody. If I retain my leadership I may help to guide the party aright in some graver crisis. If I throw it away, I not only destroy myself but I become powerless for good forever after."

But now, after months of defending his ideals, he had come to a different

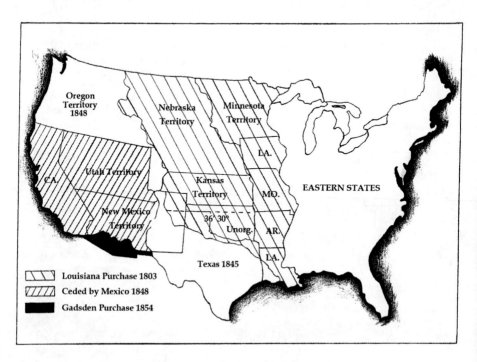

Western Expansion

conclusion. As long as southern rights were not violated, the rights of the people in the territories to decide the question of slavery through their constitutions seemed, as Douglas rationalized, to hold a compelling logic that overrode the self-interest of the northern section. It was the right thing to do, he thought. It upheld the principle of self-government, just the remedy needed to solve a very volatile issue. In the end, it was faith in this belief that enabled him to reconcile his actions and to accept the outcome as a just cause. "I passed the Kansas-Nebraska Act myself," he later remarked. "I had the authority and the power of a dictator throughout the whole controversy in both houses. The speeches were nothing. It was the marshalling and directing of men and guarding from attacks and with a ceaseless vigilance preventing surprise."

While the Democrats from both sections were nearly unanimous in favor of the bill, the Whigs demonstrated once again a glaring reminder that they were still hopelessly divided along sectional lines. Northern Whigs voted solidly in the negative, but unlike their counterparts, nearly three-quarters of the southern Whigs had voted with the Democrats.

For all practical purposes the Whig Party was now in the last throes of its existence. The painful split over the Compromise of 1850 and now the Kansas-Nebraska Act had done irreparable damage to the unity of the two sections. "We Whigs of the North," one bitter politico complained, "are unalterably determined never to have even the slightest political correspondence or connection" with the southern Whigs. Sadly, on the southern side, the feeling was mutual.

15

Political Realignment (1854 to 1856)

As the state and congressional elections approached, the northern furor over the acceptance of the Kansas-Nebraska Act was instant and divisive. The northern Whigs were infuriated not only over the obscenity of the measure itself but also with their own southern wing for supporting it. Particularly repulsive was the realization that with the 1820 restriction repealed there was the haunting possibility to many free-soilers that slavery could still extend its reach much farther north, even to the Canadian border. Considering the potential and devastating repercussions from this latest legislation, the northern Whigs felt justified in their hostility toward the South and everything the South stood for. Besides, it wasn't just the hatred of slavery and the southern goal to extend its boundaries that riled the North but also the fear that the introduction of slave labor into such a close proximity to northern borders would inhibit the further growth of the northern economy.

In assessing the northern bitterness toward the South, Senator Douglas refused to concede that his bill was the motivating factor. The Little Giant strenuously argued that northern bitterness was not intended to offend the South for "the North are Union people, a law-abiding people, a people loyal to the Constitution and willing to perform its obligations." Instead he insisted the damage was the work of the abolitionists and the Know-Nothings, and that the opposition to his bill had been largely motivated by "abolitionism, Maine liquor-lawism, and what there was left of Northern Whiggism, and then the Protestant feeling against the Catholic and the native feeling against the foreigner."

Nevertheless, Douglas was subjected to wide-spread abuse for his role in bringing the Kansas-Nebraska Act to fruition. He often remarked how he traveled from Boston to Chicago by the light of his burning effigy, and how he was booed in Trenton, jeered in New York City, hissed at in Philadelphia, and that he was called "Arnold" and "Judas." In Chicago every newspaper had turned against him, raucous and hostile mobs prevented him from speaking, and flags on the ships at dockside were lowered to half-mast.

So great was the opposition to the Kansas-Nebraska Act that from Cairo, Illinois, to Boston, Massachusetts, a plea to fight this recent attack by the South resonated from the podium, the pulpit, and the press. Indeed, it was this very anger against the Kansas-Nebraska Act that motivated a group of seething dissenters to meet and vent their outrage at the first anti–Nebraska venue back in February of 1854, three months before the law was enacted. Committed to the principle of free soil, these die-hard advocates met twice that February, first in Jackson, Michigan, and then in Ripon, Wisconsin. At these meetings, attended by a coalition of the Free Soil Party, abolitionists, Nativists, and anti–Nebraska Democrats, the alliance vowed to resist the slave-power conspiracy and the spread of its cancerous growth. Calling themselves Republicans, the new party label was officially accepted in Washington the following May. Two months later, the first Republican state platform was adopted at Jackson, Michigan. Like the Whigs, the Republicans endorsed the free labor philosophy whereby equal opportunities and a good education, together with hard work and self-discipline, could enable one to rise above wage-dependency to entrepreneurial success. As Lincoln would later conclude, "The free labor system opens the way for all—gives hope to all, and energy, and progress, and improvement of condition to all." The Republicans also appealed for continued northern resistance to the Fugitive Slave Act, for congressional prohibitions on the expansion of slavery, and criticized the Kansas-Nebraska Act as one designed to "give to the Slave States such a decided and practical preponderance in all measures of government as shall reduce the North ... to the mere province of a few slaveholding Oligarchs of the South— to a condition too shameful to be contemplated."

Following the acceptance of the Kansas-Nebraska Act the Whig Party was in serious trouble. In the North the disagreements with the southern wing, first over the Compromise of 1850 and now over the Kansas-Nebraska Act, damaged the Whig Party beyond repair. As a result, its northern members were becoming more disillusioned and fragmented, most searching for a new identity.

Not wanting to be affiliated with the Whig Party, a name tainted by the betrayal of their southern brothers, scores of disgruntled free-soil Whigs began to coalesce into small anti–Nebraska coalitions taking on such names as the People's Party, the Independent Party, and the Fusion Party, all seeking a common voice and a common banner under which to vent a common anger. Also attracted to the anti–Nebraska coalitions were irate free-soil Democrats in the North, those seeking a new political affiliation that was less conciliatory on the slavery issue.

In time, the scope and breadth of the anti–Nebraska movement would overwhelm the northern political stage. In some areas being anti–Nebraska translated into being anti–Whig, rendering the reunification of the Whig Party nearly impossible. Consequently, party loyalty began breaking down. One faithful Whig lamented in despair, "There never was a time when party ties seemed of so little account. The new questions have destroyed everything like party discipline, and many staunch old Whigs are floating off they don't know where." While many diehard Whigs, like Seward, believed they were much stronger than before and could ride the wave of anti–Nebraskaism to power in 1856, there were greater numbers within these coalitions whose ultimate motive was to form a new political party so as to rid themselves of the tarnished Whig identity.

Fiercely anti–South, the new coalitions maintained much of their support by preaching the evils of the slave-power conspiracy. They went to great lengths to exploit this new sectional conflict by continually reinforcing the negative repercussions the perceived southern conspiracy would have on the well-being of the nation. And for those who had heretofore refused to believe in its existence, there was the sudden and rude awakening that before their very eyes the conspiratorial plot had been boldly demonstrated by the success of the Kansas-Nebraska Act. And now it was threatening to spread its evil institution into their remaining lands. Northern animosity had become so intense against the South that it reached new heights and could, if left unchecked, disrupt the very bonds of the Union. It was now a battle between the northern free-soil foes of the Kansas-Nebraska Act and the southern perpetrators of this perceived slave-power conspiracy.

If matters were not discouraging enough for the Whigs, the southern wing was also breaking apart. More politically divided than ever before, the southern branch was angered as well over the anti-southern sentiments of their northern colleagues. As a consequence, they disavowed any further loyalty to the national party with many of its defecting members being adopted by the increasingly popular Know-Nothings and even the Democrats, their one-time political foe. As a result, the Democrats now ruled in the South.

Although Whig leaders like Senator Seward attempted to salvage the splintered party for their upcoming midterm elections, it proved to be a futile effort. The northern and southern Whigs were still much too divided and too detached to resolve differences that were too deep and too irreconcilable. The efforts made by the various coalitions toward draining the Whigs of their grass roots constituency, their very life-blood, proved to be instrumental in the ultimate demise of the Whig Party as a political organization.

Ultimately, the remaining Whigs recognized the further futility of supporting a party that existed in name only and they too had no other choice but to abandon the party as well. "There are about enough Whigs left to keep us in remembrance that there was once such a party, and no more," observed one Democrat. His fellow Democrat wholeheartedly agreed, replying, "The Whig party is defunct."

Besides the losses to the new Republican Party, the remaining die-hard Whigs were faced with yet another obstacle to overcome as support from their voting constituency was noticeably declining—avoiding further losses to the Know-Nothings, a political organization that had soared in popularity since its formation in 1849. Now calling themselves the American Party, this alliance of white, native-born Protestants was extremely active in both sections, attracting not only Whigs and Democrats, but also taking advantage of a large pre-existing base of anti–Catholic and anti-immigrant sentiment rampant from the Midwest to the East Coast. As a result, by 1854, the American Party's membership had grown to an estimated one and a half million faithful disciples in the principles of Nativism.

Nevertheless, there were many who disagreed with the philosophy of the American Party and were especially concerned over its possible impact on the upcoming state elections. In Pennsylvania, for instance, cries of trepidation clearly reflected the nationwide reaction to the sudden popularity of the American Party. "The Know Nothings fever is epidemic here," one Democrat lamented, while from another part of the state the mood was just as dire: "Nearly everybody appears to have gone altogether deranged on Nativism." And in New York, a Whig expressed the mood in his district when he exclaimed it "was badly infected with Knownothingism."

Back in his Springfield law office following his single term in the House, Lincoln remained absorbed in the ever-volatile Washington political scene. Voicing his concern over the new American Party, Lincoln not only opposed the bigoted doctrine of Nativism, but also the hypocrisy of its members. This was clearly expressed when he wrote to a friend, "How can anyone who abhors the oppression of negroes be in favor of degrading classes of white people? Our progress in degeneracy appears to me to be pretty rapid. As a nation we began by declaring that 'all men are created equal.' We now practically read it 'all men are created equal, except negroes.' When the Know-nothings get control, it will read 'all men are created equal, except negroes and foreigners and Catholics.'"

Like the thousands of people throughout the North in 1854, Lincoln was also disturbed by the signing of the Kansas-Nebraska Act. As the future would ultimately demonstrate, an indirect but significant benefit from the passage of the new law was that Lincoln was drawn out from his self-imposed political exile. To his childhood friend he wrote that he was "thunderstruck and stunned" by the passage of such wicked legislation and that recent measures, particularly Senator Douglas's new law, had aroused him "as he had never been before." In fact, he said, the latest events in Congress were incentive enough for him to consider returning to politics.

Coincidentally, Lincoln's opportunity to return to politics came that very summer when he ran for an open seat in the Illinois State Assembly, a mostly Democratic enclave. Soon after winning the election, however, he had a change of heart. Lincoln discovered he wasn't quite satisfied with being an obscure assemblyman far from the real action in Washington. In November, he resigned from the Illinois legislature to launch a campaign for an open seat in the U.S. Senate where he felt the more critical problems lay and where he could do the most good for the country.

Lincoln was elated at being back on the stump. Still running as a Whig, he wrote to a friend of his, "I think I am a Whig; but others say there are no Whigs, and that I am an Abolitionist. When I was at Washington, I voted for the Wilmot proviso as good as forty times; and I never heard of anyone attempting to unwhig me for that."

As the voting got underway, it appeared after each successive ballot that one of the Democratic candidates, Gov. Joel A. Matteson, might win the Senate seat. It seems Gov. Matteson advocated popular sovereignty in the territories, a principle the Democrats consistently pursued and one Lincoln loathed. To prevent Matteson from winning, Lincoln transferred all of his votes to another candidate, Lyman Trumbull, an anti–Nebraska Democrat, who ultimately won the election on the tenth ballot. Later, in a letter explaining his actions to his friend and confidant Congressman Elihu B. Washburne, Lincoln wrote, "Such is the way the thing was done. I regret my defeat moderately, but .. his [Matteson's] defeat now gives me more pleasure than my own gives me pain." Despite his loss, Lincoln continued to play an active role in politics by supporting the party and its candidates in Illinois.

In October 1854, Lincoln and Douglas, the leading Democratic statesman in Illinois, met on two separate occasions, once at Springfield and the other at Peoria. Lincoln was on the stump campaigning for anti–Nebraska candidate Richard Yates. In his memorable speech at Peoria, Lincoln devastated the logic of Douglas's views, established the tone of his political ideology, and in turn, placed himself squarely on the road to the White House.

On the repeal of the Missouri Compromise Lincoln said," I think ... that it is wrong—wrong in its direct effect, letting slavery into Kansas and Nebraska, and wrong in its prospective principle, allowing it to spread to every other part of the wide world where men can be found inclined to take it." And to counter Douglas's contention that popular sovereignty, as legislated for Nebraska and Kansas, allowed the people in the territories the "sacred right of self government," Lincoln scoffed and corrected his old friend by reminding him, "When the white man governs himself, that is self-government; but when he governs himself and also governs another man, that is more than self-government— that is despotism.... The negro is a man.... There can be no moral right in connection with one man's making a slave of another...." On this point Lincoln not only continued to berate Douglas but also to capture the attention and admiration of his enthralled listeners. "Another important objection to this application of the right of self-government," Lincoln declared, "is that it enables the first few to deprive the succeeding many of a free exercise of the right of self-government. The first few may get slavery in, and the subsequent many cannot easily get it out.... But you say this question should be left to the people of Nebraska, because they are more particularly interested. If this be the rule, you must leave it to each individual to say for himself whether he will have slaves. What better moral right have thirty-one citizens of Nebraska to say that the thirty-second shall not hold slaves than the people of the thirty-one States have to say that slavery shall not go into the thirty-second State at all?" Lincoln also went to great lengths to explain that he had "no prejudice against the Southern people." "When Southern people tell us they are no more responsible for the origin of slavery than we are," he said, "I acknowledge that fact. When it is said that the institution exists, and that it is very difficult to get rid of it in any satisfactory way, I can understand and appreciate the saying. I surely will not blame them for not doing what I should not know how to do myself."

In the final analysis, Lincoln's eloquence clearly expressed the views of the new Republican Party: that slavery must not be perpetuated, that it must not expand into the territories, and that all anti-slavery forces must unite to stomp out the southern conspirators responsible for this terrible injustice.

Within this atmosphere of hostile and bitter rhetoric, northern voters were left in a dilemma. They were offered a choice to support the American Party and their plea for Protestants to unite against a foreign and Catholic conspiracy to dominate the U.S. government, to support the new Republican Party, at times referred to as a northern or sectional party, to maintain their loyalty to the much weakened Whigs, or to support the Democratic Party, distinguished as pro–Southern and pro-slave.

In the end, unable to purge the bitter taste of the Kansas-Nebraska Act from their palates, northern voters took out their resentment at the polls and especially on the northern Democratic wing that had supported the very law they abhorred.

As the 1854 mid-term elections concluded, the vengeance metered out by voters on the northern wing of the Democratic Party was nothing short of devastating. If defeating every northern Democrat was meant to be a payback message, it was achieved in spades. Not only did northern Democrats lose control of state legislatures in all but two free states, but in Washington, their representation in the House plummeted from 91 seats to only 25. With the exception of the Civil War years when southern Democrats were absent from the Washington political scene, this minority status of northern Democrats within their own party would remain for over 70 years.

It also became apparent that the Know-Nothings of the American Party had emerged as a major political influence. They astounded everyone by capturing the mayor's seat in Philadelphia. And in Massachusetts, not only did they elect the governor but also won every seat in the State House except for two of the 378 representatives. This surprising performance prompted one Massachusetts Whig to admit, "I no more suspected the impending result than I looked for an earthquake which would level the State House and reduce Faneuil Hall to a heap of ruins." Strangely enough, one of the most significant pieces of legislation enacted by the Know-Nothings in Massachusetts was a bill outlawing racial segregation in public schools, the first such law in the country.

By 1855 the American Party also controlled Rhode Island, New Hampshire, and Connecticut in New England, as well as California and the legislature in Tennessee. They were also making inroads in traditional Democratic southern states as Virginia, Georgia, Alabama, Mississippi, and Louisiana, as well as northern states like New York, New Jersey, and Pennsylvania.

This sudden avalanche of Nativist popularity even prompted a newspaper editorial to predict that the American Party would capture the next presidential race in 1856. But more telling was that besides the spread of slavery into the northern territories, there was also the lingering, real, and pervasive fear among concerned Whig and Democratic voters over the potential political influence foreigners and Catholics could have on the country.

With the Republicans and the American Party vying for dominance as a sectional party in the North and the Democratic Party firmly in control in the South, it seemed the political landscape had been altered once again by sectionalism to a point where the question now was, not what party would control Congress, but what section.

Despite the American Party's unifying tactics of secret rituals and its singular position on Nativist principles, however, the effects of the Kansas-Nebraska Act were also penetrating the party's solidarity. In June of 1855, at their first national gathering in Philadelphia, sectional cracks appeared when a large contingent of northern delegates stormed out of the proceedings, outraged that the southern delegates, along with several northern conservatives, voted to support the Kansas-Nebraska Act. Not intending to split from the party permanently, the northerners returned when the presidential nominating convention opened in February of 1856. Again a resolution was passed which unequivocally demonstrated the support of the southern contingent for the Kansas-Nebraska measure by refusing to endorse a restoration of the Missouri Compromise. And again the northerners left the proceedings, this time vowing never to return. Instead, the group of self-exiled Know-Nothings organized into a new political entity called the North American Party. Meanwhile, the remaining southern members of the American Party threw their full support to former president Millard Fillmore as would the remnants of the Whig Party at their convention in Baltimore.

Four months later, on June 17, the Republican Party held its first presidential convention. Meeting at the Musical Fund Hall in Philadelphia for three days, the leading candidates were Senator Seward, who had by now abandoned his Whig roots; Salmon P. Chase, the senator from Ohio; and 43-year-old John C. Frémont of Georgia, a hero in the military occupation of California during the war with Mexico. Although Seward and Chase were political veterans, they carried too many liabilities for the party to support them. Conversely, Frémont's only political experience was six months in the U.S. Senate where he represented California back in the early 1850s. Nevertheless, with scant political background to defend against and no political enemies to speak of, Frémont appealed to the delegates as the ideal person to lead the party to victory. His celebrity status as the popular "Pathfinder," a moniker received from his earlier efforts to find a route for the transcontinental railroad, wouldn't hurt either, the delegates confidently predicted.

Since the Republican Party was an amalgamation of disgruntled Whigs and Democrats, free-soilers, Nativists, and abolitionists, one of the most challenging problems the delegates faced was to tailor a platform that each of the various coalitions would accept. After many heated hours of debate, proposals, and concessions, they came up with a platform that deplored the doctrine of popular sovereignty, insisting that only Congress had the right to ban slavery in the territories, and demanded the admission of Kansas into the Union as a free state. The platform also supported the principles of free-soil and the old issue of federal subsidies for internal improvements, particularly for a transcontinental railroad. Lastly, the delegates ambiguously alluded to the Republican resentment of Catholic efforts to ban Bible reading in public schools, and as a mere superficial gesture, supported the American Party's efforts to increase the waiting period for naturalization to 21 years. The Republicans were satisfied with their chances of winning the election, and their campaign slogan, "Free Speech, Free Press, Free Soil, Free Men, Frémont, and Victory," began to appear throughout the North.

Despite their displeasure over Frémont's ties to the Catholic Church (they erroneously thought he was a Catholic because he married a Catholic woman in a Catholic ceremony), the anti–Nebraska Know-Nothings of the North American Party were persuaded by the Republicans to throw their support behind Frémont in order to unify the antislavery forces against the slave-power conspiracy. The Republican leaders were quite forceful in this political maneuver, needing all the support they could get to establish themselves as a national party. There was, however, one condition—although the Republicans would inherit the North American Nativists, the party would not openly endorse their principles of Nativism. As a consequence, northern congressmen with both Nativist and anti–Nebraska sentiments joined the Republican ranks fully prepared to align themselves primarily with the Republicans' free-soil and antislavery position. As noted by one editor, "Some who came here more 'American' than Republican are now more Republican than American." With this move, the Know-Nothing phase in American politics was about to end.

Described by some historians as a transitory chapter in the nation's political history, the Know-Nothings were seen as a bridge from the demise of the Whigs into the new Republican Party.

With a Republican elected as the U.S. House speaker (Nathaniel Banks) and Frémont selected as its first presidential nominee, the northern-dominated Republican Party appeared to be progressing toward becoming the majority opposition party.

Two weeks earlier, on June 2, the Democratic Party met in Cincinnati for its nominating convention. In the running was President Pierce, vying for a second term; Senator Douglas, whose political popularity in the South was steadily growing since passage of the Kansas-Nebraska Act; and Pennsylvanian James Buchanan, the U.S. minister to Great Britain.

The contrast between the three in terms of voter appeal was quite significant and mostly reflected the degree of their participation in the Kansas-Nebraska saga. While Pierce and Douglas were the favorites of the southern delegates for their roles in repealing the Missouri Compromise, in the North they were perceived as tarnished by the very same efforts that approved the Kansas-Nebraska Act. At the same time, Buchanan gained much of his endorsement from the North. Since he was stationed in Europe during the Nebraska business his hands were clean, a factor many northerners considered in giving Buchanan their vote of approval. But as the balloting progressed through a dozen roll calls, it became apparent that the Democrats were much too divided to select any one of the three men. To avoid a fracture within the party, both Pierce and Douglas removed their names from the balloting enabling Buchanan to win the nomination on the seventeenth ballot. To balance the ticket, his vice-presidential running mate was John C. Breckinridge, an avid secessionist from Kentucky.

In a mirror image of the Republican platform, the Democrats endorsed popular sovereignty, limited federal power over slavery in the territories, and disapproved of any government aid for internal improvements which they considered "dangerous to our republican institutions and the liberties of the people." On the critical issue of government interference with slavery in the territories, the platform endorsed the "right of all territories ... acting through the legally and fairly expressed will of a majority of actual residents ... to form a Constitution, with or without domestic slavery, and be admitted into the Union upon terms of perfect equality with the other states."

As the presidential campaign progressed, the stark contrast between Buchanan and Frémont became exceedingly evident. While Frémont was the youngest presidential candidate, Buchanan was the oldest at sixty-five. The Republican candidate had almost no political experience, but Buchanan's résumé reflected his twenty years as congressman and senator, five years as minister to Russia and Great Britain, and four years as secretary of state under Polk. So diverse was his political experience that Buchanan called himself the

"Old Public Functionary." Even their personalities were offsetting. Frémont was still quite popular and charismatic while Buchanan displayed the demeanor of an aloof and a stern bachelor. Arguably the biggest difference between the two was their principal campaign argument. Republicans believed the Constitution permitted the Congress to decide the slavery question in the territories while Buchanan and the Democrats were just as convinced that Congress had no right to interfere, that it was up to the residents of the territories themselves, in other words—popular sovereignty.

Frémont's anti-slavery and free-soil position as well as his perceived Catholicism were looked upon with some disdain in the Democratic South. So adamant were they against his candidacy for these reasons that his name never appeared on the election ballots of most southern states. More significantly, many southern states vowed to secede from the Union if Frémont was elected. Robert Toombs, an old line Whig senator from Georgia, was one of many that helped propagate that point when he wrote, "The election of Frémont would be the end of the Union, and ought to be."

To capitalize on the fears some northerners held over secession, throughout the campaign the southern Democrats consistently portrayed Republicans, by their efforts to elect Frémont, as the party of disunion and as "Black Republican Abolitionists" and "nigger lovers" who were planning to "turn loose ... millions of negroes, to elbow you in the workshops, and compete with you in the fields of honest labor." This inflammatory political rhetoric appeared to carry out Buchanan's own declaration that "the Black Republicans must be ... boldly assailed as disunionists, and this charge must be re-iterated again and again."

The Republicans tried, albeit unsuccessfully, to counter the Democratic smears, insisting that Democratic threats of secession proved they were the real instigators of disunion. The Republicans, they added, were attempting to prohibit slavery in the territories merely to protect white workers from having to compete with negro labor. In another statement the Republicans declared the slave-power conspiracy seeks "to make our country a great slave empire: to make slave breeding, slave selling, slave labor, slave extension, slave policy, and slave dominion, forever the controlling elements of our Government." Also assisting to counter the Democratic charges was Abraham Lincoln, actively campaigning for Frémont and the Republican ticket in Illinois. "We, the majority, would not strive to dissolve the Union;" he remarked at Galena, "and if any attempt is made it must be by you, who so loudly stigmatize us as disunionists. But the Union, in any event, won't be dissolved. We don't want to dissolve it, and if you attempt it, we won't let you. With the purse and the sword, the army and the navy and the treasury in our hands and at our command, you couldn't do it.... All this talk about the dissolution of the Union is humbug—nothing but folly. We won't dissolve the Union, and you shan't."

Despite the efforts of the Republicans to defend themselves, many conservative and former Whig voters in the lower North took the threats of secession seriously enough to switch their votes to Buchanan. Under this perception, the election was tantamount to a referendum on secession. If Frémont wins, the South secedes; if Buchanan wins, the Union is saved. Indeed, Buchanan recognized the significance of secession in the campaign when he wrote, "I consider that all incidental questions are comparatively of little importance ... when compared with the grand and appalling issue of Union or disunion.... In this region, the battle is fought mainly on this issue."

When the votes were counted, Buchanan won decisively. He captured 174 electoral votes by winning 14 of the 15 southern states (except Maryland, which went to Fillmore) and four of the 15 northern states plus California. It was a reassuring and extremely satisfying victory for the northern Democrats not only for winning the White House but also for regaining seats previously lost in Congress. In the House particularly, where the northern wing had lost 66 seats after the ruinous 1854 election, northern representation now stood at 53 seats.

Failing to appear on most of their ballots accounted for Frémont's inability to get a single vote from the South. On the other hand, Frémont carried 11 of the 15 northern states for a total of 114 votes. Despite their loss the Republican leaders were quite pleased with their performance. Looking ahead four years, they believed the party would be able to retain the same 11 northern states they had won, and if they could capture Pennsylvania and Illinois, both Democratic strongholds, they would win the 1860 presidency.

One aspect of this election remained crystal clear. The fact that Buchanan won big in the South and Frémont captured most of the North was an indication of the degree sectionalism played in the vote for our nation's leader.

16

The Fight for Kansas (1854 to 1858)

During the year of 1854, even before final passage of the Kansas-Nebraska Act, hundreds of settlers from points around the country were already rolling into the Kansas Territory. Most came in wagons crowded with kinfolk and all their worldly possessions longing for a homestead on virgin land they could farm and call their own. With little regard for the legality of their actions, these so-called squatters simply staked out claims on the piece of land they fancied to begin a new life for themselves and their families.

As northern newspapers continued to urge people to move to Kansas, interest in the potential benefits of owning a piece of this vast territory steadily grew. So too was the need to provide financial assistance to those willing to relocate. One charitable organization that responded to this need was the Massachusetts Emigrant Aid Company which subsidized an estimated 600–700 pioneers, mostly midwestern farmers, to settle the area in and around Lawrence in just 1854 alone. In fact, the town was named after Amos Lawrence, a wealthy textile businessman, to honor his unique and appreciated role in financing the assistance program. With more and more squatters staking claims and setting up make-shift tents and crude cabins, it wasn't long before the first signs of violence began to appear. The frequent quarrelling and posturing was seldom over the issue of slavery per se, but usually resulted when several land-hungry squatters tried to gain a foothold on the same piece of real estate. The resultant disputes, often settled with firearms, would be particularly troublesome if the confrontations were between Yankee settlers and irate southerners who believed they had more right to the land than the subsidized northern riffraff. Making a bad situation even worse was that since all the land had yet to be surveyed, nobody possessed a lawful title to any of it.

In time the increasing number of outsiders invading Kansas began to rankle the sensitivity of many western Missourians that lived along the invisible border with Kansas as well as the proslavery squatters moving into the Leavenworth area. Although the Missourians were generally scrawny in appearance, dirty, unshaven, foul mouthed, and drunkards, they were also tough, gritty, and enormously determined to keep the Yankees and their "sickly sycophantic love for the nigger" out of Kansas. As the settlers continued to arrive in "their territory," the frontier-tough Missourians, acting on a possessive impulse, established various societies and associations to combat this unseemly incursion. At their raucous gatherings they stirred up even more resentment with wild and inflammatory speeches to the point where plans were made to ride into Kansas and to drive out the unwanted settlers. "We are threatened ... [with] being made the unwilling receptacle of the filth, scum and offscourings of the East ... to pollute our fair land ... to preach abolitionism and dig underground Rail-roads," wrote a troubled friend to Missouri senator David P. Atchison.

Thus, in this unsettled climate, the first territorial governor arrived in Kansas in October of 1854. Appointed by Pierce, one of Andrew Reeder's first acts as governor was to call for an election of a congressional delegate to Washington. And to implement the requirements of popular sovereignty, he set aside March 30, 1855, as the date the people of Kansas would vote to elect a legislature. At that point the legislature would begin the all-important process of establishing a constitution for or against slavery, a process heavily weighted by the political philosophy of its members. The question was, would it be a slave-state or a free-state legislature? Almost immediately after Reeder's announcement became known, a frenzy of activity suddenly erupted among both the proslavery Missourians and the advocates for a free-state Kansas.

Recognizing a loophole in the voting procedure, one that permitted any resident the right to vote regardless of the length of time in the territory, both sides ratcheted up their efforts to bring in more residents to vote for their cause. In the North the immediate concern was not so much the morality of slavery but primarily the expansion of slavery into the Kansas territory. For inspiration northerners had only to recall Seward's challenge to the slave-states made back in May. "We will engage in competition for the virgin soil of Kansas," he said, "and God give the victory to the side which is stronger in numbers as it is in right." Senator Atchison, one of the principal leaders for a slave-state Kansas, understood the ramifications of a proslavery victory as well. "The game must be played boldly," he said. "If we win, we carry slavery to the Pacific Ocean, if we lose we lose Missouri, Arkansas, Texas, and all the territories." Consequently, in an enormous mid–19th century get-out-the-vote campaign, the pro-slavery leaders rounded up thousands of supporters from Missouri, exhorting them to "enter every election district in Kansas ... and vote at the point of a Bowie knife or revolver!" Eager to demonstrate their unwavering resolve, the Missourians rode into Kansas on horseback, mule, and in wagons prepared to stuff the ballot boxes with hundreds of fraudulent votes. Needless to say, because of their numerical superiority, the proslavery crowd ultimately stole the elections. Since this was interpreted as election fraud in its most egregious form and not wanting to give credence to the results, Reeder traveled to the White House and asked Pierce to negate the elections. With Pierce openly siding with the South, however, Reeder's plea had little impact and was politely refused. Since there were so few complaints officially filed from the voting precincts themselves, the governor was more or less duty-bound to uphold the results and a proslavery legislature was now seated in Lecompton and pursuant to the Northwest Ordinance of 1787, a non-voting proslavery delegate was sent to Congress.

And that's when the political situation in Kansas took on a more radical proslavery tone.

Once in place the legislature was quick to prepare a proslavery constitution and to enact laws that protected slavery in Kansas. Under the new laws anyone defying a person's right to own slaves, either verbally or physically, would be penalized. Encouraging or abetting slaves to escape was punishable by death, only proslavery men could hold office or serve on juries, and the law even required everyone to take an oath that they would abide by these rulings. In Washington, meanwhile, Senator Atchison still had the president's ear and was able to persuade Pierce to replace Reeder, a Pennsylvanian, with a governor more receptive to proslavery principles.

The free-state pioneers, meanwhile, were extremely angered over the bogus election and its shameless mockery of popular sovereignty. With no intention of acknowledging the newly elected government, they met in Topeka in the autumn of 1855 and wrote their own antislavery constitution for Kansas and in January 1856, elected their own legislature and governor, one Charles Robinson. And contrary to the existing territorial laws on slavery, the free-soilers also enacted laws that not only prohibited slavery in Kansas but also prohibited the entry of any free blacks into the territory. Since all these actions were not officially sanctioned or recognized by the presidential-appointed governor, it was even more illegitimate than the one in Lecompton. Nevertheless, there were now two territorial governments in Kansas, one official that advocated slavery, and one unofficial that banned slavery.

The effect of having two rival governments at this point had not yet advanced into any serious violence. But the continuous threats and counter-threats were having an effect on the people by polarizing the residents of Kansas into two separate and hostile camps—free-state advocates versus the proslavery faction.

As the verbal agitation between the opposing sides increased and the division between them widened, the antislavery forces began to prepare for an even greater confrontation. Appeals were sent to the Northeastern states for hundreds of rifles and several pieces of artillery while the slavery advocates, routinely armed from the outset, brought in thousands of equally armed and ruthless Missourians led by Senator Atchison and others to counter the opposing threat. The Missourians were organized into raiding parties with names such as the Atchison Guards, the Doniphan Tigers, and the Kickapoo Rangers. With both camps equipped and poised for combat, the situation had gradually escalated into an armed conflict waiting to happen.

During this highly volatile period the spark that ignited hostilities occurred when a free-stater was shot and killed over a land claim. Incensed that no action was taken by local law enforcement, a group of Lawrence residents burned down the homes of the proslavery murderer and his two witnesses as retribution. Within days, County Sheriff Samuel Jones, also a slave-state proponent, apprehended one member of the Lawrence gang suspected of being involved in the cabin burning incident. The entire matter escalated when the suspected arsonist was rescued by the Lawrence gang while being escorted to jail. Extremely angered over this blatant and bold abduction, Jones recruited a posse of several thousand of Atchison's Missourians to exact revenge on the guilty parties in Lawrence. In Lecompton, meanwhile, the new territorial governor, Wilson Shannon, learned of the sheriff's intentions and moved quickly to head off any further violence. Traveling to Washington he appealed to Pierce for U.S. troops from Fort Leavenworth to keep the peace. Although Pierce refused to intercede with federal soldiers, he met with Senator Atchison and his associates and persuaded them to disband their followers and return to Missouri. Heeding the president's advice, Atchison explained to his men that it was in the best interest of the South to postpone further agitation in order to assure the election of a proslavery Democrat in the upcoming presidential election.

Obviously, the news from Kansas had not gone unnoticed in the nation's capital. Debates over the slavery issue in Kansas, a topic extremely disruptive by its very nature, afforded the Congress little respite. This was especially true when Seward unsuccessfully attempted to admit Kansas as a free-state based on the unlawful constitution. There was also a bid to establish a federal commission that would not only supervise new voter registrations but also monitor an election of delegates. The delegates would then begin the process of framing a new constitution for Kansas. That bill also failed.

Like their counterparts in the North, southern lawmakers were taking the situation in Kansas very seriously as well. Congressman Preston Brooks of South Carolina, for example, expressed what most of his constituents were thinking when he wrote in March 1856, "The admission of Kansas into the Union as a slave state is now a point of honor. The fate of the South is to be decided with the Kansas issue. If Kansas becomes a [free] State, slave property will decline to half its present value in Missouri ... [and] abolitionism will become the prevailing sentiment. So with Arkansas; so with upper Texas."

With attitudes on both sides brimming with resentment, only the severe winter of 1855–56 managed to keep them apart. But like the snow in the springtime thaw, the status quo also evaporated in the spring of 1856 when Sheriff Jones, still seeking revenge for the injury to his ego, conducted several unsuccessful attempts to make arrests in Lawrence, the center of free-state activity. The entire episode turned even uglier when Jones was wounded several nights later as he rested in his tent. And to make matters worse, the unknown shooter, thought to be a free-stater, was never apprehended.

Compounding the animosity toward the free-staters was the dissatisfaction of the Missourians with the publication of several Republican antislavery newspapers in Lawrence. Proslavery leaders, such as Atchison, were particularly annoyed that inflammatory and partisan articles being printed in these papers, along with highly slanted reports by biased correspondents from the major press, was giving the free-state proponents an unfair public relations advantage. This advantage, they complained, stemmed from the fact that all the news to the outside world was one-sided and prejudicial to the views of pro-slavery advocates. And by pursuing this form of propaganda, the anti-slavery leaders were able to drum up sympathetic support for their agenda from a large segment of the northern public and particularly from Washington. In fact, the oft-repeated verbiage "Bleeding Kansas" and Horace Greeley's "Border Ruffians" were examples of these literary exaggerations and distortions.

Furthermore, the efforts by the free-staters to arm and train a rebel army bent on the overthrow of the territorial government forced the chief justice of the territorial Supreme Court, Samuel Lecompte, to proclaim the inhabitants of Lawrence in violation of the laws of Kansas. He called the Topeka government "an unlawful and hitherto unheard-of organization" made up of men "who are dubbed governors, men who are dubbed lieutenant governors ... and men who are dubbed all the other dubs with which the territory is filling." As a result, a grand jury indicted the free-state leaders for treason, along with two newspapers and the Free State Hotel. According to the grand jury indictment, the hotel was in reality a fort purposely designed to provide fortress-like protection for the agitators if and when they were attacked. As ordered, within days of the indictment a group of Missourians were assembled to ride out to Lawrence to carry out the court's arrest warrant. Learning of the approaching posse of Missourians, however, now led by a federal marshal, the leaders of the free-soilers quickly left Lawrence and the whole dramatic confrontation fizzled.

Despite the failure by the marshal to capture the free-soil leaders, Sheriff Jones would not be denied the opportunity to enforce the grand jury's indictment. Taking matters into his own hands, he recruited about 800 men from the returning posse to settle this matter once and for all. On May 21, 1856, the sheriff and his newly deputized men confidently rode into Lawrence with the air of conquering warriors. With the innocent townspeople fleeing in terror, the posse raided the newspaper offices, destroyed the printing presses, and then following a wild escapade of looting, set both the hotel and the governor's house ablaze, all without a loss of life. Called the Sack of Lawrence, the raid was wildly exaggerated for political points in the Republican press with glaring headlines that read, "Triumph of the Border Ruffians—Lawrence in Ruins—Several Persons Slaughtered—Freedom Bloodily Subdued." Again, the exaggerated stories of fighting and bloodshed in Kansas made great headlines and provided fascinating reading in the North, but in turn they continued to create further hatred in the South for the free-soil cause.

Adding significantly to this sectional loathing was an episode that occurred in Washington the day after the sack of Lawrence. On May 19 Senator Charles Sumner of Massachusetts vented his pent-up anger when he unleashed a scathing two-day attack against the abuses of the proslavery faction in Kansas and of the evils of slavery in general. Called "The Crime against Kansas," Sumner's criticism of the Missourian insurgency and of the outrageous and incendiary comments made by members of the South Carolina delegation even shocked some Senate Democrats. Not mincing words, during his speech Sumner reminded the crowded gallery that "murderous robbers from Missouri, hirelings picked from the drunken spew and vomit of an uneasy civilization" had carried out a "rape of a virgin territory, compelling it to the hateful embrace of slavery." He also attacked Anthony P. Butler of South Carolina, a member of the F Street Mess, for the "loose expectoration of his speech" and described him as a "Don Quixote" sent to the Senate by a state with its "shameful imbecility from Slavery." Taking Sumner's attack personally and feeling compelled to express his own anger was Congressman Preston Brooks, Senator Butler's nephew. Two days after the speech, Brooks approached Sumner in the nearly empty Senate chamber and without warning severely beat the Massachusetts senator with his gold-tipped cane as Sumner sat at his desk. Leaving Sumner "as senseless as a corpse for several minutes, his head bleeding copiously from the frightful wounds, and the blood saturating his clothes," Brooks quietly left the Senate Chamber. So disabling were Sumner's injuries, resulting from at least thirty blows about the head, that the Massachusetts senator was unable to return to the Senate for three years.

Understandably, it wasn't long before Southern resentment over Sumner's speech blared out from banner headlines in the southern press. The *Richmond Enquirer* denounced Sumner and his northern anti-slave rhetoric and praised Brooks as a true hero for defending the honor of South Carolina and all southern gentlemen, which of course only infuriated the northerners even more. The *Enquirer* described the beating as "good in conception, better in execution, and best of all in consequence. The vulgar Abolitionists in the Senate are getting above themselves.... They have grown saucy, and dare to be imprudent to gentlemen...! The truth is, they have been suffered to run too long without collars. They must be lashed into submission."

The people of the North were incensed over this vile and unjustified assault in the revered halls of Congress and the northern press was just as outspoken as that of the South. "Has it come to this," asked the *New York Evening Post*, "that we must speak with bated breath in the presence of our Southern masters...? Are we to be chastised as they chastise their slaves? Are we too, slaves, slaves for life, a target for their brutal blows, when we do not comport ourselves to please them?" Condemning the attack one Massachusetts woman remarked of Brooks, "If I had been there I would have torn his eyes out and so I would now if I could."

The House members tried to expel Brooks, but when southern votes prevented the necessary two-thirds majority Brooks chose to resign following his censure. When he returned home to South Carolina not only was he wined and dined and applauded as a true southern patriot but to add insult to injury, Brooks was reelected and sent back to the House by a vindictive South Carolina legislature. Northern moderates who were once sensitive to the plight of the southerners and their need to maintain slavery were now so repulsed by their aggressive behavior and arrogant manner that many withdrew their support for the southern cause.

The raid on Lawrence, while escalating tensions in Kansas, also inflamed the growing passions of one particular Kansas resident—John Brown. Born in Connecticut in 1800, he was brought to Ohio as a toddler where his father opened a tannery in Hudson. As a young teen, Brown left the security of his family to enroll in a school in Plainfield, Massachusetts. Hoping to become a Congregationalist minister, he transferred to an academy in Litchfield only to leave a short time later when his money ran out. Returning to Hudson, Brown and his brother opened their own tannery and in 1820 he married his first wife. Five years later, with a wife and four year old son in tow, Brown moved to Meadville, Pennsylva-

John Brown, a fanatic anti-slavery advocate. His ultimate sacrifice to free the slaves further intensified the sectional conflicts raging between the North and South. Photograph circa 1859. Courtesy of the Library of Congress.

nia, where he bought some 200 acres of land and built a cabin and a new tannery. For the next six years the tannery grew into a successful business until Brown fell ill in 1831 and he saw his debts continue to mount. Following the loss of his business and the death of his wife, in 1833 he remarried and moved back to Ohio where over the next twenty-two years, after fathering twenty children, he suffered repeated business failures, frequent bankruptcies, and numerous court litigations. By 1854 the Brown family was living in North Elba, New York, when four of his sons, caught up in the Kansas migration craze, decided to pull up roots and head west and asked their father to join them.

Together with his eldest sons, the fifty-six-year-old Brown traveled to Kansas in October of 1855. Their motives, however, were quite different. The boys, full of youthful exuberance and ambition, wanted to stake a claim in a developing territory. The father, a staunch abolitionist, saw this move as a chance to fight against the proslavery element in Kansas he heard so much about. One of Brown's old acquaintances was Frederick Douglass, an ex-slave and fellow abolitionist, who said of Brown, "Though a white gentleman, he is in sympathy a black man, and as deeply interested in our cause, as though his own soul had been pierced with the iron of slavery." A devoted supporter of the abolitionist movement, Brown was a Bible-quoting Calvinist and an obsessed antislavery fanatic who often worked as a conductor in the Underground Railroad, guiding fugitive slaves to freedom. What struck many visitors to the Brown household was that the hired black help were referred to as Mr. and Mrs. and were always seated together with the Brown family at the supper table.

With a perpetual aura of sternness and a hypnotic stare few men were able to gaze into, John Brown was not a man to cross. Over many years, deep down in his soul, Brown harbored an immense hatred for slavery and the injustices inflicted on the black population. With these festering emotions raging within, as tensions escalated in Kansas Brown became extremely frustrated over the apparent lack of resolve the free-state forces displayed against the frequent raids on Lawrence by the proslavery proponents. Consequently, to become active in the defense of Lawrence, shortly after their arrival Brown and his sons joined the local volunteer company, the Pottawatomie Rifles, and Brown was named captain of a company of Liberty Guards. Before they arrived in Lawrence, however, Sheriff Jones had already inflicted the infamous sack and again the people of Lawrence offered no resistance and no reprisals against the responsible proslavery forces. Fed up with the impotency of the antislavery faction, Brown decided to take matters into his own hands. With a thirst for vengeance and with that wild look in his eyes, he declared that he must "fight fire with fire" and "strike terror in the hearts of the proslavery people..... Something must be done," he added, "to show these barbarians that we, too, have rights." Brown and seven others, including his four sons and his son-in-law, rode out to Pottawatomie Creek armed with guns and razor-sharp broadswords. On the night of May 24, 1856, Brown stopped at the modest cabin of his first unlucky proslavery victim, one James Doyle. With his family watching in utter terror, they dragged the defenseless man out to the front yard where he was shot, then returned inside for his sons. Leaving the youngest son behind with his frantic mother, Brown and his vigilantes took the two elder boys outside and with a heartless display of pure evil, split the skulls of the two hapless souls with their swords. And if that wasn't enough, they hacked the bodies to pieces. Now possessed with a taste of blood, the nineteenth-century terrorists moved on to two additional homes where they ended the lives of two other proslavery men with broadsword blows to the head. The horror of that night, the latest senseless vengeance over the Kansas-Nebraska Act, would be remembered forever as the Pottawatomie Massacre. With their lust for retribution temporarily appeased, Brown and his men went into hiding.

Despite sworn testimony from several witnesses and an outstanding warrant for Brown's arrest, many of the mainstream Republican newspapers refrained from reporting the slayings and those that did discounted the reports that Brown and his sons were the murderers. Instead they either shrugged it off as just one more example of the wild and distorted claims Kansas was notorious for, that Brown must have acted in self defense, or if the killings and mutilations did occur they were more than likely carried out by Indians.

Nevertheless, the country had not heard the last of John Brown.

Unable to remain in hiding for long, the following month his defeat of a much superior force of Missourians committed to his capture was added to the news of his exploits. Brown also successfully defended the free-soil town of Osawatomie against several hundred proslavery gunmen in the fall with about two dozen men. It was a skirmish that earned him the moniker "Old Osawatomie Brown." In this fight one of Brown's sons was killed. With tears welling up in his eyes and even more rage in his heart, Brown vowed to his dead son that "I have only a short time to live—only one death to die, and I will die fighting for this cause. There will be no peace in this land until slavery is done for. I will carry the war into Africa."

Indeed, John Brown would spend the rest of his life committed to fulfilling his own personal war against the evils of slavery. To help finance his war, in the fall of 1856, he returned to the East to solicit funds for the supplies and arms he would need to carry out his military operations, an event that would shock the nation.

In the meantime, with the bitter memory of the Pottawatomie Massacre lingering like a bad nightmare, the mood in Kansas began to grow increasingly ominous. The northern free-staters and the southern proslavery radicals recognized the inevitability of armed conflict to settle the question of slavery in Kansas once and for all. To prepare for this eventuality, the so-called "border ruffians" from Missouri were organized into an armed mob of resistance fighters while in the antislavery camp, a new and more aggressive leader, Jim

Lane, vowed to rid Kansas of each and every supporter of the peculiar institution.

Throughout the summer of 1856 both sides continued to intimidate their enemy not only with exaggerated threats and counter-threats but also in the all too frequent instances of bloodshed. Random and frequent bushwhacking were beginning to be routine as free-soilers and proslavery forces often clashed in sudden and deadly guerilla warfare.

Fortunately, arriving in Kansas that fall was John W. Geary, the third appointee to move into the governor's office in Lecompton in two years. A veteran of the Mexican War and the first mayor of San Francisco, Geary was appalled over the "pernicious complicity of public officials" to make Kansas a slave state. He had become weary of the senseless loss of life and with the help of 1,300 federal troops standing by, the 36-year-old governor managed to negotiate a truce between the two warring factions.

Over the following months, as the tenuous truce continued to hold, it became increasingly evident that other forces were now at work. The once bitter outcry over slavery in Kansas was significantly diluted by the ravenous desire by both sides to speculate in Kansas land deals. Financial greed had overtaken the leaders of both factions who quickly recognized the opportunities for making a fortune in land grants and railroad charters. The *New York Tribune* acknowledged this latest twist when it wrote, "The love of the almighty dollar had melted away the iron of bitterness and Anti-Slavery and Pro-Slavery men were standing together as a unit on their rights as squatters."

Following the presidential election, attention was drawn to the inauguration of James Buchanan, the fifteenth President of the United States. It was March 4, 1857, and with all the traditional pomp and circumstance before a large and enthusiastic crowd, the oath of office was duly administered by Supreme Court Justice Roger Taney on the East Portico of the Capitol. In his inaugural speech Buchanan recognized the terrible strain the fight over territorial slavery was having, not only on the inhabitants of the territory itself, but also on the country as well. "Throughout the whole progress of this agitation, which has scarcely known any intermission for more than twenty years," he began, "whilst it has been productive of no positive good to any human being it has been the prolific source of great evils to the master, to the slave, and the whole country. It has alienated and estranged the people of the sister States from each other, and has even seriously endangered the very existence of the Union." The fight for and against slavery in the territories and his advocacy for popular sovereignty received the primary focus at the very beginning of his address. Buchanan reminded his listeners that it was the "voice of the majority" that had placed him in this esteemed office and alluding to Kansas, he cleverly suggested that in America majority rule was always the proper constitutional form. "What a happy conception, then," he said, "for Congress to apply this simple rule, that the will of the majority shall govern, to the settlement of the question of domestic slavery in the Territories. Congress is neither to legislate slavery into any Territory or State nor to exclude it therefrom, but to leave the people thereof perfectly free to form and regulate their domestic institutions in their own way, subject only to the Constitution of the United States." He went on to address the right each resident of a territory should have to form a "free and independent expression of his opinion by his vote." And that "nothing can be fairer than to leave the people of a Territory free from all foreign interference to decide their own destiny for themselves."

As he entered the White House, Buchanan was convinced the principles of popular sovereignty in Kansas would settle the territorial slavery issue once and for all and as a consequence sectional strife would finally be over. As for the central question of when the territory could apply popular sovereignty, southerners of both parties always held the opinion that the Kansans could decide the fate of slavery in their territory when they were ready to apply for statehood, and in the meantime slavery was free to flourish there. Northerners, on the other hand, thought the people should decide much earlier to prevent slavery from becoming too well established in the territory, a condition that could influence the vote for a state constitution. This question, Buchanan reminded his listeners, was a "judicial question, which legitimately belongs to the Supreme Court of the United States" In return for their support for his nomination and the support he received in the presidential race, Buchanan favored the southern view, but in doing so he failed to recognize that his actions could alienate the northern Democratic wing and further divide the party. For the moment, however, how the territorial government in Kansas decided to implement popular sovereignty was the principle focus in the early years of his administration.

By this time Governor Geary, despite the truce, found it nearly impossible to do his job without the backing he expected from Washington. When he attempted to reform the territorial court system, he was thwarted by Chief Justice Samuel Lecompte. When he tried to replace Lecompte, the U.S. Senate refused to confirm a replacement. And his efforts to bring stability to the territory only brought threats against his own life. Fed up with the lack of support, on the day Buchanan was inaugurated, Geary resigned. (As a major general in the Union army, Geary went on to fight at Gettysburg before becoming governor of Pennsylvania.)

Geary's departure played right into the hands of Buchanan. His administration could now deal with a governor of his own choosing. Therefore, one of Buchanan's first appointments was to select a new territorial governor for Kansas, one that he knew well and who could be trusted in fulfilling his promise to bring peace to Kansas. His choice to replace Geary was former Mississippi senator Robert J. Walker, a no-nonsense bureaucrat from the Polk administration where he served as secretary of the treasury.

The new governor arrived in Kansas in May 1857 when it was still relatively calm and in his inauguration speech declared, "In no contingency will Congress admit Kansas as a slave state or free state, unless a majority of the people of Kansas shall first have fairly and freely decided this question for themselves by a *direct vote on the adoption of the Constitution,* excluding all fraud or violence" [italics added]. Walker's point that the constitution would be submitted to the voters received Buchanan's blessing beforehand and was taken quite literally by the free-soilers in Kansas. In time, however, and like his predecessor, Walker would find the Kansans and the issues there much too volatile for administering a stable government.

In February, several months before Walker arrived, the Lecompton proslavery legislature authorized a June election of delegates for a constitutional convention. The delegates would then meet in September to begin framing a constitution, one of the primary steps in the process leading to statehood. The free-staters, of course, suspected this election would be just as fraudulent as those in the past. To eliminate the perception of legitimacy they refused to participate, with the exception of the Democratic free-staters already working in the Lecompton government. And as expected, a majority of proslavery men were elected as delegates to the convention.

Since the constitutional convention was legally authorized by the Lecompton territorial government, Walker was powerless to do anything about it. However, because he had promised the "bona fide residents" that they would have an opportunity to personally ratify their constitution, something the proslavery delegates were uneasy with; the new governor was renounced by those in the very government he now led.

In the White House, Buchanan thought the decision to push for Kansas statehood was a good idea and reiterated how he "rejoiced ... that the convention of Kansas will submit the Constitution to the people," a position that caught the southerners off guard. He further solidified his position on the matter when he wrote a letter to Walker and declared, "On the question I am willing to stand or fall." Obviously, the proslavery crowd was in a tiff over Buchanan's position. "We are betrayed," they complained, "by an administration that went into power on [southern] votes." Resorting to their time-tested strategy, the proslavery southerners threatened to secede if the constitution was presented to the people for approval.

Of equal importance to the administration, Buchanan was also conspiring in the background with popular sovereignty advocates, like Senator Douglas, to implement strategies for bringing Kansas into the Union as a Democratic state, even if some compromise with the free-staters was necessary to accomplish that end.

The constitutional convention met on September 7 and ran through the eleventh at which time the convention president, John Calhoun, called for an adjournment. Evidently Calhoun was aware that an election to seat a new territorial legislature had been previously scheduled for early October and thought it prudent to postpone the convention until October 19, after the results of that election became known.

This time the advocates for a free Kansas voted in the October election but yet again the result was a proslavery victory. Nevertheless, in his Lecompton office Walker became highly suspicious of the vote count and in direct violation of the law, which permitted only the courts to review election returns, he examined the ballot totals for each district. As he suspected, his review revealed that from two remote counties where less than a hundred votes combined were actually cast, the tally sheets showed some 2,800 votes. In a bold and decisive action, Walker disqualified these ballots which left the free-soilers in the majority. With Walker's decree, the free-staters were now authorized to control the legislature in Lecompton. Walker's tampering with the election, of course, only drew additional wrath from the proslavery residents.

Following the election of the new anti-slavery legislature, the constitutional convention reconvened as scheduled on October 19 and following the typical parade of speeches, amendments, and votes, the delegates began to discuss the proslavery constitution for Kansas. One of the articles directed that no free blacks would be permitted to enter Kansas, an edict similar to a provision of the Topeka constitution but with one caveat, it allowed the right of slave owners to retain their slaves already residing in Kansas, as well as any future offspring. Also included was a request for a land grant of over 20 million acres, over five times the amount normally granted to new states, and a constitutional guarantee that slavery would be retained. Specifically, the constitution declared that "the right of property is before and higher than any constitutional sanction, and the right of the owner of a slave to such slave and its increase is the same and as inviolable as the right of the owner of any property whatever," and that "no alteration shall be made to affect the rights of property in the ownership of slaves." As for allowing or denying the further importation of slavery into the territory, the delegates decided to submit only that single question to the voters in the form of a referendum in December. Thus, contrary to statements made by the governor and the president, the voters would not be voting on the entire constitution as promised. Instead they would be voting on a single clause of that constitution. The obscenity of that vote was that regardless of the outcome, the constitution would still allow the continuation of slavery already existing in the state. Free-staters from both parties were infuriated over this sleight of hand especially since laws against smuggling slaves into Kansas would be largely unenforceable.

Buchanan immediately demonstrated the weakness of his leadership by acquiescing to this new arrangement. He was reluctant to challenge the convention for two reasons. He feared the South would carry out its threat to secede if he did not agree with this scheme, and because the delegates might refuse to submit any part of the constitution to the voters. He was convinced this so-called "partial submission" was better than nothing at all and therefore his pledge to the voters had actually been fulfilled. When faced with new criticism over this latest fiasco, he simply began to backtrack. He said that he never "entertained or expressed the opinion that the convention were bound to submit any portion of the constitution to the people except the question of slavery." Walker, on the other hand, was so outraged over Buchanan's betrayal for supporting the partial submission and its misinterpretation of popular sovereignty that in November he packed his bags and left Kansas for good. The following month Buchanan accepted his resignation and appointed the territorial secretary and proslavery Democrat, Frederick Stanton, as acting governor.

At this point the free-state faction was growing increasingly distressed not only over the numerous fraudulent elections but now over the bogus convention and the so-called Lecompton Constitution. Stanton sensed their growing frustration and to preclude a return to civil unrest he called on the newly elected legislature to enact a law that would give the voters another chance to vote on the entire Lecompton Constitution, something that was promised to them from the very beginning. Even though the partial submission vote would proceed as scheduled in December, the free-state legislature agreed and declared January 4, 1858, as the date for the new and separate vote.

In Washington, Buchanan quickly learned of Stanton's agreement with the free-state legislature. In a fit of rage, two days after Stanton's recommendation for a new law, he issued orders for his dismissal, replacing him with John W. Denver, the sixth governor of the territory.

On December 21, the voters of Kansas went to the polls to vote on the single slavery article of the Lecompton Constitution except for most of the free-staters who stayed home for obvious reasons. As a result, the returns were quite predicable. The importation of slavery won handily, receiving roughly six thousand votes to approximately 570. Two weeks later, however, with cries of fraud still resonating in Lawrence, the vote to accept or reject the Lecompton Constitution in its entirety was held as mandated by the anti-slavery legislature. This time the proslavery faction abstained and again the results were predicable. The vote for rejecting the Lecompton Constitution in its entirety won overwhelmingly, receiving over 10,200 votes to a mere 162.

Buchanan was taken aback by the separate free-state vote but he had already endorsed the actions of the convention and committed his support for the partial submission in his annual message to Congress in early December. Therefore, despite the official and authorized ruling of the Kansas legislature and the mandate of the voters, on February 2, 1858, Buchanan forwarded the proslavery Lecompton Constitution to the Congress with a recommendation for its approval. Buchanan had now shown his true colors by not only abandoning his principles on popular sovereignty but also his credibility to the free-staters in Kansas.

In Congress, the fight between the two sections was monumental. Buchanan fully anticipated a stiff fight in the House where, unlike the Senate, the Democratic majority was slim. Proponents from the northern and southern wings of both parties struggled mightily to win their cause while at the same time trying to minimize the potential hazard of splitting their party. Senator Douglas, as chairman of the Senate Committee on Territories and a principal advocate of popular sovereignty, was one lawmaker placed squarely in the middle of this sectional struggle. As you recall, being a loyal Democrat and party leader, he withdrew from the presidential race in 1856 to unite the party around Buchanan and to further the popular sovereignty principles both men had championed for many years. And shortly after the free-staters won control of the Kansas legislature he asserted that the voters in Kansas would agree to "nothing less than a constitution which shall exclude and prohibit slavery." But under the present circumstances he was unable to support the president or the Lecompton Constitution because of Buchanan's misguided advocacy for such a convoluted application of popular sovereignty. Douglas had to protect his own integrity, and to some degree, his own political survival. The cordial working relationship between Douglas and Buchanan received its coup de grâce when the Illinois senator met Buchanan in the White House shortly before Buchanan's annual message to Congress. Thoroughly frustrated that Buchanan disregarded his plea to withhold the endorsement of the Lecompton Constitution in his message, Douglas informed Buchanan that he could no longer continue providing the congressional support he was accustomed to on this issue. Furthermore, he was fully prepared to denounce the president's position from the podium of the U.S. Senate. At that point Buchanan became clearly irritated and in no uncertain terms, replied bitterly, "Mr. Douglas, I desire you to remember that no Democrat ever yet differed with an administration of his own choice without being crushed."

Undeterred by Buchanan's threat, the powerful Democratic leader had become a significant influence in the Senate and through his energetic application of political and oratorical skill persuaded those like-minded individuals to break with Buchanan. By working together, he explained, they could establish an alliance with the Republicans to attack Buchanan and to outline a strategy for defeating the Democratic proslavery measure. He could never "force this constitution down the throats of the people of Kansas," Douglas declared to the Senate, "in opposition to their wishes and in violation of our pledges." To the astonishment of those present, Douglas's battle with the president had crossed the line and in doing so he was placing his political future on the line as well. In fact, Douglas was so persuasive in furthering their own point of view on this matter that many Republicans wanted to bring him into the party as one of their own. At the same time, however, southern Democrats were furious with Douglas for turning his back on them. In carrying out their wrath the Senate Democratic caucus removed him as chairman of the Committee on Territories and vowed to get even in the next presidential election. Senator Jefferson

Davis added the exclamation point when he directed an attack on Douglas in the Senate. "We are not to be cheated," the Mississippian declared, by those who "seek to build up a political reputation by catering to the prejudice of a majority to exclude the property of a minority."

The fierce debates droned on and on for several weeks before the southern-dominated Democratic Senate agreed in March to accept the Lecompton Constitution and to accept Kansas into the Union as a slave state. But in the House, as Buchanan had predicted, the fight had a somewhat different outcome. Despite reports of shameless bribery from the administration, 22 northern Democrats out of 53 threw in with the Republicans to reject the Lecompton issue by a vote of 120 to 112. With both Houses in a standoff, the administration was in a serious dilemma.

Needing a compromise to save face, the administration threw its support behind an alternate measure that reduced the requested land grant from over 20 million acres to 4 million. Consequently, as part of the compromise, the entire Lecompton Constitution would not be resubmitted to the voters, a concession to the administration. Instead, only the provision for reducing the land grant would be presented for their consideration. The Kansans would then vote to accept the Lecompton Constitution with or without the reduced land grant. If the compromise passed, Kansas would be admitted into the Union as a slave state and enlarged by 4 million acres. On the other hand, if it was rejected, a new stipulation in the compromise required that a sufficient increase in the population of the territory would have to be demonstrated before statehood could be reconsidered. The House agreed and with administration pressure the Senate concurred in April of 1858. On August 2, for the third time, the residents of Kansas went to the polls to vote on the constitution via the land grant provision. When the final vote was totaled the compromise, and by implication the constitution, was soundly rejected by nearly 10,000 votes. For the time being the Kansas saga was over.

There were no winners in this sectional tragedy and neither side was truly satisfied. Buchanan and his administration, of course, were convincingly defeated. So too was the northern wing of the Democratic Party. Following the Kansas-Nebraska Act the northern Democrats had suffered a humiliating defeat in 1854 when the voters threw out seventy representatives as retribution for their disloyalty to the North. Two years later the northern Democrats were able to recover thirty of their previously lost seats and appeared to be regaining their sectional strength within the party. Now, however, they again were repudiated in the mid-term elections of 1858 when their numbers were further reduced to only thirty-two, leaving the concentration of Democratic sectional power still in the South. On the other hand, the Democrats in the South, despite the damage they knew would be inevitable to their northern members, were committed to fight for Kansas as a slave state. They ended up losing as well and the severity of the damage to their party would be evident in two years when the Republicans would take over the reins of power in Washington. And finally, the free-state advocates had to abide by the congressional proviso in the compromise for disapproving the Lecompton Constitution, one which required application for statehood only after the population of the territory reached 90,000. Ultimately, three years later Kansas became the nineteenth free state and the thirty-fourth in the Union.

Nevertheless, although the northern anti-slavery forces could claim a victory over the dreaded slave-power conspirators, the sectional struggle and loss of Kansas left the southern proslavery coalition extremely bitter. This bitterness translated into a deeply-rooted animosity that continued to strain the relations between the two sections.

17

From Brown to Lincoln (1856 to 1860)

While the political battle in Kansas was playing itself out, in the fall of 1856 John Brown was traveling throughout the East seeking moral, financial, and material support for his self-proclaimed war on slavery. Although Brown's fanatic commitment to rid the stigma of slavery from the country had been a lifelong quest, his focus had taken on a whole new dimension following the pledge he made to his dead son, Frederick, shot by a proslavery gunman at Osawatomie. "There will be no peace in this land until slavery is done for," Brown promised his boy, and now he prepared to fulfill that pledge.

In Chicago, New York and Boston, Brown was well received by abolitionist sympathizers who were wholeheartedly in favor of his cause, as least philosophically. But with little to show for his efforts in cash contributions, around one thousand dollars, Brown returned to Kansas a year later. By that time fighting had noticeably subsided, undoubtedly influenced by the tenuous truce arranged by Governor Geary. And even more significant, since the territorial legislature was now in the hands of the free-staters there was, it seemed to Brown, little that could be gained.

More intent than ever to begin his campaign, Brown pulled up stakes and with his small group of followers moved his base to Tabor, Iowa, a tiny isolated town in the southwest corner of the state. It was there that Brown's true objective became known, one that would take him to the foothills of the Appalachian Mountains in Virginia where he would launch his crusade to free the slaves.

Brown had previously dispatched one of his men to live in Harpers Ferry as a spy and an Englishman was hired as a drill instructor for the runaway slaves he expected to join him. But he still needed additional weapons to arm his army before they could advance southward. Consequently, the first step in this bold venture called for a break-in at the U.S. armory at Harpers Ferry to steal the guns stored there. Then, moving along the mountains, Brown's plan was to welcome the hundreds of runaway slaves as he traveled southward. Disregarding advice from abolitionist groups that his actions would develop into a bloody insurrection, Brown angrily remarked, "Talk! talk! talk! That will never free the slaves. What is needed is action—action." Brown even tried to enlist the support of his close friend, Frederick Douglass. "I want you for a special purpose" he said. "When I strike, the bees will begin to swarm, and I shall want you to help me hive them." Douglass tried to dissuade Brown, remarking that "an attack on the federal government would array the whole country against us." And that he would never get out of Harpers Ferry alive. But it was all to no avail.

Instead, Brown returned to the East to obtain rifles and pikes, secretly financed by six wealthy and avid extremist benefactors called the Secret Six. Following this visit Brown traveled to Chatham, Canada, in May 1858 where a vast enclave of fugitive slaves had taken refuge. There, along with a group of his followers, he met with nearly three dozen ex-slaves. At this clandestine meeting an attempt was made to recruit more blacks for his emancipation effort and a provisional constitution was drawn up, one designed to establish a government in the mountains of Virginia for the slaves Brown would soon set free. Although Brown, in his own inimitable fashion, persuaded the fugitives to agree to the constitution, he failed miserably to convince them that his liberation campaign would succeed. Only two recruits signed on with Brown, one of which soon returned to Canada after realizing the folly of his decision.

Brown, however, was not quite finished with his initial goal. Still hankering for a fight, he returned to Kansas the following month and in December led a successful raid into Missouri where one slaveholder was killed and eleven slaves liberated. Finally satisfied that his personal vendetta against the proslavery forces had been fulfilled, Brown and his men returned to the East where he rented a house at the Kennedy farm in Maryland, only five miles from Harpers Ferry.

With no plans for feeding his men or the slaves he expected to flock to his side, and no thought as to how he would conduct his troops southward, on the night of October 16, 1859, Brown set out from his Maryland hideaway. Under cover of darkness Brown and eighteen of his followers, including three of his sons, filed across the Baltimore and Ohio railroad bridge that spanned the Potomac and quietly slipped into Harpers Ferry, captured the night watchman, and easily gained entrance to the federal arsenal and armory. Once inside, Brown ordered several of his men to fan out across the town to bring back hostages, one of which turned out to be Colonel Lewis Washington, the great-grandnephew of George Washington. For no apparent reason the midnight train to the East Coast was stopped for several hours and then released, a move that undoubtedly exposed their escapade to the authorities. The only casualty in that incident was a free black baggage worker mistakenly shot and killed by Brown's men as he looked for the watchman in the fog-shrouded darkness. By the early morning hours of the 17th additional prisoners were taken when the acting superintendent, master armorer, and master machinist reported for work. With everything going smoothly Brown sat back to wait for the runaway slaves to arrive. But although Brown's intent was to draw the slaves away from their masters and to freedom, he omitted one crucial point. Inexplicably, he failed to communicate his plan to the slaves beforehand and what he intended to accomplish. As a result not a single slave showed up to join the rebellion.

Meanwhile, as Brown patiently bided his time in the armory, news of the break-in had spread throughout Harpers Ferry. Immediately responding to the threat to their community, irate locals took up arms and assembled outside the thicker brick-walled firehouse where Brown and his men had now retreated. Soon the morning stillness was shaken as gunfire began to reverberate across the hills. By the early afternoon, as the standoff between the townspeople and Brown's men continued, militia troops from Virginia and Maryland arrived, taking up positions that cut off escape across the bridge, and that night federal troops marched into town under the command of Brevet Colonel Robert E. Lee and his aide, Lieutenant James E. B. Stuart.

In the morning, following Brown's refusal to surrender, Stuart ordered a detachment of marines to storm the firehouse with their bayonets drawn for close combat. In a very short time the building was breached and during the ensuing fight one marine was killed. The intruders were ultimately captured, but in the struggle Brown received a severe wound from the dress sword of the detachment's commander and had to be carried from the building bleeding profusely. All told, of the nineteen men taking part in the raid two escaped, ten were killed, including two of Brown's sons, and seven were captured, all of whom would meet their fate on the gallows. Taken to Charleston to stand trial, the nation would soon learn the latest exploits of the notorious abolitionist John Brown.

When asked his opinion on Brown's capture, Lincoln remarked, "It was not a slave insurrection. It was an attempt by white men to get up a revolt among slaves, in which the slaves, with all their ignorance, saw plainly enough it could not succeed."

One week after his capture John Brown was brought before the court. Still ailing and frail from his injuries, he lay wounded on a pallet, his long white beard adding a peculiar dignity to his character. Throughout his weeklong trial Brown bravely withstood not only the pain of his wounds but also the pain of having to defend himself against charges of treason, murder, and inciting an insurrection, charges he categorically denied were ever his intent. He never wavered in pleading his innocence and never once complained of his treatment from the time of his capture to the hour of his death. He was stoical in his composure, eloquent in his defense, and courageous in the face of certain death. Even Virginians, despite his appalling goals, were awed by the strength of Brown's courtroom demeanor in an age where such raw courage demonstrated supreme manliness. For this he was greatly admired.

On the other hand, many in the North, either for their own political agendas or perhaps in hopes of saving his life, insisted he was deranged, especially those pointing to his atrocious acts at Pottawatomie as one not expected from a normal person.

Responding to the charges against him Brown exclaimed, "I deny everything but what I have all along admitted: of a design on my part to free slaves.... Had I interfered in the manner which I admit ... in behalf of the rich, the powerful, the intelligent, the so-called great ... every man in this Court would have deemed it an act worthy of reward rather than punishment.... I believe that to have interfered as I have done, as I have always freely admitted I have done, in behalf of His despised poor, is no wrong, but right. Now, if it is deemed necessary that I should forfeit my life for the furtherance of the ends of justice, and mingle my blood further with the blood of my children and with the blood of millions in this slave country whose rights are disregarded by wicked, cruel, and unjust enactments, I say, let it be done." Before his death, Brown prophetically uttered, "I, John Brown, am now quite certain that the crimes of this guilty land will never be purged away but with blood."

At the conclusion of his trial the court sentenced John Brown to be hanged on December 2, 1859. And so it was done.

Above the Mason-Dixon Line, Brown's death was devastating news. The sacrifice of his own life for the cause of freeing the slaves captured the imagination of most northerners. And in its aftermath he was mourned as a fallen national hero and eulogized as a true martyr. Prayer services were held in his honor, homes and shops were draped in black bunting, his picture prominently displayed in their front windows and mass pilgrimages to his gravesite in North Elba, New York, were a daily occurrence. "History, forgetting the errors of his judgment in the contemplation of his unfaltering course ... and of the nobleness of his aims," said William C. Bryant, "will record his name among those of its martyrs and heroes." In the northern press the moral censure of slavery was ratcheted up to a new level in tribute to Brown's memory and the cause of his enormous sacrifice. The *Liberator*, for example, declared that "John Brown has twice as much right to hang Governor Wise as Governor Wise has to hang him."

Slave insurrection was now advocated openly not only in the press but also from the pulpit as a necessary weapon of the antislavery movement and that northerners should not "shrink from the bloodshed that would follow." As a further memorial to Brown, in two years hence "John Brown's Body" would become the Union army's most popular marching song.

Of equal proportion to the grief expressed in the North was the condemnation of Brown from the southern aristocracy. To the rich and powerful in the South, Brown not only represented the extremist antislavery position of one man but also epitomized the unspoken desire of many northerners to cut the throat of the southern slave society. Furthermore, they explained, the sympathy expressed over his death actually expressed the disappointment over his failure to succeed. Although slave insurrection was their worst nightmare, one that sent shivers of anxiety throughout the slave community over the thought of such an event, many slaveholders were elated that not one slave had joined Brown's crusade. It was a vindication of what they professed for years, they proudly exclaimed. The slaves were indeed satisfied with their station in life and now they were proven right. Nevertheless, still fearful that other abolitionists would take up Brown's cause, the South began to organize and strengthen state militias to defend against such a possibility. With this gesture, the South was unwittingly building an armed force destined for a greater role in the Confederate army several years hence.

In a number of southern towns mass hysteria still prevailed despite the armed precautions. At these locations, just picking up a suspected insurrectionist was enough to warrant enforcement of their new vigilante lynch laws with questions asked later. "It is better for us to hang ninety-nine innocent men," explained a Texan, "than to let one guilty one pass, for the guilty one endangers the peace of society."

In the political world, the Democrats saw an enormous opportunity to capitalize on this latest sectional issue by connecting the Republican Party to the Brown incident. One of the tactics they used was to simply blame Seward, a leading Republican candidate to replace Buchanan in the White House. He was the real instigator of the Harpers Ferry tragedy, they claimed, by virtue of his inflammatory and irresponsible rhetoric. It was Seward's despicable oratory that incited Brown to react as violently as he did. Naturally Seward denied these charges as the Republicans began to circle their wagons, frantically denouncing Brown and his treasonous actions. From Springfield, Lincoln also offered his support by condemning Brown's actions. Although he "agreed with us in thinking slavery wrong, that cannot excuse violence, bloodshed and treason."

Most southerners, however, flatly rejected all attempts to appease them as nothing more than "gas and vaporing." In fact, merely coming from the North, regardless of one's abolitionist philosophy or one's opinion of the Brown affair, was enough in some places to warrant an eviction by one's southern host. Many of the more obstinate northerners who refused to leave were simply picked up, tarred and feathered and unceremoniously run out of town.

Feeling more and more alienated in a country they felt was against them and their way of life, talk of disunion was again discussed in more serious tones as a means to shield themselves from the hate, the injustices, and the intrusiveness of the North. The slaveholders cried that under these conditions they could no longer "live under a government, the majority of whose subjects or citizens regard John Brown as a martyr and a Christian hero." Editorials in the Richmond press agreed with the latest outcry for secession. "The Harpers Ferry invasion has advanced the cause of disunion," the *Enquirer* asserted, "more than any other event that has happened since the formation of the government." The *Whig* also added its voice to the growing chorus of secessionists by declaring, "There are thousands of men in our midst who, a month ago, scoffed at the idea of a dissolution of the Union ... who now hold the opinion that its days are numbered."

A few days after Brown was executed, the first session of the Thirty-sixth Congress met in an atmosphere filled with sectional animosity so thick many members arrived armed with pistols. Aghast over what he was witnessing, one senator remarked, "The only persons who do not have a revolver and a knife are those who have two revolvers."

Despite the unsettling anxiety that permeated the Congress over Brown's execution, lingering economic issues still afforded Congress little respite. A mild economic depression had occurred in 1857 which lasted until the following spring. The generally accepted immediate cause was the cascading effect from fiscal policies in Europe brought about by the Crimean War. Those policies snowballed out of control and had seriously impacted the U.S. stock market, western investments, and banks. One of the first items that warranted attention, therefore, was to assist those hurt most by the latest economic downturn.

To help in the recovery, the Republicans resubmitted a bill that provided free one hundred and sixty acre homesteads in the western territories to impoverished workers and farmers to give them a chance to begin anew. The measure had been initially introduced in the previous Congress, but in the Senate Vice President Breckinridge had cast the tie-breaking vote for its defeat. Southern values dictated that under no circumstances would they endorse the idea of allowing northerners, who in all likelihood would be antislavery advocates, to inundate the territories with their opposing philosophy. This time the new Homestead Bill was passed by both houses along sectional lines, but again its ultimate fate was determined by a Buchanan veto and his loyalty to the South.

To illustrate the degree of sectionalism that permeated the House, when the votes were tallied, 114 of the 115 yea votes came from the free-staters in the North, while 64 of the 65 nay votes were cast by the slave-state members from the South. Sectional considerations in the Senate were also faithfully maintained when the South blocked efforts to override Buchanan's veto.

During this session, the Southerners also opposed building a railroad to the Pacific since the probable eastern terminal would not be located in a southern city, and killed a protective tariff bill because, as they stated repeatedly over the past three decades, it was a federal subsidy that benefited only northern manufacturers at southern expense. To the dismay of many northerners in

Congress, the southern Democrats had now taken on the role of obstruction-ists.

Paranoid more than ever since the Harpers Ferry incident, Southerners realized they had to safeguard everything they stood for—their slave society, their way of life, their property, and their very existence. The Republican Party was seen as a northern-inspired antislavery federation that had to be defeated in the upcoming presidential election by a united southern front.

In this setting the South prepared for the 1860 Democratic National Convention at the Institute Hall in Charleston on April 23 where the southern Democrats would attempt to assert their goals for the upcoming campaign and also to attend to some unfinished business against one of their own.

The southern delegates arrived champing at the bit to bring down Senator Douglas, the potential Yankee nominee the southern Democrats reviled for his insult to the president and for refusing to support them during the Lecompton convention. Not long after the proceedings were gaveled into session it became fairly evident that the delegates were essentially divided between northerners supporting Douglas and southerners primed for battle not only against Douglas but also over the party platform.

On this point, southerners were unanimous in their demand for a proslavery plank written into the Democratic platform that guaranteed federal protection for slavery in the territories. This demand resulted primarily from the U.S. Supreme Court ruling in 1857 which declared blacks could never be considered American citizens, that Congress had no right to exclude slavery from the territories, that barring slaves from the territories was unconstitutional, and most significantly that the doctrine of popular sovereignty was unconstitutional as well, meaning territorial legislators had no right to prohibit slavery within their borders. This decision, the culmination of the famous *Dred Scott* case, sought to resolve in one sweeping decision the principal constitutional issues raised by slavery. Instead, the ruling only exacerbated sectional discord and created a whole new round of sectional strife.

Jefferson Davis, the southern spokesman since Calhoun's death and the South's principal voice in the Senate, rejected popular sovereignty and insisted that the Supreme Court's decision was final. If the mighty U.S. Congress itself was prohibited from excluding slavery in the territories, he exclaimed, so too were the lowly territorial legislators. As Davis pointed out, the territorial legislators could not "impair the constitutional right of any citizen of the United States to take his slave property into the common territories.... It is the duty of the federal government there to afford, for that as for other species of property, the needful protection." The southern delegates had agreed beforehand that if no acceptable agreement was made on this point, they would leave the hall immediately.

Northern Democrats, primarily the Douglas supporters, opposed this plank intensely not only because of their antislavery views but also for their own political survival. They considered the Supreme Court's ruling a travesty of justice, preferring instead a platform pledging continued support for the doctrine of popular sovereignty and the powers of territorial legislatures. Subsequently submitted to the southern controlled platform committee to decide, the 17 to 16 vote resulted in a win for the southern point of view but the platform still had to be approved by the convention at large.

Following a week-long and bitter debate in which neither side would budge on the final version of the platform, the Douglas contingent, while continuing to endorse popular sovereignty, offered to compromise for the sake of party harmony. They would agree to the platform adopted in 1856, and to attract more southern voters they offered the vice presidency to Congressman Alexander Stephens of Georgia. However, the Douglas Democrats could not and would not give in to southern demands for federally guaranteed slavery protection in the territories.

When the voting concluded a further modified platform was approved, one that continued to leave the power of territories over slavery in the hands of the Supreme Court. No one was satisfied. The Douglas camp was exasperated that its compromise was ignored and the southern delegates from the Deep South were unhappy as well. Incensed that they had not received all of their demands, on April 30, Senator William L. Yancey and the Alabama delegation stormed out of the convention hall, as previously planned, followed by the delegates from the other Deep Southern states.

Despite this unruly disturbance, the balloting for the Democratic nominee got under way. Soon it became obvious that even with Yancey's followers absent, the remaining southern vote was still hurting Douglas's chance for a first ballot victory. Over the days ahead, as successive roll calls continued, the incredulous managers in the Douglas camp realized it would be impossible to gather the necessary two-thirds majority for the nomination. Although Douglas maintained his lead over fifty-seven ballots, he was unable to gather enough votes from those scattered among the other candidates to capture the nomination. These included Senator Robert M.T. Hunter of Virginia, James Guthrie of Kentucky, the former treasury secretary under Pierce, and several other lesser known politicians. Extremely frustrated over this impasse and in utter desperation, on May 3 an agreement was mercifully reached to adjourn the proceedings until June 18 at which time the delegates would resume their deliberations in Baltimore, a location perceived to be less volatile and more conducive to sectional harmony.

Even before the convention began in Baltimore another conflict quickly ensued between the two sections. This time it was over the credentials of the southerners who had left the convention in Charleston and were being replaced. When discussions with the Douglas people pointed toward admitting only a portion of their delegates, the southerners became outraged over this affront to their honor and walked out a second time, followed by most of the delegates from the upper south as well. With one hundred and ten southern delegates absent from the convention, on the 23rd of June, the champion of popular sovereignty, Stephen A. Douglas, received the nomination after only two ballots. The southern quest for revenge against Douglas and a united front against the North had failed.

Following their walkout, the rebellious southerners organized their own convention in Cincinnati and nominated Buchanan's vice president, John C. Breckinridge of Kentucky. Breckinridge would run on a proslavery platform which stated in part, "That the Government of a Territory organized by an act of Congress is provisional and temporary, and during its existence all citizens of the United States have an equal right to settle with their property in the Territory, without their rights, either of person or property being destroyed or impaired by Congressional or Territorial legislation. That it is the duty of the Federal Government, in all its departments, to protect, when necessary, the rights of persons and property in the Territories, and wherever else its constitutional authority extends." A staunch proslavery secessionist, Breckinridge was once described by diarist George Templeton Strong as "the most cruel, blind, unreasoning, cowardly, absolute despotism that now disgraces the earth." On this note the southern extremists were confident that Breckinridge would fight for their cause. But what exactly was their cause and what was the tone of the South in 1860?

Simply stated, the mood in the South was going from bad to worse. Among many other injustices they claimed were perpetrated against them by the North, Southerners were fed up with the years of anti-slavery rhetoric and fed up with outside meddling from abolitionists culminating with John Brown's raid on Harpers Ferry. Also, they were fed up with years of not having their runaway slaves returned in clear defiance of federal law, and all the other northern inspired laws including those on tariffs, banking, land sales, and states' rights which they felt were designed against their slave society.

But also of great concern was the perception that even after the long and bitter sectional conflicts over the right to extend slavery into the territories, they were still destined to lose voting power in Congress.

Following the Compromise of 1850 and the Kansas-Nebraska Act of 1854 with its mandate of popular sovereignty, the South envisioned itself on the losing side of the argument. In the past fifteen years not one slave state had been admitted to the Union, Texas being the last in 1845. During this time Iowa, Wisconsin, California, and most recently, Minnesota and Oregon, all free states, had joined the Union where now there were 18 free states and only 15 slave states. Southerners resented this trend because they knew it meant that voting power in Congress would eventually favor the northern point of view, and the northern point of view, of course, was anti–South and anti-slave. The South needed free and unrestricted access to the territories and as Jefferson Davis demanded, federally guaranteed rights for slaveholders. With Breckinridge in the White House, the process to achieve that end would now begin. If they lost the election, to many southerners unable to coexist with the North in the expected hostile climate, secession was still the only viable option.

Sectionalism continued to divide the political landscape and the Democratic ideology was still widely split between the northern and southern wings. It was a virtual guarantee that the Republicans would gain the White House and it would also portend a time for the South to reach a monumental decision. "The party is split forever," predicted Alexander Stephens. "The seceders intended from the beginning to rule or ruin.... In less than twelve months we shall be in a war, and the bloodiest in history." In accessing the years of sectional conflict that seemingly brought the nation continuous struggle, particularly over the contradictory systems of labor, Senator Seward suggested that its roots lay deep in the inner psyche of American society, and that it was "an irrepressible conflict between opposing and enduring forces, and it means that the United States must and will ... become either entirely a slave-holding nation, or entirely a free-labor nation." In its editorial the *New York Tribune* agreed, "We are not one people. We are two peoples. We are a people for Freedom and a people for Slavery. Between the two, conflict is inevitable."

Born in a primitive dirt-floor log cabin in 1809, Abraham Lincoln had little formal schooling, about a year in aggregate owing to the priorities on an early nineteenth-century Kentucky farm. Nevertheless, by diligently applying himself at home he learned to read and write, a welcomed diversion from the hard and tedious chores of everyday farm life. Nearly six feet tall at fifteen years of age, Lincoln earned money by cutting and selling wood and ferrying passengers across the Ohio River. Later he accepted employment as a surveyor and running a local store in New Salem, Illinois, where he also served as its postmaster. In 1834 he won a seat in the Illinois legislature at Vandalia and spent many hours between sessions learning the nuances of the law by studying borrowed law books. Three years later, after the state capital was moved to Springfield, Lincoln received his license to practice. With the vision of a successful new vocation, Lincoln rode into Springfield on a borrowed horse to begin a new career as a frontier lawyer.

Soon Lincoln caught the eye of a 21-year-old socialite from Kentucky and after several years of courtship married Mary Todd in 1842. He opened his own law firm with partner William H. Herndon two years later. Now earning a comfortable income the young couple bought a new house for $1,500 where they raised four boys, although only one, Robert, lived to adulthood.

Despite the good life in Springfield, Lincoln longed for the exhilarating battles found only in the chaos of national politics. Therefore, following a successful run for a vacant seat in the U.S. House of Representatives, in 1846 he moved to Washington where he served from 1847 to 1849 and gained considerable respect for his antislavery views.

With the country steeped in sectional difficulties over the Kansas-Nebraska Act and the spread of slavery, Lincoln again found it extremely difficult to sit idly by in his law office as the country was being wrenched apart. As stated earlier, Lincoln's attempt to return to politics in 1854 ended in a loss for a vacant seat in the Senate, but his true reemergence into the political arena and his subsequent acclaim as a rising star in the Republican Party came about four years later when he delivered a speech at the Illinois Republican Convention.

Standing before the Illinois Republicans Lincoln eloquently stated his views on the nation's slavery issue by declaring, "We are now far into the fifth year since a policy was initiated with the avowed object and confident promise of putting an end to slavery agitation. Under the operation of that policy, that agitation has not only not ceased, but has constantly augmented. In my opinion, it will not cease, until a crisis shall have been reached and passed. 'A house divided against itself cannot stand.' I believe this government cannot endure permanently half slave and half free. I do not expect the Union to be dissolved; I do not expect the house to fall; but I do expect it will cease to be divided. It will become all one thing, or all the other." It was a striking demonstration of Lincoln's simple but logical oratory and catapulted the Springfield lawyer into the national spotlight. The delegates were so impressed that Lincoln won the Republican nomination to challenge Douglas for his Senate seat.

Despite his loss to Douglas, Lincoln's outstanding performances during their campaign debates mesmerized audiences and won him rave reviews for his persuasiveness, his wit and debating skills, his understanding of the issues, and his down to earth common sense. His political speeches in the Midwest as well as in New England and New York City also enhanced his image as a man capable of capturing the Republican presidential nomination. Furthermore, there was nothing in his political past that could be attacked—an excellent prerequisite for a potential presidential nominee.

In 1860 the Republican National Committee chose Chicago to hold the nomination convention. Since Chicago lacked a public building large enough to accommodate the expected throng of party faithful, the city built one they called the Wigwam at a cost of some $5,000.

During the months leading up to the convention, New York senator William H. Seward was the most likely choice to represent the Republicans despite the numerous enemies he had accumulated from his life in New York and Washington politics. The reputation he had acquired from merely his association with some New York legislators suspected of corruption was enough to concern many in the party as well as his image as an anti-slavery radical for his outspoken criticism of the Fugitive Slave Law and his disapproval of the Kansas-Nebraska Act. His speech some years earlier during the debates on the Compromise of 1850 was particularly disturbing to the South and to many northern conservatives within the party. In that presentation before the Senate, Seward not only defended the right of Congress to exclude slavery from the territories as a constitutional right, but also insisted quite forcefully that "there is a higher law than the Constitution, the law of God" which condemned slavery to an eventual death. It was an image Seward was now trying hard to veil over, to moderate in order to win the nomination, but by this time few were buying into it. Horace Greeley, the influential editor of the *New York Tribune*, summed up the general feeling of the Republicans when he wrote, "I know the country is not Anti-Slavery. It will only swallow a little Anti-Slavery in a great deal of sweetening. An Anti-Slavery man per se can not be elected; but a Tariff, River-and-Harbor, Pacific-Railroad, Free Homestead man, may succeed although he is Anti-Slavery...." Another obstacle was the lingering doubt among the party strategists whether Seward could win those very critical battleground states.

Nevertheless, after four years as governor of New York and twelve in the U.S. Senate, Seward was the most prominent Republican in the country and a political power to be reckoned with. And not to be overlooked, he was still the frontrunner.

In addition to Seward, the other candidates in the running were men like Simon Cameron of Pennsylvania, Salmon P. Chase of Ohio, and Edward Bates of Missouri. Unfortunately, their résumés all contained a few political enemies and other handicaps that would leave them vulnerable to attack by the Democrats. In that light they were more or less the so-called favorite sons.

On May 16 the Honorable George Ashmun of Massachusetts opened the Republican National Convention to a swarm of noisy delegates and spectators. Although the two-story Wigwam had a capacity of ten thousand people, there were many thousands more who were unable to get inside that gathered in the adjacent town square to await the state-by-state results to be announced by a clerk from the rooftop. The noise and excitement inside was deafening as shrill brass bands competed with the cries of the delegates, a great portion of which were in varying stages of inebriation. With perhaps as many as 20,000 curious onlookers also crowded outside, it was reported to be the largest political event ever witnessed to that time in the U.S.

Over the next two days the real business of the convention was carried out as campaign managers lobbied the various delegations, searching for deals. Caucuses were held to discuss various strategies for the inevitable wheeling and dealing that occurs in all conventions, including patronage and other enticements to sway the delegates to vote for their candidate. It was during these meetings that Illinois gained the backing from the Pennsylvania and Indiana delegations to place Lincoln's name in nomination.

On the morning of the eighteenth, Seward supporters formed a procession to demonstrate their unwavering support for their candidate. The Sewardites marched to the Wigwam waving to tremendous cheers and accompanied by a shrill brass band playing "O, Isn't He a Darling?"

Following the first ballot that included symbolic votes for the favorite sons, Seward, as expected, was in the lead with Lincoln a surprisingly close second. For Lincoln the tide began to change when Indiana pledged to join Illinois in granting its full support. By the end of the second ballot, after Pennsylvania followed suit, Lincoln and Seward were nearly tied towards reaching their goal of 233 votes. As the noise and excitement escalated in the Wigwam, so too did the enthusiasm and faith of the Lincoln supporters. "Imagine all the hogs ever slaughtered in Cincinnati giving their death squeals together," one reporter described the scene, "[and] a score of big steam whistles going ... and you conceive something of the same nature." During the third round of balloting several Ohio delegates switched their votes to Lincoln; that incited a sudden avalanche of other delegates to switch to Lincoln as well. With the key northern states of Pennsylvania, Ohio, Illinois, and Indiana in their camp, the Lincoln delegates were confident they would not only win the nomination but also the ultimate prize. By this time the excitement in the hall had reached a crescendo with thousands of spectators voicing their approval in an unprecedented demonstration of support.

Lincoln won the nomination and somehow most people in the Wigwam knew, except perhaps for a few of Seward diehard supporters, that this was indeed the right man to address the sectional conflicts confronting the nation in these trying times.

The following day a committee led by Mr. Ashmun arrived in Springfield to formally inform Lincoln of his nomination. One of the committeemen, a very tall Pennsylvanian, was asked by Lincoln how tall he was. His reply was six-feet, three inches, at which point Lincoln responded that he was six-feet four. Clearly thrilled, the man exclaimed, "For years my heart has been aching for a president that I could look up to; and I've found him as last, in the land where we thought there were none but little giants."

In contrast to the Democrats, the Republican Party would run on a platform that, among other planks, included its denunciation of slavery in the territories. It also demanded a renewed effort toward a homestead bill, additional tariff legislation "to encourage the development of the industrial interests of the whole country," and more funding for internal improvements. The platform also opposed any changes to the naturalization laws, insisted that Kansas "should, of right, be immediately admitted as a State under the Constitution recently formed," strongly opposed anyone contemplating treason by advocating secession, and offered a pledge to provide government funds to build the long-delayed "Railroad to the Pacific." Unlike the Democrats as well, the Republicans were fully united behind their candidate.

There was also a fourth candidate running for president by the name of John Bell, a wealthy and major slaveholder from Tennessee. He was nominated by a group of leftover Whigs, Know-Nothings, and pro–Union Democrats at a separate convention in Baltimore. Their political federation, called the Constitutional Union Party, held its convention in Baltimore on May 9 and based its campaign solely on the interpretation of the U.S. Constitution and the solidarity of Union. Their platform was one that advocated compromise to save the Union, denounced both of the major parties, and recognized "no political principle other than the Constitution ... the Union ... and the Enforcement of the Laws." Although they had little chance to win, their hope was to capture enough electoral votes to throw the election into the House. Under this scenario, they felt a subsequent union with the Democrat Party would be sufficient to elect either Breckinridge or Bell to the presidency.

With four candidates, two from the North and two from the South, it was a foregone conclusion that sectionalism would again seep into the presidential election process as it had done in 1856. It was not surprising, therefore, that as the race got underway the campaigns evolved into two separate contests. Since Breckinridge and Bell would do poorly in the North they campaigned exclusively in the South, and in the North the challenge pitted Douglas against Lincoln. The hostile climate against the Black Republicans was so great, in fact, that Lincoln's name never appeared on the ticket in ten slave states, which forced the Republicans to bypass the South entirely.

Anticipating they could win the same northern states that Frémont won in 1856, the Republicans set their sights on capturing the northern states the party lost, states like Pennsylvania, Indiana, and New Jersey. Still considered a long shot, however, was Illinois, a Democratic state where Douglas was a leading candidate for the Democratic nomination.

For the three major candidates the principal question on the minds of the voters was quite clear—what policy should the government endorse concerning the status of slavery in the territories. Douglas still sought to institute popular sovereignty as a means for the territorial residents to decide the question themselves, Breckinridge was striving to guarantee congressional protection for slavery in the territories, and Lincoln thought it best to prohibit any further expansion of slavery at all. However there was another equally significant issue which many, including Lincoln and his strategists, had dismissed—southern secession. To these cynics the threat of secession was the same "old game of scaring and bullying the North into submission to Southern demands and Southern tyranny."

From the beginning of the campaign Douglas had a hunch that Lincoln would be the ultimate victor. Nevertheless, for the sake of the Democratic Party he decided to launch a vigorous campaign to warn the voters of the impending threat of secession and the repercussions from a Republican victory. Douglas took the southern threat seriously and expended considerable time and effort in his campaign attempting to convince others that if Lincoln was elected the South would, in all likelihood, carry out its threat. In a speech in Chicago he stated, " I believe that this country is in more danger now than at any other moment since I have known anything of public life." Throughout the sweltering summer months and right up to election day the forty-seven-year-old Senator campaigned relentlessly across the country, the first presidential candidate in history to do so. Although in poor health he somehow mustered the same tireless energy on the stump as he would have in a fight on the Senate floor, a move that in all likelihood contributed to his untimely death from typhoid fever one year later. As he crisscrossed the eastern half of the country his principal theme was always the same: the Union was in dire peril. The country was at the crossroads of a severe crisis, he preached. With Lincoln in the White House the country would be on the verge of dissolution, but if he, Douglas, became president his policy of popular sovereignty would save the Union. He insisted that matters concerning slavery should be left exclusively to the state or territorial legislatures. "If each state will only agree to mind its own business and let its neighbor alone," he railed, "this republic can exist forever divided into free and slave states, as our fathers made it, and the people of each state have decided." Lincoln's presidency and congressional interference, he asserted, would only lead to secession by the South and worse yet, civil war.

Despite Douglas's apparent attempt to appease the South, he was not only rejected by the Buchanan administration but in the South he was viewed by most Democrats as a traitor, a turncoat, and no better than Lincoln. This was particularly true of southern-rights advocates who were still seething over his refusal to side with them during the constitutional episode in Kansas. They were also angered over his determined adherence to popular sovereignty which only illustrated his complete disregard for the Supreme Court ruling. And his insistence that the territories should have the same political power as the states to legislate on slavery infuriated them tremendously.

The Democrats also clung to the tired charge of calling the Republican Party a northern sectional party and "nigger lovers." The Democratic *New York Herald*, for example, warned its readers that if Lincoln were elected "hundreds of thousands" of southern slaves were likely to "emigrate to their friends— the Republicans—North, and be placed by them side by side in competition with white men.... African amalgamation with the fair daughters of the Anglo Saxon, Celtic, and Teutonic races will soon be their portion under the millennium of Republican rule."

Keeping with the custom of the day and strictly reinforced by his close advisors, Lincoln made no speeches during the campaign and made no references to his candidacy in his written letters. Instead, Lincoln confined himself to his daily routine at home in Springfield while at the same time keeping in close and constant telegraphic communication with his aides in Chicago. Also adhering to political tradition, Republican speakers and party newspapers conducted the campaign on Lincoln's behalf. Leaving no stone unturned, their speeches and editorials sought to dispel the notion that Lincoln had not been proven, that his political skills had yet to be demonstrated, that he was more than a mere "country lawyer," and that he was indeed fit to be the next president. Soon, so-called Wide-Awake Clubs sprung up around the country to help promote Lincoln's candidacy by marching in parades, holding rallies, and inundating the voters with slogans such as "Honest Abe for President," "Lincoln and Free Homestead," and "No more Slave Territories." Republicans also exploited the rampant corruption and graft in the Buchanan administration. Much was made of the kickbacks and bribery of judges in return for premature naturalization of Democratic immigrants, the payoffs to Democratic congressmen to insure their votes were consistent with the wishes of the administration, as well as the embezzlement of thousand of dollars in government funds. Even several of Douglas's cronies were implicated in the House investigation of the scandals.

In the South the reaction to a potential Lincoln victory was mixed. Most southern slave owners feared for the survival of their slave society, others worried about what Lincoln's election would do to the Union, and the rest were eager to secede, a scenario they felt was even more persuasive if Lincoln moved into the White House. The secessionists were adamantly opposed to Lincoln and vowed to further their quest to secede if he was elected. They regarded Lincoln's position on prohibiting the extension of slavery as unacceptable. He was a Black Republican, they bitterly complained, a duplicate of John Brown's antislavery radicalism and therefore an enemy of the southern people.

Sectionalism had now turned into a political struggle between the radical secessionists and the northern advocates of Unionism.

On November 6 over four and half million voters, a near record of 81.2 percent, cast their ballots in thirty-three states for the sixteenth president of the United States. By midnight the totals were known and as expected the voting followed sectional lines and Lincoln had prevailed. Needing 152 electoral votes to win the election, the Republican rail-splitter captured 180 votes from all eighteen free states. On the other hand, with the Democratic Party severely fragmented, the three opposing candidates had to divide the remaining electoral votes among themselves.

Breckinridge carried all nine Deep South states plus the border states of Delaware and Maryland for 72 votes, while Bell received 39 votes from Kentucky, Virginia, and his home state of Tennessee. Douglas, on the other hand, although receiving the second highest popular vote, fared rather poorly. His totals were only the nine votes from Missouri and three of the seven votes from New Jersey.

The results of the election indicated quite clearly just how much bitterness and animosity existed between the two political sides. Northerners were ecstatic over Lincoln's win while the Southerners' pent-up anger was on the verge of exploding.

In Springfield, the townsfolk were jubilant. One of their own was now the President of the United States and how they rejoiced. Following a day of receiving visitors and well-wishers at his home, Lincoln was finally able to sit back and reflect. Gazing at a group of his friends he said, "Well, boys, your troubles are over now, but mine have just begun."

Little did he know at the time how prophetic he was.

18

The End of the Road
(1860 to 1861)

In Springfield, the hometown hero continued to be wined and dined. Lincoln was the guest of honor at numerous parties and receptions, applauded by the business community, envied by the local politicians, and beset by a seemingly endless array of well-wishers, job seekers, and the curious, all wanting to shake the hand of the new president-elect. Remaining unpretentious to his new-found notoriety, Lincoln held open house in the state Capitol each morning so he could meet the public, receive their pledges of support and share with them this moment of victory. He also traveled to Chicago to confer with party leaders over cabinet selections, all the while painfully aware of the sectional tensions in the country, tensions he suspected exacerbated by his election which, under that pretext, now threatened the very survival of the Union itself.

In solitary moments, when he could absorb the enormity of his position, he felt humbled over the scope of the responsibilities placed upon his shoulders. Although his public demeanor remained one conveying control, poise, and confidence, the rumbling taking place across the nation over disunion could not be ignored and it filled him with intense anxiety.

One episode, written some years later in *Harper's Magazine* by his Washington secretary, John Hay, dramatically reflected Lincoln's subconscious concern over his fate. Following one of his numerous and tiring days of planning for his administration, a weary Lincoln arrived home and lay upon a lounge for a nap. "Opposite to where I lay," said Lincoln, "was a bureau with a swinging glass upon it; and looking in that glass, I saw myself reflected nearly at full length; but my face, I noticed, had two separate and distinct images, the tip of the nose of one being about three inches from the tip of the other. I was a little bothered, perhaps startled, and got up and looked in the glass, but the illusion vanished. On lying down again, I saw it a second time, plainer, if possible, than before; and then I noticed that one of the faces was a little paler—say five shades than the other. I got up and the thing melted away, and I went off, and, in the excitement of the hour forgot all about it, nearly, but not quite, for the thing would once in a while come up, and give me a little pang as though something uncomfortable had happened. When I went home, I told my wife about it, and a few days after I tried the experiment again, when, sure enough, the thing came back again; but I never succeeded in bringing the ghost back after that, though I once tried very industriously to show it to my wife, who was worried about it somewhat. She thought it was 'a sign' that I was to be elected to a second term of office, and that the paleness of one of the faces was an omen that I should not see live through the last term."

In the South the reaction to Lincoln's smashing victory was anything but kind. He was hanged in effigy in some places, rewards were offered to prevent his inauguration, hate mail began to inundate the Springfield post office, and southern newspapers immediately began to spew out their poisonous diatribe over the Republican Party and the man southerners called a Black Republican. In the *Dallas Herald* the editors warned their readers, "The evil days ... are upon us." And the *Charleston Mercury* announced, "The tea has been thrown overboard; the revolution of 1860 has been initiated." Joining in the fray of disappointment and anger was the *Richmond Examiner*. Its editorial bitterly lamented over the South's worst fear, that the Republican Party was "a party founded on the single sentiment ... of hatred of African slavery, [and] is now the controlling power."

Therefore, in their final analysis, Lincoln's election to the presidency was the final blow against their way of life. Southern radicals saw their slave society threatened like never before. They were convinced that Lincoln, his administration, and the members of his party, which would now constitute three-quarters of the Congress, stood for everything that was anti–South and anti–slave. They would never forget Lincoln's insistence that although he could tolerate slavery within its current borders, he refused to accept on any condition an expansion of slavery to the territories. And that he sincerely believed by containing the South's peculiar institution it would eventually cease to exist. It didn't matter much that Lincoln admitted the South was not responsible for slavery or that he could not blame them for not ending something he wouldn't know how to end himself. What mattered was that he and his administration opposed states' rights and especially the right of slaveholders to take their slaves into the territories. Northern injustices against them had gone on for too long, they said, and this was the final straw. The time had finally arrived to strike back.

To these southern extremists bent on preserving their way of life, seceding from the Union now seemed the only viable option. With Lincoln in the White House and southern views castigated in Congress, control of southern interests and southern principles would be forever lost by the actions of outsiders. They sincerely believed that the right of each state to govern itself under its state constitution and state laws had to be upheld. So with their right to expand slavery denied, persistent northern resistance to the Fugitive Slave Act, interference from outside agitators in their affairs, and prospects for their future uncertain, Southerners ran out of options, ran out of patience, and ran out of loyalty to their country.

But, as in the past, there was still the lingering question of southern solidarity over secession, not only with the question of disunion itself but also on the means to accomplish this drastic action. Should the states cooperate with each other and act as a united body or separately, each state seceding when its legislators deemed it appropriate? These two scenarios divided the South, each state assuming the role of one or the other, either a cooperative or as a separative.

As in the past, South Carolina was the breeding ground and principal instigator in the drive for disunion. The state had been at the forefront of the secessionist effort on two previous occasions, first during the nullification crisis of 1832 and then in 1851 over its interpretation of the Compromise of 1850.

In a test of southern will for secession, the proactive radical legislature in South Carolina took the first step once again to fashion a cooperative effort among the southern states. At the request of the legislature, in December of 1859, Governor William H. Gist dispatched a representative to Virginia to discuss mutual grievances with the governor and the lawmakers and to outline remedies for the two states to act upon. Gist also called on the other southern states to meet together as well and to arrive at a similar common course of action against northern injustices, hopefully expecting them to propose secession. Although the agent from South Carolina was well received and politely heard, no further action resulted from his meeting. Apparently, since two very influential Virginians, Robert M. T. Hunter and Henry Wise, were being proposed as Democratic presidential candidates for the 1860 election, no one wanted to jeopardize their chances by bringing up such a controversial issue as secession at this time. For various reasons several other southern states also respectfully declined to participate in such a venture. It appeared as if all the fire-eaters calling for secession had suddenly become frozen with doubt when proposals to initiate their oft-repeated threats were on the table.

South Carolina, however, had always been unique among the southern states, a perception accurately pointed out in one sentence written by a reporter for the *London Times:* "There is nothing in all the dark caves of human passion so cruel and deadly as the hatred the South Carolinians profess for the Yankees." The Palmetto State had always been a strict proponent of states' rights, namely the right of any state to govern as a sovereign entity. And the rationale for the right to secede, South Carolinians claimed, derived from the wording of the Declaration of Independence which stated that the colonies, "are, and of right ought to be, Free and Independent States, that they have full power to levy war, conclude peace, contract alliances, establish commerce, and to do all other acts and things which independent States may of right do." And that whenever any "form of government becomes destructive of these ends for which it was established, *it is the right of the people to alter or abolish it, and to institute a new government*" (italics added). Furthermore, in their opinion the U.S. Constitution supported the principles of the Declaration and retained the states as the primary voice of the people.

When it became apparent that a cooperative effort would be difficult to organize, Governor Gist realized that someone would have to lead the way and hopefully the other southern states would follow. Therefore, with a Lincoln presidency becoming more and more likely, Gist made one last attempt in October of 1860 to gain support for secession. Writing to the other governors Gist explained, "It is the desire of South Carolina that some other state should take the lead, or at least move simultaneously with her. She will unquestionably call a convention as soon as it is ascertained that a majority of the electors will support Lincoln. If a single state takes the lead, she will follow her. If no other state secedes, South Carolina will secede (in my opinion) alone if she has any assurance that she will be soon followed by another, or other states; otherwise, it is doubtful." With the exception of Florida, Alabama, and Mississippi, which responded that they would follow the lead of South Carolina, no other southern state would agree to the governor's proposal. Several spoke of preferring to discuss the matter further at a convention while others opined that merely the fact that Lincoln was elected was not sufficient grounds to leave the Union, and others just flatly refused to take part at all.

Support for a united effort to secede failed once again. Because of that failure and all the other previous idle threats to secede, northerners had become immune to their legitimacy and brought to mind Clay's dressing down of southern senators back in 1850 when he told them, "We ought not to be perpetually exclaiming wolf, wolf, wolf."

In the opinion of most northerners all the talk about disunion was just that, all talk, and not taken very seriously. South Carolina, they thought, was acting like a "spoilt child wandering from the fold of a paternal government." Even Lincoln himself thought it unlikely the South would secede. "The people of the South have too much sense," he opined, "to attempt the ruin of the government." Yet, there were many who feared the consequences of such a move. In fact, several states that had passed personal liberty laws and other measures that offended the South hastened to repeal them in hopes their actions would allay the threat of secession. On the other hand, some northerners received these latest threats with a grin and a shrug, their inner soul torn between a fear of disunion and the relief of ridding the country of such a long-standing irritant, while others were simply willing to step aside and "let the wayward sisters depart in peace." Horace Greeley, the editor of the *New*

York Tribune, for example, shamelessly printed his sentiments for all southerners to heed: "There's the door—go!"

President Buchanan took the threat of secession very seriously and it was foremost on his mind. So much so that on December 3 his entire annual message to Congress was devoted to the issue. In his message, he questioned, "Why is it [with all the prosperity the country was blessed with] that discontent now so extensively prevails, and the Union of the States..., is threatened with destruction?" Further into his message he replied to this question by blaming the North for causing all the current unrest. "But let us take warning in time, and remove the cause of danger.... It cannot be denied that, for five and twenty years, the agitation at the North against slavery in the South has been incessant.... This agitation has ever since been continued by the public press, by the proceedings of State and county conventions, and by abolition sermons and lectures.... How easy would it be for the American people to settle the slavery question forever, and to restore peace and harmony to this distracted country! They, and they alone, can do it. All that is necessary to accomplish the object, and all for which the slave States have ever contended, is to be let alone, and permitted to mange their domestic institutions in their own way."

Following the announcement of the Republican victory, large secessionist rallies suddenly and quite unexpectedly sprang up in Charleston, Montgomery, and Mobile. At these rallies highly irresponsible and inflammatory rhetoric goaded the citizens to support the drive for disunion. With an apparent awakening of political expediency, secession had now replaced slavery as the principal and most controversial issue between the two sections. Taking note of the renewed enthusiasm for secession, and despite South Carolina's half-hearted reluctance to resume the lead in the secessionist movement, on November 10, the state legislature called for a convention to meet in Columbia on December 17 to settle the secession issue once and for all. Within several days five additional Deep South states, Alabama, Mississippi, Georgia, Louisiana, and Florida, now spurred on with renewed passion in light of South Carolina's declaration, also called for state conventions as well.

Meanwhile, South Carolina's congressional delegation in Washington, working on the assumption that their state would vote to secede, began to prepare the way for transferring custody of the federal forts protecting Charleston over to state jurisdiction. These forts included Fort Moultrie, presently garrisoned by a small number of regular army troops under Major Robert Anderson; Castle Pinckney, a modest stone fort under the watch of one Union military caretaker; the abandoned Fort Johnson on James Island; and Fort Sumter, a state-of-the-art fortress in the shape of a pentagon still under construction on a small man-made island in Charleston Harbor. The southern delegation surmised that to avoid the possibility of trouble after South Carolina seceded, it would be best to obtain an agreement for an orderly transfer of ownership before the actual declaration of secession occurred. Therefore, on December

8, several congressmen met with President Buchanan to discuss documenting an agreement that would be satisfactory to both sections. At the end of the meeting the southern delegation possessed a document, signed by five of the congressmen, which they understood to be acceptable to Buchanan. The agreement pledged that neither side would attack, fire on, or reinforce any of the forts in and around Charleston Harbor before the convention committed itself and that "we hope and believe not until an offer has been made through an accredited Representative to negotiate for an amicable arrangement of all matters between the State and Federal governments, provided that no reinforcements shall be sent into those Forts & *their relative military status remains as at present*" (italics added).

With this signed letter in hand, the authorities in South Carolina were under the erroneous perception that a preliminary gentlemen's agreement or memorandum of understanding had been reached with President Buchanan over the transfer of the forts. Delighted over their success, a three-member commission was promptly dispatched to Washington to pursue further negotiations in the transfer. In the White House, President Buchanan reconsidered the intent of the letter and thought otherwise. He refused to agree with the wording of this document and as such felt he was under no obligation to adhere to its provisions, especially if South Carolina voted to leave the Union.

Meanwhile, with tensions riding high and the talk of secession on everyone lips, numerous last minute proposals were introduced in the Thirty-sixth Congress. They were the final attempts to reduce the possibility of war by encouraging South Carolina to reconsider her threat of secession. Since there were so many offers of compromise each chamber elected a special committee, called the Committee of Thirteen, to sort through them all. One such plan delivered to the floor of the Senate was called the Crittenden Compromise after its author, John J. Crittenden of Kentucky. This so-called final compromise called for several constitutional amendments that guaranteed the federal government would not interfere with slavery in the states, that prohibited Congress from abolishing slavery in the District of Columbia unless certain conditions were met, and quite significantly, protected slavery in all the territories "now held, or hereafter acquired." In Springfield, Lincoln was briefed on the proposal and remaining firm in his repeatedly stated position quickly sent a message to the Republicans to "entertain no proposition for a compromise in regard to the extension of slavery...." He further stressed that to compromise on this matter "acknowledges that slavery has equal rights with liberty, and surrenders all we have contended for.... We have just carried an election on principles fairly stated to the people. Now we are told in advance, the government shall be broken up, unless we surrender to those we have beaten.... If we surrender, it is the end of us." Heeding the advice of their new leader, the proposal was rejected in both houses of Congress by a solid Republican vote.

With no compromise likely to come from Congress, an open letter to the southern people was signed by nearly every congressional representative from seven southern states. "The argument is exhausted," they wrote. "All hope of relief in the Union, through the agency of committees, Congressional legislation, or constitutional amendment, is extinguished.... The honor, safety, and independence of the Southern people are to be found in a Southern Confederacy."

On December 17, shortly after their arrival at the Baptist Church in Columbia, the delegates, an assemblage of South Carolina's finest, including five former governors, soon learned that a severe outbreak of smallpox had imperiled the city. Choosing not to expose themselves unnecessarily to this life-threatening disease, they voted to relocate their deliberations to Charleston. Before adjourning, however, they quickly voted to appoint a select committee to draw up the document that would change the course of history—an ordinance of secession.

The following day, a clear and crisp December Tuesday, one hundred and seventy delegates arrived in Charleston, a thriving seaport of 40,000 people. As the delegates took their places in Institute Hall, the seriousness of their purpose was clearly etched in their faces. The delegates were absolutely certain that Lincoln's policies would not only prohibit the South from extending slavery into the territories, but in turn would also deprive them of their constitutional right to further their peculiar institution, their prosperity, and their heritage. It was because of these perceived policies that they were brought to this historic gathering and that they were the instruments to decide the fate of their state and as a consequence the future of the Union. Following a day of seemingly endless speeches, motions, and reports, a vote was taken to reassemble in two days at St. Andrew's Hall.

The opening gavel on December 20 brought the convention to order and the moment each had been waiting for. Uncharacteristically silent, the delegates were transfixed as the speaker took his place at the podium. Sensing the growing tension in the hall, the chairman of the Committee to Prepare an Ordinance of Secession launched immediately into his short presentation, a resolution that read, "We, the people of the State of South Carolina, in Convention assembled, do declare and ordain, and it is hereby declared and ordained, that the Ordinance adopted by us in Convention on the twenty-third of May, in the year of our Lord one thousand seven hundred and eighty-eight, whereby the Constitution of the United States was ratified, and also, all Acts and parts of Acts, of the General Assembly of this State, ratifying amendments of the said Constitution, are hereby repealed; and that the union now subsisting between South Carolina and other States, under the name of 'The United States of America,' is hereby dissolved." The resolution for secession was now cast and the delegates wasted little time in affirming their approval by a vote of 169 to 0.

That evening at St. Andrew's Hall, hereafter called Secession Hall, amid the sheer pandemonium of scores of political and public witnesses, the delegates signed the parchment that officially severed the ties between South Carolina and the rest of the Union. At that point the convention president declared South Carolina an "Independent Commonwealth," triggering widespread celebrations and rejoicing throughout the South. South Carolina had led the way and there was no turning back.

On the streets of downtown Charleston, with the storefronts festooned in colorful bunting, there were parades, bonfires, and salvos of artillery by the Citadel cadets. People ran wildly through the streets waving palmetto flags, dancing and cheering for a cause that at the moment had little impact on their sensibilities for the future ahead. The festivities were repeated in other major southern cities as well, cities such as Montgomery, Mobile, Wilmington, and New Orleans, all jubilant reactions to the moment at hand, totally insensitive to the darker clouds of war thundering over the horizon. War was inconceivable, most southerners alleged, because the "Yankees were cowards and would not fight." In fact it was widely believed that "a lady's thimble will hold all the blood that will be shed."

Now that South Carolina had withdrawn from the Union, the federal troops at Fort Moultrie were considered a threat to its sovereignty. So much so that within a few days secessionists were now patrolling near the fort night and day. With the patrols clearly a threat and the garrison under such close scrutiny, Major Anderson became increasingly concerned for the safety of his men. He knew that shortly the Carolinians would organize a substantial armed force to assert their claim to the old fort. To avoid this confrontation and to spare any loss of life, Anderson decided to evacuate Fort Moultrie immediately and to move his entire command across the harbor to Fort Sumter.

After packing the wives and children off to Fort Johnson with six months of supplies, in the waning sunset of December 26, Anderson, his 65 regulars and eight members of the band quietly made their way through the small town of Moultrieville and to their four hidden boats bobbing lazily at the seawall. With their baggage stowed out of sight they slid into the harbor and began to row the one mile to Fort Sumter. Suddenly a light appeared, piercing the darkness that had once hidden the escaping vessels. Within moments a secessionist guard boat on patrol in the harbor, manned by troops of the Washington Light Infantry, pulled alongside Anderson's boat to inspect the shadowy inhabitants now frozen in silence by the glaring light of the lanterns. Anderson, however, had the foresight to open his coat to conceal his brass military buttons and had ordered his men to hide their weapons under their own coats. Assuming the men were workmen going to the fort and seeing nothing that aroused their suspicions, the guard boat waved the men on and continued with its rounds. Within a few minutes the triple-tier fort, four times as large as Fort Moultrie with walls 40 feet high and up to 12 feet thick, loomed into view and the men were safely inside.

Once inside the troops rounded up the workmen. Those loyal to the Union were kept at the fort, the others sent ashore. Since the transfer had gone so well a second trip was made, this time to get additional supplies. And once everyone was safely back, two guns were fired to signal the families at Fort Johnson that everything had gone well and to also signal the two men left behind at Fort Moultrie to spike the guns. At the same time the shots created much confusion in the harbor causing the patrols to blow their alarms, fire off signal rockets, and set bonfires on shore.

The next day a telegram was sent to Washington. "I have the honor to report," Anderson wrote, "that I have just completed, by the blessing of God, the removal to this fort of all my garrison."

Needless to say when the authorities in Charleston learned that the federal troops had occupied "their fort," reaction was swift. The three-member commission met with the president on December 28 and angrily denounced the occupation of Fort Sumter as a violation of their agreement that the "forts & their relative military status remains as at present." With that said, they demanded Buchanan honor his agreement by immediately withdrawing the troops from the fort. Much too weak to take a position against them, Buchanan insisted on more time to study the matter. Over the next two days Buchanan met with his Cabinet to consider the government's next move. The advice of three southern Cabinet members, particularly those involved in behind-the-scenes schemes to undermine the administration, was so assertive against any action detrimental to the South that Buchanan became confused and indecisive. At that point, the new attorney general, Edwin M. Stanton, rose and told Buchanan, "Mr. President, it is my duty, as your legal adviser, to say that you have no right to give up the property of the government, or abandon the soldiers of the United States to its enemies; and the course proposed by the Secretary of the Interior, if followed, is treason, and will involve you and all concerned in treason." For the first time, to the outrage of the southern members present in the room, the word treason was used to describe their unseemly efforts.

Bolstered by Stanton's recommendation, Buchanan simply shrugged off the demands of the southern commissioners and with a newfound confidence reminded the Carolinians that since they had seceded from the Union and had already seized Castle Pinckney, Fort Moultrie, and every other federal property within their borders, except Fort Sumter, he was under no obligation to honor anything. Major Anderson and his garrison would continue to occupy Fort Sumter.

Learning of Buchanan's defiant attitude, an extremely irate Jefferson Davis sent Buchanan an angry letter suggesting that he was "surrounded with blood and dishonor on all sides."

As the revelry wound down and the novelty of their actions faded into reality, the seriousness of their bold decision and its inherent responsibilities was beginning to become evident to the South Carolina delegates. In an effort to explain the rationale for their actions an explanation was published to the "remaining United States of America, and to the nations of the world." In their view, the South Carolinians declared, the free states of the North had "assumed the right of deciding upon the propriety of our domestic institutions; and have denied the rights of property established in fifteen of the States and recognized by the Constitution; they have denounced as sinful the institution of Slavery; they have permitted the open establishment among them of societies, whose avowed object is to disturb the peace and to eloign [steal] the property of the citizens of other States. They have encouraged and assisted thousands of our slaves to leave their homes; and those who remain, have been incited by emissaries, books, and pictures, to servile insurrection. For twenty-five years this agitation has been steadily increasing, until it has now secured to its aid the power of the common Government.... A geographical line had been drawn across the Union, and all the States north of that line have united in the election of a man to the high office of President of the United States whose opinions and purposes are hostile to Slavery ... and that a war must be waged against Slavery until it shall cease throughout the United States. The guarantees of the Constitution will then no longer exist; the equal rights of the States will be lost. The slave-holding states will no longer have the power of self-government, or self-protection, and the Federal Government will have become their enemy."

At the White House Buchanan was well aware of the predicament Major Anderson was in at Fort Sumter but had always hesitated to get involved in a crisis he blamed on Lincoln. But, with only weeks left in his tenure, on December 31 he reluctantly gave the order to send a relief ship to the fort with additional troops and provisions. It was a decision made following long consultations with the conqueror of Mexico City, 74-year-old Gen. Winfield Scott, now commander and general-in-chief of the Union army and Buchanan's military advisor.

The relief ship selected for the mission to Charleston was the *Star of the West*, presently moored at Governors Island in New York Harbor. A side-wheel merchant steamship, the vessel was unarmed to avoid any demonstration of hostility and her shallow draft made her suitable for the venture into Charleston Harbor. Loaded with provisions and between 200 and 250 army troops under the command of Lt. Charles R. Woods, the ship set out for Fort Sumter on January 5, arriving at the entrance to the harbor four days later at 1:30 A.M. As the blanket of fog dissipated in the early morning sun the cadets from the Citadel, who were manning the batteries hidden among the sand dunes on Morris Island, spotted the *Star of the West* as she steamed inside the main channel toward Fort Sumter. Following three direct but non-fatal hits from the batteries on Morris Island and Fort Moultrie, the captain of the relief ship prudently chose to abort the mission and return to New York, ingloriously ending Buchanan's relief effort to Fort Sumter.

The Charleston newspapers rejoiced over this victory. This was proof, they claimed, that South Carolina was quite capable of defending its honor and its sovereignty against the might of the federal government. Encouraged by the successful defense of Charleston Harbor, within the next three weeks six additional states from the Deep South voted to join South Carolina. In quick succession, Mississippi seceded on January 9, 1861, then Florida the following day and Alabama on the eleventh. On January 19, Georgia cast its votes for secession, with Louisiana and Texas leaving the Union on January 26 and February 1 respectively. Eight southern states were left, four from the upper South (Virginia, Arkansas, Tennessee, and North Carolina) and the four border states of Missouri, Maryland, Delaware, and Kentucky. Each voted to reject secession at this time, preferring to take a wait and see attitude. In Washington, Buchanan woefully lamented, "Are calamities never to come singly!"

On February the fourth, thirty-eight delegates from six of the ceded states met in Montgomery, Alabama, to frame a constitution for a new government and to select the president and vice president who would implement it. (Having left the Union only three days earlier, Texas was unable to send delegates.) Although the provisional constitution was based primarily on the U.S. version, among other provisions it guaranteed the protection of slavery in any new territory, and disallowed government funding for internal improvements as well as protective tariffs as opposed to revenue producing tariffs. The constitution was adopted and on February 9, Jefferson Davis was unanimously elected the first provisional president of the Confederate States of America. Nine days later, on the steps of the Capitol building in Montgomery, he was inaugurated for a six-year term.

The youngest of ten children, Davis, like Lincoln, was born in Kentucky. Moving to Mississippi at a young age, he too was raised on the family farm and attended a local log-constructed school. But unlike Lincoln, Davis went on to receive a much better education by attending such elite schools as St. Thomas College in Kentucky, Jefferson College and Wilkinson County Academy in Mississippi, as well as Transylvania University, also in Kentucky. And in 1824 he entered West Point Academy for four years, graduating at the ripe age of twenty. Attaining the rank of first lieutenant in 1834, Davis resigned his commission and a year later and married Sarah Taylor, the daughter of Colonel Zachary Taylor, then the commander of Fort Crawford in the Wisconsin Territory. Tragically, three months after their wedding, Sarah died of malaria. Heartbroken, Davis attempted to get on with his life by traveling aimlessly around the South, but eventually he went back home and spent his time studying history and government and discussing politics. During this period Davis also became a cotton planter and worked the fields with his slaves as his father once did, as well as becoming more involved in local politics.

With his new wife, Varina, Davis arrived in Washington in March of 1845 to represent Mississippi in the House of Representatives. After only seven months in Congress, with the war raging in Mexico, Davis decided to rejoin the army where he served with distinction as a member of the Mississippi Rifles at Monterrey and Buena Vista under the overall command of his former father-in-law.

Following the war he was elected to fill a Mississippi Senate seat in 1849 but resigned two years later to make an unsuccessful bid for governor of Mississippi. During the next two years, Davis maintained his political connections by actively advocating for various causes and campaigning for Franklin Pierce in his presidential bid. To reward Davis for his support, in 1853 the new president selected him to be his secretary of war. Davis returned to the Senate four years later when the Buchanan administration came into power but in January of 1861, when Mississippi seceded from the Union, Davis resigned.

Now, as the president of the Confederate States of America, in his brief inaugural address Davis reminded his listeners, "You will see many errors to forgive, many deficiencies to tolerate, but you shall not find in me either a want of zeal or fidelity to the cause." And, he implored other states to join the confederacy so they "may seek to unite their fortunes to ours." Also taking the oath of office that morning was Vice President Alexander H. Stephens of Georgia.

In Fort Sumter meanwhile, after taking stock of his predicament, Major Anderson notified the War Department that with the limited rations on hand he expected his food to run out by April 15, at which time he would evacuate the fort. Additionally, the buildup of Confederate forces was progressing at an alarming rate with scores of batteries and an estimated 10 regiments of 8,000 troops now surrounding Fort Sumter. Under the command of Gen. Pierre G. T. Beauregard, a former gunnery student of Major Anderson's at West Point, the threatening guns were positioned on Morris, James, and Sullivan's Island, at Fort Moultrie, Castle Pinckney, and Cummings Point as well as on a floating battery in Charleston Harbor. Ironically, in January, Beauregard was appointed superintendent of West Point. Five days later, following the secession of his home state of Mississippi, Beauregard chose to resign his position to fight for the honor of his fellow southerners With this move, Beauregard claimed the distinction of having served the shortest tenure as superintendent in the academy's history.

Suspecting that he and his men were in imminent danger, Anderson ordered the defenses of the fort strengthened in anticipation of an attack. Accordingly, guns were mounted in the lower two tiers, embrasures bricked up, sandbags stacked at critical locations, wire traps laid around the perimeter of the fort, and a cheval-de-frise constructed to impede the expected land assault. Also, on the parade grounds, five massive Columbiad cannon barrels were positioned in dug-out trenches to serve as makeshift mortars.

During this tumultuous period and in parallel with his increasingly demanding political schedule, Lincoln and his wife, Mary, sold their furniture, rented out their house, moved into an apartment in the Chenery House, a local hotel, and prepared for their departure for Washington. With the threat of violence becoming more pronounced during these turbulent days and with rumors of a possible assassination attempt on the president-elect, plans called for Lincoln to board the train accompanied by security forces. Besides these rumors against Lincoln, General Winfield Scott also claimed to have convincing evidence of a "widespread and powerful conspiracy to seize the capitol."

Finally, it was time to leave Springfield. On the cold and rainy morning of February 11, 1861, Lincoln's carriage arrived to transport the president-elect to the local railroad station. Despite the severe weather the streets were lined with friends and neighbors all waving their good-byes as the soon to be president rode past them to the Great Northern Railroad Depot. With a four-man security force at his side, at nearly 8 A.M. Lincoln climbed onto the steps of his special Pullman sleeper and with a heavy heart delivered a brief, poignant farewell address that reflected his inner fears of the many dire problems facing not only the nation but himself as well. "My friends," he sadly told his audience, "no one, not in my position can appreciate the feeling of sadness I feel at this parting ... I now leave not knowing when, or whether ever, I may return, with a task before me greater than that which rested upon Washington."

Despite fears for his life and reports of an assassination plot in Baltimore, Lincoln chose to ignore the threats and ordered his train on a roundabout route, stopping in such cities as Indianapolis, Cincinnati, Cleveland, Pittsburg, Albany, New York City, and Philadelphia, so that he could meet and speak to his many supporters that thronged the stations. As a result, the journey took twelve days and traveled some two thousand miles. In a last minute change of heart, however, in Philadelphia Lincoln agreed to secretly board a train in the early morning hours before dawn. Hidden in a darkened sleeping berth, he was moved quietly through Baltimore and into Washington unnoticed.

At last the big day arrived. On March 4, Buchanan and Lincoln took the customary open carriage ride up Pennsylvania Avenue from Willard's Hotel. Standing before an enormous crowd, the oath of office was administered by Chief Justice Roger Taney.

Earlier that day Hannibal Hamlin, of Maine, had taken his oath in the Senate chamber as the new vice president.

It was a cold and blustery afternoon as Lincoln gazed out at the throng of Americans waiting eagerly to hear his reassuring and comforting words, something they needed in these uncertain times. Since assassination threats were still rumored, especially in Washington, a city sympathetic to the South, security was extremely tight with some six hundred troops scattered throughout the area and nearly two thousand volunteer policemen deployed to keep the peace.

Now sporting his trademark beard, the president turned to the crowd and began his inaugural address. At the very beginning of his speech Lincoln made a special point to address the concerns of the southern people. "Apprehension seems to exist among the people of the Southern States that by the accession of a Republican administration their property and their peace and personal security are to be endangered.... I declare that I have no purpose, directly or indirectly, to interfere with the institution of slavery where it exists. I believe I have no lawful right to do so, and I have no inclination to do so." But in a veiled threat he reminded the rebellious southern states, "In your hands, my dissatisfied fellow-countrymen, and not in mine, is the momentous issue of civil war. The government will not assail you. You can have no conflict without being yourselves the aggressors. You have no oath registered in heaven to destroy the government, while I shall have the most solemn one to preserve, protect, and defend it."

In the White House, Lincoln's first day in office was just as he had feared. Besides the constitutional issues over secession, Lincoln was also confronted with a developing incident in Charleston Harbor that he knew would have dire implications for the future of the country.

As the new president, Lincoln felt compelled to respond immediately to the growing threat against Fort Sumter but received contradictory advice on what to do. While there were those in his Cabinet who proposed immediate military action, General Scott, his military advisor, saw "no alternative to surrender" since it would take too long to assemble the ships and to train the 20,000 troops he estimated it would take to carry out a military expedition. Even Seward, his secretary of state, preferred to abandon the fort so as to prevent a civil war. But Lincoln had pledged in his inaugural address to defend and protect government property, and because of that pledge, he felt very strongly that he was obligated to carry out his duties even at the risk of a military confrontation. Finally, after moments of sober contemplation, Lincoln ordered a second attempt to deliver relief supplies to the fort and insisted the mission be carried out as a non-aggressive gesture. If the South chose to fight, however, he insisted that warships be stationed outside the harbor ready to respond.

In early April, a plan to launch a flotilla of seven warships and transports carrying troops, artillery, and supplies was put into action. As a goodwill gesture, Lincoln decided to inform the governor of South Carolina, Francis Pickens, that the ships en route were on a relief effort, under the command of Gustavus F. Fox, and no more unless they were impeded from carrying out their mission. The letter read, "An attempt will be made to resupply Fort Sumter with provisions only; and that, if such attempt be not resisted, no effort to throw in men, or ammunition, will be made, without further notice, [except] in case of an attack on the Fort." Distrustful of Lincoln's message, Pickens was not convinced of its sincerity, and declared bitterly, "Nothing can prevent war except the acquiescence of the President of the United States in secession and his unalterable resolve not to attempt any reinforcement of the Southern forts."

Even the *Charleston Mercury* contributed to the increasing war fever by writing, "Border southern States will never join us until we have indicated our power to free ourselves—until we have proven that a garrison of seventy men cannot hold the portal of our commerce. Let us be ready for war."

In Montgomery, President Davis was duly briefed on the Union relief expedition but had already made up his mind on how he was going to proceed. Instead of merely waiting for Anderson to evacuate the fort on April 15, he was prepared to issue orders for the attack on and capture of the Union garrison before the flotilla arrived with additional supplies that would only extend the occupation. Davis also refused to have the fort simply handed over to him, preferring instead to capture it in a sheer show of force. It would demonstrate to the other southern states, as well as to the world, that the Confederacy could stand up for its principles and its ideals. On April 10 the order was forwarded to General Beauregard.

During the afternoon of the following day three Confederate agents rowed out to the fort under a white flag and demanded the immediate surrender of the fort. Anderson refused, telling the Confederates, "Gentlemen, if you do not batter the fort to pieces about us, we shall be starved out in a few days." Early the next morning, around 12:45 A.M., the emissaries returned and a second request was communicated to Anderson which was again rejected. Finally, retiring to an adjoining room in the fort, the Confederates wrote a letter to the commander. Handed over to Anderson at 3:30 A.M., the letter stated, "By authority of Brigadier-General Beauregard, commanding the Provisional Forces of the Confederate States, we have the honor to notify you that we will open the fire of his batteries on Fort Sumter in one hour from this time." With the message delivered, the men departed and as promised General Beauregard's artillery commenced fire on the fort at 4:30 A.M. on April 12, 1861.

The bombardment continued throughout the day as well as the next. In the meantime the naval flotilla had rendezvoused outside the harbor but instead of seven ships only four had arrived. Without the full contingent of vessels to successfully attempt the relief effort, particularly the warship *Powhatan* that carried the landing craft for the men and supplies, the mission had to be aborted.

With portions of Fort Sumter ablaze from the red-hot shot raining down from Fort Moultrie, the powder magazine threatening to explode, and the impotent relief ships anchored helplessly outside the harbor, on the evening of April 13 Major Anderson finally surrendered. The next morning the garrison marched out of the fort to the strains of Yankee Doodle. Ironically, the only casualty occurred after Anderson had capitulated. During the ceremonial 50-gun salute to their flag, cartridges stacked in the open ignited from falling sparks, killing one soldier, fatally wounding another, and injuring four.

Told of the surrender, Governor Pickens was overjoyed and happily exclaimed, "We have met them and we have conquered."

Following years of sectional battles between the two sides, the confrontation at Fort Sumter was the spark that started a new and bloody chapter in American history. As a result, over the next several days political maneuvering on both sides rapidly escalated out of control.

Word of Anderson's departure from Fort Sumter reached the White House that evening and a Cabinet meeting was urgently called into session. The following day, April 15, Lincoln called on the governors of all the states, including the South, for 75,000 troops to serve a 90-day tour of duty. Their assignment was clearly delineated in his proclamation, "to repossess the forts, places, and property which have been seized from the Union...." The governor of Virginia, John Letcher, was outraged that Lincoln had the audacity to expect he would send troops against fellow southerners and angrily responded to Lincoln in no uncertain terms. In his letter Letcher wrote, "In reply to this communication, I have only to say that the militia of Virginia will not be furnished to the powers at Washington for any such use or purpose as they have in view. Your object is to subjugate the Southern States, and a requisition made upon me for such an object—an object, in my judgment, not within the purview of the Constitution or act of 1795—will not be complied with. You have chosen to inaugurate civil war, and having done so, we will meet it in a spirit as determined as the Administration has exhibited towards the South." The governors of Kentucky, North Carolina, Tennessee, Missouri, and Arkansas all sent similar sentiments. In fact, to Litcher, Lincoln's impudent request to pit the southern states against each other was enough to drive Virginia out of the Union on April 17. Following her lead, Arkansas, North Carolina, and Tennessee also voted to join the southern Confederacy. In turn, Lincoln's request for troops provoked Jefferson Davis to react by calling for privateers—privately owned ships sanctioned by the Confederate government—to attack and capture U.S. merchant vessels at sea, a form of legalized piracy. Two days later, on April 19, Lincoln retaliated by imposing a naval blockade of all southern ports from South Carolina to Mexico, some 3,500 miles, and requested 42,000 more troops to serve for 3 years. And that same day, four Union soldiers from the 6th Massachusetts Infantry Regiment and thirteen civilians lay dead after an angry mob rioted in Baltimore over the army's presence in their city.

By this time, it was quite apparent that sectional posturing was gaining more and more momentum as each side began to impose increasingly hostile actions against the other. Gosport Naval Yard in Virginia was seized which, in turn, triggered an advance by Union troops across the Potomac on May 24. Apprehensive over the close proximity of the Confederate border and the security of the capital, the move to occupy the port city of Alexandria was taken to establish a buffer zone between Richmond and Washington.

As the slide to war progressed, further attempts at diplomacy were clearly out of the question. Most southerners were fed up with everything northern. They despised all the years of arrogant resistance to everything they demanded as fair and equitable treatment, and despised Lincoln not only for his disapproving position on southern expansionism, but now also for his growing militancy toward the South.

Northerners, on the other hand, after years of insane bickering, were tired of southern intransigence. They were also outraged over the treasonous act of secession and the aggressive attack in Charleston Harbor, both, they claimed, a desecration of the American flag. To both sides, therefore, the time had come to resolve their differences once and for all.

The nation had now reached the point where reactionary events were overtaking the dialogue and compromise of a democratic society. This journey had begun long ago and its steady advance through a series of political, economic, cultural, and territorial conflicts had established a psychological mindset unalterably conducive to armed hostilities. Since these conflicts had positioned the nation on an unalterable course no one could reverse, in the end the people were confronted with the greatest sectional conflict of them all—the American Civil War.

Chronology

August 1619—The first 20 Africans are brought to Jamestown, Virginia, by the Dutch.

October 1705—The Virginia General Assembly declared all slaves were considered to be "real estate."

April 1775—The Quakers established the Society for the Relief of Free Negroes Unlawfully held in Bondage, the first anti-slave organization in U.S.

May–September 1787—The Constitutional Convention agreed that Congress could outlaw the importation of slaves but only after twenty years had passed. Also, as a result of the convention's tax law requirements, each slave would be counted as three-fifths of a person for representation purposes.

July 1787—The Northwest Ordinance was enacted by Congress. All territories (Northwest Territory) north of the Ohio River would be free—land now occupied by Indiana, Michigan, Illinois, Wisconsin, and Ohio, and those to the south would be slave.

March 1794—Eli Whitney's cotton gin patented. Being a faster and more efficient method for processing cotton, the new gin revolutionized the industry and created an enormous demand for more slaves.

May 1803—The Louisiana Purchase is signed. U.S. acquired 800,000 square miles from France for $15 million, land now occupied by Arkansas, Missouri, Iowa, Minnesota, North Dakota, South Dakota, Nebraska, Oklahoma, Kansas, Louisiana, and parts of Montana, New Mexico, Texas, Wyoming, and Colorado.

March 1807—Congress abolished the African slave trade effective January 1, 1808.

June 1812—Congress declared war on Great Britain. Naval blockade imposed by British from New York to New Orleans motivated the creation of many new U.S. manufacturing ventures.

Tariff of 1816—Signed by President James Madison, it was the first tariff designed to offer protection to the new U.S. industries from the onslaught of post-war foreign competition.

283

April 1816—Congress approved charter for the Second Bank of the United States effective the following January. Central bank would deal with enormous war debts.

March 1817—James Monroe inaugurated as fifth president of U.S.

April 1817—Rush-Bagot Agreement. Accord with Britain halted naval arms race on the Great Lakes.

March 1818—Missouri's petition to join the Union as a slave state presented to the U.S. House. Annexation would be in violation of the Northwest Ordinance since most of the state was located north of the Ohio River (Mason-Dixon Line).

October 1818—Anglo-American Convention. Treaty signed between U.S. and Great Britain allowed joint occupation of the Oregon Territory.

December 1818—Illinois joined the union of states. Senate parity is broken in favor of the free states (11 to 10).

February 1819—Adams-Onís Treaty. The Spanish government relinquished its claim to a portion of the Oregon Territory and ceded the eastern half of Florida. In return, the U.S. renounced its claim to territory of present-day Texas west of Sabine River.

December 1819—Alabama annexed as the eleventh slave state.

March 1820—The Missouri Compromise is approved. The compromise established the line between free and slave states at 36° 30', the southern border of Missouri. The measure also admitted Maine as a free state on March 15 and Missouri as a slave state on August 10, 1821. Senate parity remained intact at 12 free and 12 slave.

December 1821—The first of the "Old Three Hundred" settle on Mexican land in present-day Texas under the guidance of Stephen F. Austin. In ten years the population would grow to some 20,000 people, mostly southerners, along with 4,000 slaves.

December 1823—The Monroe Doctrine enacted. Essentially a set of principles designed to restrict further foreign colonization of the western hemisphere.

May 1824—Tariff of 1824 (Sectional Tariff). The new levy was an exclusive protectionist tariff ranging between 23 percent and 37 percent in order to safeguard U.S. industries and jobs.

February 1825—The House of Representatives elected John Quincy Adams president of the U.S. as directed by the 12th Amendment.

May 1828—"Tariff of Abominations." The levy on raw materials and manufactured goods would increase to nearly 50 percent. The South threatened nullification.

February—August 1828—The Anti-Masonic Party is formed in New York to protest the existence of the Freemasonry organizations and to withhold all political support for Masons running for office.

September 1829—Mexico banned slavery.

March 1829—Inauguration of Andrew Jackson as seventh president.

May 1830—The Indian Removal Act became law. Resulted in the displacement of thousands of Indians to land west of the Mississippi, and in the Trail of Tears where an estimated 4,000 Cherokee Indians died of hypothermia, starvation, and disease.

May 1830—Jackson signed Preemption Bill which forgave trespassing charges on land- squatters and allowed sales of up to 160 acres at $1.25 an acre.

January 1831—William Lloyd Garrison began publishing his anti-slave journal, the *Liberator*.

August 1831—Nat Turner, slave and religious fanatic, massacred over 50 white men, women, and children. Exploited by abolitionists, the episode caused the South to become increasingly apprehensive over the potential of slave insurrections.

July 1832—President Jackson vetoed the attempt to re-charter the Second Bank of the United States.

July 1832—Tariff of 1832 (McLane-Adams Tariff). Law reduced high tariffs of 1828 to the 1824 levels.

November 1832—South Carolina imposed "Nullification Ordinance" which declared the tariffs of 1828 and 1832 null and void.

December 1832—President Jackson was elected to a second term. It was the first victory for the new Democratic Party and was also the first election with a third-party candidate on the ballot (Anti-Masonic Party).

March 1833—Compromise Tariff approved. As a means to resolve the nullification crisis, the new law reduced tariffs over a period of 9 to 10 years from an average of 33 percent down to 1816 levels of about 20 percent.

September 1833—Without congressional approval, President Jackson ordered all government funds transferred from the Second Bank of the United States into smaller state banks.

October 1833—Formation of the American Anti-Slavery Society.

March 1834—President Jackson censured by the U.S. Senate for refusing to return government funds to the Second Bank of the United States.

March 1836—Texas declared its independence from Mexico.

March 1836—Mexican president and general Antonio López de Santa Anna defeated Texans at the Alamo in San Antonio. All 187 Texas defenders were slain.

April 1836—Santa Anna defeated at San Jacinto by Texans commanded by Sam Houston. Santa Anna grants Texas her independence as condition for his release from custody.

May 1836—A "Gag Rule" issued by a House committee declared all petitions submitted to the House on slavery would be tabled without debate.

June 1836—Jackson signed the Deposit-Distribution Act. The act improved regulation of federal deposits, restricted the use of small bank notes of $5 or less, forbade suspension of specie payment in banks holding federal funds, and required banks to distribute surplus government funds to state treasuries.

June 1836—Arkansas admitted to the Union.

July 1836—President Jackson's Specie Circular was approved. The law was designed to curb enormous speculation in western land by prohibiting all government land-office personnel from finalizing public land sales unless they were transacted in gold or silver.

January 1837—Michigan annexed as 26th state.

March 1837—U.S. recognized the Republic of Texas.

March 1837—Martin Van Buren inaugurated as the eighth president of U.S..

May 1838—Jackson's Specie Circular repealed by the Congress.

June 1838—President Van Buren's attempt to pass his Independent Treasury Act failed in the House.

July 1840—Van Buren's Independent Treasury Act became law. Since banks holding government funds violated the Deposit-Distribution Bill by withholding specie payments, Van Buren ordered all government deposits transferred to government-owned repositories or sub-treasuries.

March 1841—William H. Harrison, the first Whig to win the presidency, was sworn in as ninth president. Harrison would succumb to pneumonia one month later.

April 1841—Vice President John Tyler ascended to the presidency following the death of Harrison, the first such occurrence in U.S. history.

August 1841—Van Buren's Independent Treasury Act repealed by Congress.

August 1841—President Tyler vetoed Henry Clay's Fiscal Bank Bill, a measure to establish a new Bank of the United States.

September 1841—Tyler vetoed Clay's bank bill a second time despite modifications.

September 1841—Angered over Tyler's intransigence, the Cabinet resigned with the exception of Secretary of State Daniel Webster.

June 1842—Tyler vetoed the so-called "little tariff" that would have enabled the treasury to acquire more needed revenue while Congress debated a replacement for the Compromise Tariff of 1833.

August 1842—Tariff of 1842 was signed into law. Recognizing the government could not be sustained on the Compromise Tariff level of 20 percent, the new tariff returned the levy to the 30 percent levels of 1833.

September 1843—Secret negotiations began between the Tyler administration and President Sam Houston of Texas on potential statehood. Mexico threatened war if Texas annexed.

April 1844—Tyler forwarded Texas annexation treaty to the Senate for ratification.

June 1844—Senate rejected Texas annexation treaty. The House would also disapprove.

March 1845—Tyler, in final act as president, signed bill granting statehood to Florida.

March 1845—Democrat James K. Polk was sworn in as 11th president of U.S. A staunch proponent of expansionism, Polk was the first dark-horse candidate to be elected.

July 1845—Alarmed over the growing presence of Mexican troops along the Rio Grande, Gen. Zachary Taylor was dispatched to Corpus Christi.

December 1845—John Slidell was dispatched to Mexico City in a failed attempt to purchase Mexican territory ranging from New Mexico and California to Oregon for $30 million. Tensions between the two nations worsened.

December 1845—Texas annexed as fifteenth slave state. Mexican troops assemble along the Rio Grande in threatening show of force.

March 1846—Gen. Taylor's Army of Occupation arrived near the Rio Grande and built Fort Texas opposite Matamoros, Mexico.

April 1846—U.S. reconnaissance force ambushed by Mexican cavalrymen. Sixteen American troops killed.

May 1846—Taylor defeated Mexican army in Battles of Palo Alto and Resaca de la Palma.

May 1846—U.S. Angered over the Mexican invasion of Texas and the resultant U.S. casualties; a state of hostilities with Mexico was declared. Hostilities with Mexico would continue until Gen. Winfield Scott occupied Mexico City in September 1847.

June 1846—Oregon Treaty was signed by President Polk. As a result, a potential war with Great Britain was averted.

July 1846—The Walker Tariff was signed into law. It lowered rates to stimulate trade, increased revenue to the Treasury, and improved relations with Britain.

August 1846—Van Buren's sub-treasury system was reinstated. Now called the Constitutional Treasury Act, all government funds would be deposited in federal vaults. It was the forerunner of the Federal Reserve System.

August 1846—Rep. David Wilmot of Pennsylvania introduced his Wilmot Proviso to combat fears over the so-called slave power conspiracy.

December 1846—Iowa admitted to Union (15 slave states to 14 free states).

January 1847—To resolve the dispute over post-war territorial apportionment, Secretary of State James Buchanan proposed to extend the Missouri line dividing free and slave states to the Pacific. His recommendation raised fears in the North of an "All Mexico" scenario and was tabled.

December 1847—Abraham Lincoln took his seat in the U.S. House of Representatives. He would serve for two years.

December 1847—Sen. Lewis Cass of Michigan proposed the concept of popular sovereignty. His bill would have given the residents of a territory the right to decide whether to accept or reject slavery. The bill was never acted upon.

February 1848—The Treaty of Guadalupe Hidalgo was signed ending the war with Mexico.

March 1848—The Mexican treaty was ratified by the Senate. U.S. paid $15 million plus assumption of Mexican debt to American citizens. Mexico recognized the Rio Grande boundary of Texas and ceded 525,000 square miles, comprising present-day California, Utah, Arizona, New Mexico and parts of Colorado and Wyoming west of the Rockies.

May 1848—Wisconsin admitted to the Union (15 free and 15 slave states).

June 1848—Free Soil Party formed when the Liberty Party joined forces with anti-slave Democrats and Whigs.

July 1848—First women's rights convention held in Seneca Falls, N.Y. Organized by Elizabeth Cady Stanton and Lucretia Mott.

August 1848—Oregon granted territorial status on land comprising present-day Idaho, Oregon, Washington, and parts of Wyoming and Montana.

1849—Secret society of nativists called the Know-Nothings was formed to prevent Catholics and immigrants from participating in the political process.

March 1849—Gen. Zachary Taylor was inaugurated as the twelfth president of U.S.

July 1850—Zachary Taylor died. Vice President Millard Fillmore assumed presidency.

August—September 1850—Five new laws comprising the Compromise of 1850 were signed by President Millard Fillmore.

September 1850—California is accepted for statehood (16 free states to 15 slave states).

December 1850—As a result of their opposition to the Compromise of 1850, delegates from four southern states met to consider seceding from the Union. No agreement was reached.

August 1851—Narciso López and his filibusters fail in their third attempt to capture Havana, Cuba. López was subsequently executed by the Spanish government.

March 1852—Democrat Franklin Pierce inaugurated as the 14th president of U.S..

April 1854—Pierce failed in a bid to purchase Cuba from Spain.

April 1854—The Gadsden Treaty accepted by the Senate.—U.S. purchased about 46,000 square miles of land in the Southwest from Mexico.

May 1854—President Pierce signed the Kansas-Nebraska Act into law. This single piece of legislation, arguably the most controversial measure passed by Congress, fractured the Democratic Party, dismembered the Whigs, initiated a new national party, and launched Abraham Lincoln into political prominence.

October 1854—The Ostend Manifesto against Cuba was issued by U.S. ministers in Belgium.

March 1855—To implement the requirements of popular sovereignty, Kansans voted to elect either a free-state or slave-state legislature. Missouri border ruffians posing as residents inundated the voting process and fraudulently elected a pro-slave legislature.

May 1856—The Sack of Lawrence. Tensions rise in "Bleeding Kansas."

May 1856—In the Senate, Charles Sumner of Massachusetts was beaten senseless by Rep. Preston Brooks of South Carolina over Sumner's remarks on the evils of slavery.

May 1856—John Brown and seven men butchered five proslavery advocates in the Pottawatomie Massacre.

June 1856—Democratic National Convention nominated Pennsylvanian James Buchanan for president.

June 1856—First Republican National Convention nominated John C. Frémont of Georgia for president

July 1856—Filibuster William Walker proclaimed himself president of Nicaragua after defeating the Nicaraguan army and the defection of its president.

March 1857—James Buchanan was sworn in as the fifteenth president of U.S.

March 1857—U.S. Supreme Court denied Dred Scott his freedom from slavery.

May 1858—John Brown, preparatory to his campaign to free the slaves, met with fugitive slaves in Chatham, Canada. They drew up a provisional constitution for a proposed government for freed slaves in the mountains of Virginia.

May 1858—Minnesota admitted to the Union (17 free states to 15 slave states).

August 1858—Kansas residence, voting for the third time, rejected the state's proslavery constitution.

August 1858—First of seven Lincoln-Douglas debates extending to October 15.

February 1859—Oregon is granted statehood (18 free states to 15 slave states).

October 1859—John Brown and eighteen followers broke into the federal arsenal and armory in Harpers Ferry, Virginia, to steal weapons for their campaign to free the slaves. Two days later Brown was captured and imprisoned.

December 1859—John Brown was hanged for treason.

May 1860—Abraham Lincoln won the Republican nomination for president.

June 1860—Northern Democrats selected Illinois senator Stephen A. Douglas as their candidate in the presidential campaign. At a separate convention southern Democrats chose John C. Breckinridge of Kentucky.

September 1860—Filibuster William Walker was executed following fourth attempt to take over Nicaragua.

October 1860—Fearful that Lincoln would win the presidency, South Carolina governor called for a convention to support secession.

November 1860—Abraham Lincoln was elected 16th President of the U.S. Outraged southerners talked increasingly of secession.

December 1860—South Carolina voted to secede from the Union.

December 1860—Major Robert Anderson removed his troops from Fort Moultrie and occupied Fort Sumter in Charleston Harbor.

December 1860—President Buchanan dispatched side-wheeler *Star of the West* to carry supplies to Fort Sumter.

January 1861—In Charleston Harbor, following several direct hits from coastline batteries, the *Star of the West* aborted mission.

January 1861—Mississippi, Florida, Alabama, Georgia, and Louisiana seceded from the Union.

February 1861—Texas seceded.

February 1861—At Montgomery, Alabama, Jefferson Davis was elected provisional president of the Confederate States of America.

March 1861—In Washington, Lincoln inaugurated under tight security.

April 4, 1861—Lincoln ordered a seven-ship fleet to deliver troops, arms, and supplies to Fort Sumter.

April 10, 1861—President Davis directed Confederate general Pierre G. T. Beauregard to offer ultimatum to Major Robert Anderson: surrender or be bombarded.

April 12, 1861—Confederate batteries opened fire on Fort Sumter.

April 13–14, 1861—Major Anderson surrendered and Union troops evacuated Ft. Sumter.

April 15, 1861—President Lincoln called on all states to provide 75,000 troops to "repossess the forts, places, and property which have been seized from the Union...."

April 17, 1861—Outraged over Lincoln's order for troops, Virginia seceded. Arkansas, North Carolina, and Tennessee followed on May 6, May 20, and June 8, respectively.

April 17, 1861—Jefferson Davis called for owners of private vessels to apply for letters of marque.

April 19, 1861—Lincoln ordered naval blockade of southern coastline.

Bibliography

Capers, Gerald M. *Stephen A. Douglas: Defender of the Union.* Boston: Little, Brown, 1959.

Cole, Donald B. *Martin Van Buren and the American Political System.* Princeton, NJ: Princeton University Press, 1984.

_____. *The Presidency of Andrew Jackson.* Lawrence: University Press of Kansas, 1993.

Eisenhower, John S.D. *So Far from God: The U.S. War with Mexico 1846–1848.* New York: Random House, 1989.

Epperson, James F. *Causes of the Civil War.* Stockton, NJ: OTTN, 2005.

Holt, Michael F. *The Political Crisis of the 1850s.* New York: John Wiley & Sons, 1978.

_____. *The Rise and Fall of the American Whig Party: Jacksonian Politics and the Onset of the Civil War.* New York, Oxford: Oxford University Press, 1999.

Kolchin, Peter. *American Slavery 1619–1877.* New York: Hill & Wang, 1993.

Kunhardt, Philip B., Jr., Philip Kunhardt, III, and Peter W. Kunhardt. *Lincoln: An Illustrated Biography.* New York: Knopf, 1992.

McPherson, James M. *Battle Cry of Freedom: The Civil War Era.* New York: Ballantine, 1988.

Merk, Frederick. *Manifest Destiny and Mission in American History.* Cambridge: Harvard University Press, 1963.

Oates, Stephen B. *The Approaching Fury.* New York: Harper Collins, 1997.

Peterson, Merrill D. *The Great Triumvirate: Webster, Clay, and Calhoun.* New York, Oxford: Oxford University Press, 1987.

_____. *The Legend Revisited: John Brown.* Charlottesville and London: University of Virginia Press, 2002.

Potter, David M. *The Impending Crisis: 1848–1861.* New York: Harper & Row, 1976.

_____. *The South and the Sectional Conflict.* Baton Rouge: Louisiana State University Press, 1968.

Seigenthaler, John. *James K. Polk.* New York: Times Books, 2003.

Singletary, Otis A. *The Mexican War.* Chicago and London: University of Chicago Press, 1960.

Smith, Page. *The Nation Comes of Age: A People's History of the Ante-Bellum Years.* Vol. 4. New York: McGraw Hill, 1981.

Stampp, Kenneth M., ed. *The Causes of the Civil War.* New York: Simon & Shuster, 1959.

Index